PETRARCH'S LAURELS

Also by Sara Sturm-Maddox

Petrarch's Metamorphoses: Text and Subtext in the *Rime sparse*
Lorenzo de' Medici
The *Lay of Guingamor:* A Study

Sara Sturm-Maddox

PETRARCH'S LAURELS

The Pennsylvania State University Press
University Park, Pennsylvania

Library of Congress Cataloging-in-Publication Data

Sturm-Maddox, Sara.
    Petrarch's laurels / Sara Sturm-Maddox.
        p.   cm.
    Includes bibliographical references and index.
    ISBN 0-271-00822-9
    1. Petrarca, Francesco, 1304–1374. Rime.   2. Petrarca, Francesco,
1304–1374—Symbolism.   3. Petrarca, Francesco, 1304–1374
—Characters—Laura.   4. Laura (Fictitious character)   5. Laurel in
literature.   I. Title.
PQ4479.S69   1992
851'.1—dc20   91-23489
                                                                      CIP

It is the policy of The Pennsylvania State University Press to use acid-free paper
for the first printing of all clothbound books. Publications on uncoated stock
satisfy the minimum requirements of American National Standard for
Information Sciences—Permanence of Paper for Printed Library Materials,
ANSI Z39.48—1984.

for Helen and Jimmy, Mattie and James
in memoriam

. . . ce Paradis de belles fictions,
Déguisement de nos affections . . .
  —Joachim Du Bellay, "A une Dame"

. . . dell'imago,
Poi che 'l ver m'è tolto, assai m'appago.
  —Giacomo Leopardi, "Alla sua donna"

CONTENTS

ACKNOWLEDGMENTS

The preparation of this book was assisted in a preliminary phase by a Joseph P. Healey grant from the University of Massachusetts at Amherst, then by a senior fellowship from the National Endowment for the Humanities. It was made more agreeable by discussions with colleagues in the United States and in Canada, Great Britain, France, and Italy, where some of its arguments were developed as conference presentations and as lectures, and with my husband Don, who contributed levity as well as encouragement when I most needed it. I am most grateful for both forms of support.

Earlier versions of portions of this study, now substantially revised, have appeared in the following: parts of Chapter 1 in "Petrarch's Siren: 'dolce parlar' and 'dolce canto' in the *Rime sparse*," *Italian Quarterly* 27 (1986), 5–19; of Chapter 2 in "*Antiche piaghe:* Love's Violence in Petrarch's *Rime sparse*," in *A Miscellany of Medieval and Renaissance Studies in Honor of Aldo S. Bernardo,* ed. Anthony L. Pellegrini and Bernard S. Levy (Binghamton, N.Y.: special issue of *Mediaevalia,* 1989 [for 1986]), 187–204; and of Chapter 4 in "*Rime sparse,* 25–28: The Metaphors of Choice," *Neophilologus* 69 (1985), 225–35; permission to include this material is gratefully acknowledged. The *Rime sparse* and accompanying translations, along with Petrarch's *rime disperse* and Dante's *rime petrose* unless otherwise indicated, are reprinted by permission of the publishers from *Petrarch's Lyric Poems* by Robert Durling (Cambridge: Harvard University Press, copyright © 1976 by Robert M. Durling).

Fig. 1. The Commentator Servius Points to Virgil. Simone Martini's miniature in Petrarch's Virgil manuscript. Courtesy of Special Collections, Homer Babbidge Library, University of Connecticut.

INTRODUCTION

"*. . . colsi 'l glorïoso ramo,*
onde forse anzi tempo ornai le tempie
in memoria di quella ch'io tanto amo."
—Francesco Petrarca, Trionfo d'Amore, *IV, 79–81¹*
[. . . I plucked the glorious laurel branch
wherewith—perhaps too soon—I decked my brow,
remembering her whom I so deeply love.]

The poet's laurels, the poet's Laura: exploration of this fundamental correlation has long engaged the commentators of Petrarch's collection of his vernacular lyrics known as the *Rime sparse,* his friend and admirer Boccaccio first among them.² The correlation, however, while evident to even a casual reader not only of the *Rime* but of the vernacular *Trionfi* and the Latin *Africa* and *Bucolicum carmen* as well, is problematic in nature, and it was first problematized by Petrarch himself. Consider the *Secretum,* the text in which he casts in a dialogue between himself and his spiritual mentor Augustinus the story of his uncertainties, where his revered interlocutor speaks to him pointedly concerning his love for a lady known to us only as Laura. Love is one of the chains that bind him,

---

1. The text is cited here and throughout from Francesco Petrarca, *Trionfi,* introduzione e note di Guido Bezzola (Milan, 1984), and in English from *The Triumphs of Petrarch,* trans. Ernest Hatch Wilkins (Chicago, 1962).

2. Boccaccio suggests in his biographical essay on Petrarch that Laura stands allegorically for the laurel crown: "Laurettam illam allegorice pro laurea corona . . . accipiendam puto"; see *De vita e moribus domini Francisci Petracchi de Florentia,* in *Opere Latine Minore,* ed. A. F. Masseri (Bari, 1928), 243. Among many recent discussions, see Adelia Noferi, "Il *Canzoniere* del Petrarca: Scrittura del desiderio e desiderio della scrittura," *Paragone letteratura* 296 (1974), who identifies the laurel as an emblem of poetry, through its link with the name of Laura (9).

declares Augustinus; the other is glory. And glory, symbolized by the crown conferred in antiquity upon poets as upon emperors, is related to Laura through her name. The latter, moreover, is in his analysis priori-tary, in that Petrarch's assiduous cultivation of the symbolic laurel has been inspired by its relation to the lady's name:

> . . . who could sufficiently utter his indignation and amazement at this sign of a distempered mind, that, infatuated as much by the beauty of her name as by her person, you have with perfectly incredible silliness paid honour to anything that has the remotest connection with that name itself? Had you any liking for the laurel of empire or of poetry, it was forsooth because the name they bore was hers; and from this time onwards there is hardly a verse from your pen but in it you have made mention of the laurel. . . .[3]

At this point, on the other hand, the earnest Petrarchan persona of the *Secretum* might have raised an objection in his defense: turning to the oration pronounced by Petrarch on the occasion of his poetic coronation in Rome in 1341, Augustinus would find that there the undisputed preoccupation with the laurel is never associated with the name of Laura.[4] That the argument is *not* advanced is due to the preemptive acuity of Augustinus, who displays a characteristic ability to expose the reticences of his partner in this debate:

> I clearly divine what excuse you will make. . . . You will allege that you were devoted to these [poetic] studies some time before you became a lover at all, and that desire for the glory of the poet's crown kindled your heart from childhood. [All the difficul-ties and obstacles that opposed themselves to such pursuit, how-ever,] would perhaps have broken your resolve entirely, if the

3. Throughout this study the *Secretum* is cited from *Petrarch's Secret*, trans. William H. Draper (London, 1911); here 134.

4. Petrarch connects it instead through etymology with the name of Daphne, citing Uguiccione's explanation that the Greek *daphne* has the same meaning as the Latin *laurus*. The Coronation Oration is translated by E. H. Wilkins in *Studies in the Life and Works of Petrarch* (Cambridge, Mass., 1955), 300–313; for its circumstances, see Wilkins, *The Making of the "Canzoniere" and Other Petrarchan Studies* (Rome, 1951), chap. II. The versified account of the ceremony that Petrarch addressed to an absent friend alludes to Apollo's association with the laurel wreath "first beloved of him and now—after so long—so dear to me," but does not connect the laurel with Laura; see Thomas G. Bergin, "Epistola metrica II, 1 ad Johannem Barrilem: An Annotated Translation," in Aldo Scaglione, ed., *Francis Petrarch, Six Centuries Later: A Symposium* (Chapel Hill and Chicago, 1975), 56–65.

remembrance of a name so sweet, always entwining itself with your inmost soul, had not banished every other care. . . .[5]

Despite this rather abrupt dismissal, however, it is Petrarch's poetic ambition that prompts another of his interlocutors, this one not a fictional incarnation but a noted contemporary, to advance the hypothesis opposite to that of Augustinus: that it was love for the poetic laurel that gave rise to his naming and praising of Laura. Giacomo Colonna's suggestion is energetically refuted in the poet's reply:

What in the world do you say? That I invented the splendid name of Laura so that it might be not only something for me to speak about but occasion to have others speak of me . . . that the truly live Laura by whose beauty I seem to be captured was completely invented, my poems fictitious and my sighs feigned;

and to his friend and patron Petrarch counters with the formula frequently adduced, in the absence of compelling historical documentation, as evidence of the existence of a "real" Laura: "I wish indeed that you were joking about this particular subject, and that she indeed had been a fiction and not a madness [simulatio esset utinam, et non furor]!"[6]

The opposition between the views of Augustinus and Colonna concerning Petrarch's love for Laura and his love for the symbolic laurel is of course only one of priority; they are agreed on the primacy of the correlation. What neither evokes is the further element that organizes the relation of the two terms in the collection of "scattered rhymes" through which Petrarch is forever identified with the passionate pursuit both of an inaccessible lady and of a poetic glory worthy of the laurel crown. While the Coronation Oration makes no mention of Laura, Petrarch there alludes to mythological story, and in the story to which he alludes we find the paradigm through which he will associate his pursuit of the poet's laurels with his pursuit of Laura: Apollo's consecration of the laurel results from his pursuit of a nymph who assumes its arboreal form in a metamorphosis effected to escape his possession.[7]

5. *Petrarch's Secret*, 135–36.

6. *Fam.* II, 9. Here and throughout, unless otherwise indicated, the *Familiares* are cited from Aldo Bernardo's translations: Francesco Petrarca, *Rerum familiarium libri I–VIII* (Albany, N. Y., 1975); *Letters on Familiar Matters (Rerum familiarium libri IX–XVI)* (Baltimore, 1982); *Letters on Familiar Matters; Rerum familiarium libri XVII–XVIV* (Baltimore, 1985).

7. For the primacy of this Ovidian inspiration, see Carlo Calcaterra, *Nella Selva del Petrarca* (Bologna, 1942), esp. 35–49. An important theoretical analysis of the relation of the elements of Laura and *lauro* to the Ovidian *fabula* is found in Cesare Segre, "Les isotopies de Laure," in H. Parret and H. G. Ruprecht, eds., *Exigences et Perspectives de la Sémiotique: Recueil d'hommages pour A. J. Greimas* (Amsterdam and Philadelphia, 1985), 811–26.

Readers of the *Rime* have long identified in this mythological paradigm the fundamental relation between Laura and laurel.[8] Yet in fact Petrarch seems to have hesitated before settling upon the particular casting of Laura that anchors both the symbolic and the imagistic networks of his personal mythology. Let us consider an early poem not ultimately included in the collection. Here, as the lady arms herself to inflict love's wounds, the poet represents her through a singularly direct classical allusion:

> Poi mi ricordo di Venus iddea,
> qual Virgilio descrisse 'n sua figura,
> e parmi Laura in quell'atto vedere
> or pietosa ver' me or farsi rea.[9]

> [Then I recall Venus the goddess as Virgil described her, and I seem to see Laura in that act become now pitying, now fierce toward me.]

This Laura has familiar traits of her depiction in the *Rime*—her free-flowing hair evoked as "a l'aura sparsi / i mille e dolci nodi" [the thousand sweet knots spread to the breeze]—but the allusion to Venus is limited to its iconographic suggestiveness. The direct invocation of Virgil as literary precursor affords little more than an invitation to the reader to "imagine" the new poet's lady according to a well-known model. In another sonnet not found in the *Rime*, an early composition whose archaic form has no equivalent in the poems selected for inclusion in the collection,[10] Petrarch's choice of a mythological prototype for his lady Laura falls on the goddess Aurora:

> Sì come il padre del folle Fetonte
> quando prima sentì la punta d'oro
> per quella Dafne che divenne alloro,
> de le cui fronde poi si ornò la fronte;
> e come il sommo Giove nel bel monte
> per Europa trasformossi in toro;

---

8. Carlo Calcaterra, *Nella Selva del Petrarca* (Bologna, 1942), 11.

9. The text of this poem and that of "Sì come il padre del folle Fetonte" are cited from Natalino Sapegno, *Francesco Petrarca: Rime, Trionfi e Poesie latine* (Milan and Naples, 1953). The sonnet was probably addressed to Sennuccio del Bene; see Joseph A. Barber, "Il sonetto CXIII e gli altri sonetti a Sennuccio," *Lectura Petrarce, II, 1982* (Padua, 1983), 33.

10. See Barber, "Il sonetto CXIII," esp. 25–26.

e com' per Tisbe tinse il bianco moro
Piramo del suo sangue innanzi al fonte;
così son vago de la bella Aurora,
unica del sol figlia in atto e in forma,
s'ella seguisse del suo padre l'orma.
Ma tutti i miei pensier' convien che dorma
finché la notte non si discolora:
così, perdendo il tempo, aspetto l'ora.

E se innanzi di me tu la vedesti,
io ti prego, Sennuccio, che mi desti.

[Just like the father of foolish Phaeton when first he felt the golden wound for that Daphne who became a laurel, with whose leaves he then adorned his brow; and like highest Jove who in the lovely mountain transformed himself into a bull for Europa; and like Piramus who for Thisbe tinted the white mulberry with his blood at the fountain; so am I enamored of the beautiful Aurora, the sun's only daughter in act and in form, following the trace of her father. But all my thoughts must sleep until the night loses its color; thus, losing time, I await the hour. And if you should see her before I do, I beg you, Sennuccio, to awaken me.]

Although Apollo's love for Daphne and her transformation into the laurel is recalled in this poem, the privileged status of the god among the poet's own mythological prototypes is not due to that relation but to his identification as father of Aurora, the object of the poet's love confirmed in yet another poem among the *disperse:*

Io son sì vago della bella Aurora,
unica figlia di quel che l'alloro
nobilitò in prima. . . .[11]

[I am so enamored of the beautiful Aurora, only daughter of he who first ennobled the laurel. . . .]

These poems, all of which testify to Petrarch's early experimentation with mythological models, call into question the inevitability of the Ovidian story of Daphne's metamorphosis as subtext for the poet's

11. Cited in Barber, "Il sonetto CXIII," following A. Solerti, ed., *Rime disperse di Francesco Petrarca o a lui attribuite* (Florence, 1909).

account of his own experience of love and poetry. In all of them, the distinction between the poet's experience and that of the mythological personae remains intact. In none of them, in particular, do we find the functional identity of poet and Apollo; nor, despite the experimentation with paronomastic affinities, do we find the association of Laura and *lauro* that not only Augustinus and Colonna but also commentators from Petrarch's time to our own identify as the nucleus of an entire poetic production. Or consider another early work, the third eclogue set in the year of Petrarch's coronation as poet although composed some years later, where he casts himself as a shepherd to reenact Apollo's pursuit of a nymph named Daphne. Although the reader already familiar with Petrarch's love lyrics at once identifies in this Daphne an incarnation of his Laura—she has Laura's radiant smile, her hair scattered about her shoulders by the breeze—the nymph nonetheless remains fully distinct from the symbol of poetic achievement that she bestows, a laurel branch identified not with her transformation but as a gift from the muse Calliope; here again there is no relation effected either with Laura or with her name.

The optimistic rewriting of Ovidian story in Petrarch's third eclogue, where Daphne at last ascends the Capitoline with the rustic poet-protagonist to award him the laurel crown, is made possible only through the omission of the central event of that story, the metamorphosis of nymph into laurel. Transformation into the laurel, on the other hand, is staged in one of the earliest components included in the *Rime sparse,* the opening section of canzone 23 annotated by Petrarch himself in the so-called "codice degli abbozzi," his draft manuscript, as one of his earliest compositions, "de primis inventionibus nostris":[12]

> Qual mi fec' io quando primier m'accorsi
> de la trasfigurata mia persona,
> e i capei vidi far di quella fronde
> di che sperato avea già lor corona,
> e i piedi in ch'io mi stetti et mossi et corsi,
> com'ogni membro a l'anima risponde,
> diventar due radici sovra l'onde
> non di Peneo ma d'un più altero fiume,
> e 'n duo rami mutarsi ambe le braccia!
>
> (23, 41–49)[13]

---

12. For the manuscript see A. Romanò, *Il codice degli abbozzi (Vaticano latino 3196) di F. Petrarca* (Rome, 1955). The successive phases of the canzone are examined by Dennis Dutschke, *Francesco Petrarca: Canzone XXIII from First to Final Version* (Ravenna, 1977).
13. Cf. *Metamorphoses* I, 547–52.

[What I became, when I first grew aware of my person being transformed and saw my hairs turning into those leaves which I had formerly hoped would be my crown, and my feet, on which I stood and moved and ran, as every member answers to the soul, becoming two roots beside the waves not of Peneus but of a prouder river, and my arms changing into two branches!]

Yet in these verses that closely echo Ovid's, the transformation is not that of the beloved but that of the poet himself. Its association with the personae of the mythological narrative is blocked both by this displacement and by its motivation and attribution, for while the metamorphosis of the Ovidian Daphne occurs as a response to her plea addressed to the river-god her father to effect her escape from Apollo's possession, Petrarch's unwitting poet is transformed by an alliance between the lady and Amor:

> ei duo mi trasformaro in quel ch'i' sono,
> facendomi d'uom vivo un lauro verde
> che per fredda stagion foglia non perde.
>
> (23, 38–40)

[those two transformed me into what I am, making me of a living man a green laurel that loses no leaf for all the cold season.]

Only the fact of metamorphosis into the laurel, acknowledged in the completed poem both as prioritary and as enduring ("né per nova figura il primo alloro / seppi lassar" [nor for any new shape could I leave the first laurel]), links the story of Apollo and Daphne with this event, whose significance would seem to validate the hypothesis of Giacomo Colonna: the symbolization of poetic endeavor is confirmed, albeit negatively in that the poet's voice is lost in the change.[14] And this is but the first of several Ovidian myths evoked in the canzone in the successive transformations undergone by the lyric protagonist; in the final version of the poem, moreover, it is not the myth of Apollo and Daphne but that of Acteon and Diana that affords a dramatic vehicle for the poet's own story, assigning roles both to the lover and to the lady.[15]

14. For Leonard Barkan this transformation suggests "that in the throes of passion he no longer possesses the independent identity that can make him poet"; see *The Gods Made Flesh: Metamorphosis and the Pursuit of Paganism* (New Haven, 1986), 207.

15. For the significance of this casting of the poet's amorous adventure, see Luigi Vanossi, "Petrarca e il mito di Atteone," *Romanistische Zeitschrift für Literaturgeschichte* 10 (1986): esp. 3–8.

These varied transgressions and evasions of the primary Ovidian myth
suggest again that the story of Daphne's metamorphosis affords an
inadequate measure for Petrarch's dramatic and symbolic exploitation of
the relation between Laura and the laurel. While early in the ordering of
the poems he alerts his reader to its pertinence, to Amor's attack on
Apollo, Daphne's flight, and her transformation into the evergreen laurel
sacred to the god who had unsuccessfully pursued her, for the principle
of irreversible succession through which Daphne was lost to Apollo he
substitutes a principle of simultaneity: Laura becomes the laurel, and the
laurel becomes Laura, in a vertiginous symbiosis of figures that finds
only its point of departure in Petrarch's reading of Ovidian story. The
image of Daphne-become-laurel is fractured, its two components of
elusive beloved and evergreen tree freed for independent development.
The essential elements of the Ovidian account retain their evocative
power: inflicted passion, pursuit, transformation; loss, frustration, com-
pensatory celebration by the lover. Yet each retains singly its potential as
vehicle for new content, for a plurality of new investments: the fixed
personae and events, the irreversible narrative chronology, even the
governing mythological premise of Ovid's account resolve into a set of
figures that are freed to resonate with other elements, to participate in
other chronologies. At the same time, each occurrence signals ambiguities
that are not fully resolved within the single poem, provocative notations
that are amplified, confirmed, negated, or corrected in other poems, in a
play of insufficiencies and complementarities inviting the reader to partic-
ipate in the progressive integration of the poems as a signifying system
whose dimension is the collection as a whole.[16]

The present study undertakes a reexamination both of Laura and of the
laurel. Part I, opening with a review of the Ovidian paradigm, follows
the subsequent digressive investments of its elements. Exploring the
situation of both lady and laurel in landscape and probing the multiple
functions of a descriptive system centered in light and shadow, the
discussion brings into focus a small number of motifs that recur in
patterns of dissociation and recombination throughout the collection. As
both Laura and the laurel determine the coordinates of the poet's
movement, in the fictional space and time of the lyrics as well as the inner
landscape and inner calendar that orient the real *materia* of the *Rime*

16. For reflection on the totality of independent lyric components as system, see Cesare
Segre, "Système et structures d'un *Canzoniere*," in *Recherches sur les systèmes signifiants*
[Symposium de Varsovie 1968] (The Hague and Paris, 1973), 373–78, and his "Sistema e
strutture nelle *Soledades* di A. Machado," in *I segni e la critica* (Turin, 1969), 95–134.

sparse, that movement is disclosed to be not only complex, but profoundly ambiguous.

Here once again Augustinus's assessment is suggestive. His categorical diagnosis of the obsessive correlation of Laura and *lauro* as the "sign of a distempered mind," prompting an immediate defense from the Petrarchan persona of the dialogue, casts the issue as one of more than poetic priority. In the *Rime sparse* in which most of Petrarch's verses celebrating both Laura and the laurel are collected, both the accusation and the defense are implicated in the sets of oppositions disclosed in Part I, resulting in a profound ambivalence with regard to the central question that has long preoccupied and divided Petrarch's readers: the status ultimately to be accorded the poet's devotion to Laura. Was she, like the stilnovist *donna angelicata* and like Dante's Beatrice, his guide to Heaven as well as his sublime poetic inspiration? Or was she, wittingly or no, the embodiment of an earthly beauty so overwhelming that it foreclosed for the poet on all other concerns, including concern for his salvation? Reading the contrasting and often conflicting perspectives of individual lyrics within the ordered sequence, Part II takes as its point of departure a variety of textual interventions to identify within the collection itself two "readings" of the poet's story, one a redemptive itinerary, the other a fall. Following the prompting of these digressive versions, it reconsiders Laura as the poet's guide as she affords him access to both a secular and a celestial Paradise, ultimately to challenge the assumption underlying many readings of the *Rime* that its poet's story, like his love for Laura, follows a linear itinerary from amorous passion for a mortal creature to exemplary sublimation, from *concupiscentia* to *caritas*. It proposes instead that the relation of the two parts of the *Rime sparse* is in a special sense specular, in a collection that is dominated throughout by two ultimately rival cosmologies.

The Epilogue returns to the fundamental connection of lady and laurel to reexamine Petrarch's mythmaking, through which a new myth emerges from the old: a myth of poetic origins centered in Valchiusa as the locus of an amorous epiphany, and in the shade of the laurel as the locus of writing, of the production of *rime sparse*.

PART I

1

METAMORPHOSES

Despite the conviction carried by its searching analyses, the probing in the *Secretum* of the poetically fertile correlation of *lauro* and Laura is a token not of Petrarch's autobiographical candor but of his mythmaking.[1] And so it is too in the *Rime sparse,* the lyric collection in which most of his vernacular "scattered rhymes" are brought together in a careful ordering that received his patient attention until the year of his death. Exploration of that mythmaking, however, necessarily begins with myths already made. Thus sonnet 5 opens upon the triad of Amor, lover, and beloved sketched in the initial account of the *innamoramento*—

> Quando io movo i sospiri a chiamar voi
> e 'l nome che nel cor mi scrisse Amore—

> [When I move my sighs to call you and the name that Love wrote on my heart—]

but opens further to Ovidian story to invoke another triad—Amor, Apollo, and Daphne—and to associate the poet's lady with the "eternally green boughs" sacred to the god.[2]

1. Historical inquiry, while productive of a variety of hypotheses concerning the "real" Laura, has proved frustrating. For a survey and evaluation of efforts to identify Laura and her relations with Petrarch, see Enrico Carrara, "Le leggenda di Laura," in his *Studi Petrarcheschi e altri scritti* (Turin, 1959), 79–111. For a recent biographical approach, see F. J. Jones, "Laura's Date of Birth and the Calendrical System Implicit in the *Canzoniere*," *Italianistica* 12 (1983): 13–33; "Further Evidence of the Identity of Petrarch's Laura," *Italian Studies* 39 (1984): 27–46; "An Analysis of Petrarch's Eleventh *Canzone:* 'Mai non vo' più cantar com'io soleva'," *Italian Studies* 41 (1986): 24–44.

2. For Petrarch's adoption of the mythological model, see Marga Cottino-Jones, "The

Petrarch's association of both his lyric persona and his poetic project with this specific Ovidian story, marking some of his earliest compositions, was an act of self-definition, one recognized by his poetic correspondents who were quick to note the potential of an analogy that cast him as a privileged initiate: "Ah, do not hide from others the clear lights granted you by Phoebus," one writes to him; "Ah, do not wish to conceal the power that Apollo grants you," urges another.[3] It is particularly suggestive, then, that it is precisely in terms of this privileged relation that Petrarch first distances his poet's story from the mythological paradigm. In the poem that first reveals Laura's name in the collection and first signals its association with the laurel beloved of Apollo, that new relation is fearfully, not optimistically limned, suggesting an act of presumption that may incur the god's displeasure:

> Così LAU-dare et RE-verire insegna
> la voce stessa, pur ch'altri vi chiami,
> o d'ogni reverenza et d'onor degna;
> se non che forse Apollo si disdegna
> ch'a parlar de' suoi sempre verdi rami
> lingua mor-TA-l presuntuosa vegna.
>
> (5, 9–14)

[Thus the word itself teaches LAU-d and RE-verence, whenever anyone calls you, O Lady worthy of all reverence and honor; except that perhaps Apollo is incensed that any mor-TA-l tongue should come presumptuous to speak of his eternally green boughs.]

The inadequation of the poet's status compared with that of his mythological prototype is thus posited on the instance of its introduction: the evergreen boughs remain sacred to Apollo, and the Ovidian paradigm retains its integrity against attempts at appropriation. "Se non che forse": the qualification has a premonitory force that threatens the lover's

---

Myth of Apollo and Daphne in Petrarch's *Canzoniere*," in *Francis Petrarch, Six Centuries Later*, ed. Aldo Scaglione (Chapel Hill and Chicago, 1975), 159–60, and for the assimilation of the poet to Apollo, see Alfred Noyer-Weidner, "Zur Mythologieverwendung in Petrarcas *Canzoniere*," in *Petrarca 1304–1374: Beiträge zur Werk und Wirkung*, ed. F. Schalk (Frankfurt, 1975), esp. 237–38.

3. Braccio Bracci di Arezzo, "O infiammato da' lucenti raggi"; Antonio Beccari, "O novella Tarpea, in cui s'asconde." See Annarosa Cavedon, "Intorno alle 'Rime estravaganti' del Petrarca," *Revue des Etudes Italiennes* 29 (1983): 89–90.

enterprise at the same time that it denies closure to the celebratory moment of the sonnet.

That Petrarch's poet will elude this interdiction is due in part to radical changes effected on the mythological model. The poems discover one means to circumvent the interdiction opposed to his desire and to pretend to a measure of possession by affirming that the laurel is not only that external object, eternal reminder of the flight and transformation of the beloved, but also a plant rooted in his heart. Thus, he warns Laura, her disdainful attempt to escape his pursuit is, unlike Daphne's, doomed to failure:

> Se voi poteste per turbati segni—
> per chinar gli occhi o per piegar la testa,
> o per esser più d'altra al fuggir presta,
> torcendo 'l viso a' preghi onesti et degni—
> uscir giamai, o ver per altri ingegni,
> del petto ove dal primo lauro innesta
> Amor più rami, i' direi ben que questa
> fosse giusta cagione a' vostri sdegni.
>
> (64, 1–8)

[If you could, by any angry gestures—by casting your eyes down or bending your head or by being more swift to flee than any other, frowning at my virtuous and worthy prayers—if you could ever thus or by any other strategem escape from my breast where Love engrafts many branches from that first laurel, I would say that would be a just reason for your disdain.]

Freed from the circumstances of the Ovidian account, this is no longer Apollo's laurel but Petrarch's laurel. Now the *innamoramento* is figured by its implantation in the poet's heart, where it flourishes (228, 255), part of the "double treasure" that pairs Laura with his patron Giacomo Colonna:

> Un lauro verde, una gentil colonna
> quindeci l'una et l'altro diciotto anni
> portato ò in seno, et giamai non mi scinsi.
>
> (266, 12–14)

[A green Laurel, a noble Column, the latter for fifteen, the former for eighteen years, I have carried in my breast and have never put from me.]

Another adaptation, even more poetically fertile, revises the relation of laurel and lady. The mythological paradigm is posited on succession, as indeed is any notion of metamorphosis: Daphne *becomes* a laurel. Even in the early phases of his preoccupation with the Ovidian myth, however, Petrarch experimented, on occasion boldly, with a principle of simultaneity. In a series of three early poems, effecting a narrative development that transcends the boundaries of the individual lyrics, he writes as it were a continuation of that story (41–43).[4] He expands upon its personae to include not only Apollo but Jove and Vulcan as well in a set of elaborate meteorological conceits in which the presence or absence of Laura determines fair or inclement weather. The sun remains distant in the absence of "his dear friend" (41),[5] and Petrarch writes a dramatic new scene in which a disconsolate Apollo searches for his beloved "dal balcon sovrano":

> poi che cercando stanco non seppe ove
> s'albergasse da presso o di lontano,
> mostrossi a noi qual uom per doglia insano
> che molto amata cosa non ritrove.
>
> (43, 5–8)

[when, tired with searching, he could not discover where she was dwelling, whether near or far, he showed himself to us like one mad with grief at not finding some much-loved thing.]

While this sequence built around the departure or return of Laura figured as laurel is obviously transgressive of the closure of the mythological story, Apollo's affective dependence on the laurel's presence affords an opening to a sentimental content foreign to Ovid's text, anticipating the numerous separation poems that will punctuate the *Rime* both *in vita* and *in morte de Laura.*[6]

4. See Ernesto Travi, "Il primo Petrarca volgare," *Italianistica* 4 (1975): 23. On the triad of *Rime* 41–43 as a "miniature story" telling of Laura's departure, absence, and return, see Peter Hainsworth, *Petrarch the Poet* (London, 1988), 65–69.

5. Here, as P.R.J. Hainsworth notes, Petrarch's representation contradicts reasonable assumptions about identity: "what the poem literally presents is the departure of a tree which once had human form"; see "The Myth of Daphne in the *Rerum vulgarium fragmenta,*" *Italian Studies* 34 (1979): 36.

6. "This agonistic Apollo," observes Mary Barnard, "will be Petrarch's legacy to the Spaniards Garcilaso and Quevedo"; see *The Myth of Apollo and Daphne from Ovid to Quevedo: Love, Agon, and the Grotesque* (Durham, 1987), 106. Bernhard König examines the three-poem "cycle" and its innovation with regard to the Italian lyric tradition in "Meteorologisch-Mythologische Spielereien (zu Petrarca, *Canzoniere,* XLI–XLIII)," in *Interpretation und Vergleich* (Festschrift für Walter Pabst), ed. E. Leube and L. Schrader (Berlin, 1972), 145–56.

Another strategy is suggested by that of Ovid's Apollo as he seeks a means to transcend the apparently definitive frustration of his desire in the nymph's metamorphosis: making of its leaves a garland, a crown, he explicitly confers upon it the status of symbol. "Since you cannot be my bride," he exclaims to the plant that he embraces as he had sought in vain to embrace the body of Daphne, "surely you will at least be my tree!"[7] This triumphal sublimation is a feature of the Ovidian story that has not infrequently caught the imagination of poets. Thus, for example, Andrew Marvell:

> The Gods rejoice, the Tyrant ceasing to rage,
> And although they have known nymphs and goddesses many times,
> Each one achieves his desires better now in a tree . . .
> Apollo pursued beautiful Daphne
> That she might become a laurel; but he had sought nothing more.[8]

This final observation, of course, is an interpretation belied by the Ovidian text; while more playful, it is as willfully ingenuous and suspect as Petrarch's declaration to a Laura now in Heaven that "I never wished anything from you but the sunlight of your eyes" (*Rime* 347). Nor, having read Petrarch's impassioned praises of Laura's curling golden locks and her white arms, can we agree that for the poet of the *Rime sparse*, as for Marvell's contented Apollo, "Hair cannot compete with leaves, nor arms with branches."

On the contrary: in the *Rime*, hair does indeed compete with leaves, and arms with branches, to render Laura. While Petrarch's poet will imitate Apollo's enterprise, claiming the laurel as the "slender tree that in my rhymes I beautify and celebrate" (148), his strategy is of a different order: instead of Daphne *then* laurel, he will celebrate Laura *and* laurel. Consider his startling variations on the image of bark as bodily form, as in the recollection of the body of a young Laura as

> . . . quella dolce leggiadretta scorza
> che ricopria le pargolette membra
> dove oggi alberga l'anima gentile.
>
> (127, 35–37)[9]

---

7. For this compensatory aspect of the myth, see Pier Massimo Forni, "Laudando s'incomincia: Dinamiche di una funzione petrarchesca," *Italian Quarterly* 23 (1982): 19. Here and throughout, citations are from *The Metamorphoses of Ovid*, trans. Mary J. Jones (Baltimore, 1955; repr. 1975).

8. "Hortus," in *The Latin Poetry of Andrew Marvell*, trans. William A. McQueen and Kiffin A. Rockwell (Chapel Hill, 1964).

9. The same opposition in the poet's own metamorphoses opposes "quel dentro" to "la

[. . . that lovely tender bark which covered then the little members where, today, that noble soul dwells.]

Reinterpreted in later poems in a metaphysical key, the emphasis will fall on its mortality as the "terrena scorza," the earthly vesture abandoned by the soul on the occasion of death (278). In the poem cited above, however, Ovid's notation of the bark that covered the limbs of the nymph and arrested her flight becomes sensually evocative in its contrast to the incorporeal "anima" of the beloved. No longer the end product of a metamorphosis that signals an absence, it becomes, unexpectedly, a marker of physical presence.

Daphne's female form may remain in Apollo's memory—"if you have not forgotten, with the turning of the years, those beloved blond locks," the poet of the *Rime* prompts the god in sonnet 34—but her flesh becomes bark, her hair leaves, her arms branches, her feet roots. At the completion of the transformation, there remains not a nymph, but a tree. While its nodding branches seem to signal their acquiescence to Apollo's celebratory proclamation, no human trace of Daphne remains; her transformation is irreversible, definitive.[10] In one of two early poems addressed to Apollo Petrarch styles himself the god's successor in his devotion to the sacred plant: "Life-giving sun, you first loved that branch which is all I love" (188).[11] In the other, however, that succession—"where you first and then I were limed"—yields to a project of simultaneity: "thus we shall then together see a marvel—our lady sitting on the grass" (34), and this affirmation, eradicating the distance that separates the new poet from his amorous precursor, also eradicates the "before" and "after" that separates human and arboreal forms of the beloved. The care with which Petrarch effected this adaptation is evident in the successive versions of this poem, where the early variant of Laura in shade "facendo dei suoi rami a se stessa ombra" [with her branches making a shade for herself] yields to "far de le sue braccia a se stessa ombra" [with her arms making a shade for herself]; a similar revision occurs in *Rime* 23 to render the poet's own metamorphosis, where the

---

scorza" (23), and figures in Petrarch's variation on the motif of the lover's heart separated from his body (180). On the motif, see W. Pagani, *Repertorio tematico della scuola poetica siciliana* (Bari, 1968), 172–73, and on Petrarch's use of the topos, see Rudolf Baehr, "Il Sonetto XV," *Lectura Petrarce, III, 1983* (Padua, 1984), 50–52.

10. On the Petrarchan figures as "deliberately at odds with Ovid," see Thomas M. Greene, *The Light in Troy; Imitation and Discovery in Renaissance Poetry* (New Haven and London, 1982), 128.

11. On the identification of poet and Apollo, see Cesare Segre, "La critica strutturalistica," in *I metodi attuali della critica in Italia* (Turin, 1970), 328–33.

initial casting of "et rami diventar ambe le braccia" [both my arms changing into branches], almost a literal translation of Ovid's "in ramos braccia crescunt," is replaced by a formula that insures the continued relation of arboreal and human forms in the designation of two branches: "e 'n duo rami mutarsi ambe le braccia."

In other ways too in Petrarch's portrayal of Laura, elements of the feminine figure are interchangeable with those of her arboreal equivalent. In the scene of the *innamoramento*, the snares of Amor are concealed now in Laura's golden hair, now in the shadow of the laurel. Her hair is a fateful net spread by Amor beneath the tree's branches (181); in full substitution, the branches themselves are described as enlimed, "invescati."[12] The breeze originates in the laurel (129) or moves "softly sighing" through both the green laurel and her golden hair (246);[13] the poet's "burning sighs that never moved a leaf of the lovely branches" (318) recall, in an allusion not visible on the surface of the text, the sensual suggestiveness of the moment in which Ovid's Apollo comes closest to Daphne, his breath touching "the locks that lay scattered on her neck."[14]

We have seen that in poems among the *rime disperse* Apollo figures as father of the beloved in her incarnation as the goddess Aurora. While this identification, in competition with the fundamental Ovidian paradigm of the *Rime*, is excluded from the eventual collection, "l'aurora" continues to dissimulate Laura's name while suggesting her presence. Its paronomastic play, evident in verses such as "vien poi l'aurora et l'aura fosca inalba" [then the dawn comes and lights up the dark air] (223), is a prelude to a rare direct disclosure of her name, once among the poems *in vita*,

> Là ver l'aurora, che sì dolce l'aura
> al tempo novo suol movere i fiori . . .
> Temprar potess'io in sì soavi note
> i miei sospiri ch'addolcissen Laura . . .
>
> (239, 1–2, 7–8)[15]

[At the time near dawn when so sweetly the breeze in the springtime is wont to move the flowers . . . Could I but tune in such

12. For examples see poems 59; 270; 142; 195.
13. See also 56; 127; 143; 159; 196; 197; 198; 227; 279.
14. On Petrarch's development of the erotic suggestiveness of the image, see Antonio Daniele, "Lettura del sonetto petrarchesco 'Al cader d'una pianta che si svelse' (CCCXVIII)," *Revue des Etudes Italiennes* 29 (1983): 48.
15. On "aurora" in this poem, see Adelia Noferi, "Il *Canzoniere* del Petrarca: Scrittura del desiderio e desiderio della scrittura," *Paragone letteratura* 296 (1974): 7.

sweet notes my sighs that they would sweeten the breeze
(/Laura) . . .]

and again in a poem *in morte* that recalls the sonnet among the *disperse*,
"Io son si vago della bella Aurora":

> Quand' io veggio dal ciel scender l'Aurora
> co la fronte di rose et co' crin d'oro,
> Amor m'assale ond'io mi discoloro
> et dico sospirando: "Ivi è Laura ora."
>
> (291, 1–4)[16]

[When I see the dawn coming down from the sky with rosy brow
and golden hair, Love assails me, and I turn pale and say, sighing:
"There Laura is now."]

Other sonnets, among the most affectionate and intimate of the collec-
tion, connect more directly with the myth of Aurora. *In vita* the poet
celebrates his awakening at daybreak in a poem in which only the
mythological casting distances its protagonists from those of the tradi-
tional erotic *alba*:

> Quella ch'à neve il volto, oro i capelli,
> nel cui amor non fu mai inganni né falli,
> destami al suon delli amorosi balli,
> pettinando al suo vecchio i bianchi velli.
>
> (219, 5–8)[17]

[She whose face is snow, whose hair is gold, in whose love was
never any deceit or failing, awakens me with the sound of her
amorous dance, combing the white fleece of her aged husband.]

---

16. Laura's identification as Aurora is striking in Petrarch's annotation when he looks
back at this sonnet and that concerning the death of Sennuccio del Bene as "sonitia de
morte Sennucii et de Aurora"; see Rosanna Bettarini, "Che debb'io far? (*RVF*
CCLXVIII)," *Lectura Petrarce, VII, 1987* (Padua, 1988), 190. For the repeated "naming"
of the beloved in poems written to or connected with Sennuccio, see Marco Santagata in
" 'Razo e dreyt ay si 'm chant e 'm demori': un episodio della cultura provenzale del
Petrarca," *Rivista di Letteratura Italiana* 5 (1987): 63 hr n. 55.

17. The allusion to Tithonus in this poem, Sylvia Ruffo-Fiore suggests, allows Petrarch
both to disguise his anxieties and to "broach the possibility of a mutual, sexually fulfilled
relationship"; see "A New Light on the Suns and Lovers in Petrarch and Donne," *Forum
Italicum* 8 (1974): 547–49.

It is this affection of Aurora for her aged husband Tithonus that will underline the pathos of the corresponding sonnet *in morte:*

> "O felice Titòn, tu sai ben l'ora
> da ricovrare il tuo caro tesoro;
> ma io che debbo far del dolce alloro?
> ché se 'l vo' riveder, conven ch'io mora."
>
> (291, 5–8)

["O happy Tithonus, you well know the hour when you will recover your dear treasure, but what must I do about the sweet laurel? for if I wish to see it, I must die."]

A similar wordplay characterizes the free associations worked by Petrarch on the topos, favored by his troubadour precursors, of the "aura" that originates in the vicinity of the lady and awakens in the distant lover the memory of her presence.[18] To this air, in its alternate occurrence as "aere," he attributes a comfort that sustains him.[19] The "aura" is identified not only with the region where the lady is physically present, but with her birthplace:

> Tosto che giunto a l'amorosa reggia
> vidi onde nacque l'aura dolce et pura
> ch'acqueta l'aere et mette i tuoni in bando . . .
>
> (113, 9–11)

[As soon as I reached the palace of Love and saw the birthplace of the sweet and pure breeze that calms the air and banishes the thunder . . .]

Here as in other poems, favored not only by homonymic identity but by an orthographic practice that did not consistently render the article as separate from the noun, the breeze may signify Laura herself. A veil is

18. See G. Contini, "Préhistoire de l'*aura* de Pétrarque," in *Varianti e altra linguistica* (Turin, 1970), 193–99. For an inventory, see Jean-Marie D'Heur, "Le motif du vent venu du pays de l'être aimé: L'invocation au vent, l'invocation aux vagues," *Zeitschrift für Romanische Philologie* 88 (1972): 69–104; and for antecedents of this vernacular tradition in classical Arabic love poetry, see Barbara Spaggiari, "Il tema 'west-östlicher' dell'aura," *Studi Medievali* 26 (1985); esp. 234–41. Santagata suggests that the catalyst in Petrarch's play on "aura" may have been his reading of Boccaccio's early works (" 'Razo e dreyt'," 59–62).

19. For the originality of this thematic development, see Baehr, "Il Sonetto XV," 47–49.

that object "ch' a l'aura il vago et biondo capel chiuda" [that keeps her lovely blond head from the breeze] (52); of his vacillations between ardor and suffering the poet confides that "l'aura mi volve" [the breeze turns me about] (112). So too he records her death: "è l'aura mia vital da me partita" [my vital breeze has departed from me] (278).[20]

Yet this varied paronomastic repetition, like the animation of the laurel, is productive of only a surrogate presence. In this, of course, Petrarch's Laura is like her primary mythological prototype: the casting of Laura as Daphne identifies her as an elusive object of desire, she "who has turned in flight" (6), forever just beyond the grasp of the pursuing lover.[21] The poet's wish to spend an endless night with her is the desire to truncate the Ovidian paradigm, to dissociate the outcome of his pursuit from that of his mythological precursor:

> et non se transformasse in verde selva
> per uscirmi di braccia, come il giorno
> ch' Apollo la seguia qua giù per terra!
>
> (22, 34–36)

[and let her not be transformed into a green wood to escape from my arms, as the day when Apollo pursued her down here on earth!]

It is an impossible desire, like that for a night without end: in this sense, the myth is not to be eluded. Desire and its frustration mark Petrarch's adaptations of the Ovidian story in the earliest version of the collection as it may be reconstructed,[22] and the futility of the poet's pursuit will be acknowledged again and again in *impossibilia*:

20. See Cesare Segre, "Les isotopies de Laure," in H. Parret and H. G. Ruprecht, eds., *Exigences et Perspectives de la Sémiotique: Recueil d'hommages pour A. J. Greimas* (Amsterdam and Philadelphia, 1985), 821–22, and also his "I sonetti dell'aura," *Lectura Petrarce, III, 1983* (Padua, 1984), 58–78.

21. As a recent study suggests, it is in this rendering that Petrarch "seems to have drawn most deeply on the Ovidiam myth" (Hainsworth, "The Myth of Daphne," 34); see also Norbert Jonard, "I miti dell'Eros nel *Canzoniere* del Petrarca," *Lettere Italiane* 34 (1982): 453.

22. For the reconstruction of this version, see E. H. Wilkins, *The Making of the Canzoniere and Other Petrarchan Studies* (Rome, 1951), 146–50, and on Petarch's use of the myth in this early period, see Marco Santagata, "La canzone XXIII," *Lectura Petrarce, I, 1981* (Padua, 1982), esp. 68.

Beato in sogno et di languir contento,
d'abbracciar l'ombre et seguir l'aura estiva,
nuoto per mar che non à fondo o riva;
solco onde, e 'n rena fondo, et scrivo in vento.

(212, 1–4)

[Blessed in sleep and satisfied to languish, to embrace the shadows, and to pursue the summer breeze, I swim through a sea that has no floor or shore, I plow the waves and found my house on sand and write on the wind.]

Thus he pursues "a wandering, fleeing doe with a lame, sick, slow ox" (212); thus it is that "weeping and singing our verses we shall go with a lame ox hunting the breeze [*l'aura*]" (239). These latter verses, which echo first those written by Dante for the Arnaut Daniel encountered among the lustful on the slopes of Purgatory—" 'Ieu sui Arnaut, que plor, e vau cantan' " ["I am Arnaut, who weep and sing as I go"] (*Purg.* XXVI, 142)—echo in turn Arnaut's own self-characterization as unsuccessful lover: "Ieu sui Arnautz qu'amas l'aura, / e chatz la lebre ab lo bou / e nadi contra suberna" ["I am Arnaut who gathers the breeze, and chases the hare with an ox and swims against the current"].[23]

As she eludes the enamored poet, so does this Laura elude characterization. Of her several attributes celebrated throughout the collection, only her hair receives a significant descriptive development, and that development belongs to literary tradition. Its golden color is conventional in medieval portraiture; Cino da Pistoia in particular favored it, as did Dante in his *rime petrose*, the "stony rhymes" that incontestably shaped Petrarch's early experiments with descriptive characterization.[24] To Cino

23. "En cest sonet coind' e leri," 43–45. Citations of the *Commedia*, here and throughout, are from the critical edition of Giorgio Petrocchi, *La Commedia secondo l'antica vulgata* (Mondadori, 1966–68), as reprinted with minor revisions in Dante Alighieri, *The Divine Comedy*, translated with a commentary by Charles Singleton (Princeton, Bollingen Series 80), Vol. I: *Inferno* (1970); Vol. 2: *Purgatorio* (1973); Vol. 3: *Paradiso* (1975). For Arnaut as a source of Petrarch's equivocal play with the name of Laura, see G. Contini's introduction to the Toja edition of Arnaut's poems (Florence, 1960), xiii, and for the connection Arnaut-Dante-Petrarca, see Domenico De Robertis, "Petrarca petroso," *Revue des Etudes Italiennes* 29 (1983): 28. For the relation of Petrarch's metaphors to those of Arnaut, see Shapiro, *Hieroglyph of Time*, 74–75; Marguerite Waller, *Petrarch's Poetics and Literary History* (Amherst, Mass., 1980), 61–62; Barbara Spaggiari, "Cacciar la lepre col bue," *Annali della Scuola Normale di Pisa* XII, 4 (1982): 1333–1409.

24. For Dante's *rime petrose* see Robert M. Durling, *Petrarch's Lyric Poems: The "Rime sparse" and Other Lyrics* (Cambridge, Mass., and London, 1976), from which citations and translations are taken. De Robertis discusses Petrarch's incorporation of this element in "Petrarca petroso" (27).

and other stilnovist love poets Laura is indebted for the braiding of her hair into "treccie."[25] Its free play in the breeze, on the other hand, occurring in numerous poems in the *Rime* with a minimal variation that intensifies the effect of an obsessive image, is adopted from Ovid, in whose account the nymph's hair flows loosely about her neck as she flees before Apollo (*Met.* I, 529, 542).[26] Laura's poet recalls her Ovidian prototype when he demands, "What nymph in a fountain, in the woods what goddess ever loosed to the breeze locks of such fine gold?" (159). The sight enraptures Ovid's Apollo: "He eyed her hair as it hung carelessly about her neck, and sighed: 'What if it were properly arranged!' " Not less enraptured is Petrarch's poet in his attention to Laura's hair:

> . . . le chiome, or avolte in perle e 'n gemme,
> allora sciolte et sovra or terso bionde,
> le quali ella spargea sì dolcemente
> et raccogliea con sì leggiadri modi
> che ripensando ancor trema la mente.
> Torsele il tempo poi in più saldi nodi. . . .
>
> (196, 7–12)

> [. . . her golden locks, now twisted with pearls and gems, then loosened and more blond than polished gold, which she let loose so sweetly and gathered again with such a charming manner that as I think back on it my mind still trembles. Time wound them afterward into tighter knots. . . .]

These verses suggest not only the nymph but the *dea*, the Ovidian Diana whose scattered hair is drawn up into a knot by an attendant (*Met.* III, 169–70). It is the air that ties Laura's hair in the opening verses of *Rime* 90, "erano i capei d'oro a l'aura sparsi / che 'n mille dolci nodi gli avolgea" [her golden hair was loosed to the breeze, which turned it in a

---

25. For examples, see Antonio Lanza, *Studi sulla lirica del Trecento* (Rome, 1978), 17–18. Cf. Dante in "Così nel mio parlar," vv. 66–67.

26. These elements are recombined in the Sofonisba of Petrarch's *Africa* (V, 35–42) that affords, as Ugo Dotti observes, a provisional definition of the image of Laura; see "Petrarca: Il mito dafneo," *Convivium* 37 (1969): 10, 21–22. For analysis of the "ritrattistica petrarchesca," see also Ezio Raimondi, *Metafora e storia* (Turin, 1970), esp. 180–87. The Latin text includes both "auro," gold, and "aura," breeze, in a suggestion of the wordplay that in the *Rime* will relate the color of Laura's hair to the breeze that becomes her phonic equivalent.

thousand sweet knots],[27] the air that again arranges her hair into changing patterns:

> Aura che quelle chiome bionde et crespe
> cercondi et movi et se' mossa da loro
> soavemente, et spargi quel dolce oro
> et poi 'l raccogli e 'n bei nodi il rincrespe . . .
>
> (227, 1–4)[28]

[Breezes that surround those curling blond locks and move in them and are moved by them softly, and scatter that sweet gold and then gather it again and recurl it in lovely knots . . .]

The effect of this insistent repetition is the opposite of pictorial realism. The limited elements of its repertory never coalesce to form anything that may properly be termed a portrait of Laura, even according to the standardized descriptive technique recommended by medieval rhetoric.[29] The descriptive codes that identify "Laura" in the *Rime*, focusing on the formalized representation of discrete physical attributes, result in the fragmentation of her physical image, much like the synecdochal representation of the laurel, the bark, branches, leaves, and roots all present in Ovid's account of Daphne's transformation. These are frequently added together in a catalogue, as in this lament for Laura's death:

> Gli occhi di ch'io parlai sì caldamente,
> et le braccia et le mani e i piedi e 'l viso . . .
> le crespe chiome d'or puro lucente . . .
>
> (292, 1–2, 5)

[The eyes of which I spoke so warmly, and the arms and the hands and the feet and the face that had so estranged me from

27. See Giuseppe Mazzotta, "The *Canzoniere* and the Language of the Self," *Studies in Philology* 95 (1978): 277. For a suggestive comparison of *Rime* 90 to its classical subtexts in Virgil and Ovid, see Greene, *The Light in Troy*, 112–113.

28. Adelia Noferi notes that the key to this image is found in Petrarch's exegesis of the appearance of Venus to Aeneas; see "La costituzione della parola impossibile: Note al sonetto CXLIII del *Canzoniere*," *Studi Petrarcheschi* 8 (1976): 206–8.

29. For this technique, see Alice M. Colby, *The Portrait in Twelfth-Century French Literature* (Geneva, 1965). Hainsworth observes that Petrarch's "evocations of Laura's person are less descriptions than incantatory listings" of selected physical features; see *Petrarch the Poet*, 120–21.

myself and isolated me from other people, the curling locks of pure shining gold . . .]

In this listing of attributes, each accompanied only by a definite article that serves to render them curiously autonomous and at the same time absolute, the reader recognizes the entity that bears the name "Laura."[30]

This textual Laura is, in fact, a sort of *case vide,* to be filled by the projections of the reader's imagination. Yet Petrarch's text not only invokes this figure as absence; it dramatizes too the protagonist's creation of his own Laura. This effort of creation, to which we shall return, is attributed both to the spontaneous working of his fantasy and to the careful exercise of his poetic craft. It is much of the business that he is about in the course of the collection. Thus, in the *Rime,* in the absence of Laura there is the image of Laura, evoked with a frequency that rivals the presentations of the lady herself. It is first of all an image within, "that lovely smiling face, which I carry painted in my breast and see wherever I look" (96). Elusive as a woman and defiant of descriptive characterization, Laura becomes potentially a work of art. Its canvas may be not only the poet's heart but all of nature, projected onto the familiar natural landscape of rocks, trees, water, grass, and clouds, activated at any place, any time, to the exclusion of all else:

> Dico che perch'io miri
> mille cose diverse attento et fiso,
> sol una donna veggio e 'l suo bel viso.

(127, 12–14)

[I say that although I gaze intent and fixed on a thousand different things, I see only one lady and her lovely face.]

This compensation for the insubstantial and elusive image of a "present" Laura again reveals its inadequation. If there is an agent—variously "one who," "Amor," "a thought"—depicting the lady within, there is also the imperative for the poet to render that image more concrete, to externalize the image found in his heart to give it once again presence

30. Compare sonnet 348, in which most terms of the enumeration are accompanied by a superlative: "Da' più belli occhi, et dal più chiaro viso . . . da' più bei capelli . . . da le man, da le braccia . . . da' più bei piedi snelli" [from the most beautiful eyes and the brightest face . . . the most beautiful hair . . . the hands and arms . . . the beautiful light feet], to form together "la persona fatta in paradiso," the body made in paradise.

through the medium of *rime*, and in his confessed inadequacy to that task Petrarch's lyric persona introduces the insufficiencies of the description of Laura into the overt thematics of the collection: "I am not sufficient to describe her by myself, and I come untuned because of it" (125). Following her death, when this imperative becomes one with that of bearing witness to a unique Laura, he again records his failure:

> Da poi più volte ò riprovato indarno
> al secol che verrà l'alte bellezze
> pinger cantando, a ciò che l'ame et prezze,
> né col mio stile il suo bel viso incarno.
>
> (308, 5–8)

[Since then I have often tried in vain to depict in song for the age to come her high beauties, that it may love and prize them, nor with my style can I incarnate her lovely face.]

His efforts to carry out Love's instructions to depict Laura "to whoever did not see her" are in vain, and he can only conclude, "Therefore blessed the eyes that saw her alive!" (309).[31]

Yet Laura's status as a work of art is not entirely dependent in the *Rime* on the efforts of her devoted poet to achieve her portrait; she transcends the descriptive capacity of mortals, he tells us, precisely because she is a work of art, one fashioned by a divine artist. When a mortal artist, Simone Martini, paints in her portrait a work that could not have been "imagined" on earth, the poet can only conclude that he observed his subject in Paradise (77).[32] Even Nature, the supreme artist who fashioned Laura, turned to Heaven for the creation of her face:

> In qual parte del Ciel, in quale Idea
> era l'esempio onde Natura tolse

31. See Nancy J. Vickers, "Diana Described: Scattered Woman and Scattered Rhyme," in *Writing and Sexual Difference*, ed. Elizabeth Abel (Chicago, 1982), 106; Serenella Baggio, "L'immagine di Laura," *Giornale storico della letterature italiana* 156 (1979): 334.

32. Baggio notes that Petrarch's treatment of the portrait of Laura by Simone Martini emphasizes the neoplatonic idealism of the painter's vision rather than his faithful rendering of the "bel viso" ("L'immagine di Laura," 321–25). Willi Hirdt terms this Laura a "synthetic lady" whose anatomic individuality is subordinated to her higher qualities; see "Sul sonetto del Petrarca 'Per mirar Policleto a prova fiso'," *Miscellanea di Studi in onore di Vittore Branca*, I (Florence, 1983), 435–47 (citation, 444). For a suggestion of the relation of Simone's portrait to the feminine figures in his known works, see Travi, "Il primo Petrarca volgare," 20.

quel bel viso leggiadro in ch'ella volse
mostrar qua giù quanto lassù potea?

(159, 1–4)

[In what part of Heaven, in what Idea was the pattern from which
Nature copied that lovely face, in which she has shown down here
all that she is capable of doing up there?]

When Amor in turn assumes the role of artist, creating Laura by artfully
combining the beautiful elements afforded by Nature, the natural ele-
ments *become* the lady:

Onde tolse Amor l'oro et di qual vena
per far due treccie bionde? e 'n quali spine
colse le rose, e 'n qual piaggia le brine
tenere e fresche, et die' lor polso et lena?

(220, 1–4)

[Where and from what mine did Love take the gold to make two
blond tresses? From what bush did he pluck the rose and in what
meadow the fresh and tender frost, to give them pulse and breath?]

Through this series of implicit similes, Poole points out, Petrarch inverts
the rhetorically conventional order of the *descriptio* to suggest that Laura
herself represents the entire cosmos, the created universe, of which she is
the rarest, quintessential expression.[33] Petrarch himself emulates the
creative movement attributed here to Amor, not only combining but
animating the natural elements to render Laura:

et le rose vermiglie infra la neve
mover da l'ora, et discovrir l'avorio
che fa di marmo chi da presso 'l guarda . . .

(131, 9–11)

[and I would see the scarlet roses moved by the breeze amid the
snow, and the ivory uncovered that turns to marble whoever looks
on it from close by . . .]

33. Gordon Poole, "Il topos dell' 'effictio' e un sonetto del Petrarca," *Lettere Italiane*
32 (1980): 17–18.

When they are on occasion added together, Laura's individual beauties render her image not more but less concrete; they fashion an "icon of perfection" that is both more and less than the portrait of a woman.[34] Thus the image of a weeping Laura remains in the poet's heart:

> La testa or fino, et calda neve il volto,
> ebeno i cigli, et gli occhi eran due stelle . . .
> perle et rose vermiglie ove l'accolto
> dolor formava ardenti voci et belle,
> fiamma i sospir, le lagrime cristallo.
>
> (157, 9–10, 12–14)

[Her head was fine gold, her face warm snow, ebony her eyebrows, and her eyes two stars . . . pearls and crimson roses, where gathered sorrow formed ardent beautiful words, her sighs flame, her tears crystal.]

In the well-known formulations of "Giovene donna sotto un verde lauro" [A youthful lady under a green laurel] (*Rime* 30), the lady initially described as whiter and colder than snow is substituted by a laurel "that has branches of diamond and golden locks." The full reification of the laurel in this poem as an idol sculpted in living laurel further subverts the portrayal of Laura as woman, as the lover's meditation itself gradually effects her metamorphosis.[35] As Freccero comments of this Laura, "her virtues and her beauties are scattered like the objects of fetish worship. . . . Like the poetry that celebrates her, she gains immortality at the price of vitality and history."[36] Thus is Love invited to join the poet to witness "how much skill has gilded and impearled and incarnadined that noble body never seen elsewhere" (192). In an allegorical portrait late in the collection Laura's iconic attributes render her body as a "bella pregione" inhabited by her soul:

> Muri eran d'alabastro e 'l tetto d'oro,
> d'avorio uscio, et fenestre di zaffiro
> onde 'l primo sospiro

---

34. See the observations of Leonard Forster in *The Icy Fire: Five Studies in European Petrarchism* (Cambridge, 1969), 9.

35. Robert Durling, "Petrarch's 'Giovene donna sotto un verde lauro'," *MLN* 86 (1971): 11.

36. John Freccero, "The Fig Tree and the Laurel: Petrarch's Poetics," *Diacritics* (Spring 1975): 39. For the idolatrous nature of this representation, see also Durling, "Petrarch's 'Giovene donna'," esp. 12–20.

mi giunse al cor . . .
   D'un bel diamante quadro et mai non scemo
vi si vedea nel mezzo un seggio altero
ove sola sedea la bella donna.

(325, 16–19, 24–26)

[The walls were of alabaster and the roof of gold, the entrance of ivory and the windows of sapphire whence the first sigh reached my heart . . . In the midst could be seen a proud throne of squared and faultless diamond, where the beautiful lady sat alone.]

Other poems, evading entirely the imperative to describe or re-present Laura, render her emblematically as another living creature, as phoenix or as deer. Both are marked as Laura-surrogates through descriptive attributes, the phoenix with "gilded feathers about her noble white neck" (185), the deer as "a white doe . . . with two golden horns" and a "sweet proud look" (190). Both, however, remind us also of the distance that separates the poet from his lady; the haughty phoenix takes flight, the doe disappears as he is rapt in contemplation. The inscription "Nessun mi tocchi" [Let no one touch me] about the neck of the animal, with its Biblical echoes of a creature "made free" by her creator, also invokes the myth of Diana, of whom the stag is the favored animal, and through it the violation of the prohibition against seeing already enacted in the final stanza of *Rime* 23.[37]

The portrait of Laura is yet another surrogate image through which her presence in the *Rime* assumes an almost hallucinatory status. It appears to look so kindly upon the poet that he addresses it:

ma poi ch' i' vengo a ragionar con lei,
benignamente assai par che m'ascolte:
se risponder savesse a' detti miei!

(78, 9–11)

[then, when I come to speak to her, she seems to listen most kindly: if she could only reply to my words!]

This image, an acknowledged artifact, assumes the same enabling function with regard to the expression of desire as the portrayal of Laura as

37. See the discussion of Jonard, "I miti del Eros," 462. On the multiple associations and intertextual suggestiveness of Petrarch's *cerva*, see also Maria Luisa Doglio, "Il sonetto CXC," *Lectura Petrarce, V, 1985* (Padua, 1986), 249–64.

Daphne: both afford the distancing through which alone the avowal of desire becomes possible. To the poet's fervent wish in sestina 22 that the lady not escape his embrace as she had escaped that of Apollo corresponds the equally fervent apostrophe to Pygmalion, the sculptor who fell in love with a statue of his own creation, whose desire to possess his beautiful image was satisfied when Venus gave it life:

> Pigmaliòn, quanto lodar ti dei
> de l'imagine tua, se mille volte
> n'avesti quel ch' i' sol una vorrei!
>
> (78, 12–14)

[Pygmalion, how glad you should be of your statue, since you received a thousand times what I yearn to have just once!]

Hearing another speak sweetly of love, Petrarch's poet in his own kindled desire finds his beautiful lady "present wherever she was once sweet or kind to him" (143);[38] this same "bella donna," projected onto nature, deceives both eyes and ears:

> Con leggiadro dolor par ch'ella spiri
> alta pietà che gentil core stringe;
> oltra la vista, agli orecchi orna e 'nfinge
> sue voci vive et suoi santi sospiri.
>
> (158, 5–8)

[She seems with graceful sorrow to breathe deep pity that wrings a noble heart; beyond sight, my ears seem to hear her speak aloud her eloquent words and holy sighs.]

The elusive nature of this Laura, frustrating to the poet of the *Rime sparse,* has frustrated its readers as well. Complaining of the lack of assurance with which we may speak of one of the most celebrated ladies of our poetic tradition, Günter Eich proposes to remedy this situation: "nobody knows Laura, but we want to invent her at last. She plays piano . . .";[39] before him generations of readers, many of them poets,

38. Noferi, "La costituzione della parola impossibile," 203–4, notes a similar use of "trovare" in other poems and cites Freud concerning the hallucinatory phenomenon here represented.

39. See Anselm Haverkamp, "Laura's Metamorphoses: Eich's *Lauren*," *Comparative Literature* 36 (1984): 312–27. The citation is in translation from Eich's *Moles* in *Gesammelte Werke* (Frankfurt, 1973), I, 353.

had responded to Petrarch's lady, not only by the elaboration of a pseudohistorical dimension, but by the invention of their own Lauras. Yet despite all the representations of her elusive nature noted above, despite our inability (matching the poet's) to draw a satisfactory portrait of Laura, the reading of the "absent" Laura that has become a critical commonplace is misleading: if at the close of the collection we may still say that "nobody knows Laura," it is not because the poems render her only as absence.[40] Consider a poem early in the collection in which the poet, affirming that he had indeed revealed his love to Laura, laments her response:

> Lassare il velo per sole o per ombra,
> Donna, non vi vid'io
> poi che in me conosceste il gran desio
> ch' ogni altra voglia d'entr' al cor mi sgombra.
>
> (11, 1–4)

[Lady, I have never seen you put aside your veil for sun or for shadow since you knew the great desire in me that lightens my heart of all other wishes.]

While the veil here as a figure of evasion evokes the model of Daphne's refusal to hear the pleas of her enamored suitor, the "poi che" is suggestive of an anterior time in which Laura was not so evasive. Later the poet reproaches Envy for having made her wary of his attentions:

> troppo felice amante mi mostrasti
> a quella che' miei preghi umili et casti
> gradì alcun tempo, or par ch' odi' et refute.
>
> (172, 6–8)

[you made her think me too fortunate a lover, she who for a while accepted my humble and chaste prayers and now seems to hate and refuse them.]

Allusions such as these set the poet's present lament against a time in which we are free to imagine a different response, and indications of that

40. For a recent insistence on Laura as "absence," see the chapter "The Death of Beatrice and the Petrarchan Alternative" in Robert Pogue Harrison, *The Body of Beatrice* (Baltimore and London, 1988), 93–109.

response are not lacking in the *Rime*. Consider now one of the several poems recalling Laura's greeting:

> Volgendo gli occhi al mio novo colore,
> che fa di morte rimembrar la gente,
> pietà vi mosse; onde benignamente
> salutando teneste in vita il core.

> (63, 1–4)

[Turning your eyes to my strange color, which makes people remember death, pity moved you; wherefore, kindly greeting me, you kept my heart alive.]

This scene is Petrarch's version of a motif fundamental to stilnovist poetry; in particular, it recalls Dante's depiction of Beatrice's greeting in the *Vita Nuova*. As Rainer Warning observes, however, the principal motivation of the greeting, the lady's cognizance of the poet's state and her "pietà," "would be unthinkable in the *Vita Nuova*."[41] And repeatedly in Part I of the *Rime,* as the poet declares his determination to persist in his suit as well as in his devotion, a favorable reaction from Laura is not excluded. The adjective "cortese" marks some of the lapses in her generally inflexible attitude: her early greetings are a gift described as courteous, "cortese" (37), like the open gift of *Rime* 63 cited above, and later he will recall that

> Li occhi soavi ond'io soglio aver vita
> de le divine lor alte bellezze
> furmi in sul cominciar tanto cortesi.

> (207, 14–16)

[Her gentle eyes, from which I am wont to take life, were of their high, divine beauty so generous to me at the beginning.]

"At the beginning": but there are indications that her response does not entirely alter following her discovery of his love. In a poem in which Petrarch attempts to characterize his state to his friend Sennuccio—"I

---

41. Rainer Warning, "Imitatio und Intertextualität: Zur Geschichte Lyrischer Dekostruktion der Amortheologie: Dante, Petrarca, Baudelaire," in *Imitation: Das Paradigma der Europäische Renaissance-Literatur* (Festschrift für Alfred Noyer-Weidmer) (Wiesbaden, 1983), 303; for the stilnovist and Petrarchan renderings of the lady's greeting, see 292–313.

wish you to know how I am treated and what my life is like"—he records her contradictory attitudes:

> Qui tutta umile et qui la vidi altera,
> or aspra or piana, or dispietata or pia,
> or vestirsi onestate or leggiadria,
> or mansueta or disdegnosa et fera.
>
> (112, 5–8)

[Here I saw her all humble and there haughty, now harsh, now gentle, now cruel, now merciful; now clothed in virtue, now in gaiety, now tame, now disdainful and fierce.]

Persevering with a single-mindedness that recalls the *ferm voler* of his precursor Arnaut Daniel, he proclaims that

> . . . et mansuetudine et durezza
> et atti feri et umili et cortesi
> porto egualmente. . . .
>
> (229, 5–7)

[. . . I bring away equally mildness and harshness, cruel gestures and humble and courteous. . . .]

Nonetheless, in most of the poems of Part I that move beyond the poet's subjective state to include a reaction from Laura, it is her refusal that is recalled or recorded, as in the poem that of all the collected *rime* most resembles a conventional declaration of the lover's suit:

> Mille fiate, o dolce mia guerrera,
> per aver co' begli occhi vostri pace
> v'aggio proferto il cor, m' a voi non piace
> mirar sì basso colla mente altera. . . .
>
> (21, 1–4)

[A thousand times, O my sweet warrior, in order to have peace with your lovely eyes, I have offered you my heart; but it does not please you to gaze so low with your lofty mind. . . .]

This negative reaction, however, sharply differentiates Laura from the Ovidian Daphne, foreshadowing a new role that is first limned in the metamorphosis canzone 23. While the poet's declaration of fidelity to the "primo alloro" in that poem evokes the transformed Daphne, the lady herself also appears repeatedly in the canzone, always (with one significant exception) in her recognizable human form. To effect his initial transformation into the laurel, she is enlisted by Amor, whose own attempts to overcome the "duro effetto" of his chosen victim had been unsuccessful:

> ché sentendo il crudel di ch'io ragiono
> infin allor percossa di suo strale
> non essermi passato oltra la gonna,
> prese in sua scorta una possente Donna
> ver cui poco giamai mi valse o vale
> ingegno o forza o dimandar perdono;
> ei duo mi trasformaro in quel ch'i' sono . . .
>
> (23, 32–38)

[For that cruel one of whom I speak, seeing that as yet no blow of his arrows had gone beyond my garment, took as his patroness a powerful Lady, against whom wit or force or asking pardon has helped or helps me little; those two transformed me into what I am . . .]

While the vengeful archer here recalls Cupid's attack on a scornful Apollo, the complementary role attributed to the lady significantly distances her from the Ovidian nymph who figures in that project. We recall that Daphne's rejection of Apollo's suit, like the god's passion itself, resulted from Love's machinations: she too was struck by an arrow, the leaden arrow compelling not love but aversion.[42] In Ovid's account the role of Cupid is merely initiatory: he inflicts the two wounds that impose irreconcilably opposed passions, with the inevitable outcome of pursuit by one victim, flight by the other. In *Rime* 23 the three personae are realigned, as the lady, no longer a victim, assumes a status as agent equal if not superior to that of the god himself.[43]

In Petrarch's *Trionfo d'Amore*, where the all-conquering power of Amor as "vittorioso e sommo duce" is proclaimed, it is again the lady and not the god who effects the conquest. There the narrator, initially

---

42. Petrarch mentions this aversion in the *Rime* in sonnet 206, but not as an element governing his present relation to Laura: "S'i' 'l dissi, Amor l'aurate sue quadrella / spenda in me tutte, et l'impiombate in lei!" [If I said it, let Love use all his golden arrows on me and the leaden ones on her . . .].

43. The entire burden of a later recapitulation is that without Laura Amor is powerless to touch the poet (270).

joining Love's procession merely as a spectator, is rendered captive by "una giovinetta":

> Ella mi prese; et io, ch'avrei giurato
> difendermi d'uom coverto d'arme,
> con parole e con cenni fui legato.
>
> (III, 91–93)[44]

[She took me captive: I, who would have sworn to make defense against men bearing arms, was bounden by her arms and by her ways.]

But while throughout the *Trionfi* Laura remains the implacable and eventually victorious adversary of Amor, in the *Rime* there are numerous suggestions that her collaboration is not involuntary—suggestions that give us a Laura who is not Love's unwitting instrument but his full accomplice. It is to her conspiratorial role that the poet alludes when he records that Love and madonna "have plotted wrongfully against me" (57).

Here again we may take the measure of Petrarch's elusive Laura by measuring her distance from her mythological prototype. First Daphne: "Thus the god and the nymph sped on," Ovid tells us, "one made swift by hope and one by fear." Petrarch's poet is like Apollo in this, motivated by a constant hope that is prominently thematized in the *Rime*. Laura, however, is not motivated by the fear that speeds Daphne's flight, nor is she constrained by the fear of disclosure that in the troubadour tradition frequently determined the inaccessibility of a lady subject to marital and societal censure. Like the haughty lady of Dante's *rime petrose*, her refusal is a matter of her own volition.[45] Unlike Daphne, Laura commands her own fate, and for her there are many means of evasion.

The initial characterization of Laura as a "powerful Lady" in *Rime* 23 identifies a virtuality that is realized in the action of that poem as she

---

44. The close relation of this segment of the *Trionfo d'Amore* to the account of the *innamoramento* in canzone 23 is evident in the verse ". . . so in qual guisa / l'amante ne l'amato si trasforme" [I know how I am transformed into her I love] (III, 161–62).

45. In his "Al poco giorno" in imitation of Arnaut's "Lo ferm voler" Dante omits these societal elements hostile to the lovers, with the consequence that the lady's inaccessibility becomes a matter of her own decision; see Maria Simonelli, "La sestina dantesca fra Arnaut Daniel e il Petrarca," *Dante Studies* 91 (1973): 134.

presides over the poet's metamorphoses, culminating in a scene that dramatizes her imperious control and her manipulation of his unhappy fate:

> Poi la rividi in altro abito sola,
> tal ch' i' non la conobbi, o senso umano!
> anzi le dissi 'l ver pien di paura;
> ed ella ne l'usata sua figura
> tosto tornando fecemi, oimè lasso!
> d'un quasi vivo e sbigottito sasso.

(23, 75–80)

[Later I saw her alone in another garment such that I did not know her, oh human sense! rather I told her the truth, full of fear, and she to her accustomed form quickly returning made me, alas, an almost living and terrified stone.]

This single transformation of Laura's physical form in the poem is self-willed, and it is effected in order further to disorient the suppliant poet.[46] Clearly this Laura is not cast in the role of Daphne: she is a shape-shifter who also possesses the status of judge and pardoner. We witness once again her transformative power as she, on her own initiative, restores him to human form, only to repetrify him as he resumes his plaint:

> Poi che Madonna da pietà commossa
> degnò mirarme e ricognovve et vide
> gir di pari la pena col peccato,
> benigna mi redusse al primo stato.

(23, 132–35)

[Since my lady, moved with pity, deigned to gaze on me and recognized and saw that the punishment was equal to the sin, benignly she reduced me to my first state.]

The distant mythological prototype of *this* Laura is not the defenseless but forever inaccessible nymph of Ovidian story, she who forever refuses the lover's advances; it is an imperious goddess who responds to male pursuit, not with flight, but with vengeance. When the poet at last, a

---

46. Recall of the Ovidian myth to which this passage alludes (*Met.* II, 685–707) intensifies this depiction. It likens the lady to Mercury, who first forbids Battus to speak of his theft of Apollo's oxen, then uses disguise to induce Battus to disclose that which he had seen and punishes the disclosure.

new Acteon, comes upon her naked in a spring, she resumes the role of
"powerful Lady" in the mythological guise of the powerful Diana:
splashing water over the transfixed intruder, she transforms him into a
stag, to be pursued by his own hounds into the present of the poem.[47]
What are the implications of the casting of Laura into this second, less-
noted mythological role? Ovid refuses to pronounce on Diana's transfor-
mation of Acteon: "When the story had been told, opinions were
divided: some thought that the goddess had been too cruel, others praised
her, and declared her act in keeping with her strict chastity. Both sides,"
Ovid adds before passing on to another scene with other protagonists,
"could justify their views."[48]

This division of judgment concerning the encounter between Diana's
"strict chastity" and a mortal whose accidental violation is cruelly
punished is highly suggestive for the representation of Petrarch's Laura.
Let us take for a moment the side of those fictive hearers of Acteon's
story who praised the goddess. While Petrarch's poet laments the fact
that Amor left Laura free while compelling him to bondage, in other
poems her definitive liberty is attributed not to the god's perverse
omission but to her own defenses. Like the poet and the Ovidian Apollo
before Amor's assault, this Laura is not only confident but scornful of
the god's power; her disdain, unlike theirs, proves to be well founded in
an impregnable resistance, as the poet ruefully concedes:

> . . . voi, che mai pietà non discolora
> et ch'avete gli schermi sempre accorti
> contra l'arco d'Amor che 'ndarno tira.
>
> (44, 9–11)

[. . . you, whom pity never makes pale and who have your
defenses always ready against Love's bow, which he draws in
vain.]

This singular invulnerability will be associated later in the collection with
her virtue, and specifically with a resolute chastity for which the Ovidian
laurel will again afford a new resonance. The association, found in
moralizing readings of the myth of Daphne in which the tree's evergreen

---

47. For the adaptation of this myth to represent power relations, see Vickers, "Diana
Described," esp. 103.
48. *The Metamorphoses of Ovid*, 80.

property was commonly glossed as chastity,[49] is implicit as early as *Rime* 29, where it figures among other qualities of Laura:

> ch' è stella in terra, et come in lauro foglia
> conserva verde il pregio d'onestade,
> ove non spira folgore né indegno
> vento mai che l'aggrave.
>
> (46–49)

[for she is a star on earth, and as the laurel its leaf so she preserves the worth of chastity. No lightning ever comes, or unworthy wind, to bend her down!]

In sestina 142 the laurel is acknowledged as protection from the ardent light of Venus; in sonnet 263, at the close of Part I, chastity will be proclaimed Laura's particular "treasure" as the poet celebrates the "victorious triumphal tree," and *in morte* her "unvanquished chastity" has earned for her the laurel with which the poet imagines her adorned in Heaven (313).[50]

Laura's invulnerability, however, does not uniformly receive this edifying interpretation. The inaccessible Laura has also a vernacular prototype, the sovereign lady celebrated in the cult of *fin'amors*, who rewards the suffering of her suppliant admirer only with further signs of her scorn or indifference. She is capable even of cruelty, a potential already present in the otherwise idealized lady of the stilnovisti.[51] Dante's "Così nel mio parlar," with its vehement invocation of Love's vengeance against his cruel lady Petra, affords a dramatic model for the violence of the lady who opens the lover's breast and removes his heart in *Rime* 23.[52] This

49. See Cottino-Jones, "The Myth of Apollo and Daphne," 154–57, and Sara Sturm-Maddox, *Petrarch's Metamorphoses: Text and Subtext in the Rime sparse* (Columbia, Mo., 1985), 35–40. The interpretations of the myth are traced in Wolfgang Stechow, *Apollo und Daphne* (Leipzig and Berlin, 1932) and reviewed by Aldo Bernardo in *Petrarch, Laura, and the "Triumphs"* (Albany, N.Y., 1974), 204–5.

50. In the poems *in morte*, as Cottino-Jones observes, the laurel loses all direct connection with the Ovidian myth, representing always Laura herself or her invincible virtue ("The Myth of Apollo and Daphne," 153–54). The connection of the laurel with chastity is also prominent in the *Trionfi*, where Laura after her victory over Cupid leads a triumphal procession to place her symbolic laurel crown on the altar of patrician chastity (*Tr.Pud.*, 184–86).

51. See the illustrations of the lady's cruelty in Eugenio Savona, *Repertorio tematico del Dolce Stil Nuovo* (Bari, 1973), 168–212.

52. "Così vedess' io lui fender per mezzo / lo core a la crudele che 'l mio squatra," writes Dante [Would I might see him split her cruel heart right down the middle, for she is quartering mine]. See Santagata, "La canzone XXIII," 63.

characterization of Laura is prominent in the earliest versions of Pe-
trarch's collection, as in this sonnet of singularly violent imagery:

> mi vedete straziare a mille morti
> né lagrima però discese ancora
> da' be' vostr'occhi, ma disdegno et ira.
>
> (44, 12–14)

[you see me torn asunder by a thousand deaths, but nevertheless
no tear has ever fallen from your eyes, but only disdain and
anger.]

This unfeeling Laura not only provokes the declarations of despair and
alienation characteristic of the poet of the *Rime*; she responds actively,
as in a display of anger in which he sees Amor "lightning in her piercing
angry eyes" (147), compelling his humble submission "wherever she
angrily turns her eyes, who hopes to deprive my life of light" (179). As
in the metamorphosis canzone, when he continues to entreat her it is
only to encounter again and again her prideful disdain:

> Lasso, Amor mi trasporta ov' ir non voglio,
> et ben m'accorgo che 'l dever si varca;
> onde a chi nel mio cor siede monarca
> sono importuno assai più ch'i' non soglio.
>
> (235, 1–4)

[Alas, Love carries me off where I do not wish to go, and I see
well that we are crossing beyond what is permitted; thus I am
much more troublesome than I am wont to her who is enthroned
monarch in my heart.]

This designation of Laura as "monarca," a hapax in the *Rime*, is highly
suggestive of the courtly mode, and this Laura in her "harsh pride" again
recalls the courtly lady.

While one early sonnet cited above explains Laura's lack of response
as her refusal to "gaze so low with her lofty mind" (21), in another poem
a different attitude is inculpated:

> Se forse ogni sua gioia
> nel suo bel viso è solo
> et di tutt'altro è schiva . . .
>
> (125, 46–48)

[If, perhaps, she takes pleasure only in her lovely face and flees everything else . . .]

This attitude that makes of Laura the poet's "sweet enemy" is neither the most powerful nor the most direct suggestion in the *Rime* of her preoccupation with her own beauty, signaled in other poems in a tone that is sharply accusatory. Immediately following the assertion of her impregnable defenses against Love, the first of two curious sonnets about her mirror proposes an alternative to Ovid's frightened nymph as the mythological prototype for the unyielding lady:

> Certo, se vi rimembra di Narcisso,
> questo et quel corso ad un termine vanno—
> ben che di sì bel fior sia indegna l'erba.
>
> (45, 12–14)

[Certainly, if you remember Narcissus, this and that course lead to one goal—although the grass is unworthy of so lovely a flower.]

Already in the metamorphosis canzone 23 the poet had played Echo to an inaccessible Laura, remaining a disembodied voice; here the mythological allusion casts Laura in the role of Narcissus and her mirror as the poet's adversary:

> Ma s'io v'era con saldi chiovi fisso,
> non dovea specchio farvi per mio danno
> a voi stessa piacendo aspra et superba.
>
> (45, 9–11)[53]

[But if I had been nailed there firmly, a mirror should not have made you, because you pleased yourself, harsh and proud to my harm.]

The striking harshness of this image of the poet fixed with strong nails to the lady's mirror reveals the strength of his desire to take the place of

---

53. For the various poetic adaptations of Ovid's myth in the medieval period, see Frederick Goldin, *The Mirror of Narcissus in the Courtly Love Lyric* (Ithaca, 1967), and for its medieval allegorizations, see Louise Vinge, *The Narcissus Theme in European Literature up to the Early Nineteenth Century* (Lund, 1967). On the Narcissus resonances in *Rime* 45, see Mazzotta, "The *Canzoniere* and the Language of the Self," 278–82, and Vinge, 110–12, who notes that this ambiguous compliment to the beauty of a proud lady becomes a recurrent motif in the Petrarchan tradition.

that mirror, to introduce himself as the object in which Laura may see
the beauty that gives her such pleasure. The closing of the companion
sonnet addresses to Laura an unexpected indictment of her mirrors, felt
as sharp thorns by one who finds himself ignored in favor of "micidiali
specchi / che 'n vagheggiar voi stessa avete stanchi" [murderous mirrors
you have tired out with your love of yourself]:

> questi fuor fabbricati sopra l'acque
> d'abisso et tinti ne l'eterno oblio
> onde 'l principio de mia morte nacque.
>
> (46, 12–14)[54]

[these were made beside the water of hell and tempered in the
eternal forgetfulness whence the beginning of my death was born.]

The severity of this protest has its precedent in the lyric tradition, just
as the fate of Narcissus was within that tradition an example for ladies
too haughty to respond to a suitor's plaint.[55] Reflected in these mirrors is
a Laura who remains invulnerable to Love because she loves no one other
than herself:

> Questi poser silenzio al signor mio
> che per me vi pregava, ond'ei si tacque
> veggendo in voi finir vostro desio.
>
> (46, 9–11)

[These imposed silence on my lord, who was praying to you for
me; and he became still, seeing your desire end in yourself.]

---

54. Angelo Jacomuzzi, "Il primo sonetto del *Canzoniere*," in *Letteratura e critica: Studi
in onore di Natalino Sapegno* (Rome, 1977), finds this passage the most tragic of the entire
collection (58). It may also recall the fate of Narcissus, against which the poet warns his
lady: "Even then, when he was received into the abode of the dead," Ovid tells us, "he
kept looking at himself in the waters of the Styx" (*Met.* III, 504–5). For a probable Virgilian
recall, see Adelia Noferi, *L'Esperienza poetica del Petrarca* (Florence, 1962), 194–96.

55. Andreas Capellanus recommends this appeal to a lover hoping to overcome a lady's
resistance: "se senza isperanza del tuo amore mi lasci andare . . . a morte mi costrigni . . .
e così serai micidiale chiamata" [if you allow me to depart without hope of your love . . .
you condemn me to death . . . and thus you will be called homicidal]; cited from the
Trecento translation in Andrea Capellano, *Trattato d'Amore*, testo latino del secolo XII con
due traduzioni toscane inedite del secolo XIV, ed. Salvatore Battaglia (Rome, 1947), 93.
Dante's cruel Petra is a "scherana micidiale" ("Così nel mio parlar," 58). See also Guillaume
de Lorris, *Le Roman de la Rose*, ed. Ernest Langlois (Paris, 1920), II, 1507–1510: "Dames,
cest essemple aprenez, / Qui vers vos amis mesprenez / Car, se vos les laissiez morir / Deus
le vos savra bien merir" [Ladies, who mistreat your lovers, heed this example, for if you
allow them to die, God will hold you accountable].

The disquieting indication of a self-enamored Laura "whom pity never makes pale" (44), while not frequent in the collection, is underlined by its recurrence in the canzone that opens Part II of the *Rime,* where she is dramatically identified as "quella che sol per farmi morir nacque, / perch' a me troppo et a se stessa piacque" [her who was born to make me die, since she pleased me and herself too much] (264).[56]

In one of the celebrated "canzoni degli occhi" the poet intimates that his long suffering tempts him to suicide, "and the fault is hers who does not care" (71, 42–45). Although the next stanza opens with an apparent retraction, the accusation is not unique in the collection.[57] In a few poems, moreover, her obstinate impassivity is replaced by a suggestion of hostility, as in the allusion to a punishment of the poet recalling that exacted in canzone 23:

> Giunto m'à Amor fra belle e crude braccia
> che m'ancidono a torto, et s'io mi doglio
> doppia 'l martir; onde pur com'io soglio
> il meglio è ch'io mi mora amando et taccia.
>
> (171, 1–4)[58]

[Love has brought me within the reach of lovely, cruel arms that unjustly kill me, and if I complain he redoubles my torment; thus it is still better that I die loving and be silent, as I am wont.]

Very near the end of Part I, Laura is dramatically cast as an active antagonist whose glances, speech, and sudden reticences destroy him:

> Così li afflitti et stanchi spirti mei
> a poco a poco consumando sugge,

---

56. For a Freudian reading of the lover's response to Laura's feminine narcissism and its implications, see Gordon Braden, "Love and Fame: The Petrarchan Career," in *Pragmatism's Freud: The Moral Disposition of Psychoanalysis* (Baltimore, 1986), 126–58.

57. The early commentator Vellutello concurs with a similar attribution of blame to Laura in *Rime* 224. Here, as William J. Kennedy notes, Vellutello in "focusing upon the lady's wilful obstinacy . . . demythologizes what other commentators construed as her normative forbearance"; see "Ronsard's Petrarchan Textuality," *Romanic Review* 77 (1986): 96.

58. On "le persécuteur bien-aimé" as characteristic of a poetics founded in the ambivalence of desire, see Pierre Blanc, "L'oxymoron pétrarquesque ou de l'amour fou," *Revue des Etudes Italiennes* 29 (1983): 116–17.

e 'n sul cor quasi fiero leon rugge
la notte, allor quand'io posar devrei.

(256, 5–8)[59]

[Thus little by little she consumes and saps my afflicted, tired
spirits, and like a fierce lion she roars over my heart at night,
when I ought to rest.]

Is this Laura indifferent and unfeeling, or is she cruel? Or both,
unpredictably and disconcertingly, in alternation? Is she unaware of the
poet's suffering, or does she willfully occasion and then exacerbate it? Is
she the unknowing or reluctant object of his love, or the willful manipu-
lator of his fate? This lack of resolution is all the more striking in the
light of the final mention of Laura *in vita* that renders her as "aspro core
et selvaggio et cruda voglia / in dolce umile angelica figura" [a harsh heart
and wild cruel desire in a sweet, humble, angelic form] (265). Included in
Part II of the *Rime,* following immediately upon the great canzone "I'
vo pensando" but preceding the notice of Laura's death, the strategic
placement of this poem is incontestable, and it lays bare a dynamic
operative throughout the poems of Part I. Here we witness a radical
dissociation: the positive modifiers "dolce," "umile," and "angelica," we
now recall, have been repeatedly assigned to Laura in terms of her
beauty, and here once again they render her "figura." But here that
incomparable beauty is sharply and directly contrasted to appropriate
affective referents—"core," "voglia"—and these, "aspro," "selvaggio,"
and "cruda," are negatively defined.[60]

Petrarch's reader will anticipate, and perhaps protest: in the revisionary
movement effected in Part II of the *Rime* the poet will claim that he
himself had "misread" his lady when she was alive, construing and
blaming as cruelty or indifference what had been her pious attempts to
moderate his passion:

Or comincio a svegliarmi, et veggio ch' ella
per lo migliore al mio desir contese

59. For this poem as the extreme expression of the "obsessive and demonic" image of
Laura, see Glauco Cambon, "L'eterno femminino petrarchesco: Magia e impotenza della
metafora," *Italian Quarterly* 23 (1982): 15–16.

60. Kenelm Foster finds this poem, apparently written some two years after Laura's
death, singularly disconsonant with the celebration of her chastity and virtue toward which,
in his reading, her portrayal evolves; as answer to the questions of "Why write it" and
"Why place it here," he suggests only that Petrarch was responding to a chance reading of
a line by Arnaut Daniel, which he adapted to the content of poem 264. See *Petrarch, Poet
and Humanist* (Edinburgh, 1984), 100–101.

et quelle voglie giovenili accese
temprò con una vista dolce et fella.

(289, 5–8)

[Now I begin to awaken, and I see it was for the best that she resisted my desire and tempered those burning youthful lusts with a face both sweet and angry.]

These eventual rereadings, however, occur primarily among the poems *in morte;* in Part I of the *Rime,* as Petrarch's poet struggles to interpret Laura and advances contradictory interpretations, the question remains unresolved.

These poems give us a Laura whose presence has frequently been occulted by preoccupation with her mythological prototypes. She speaks twice in canzone 23, first forbidding the poet to tell of her action in opening his breast and removing his heart as she commands him imperiously, "Make no word of this." While this act of silencing anticipates that to which the final transformation alludes in likening the poet's fate to that of Acteon, Petrarch's suppression there of the words spoken by Ovid's Diana to the unfortunate hunter, "Now you are free to tell that you have seen me unveiled . . . if you *can* tell" ("sit poteris narrare"), reserves for Laura herself the single voicing of an interdiction against speech in the collection.[61] And again she speaks, striking fear into the poet now changed into a stone, to voice a singularly appropriate warning:

Ella parlava sì turbata in vista
che tremar mi fea dentro a quella petra,
udendo: "I' non son forse chi tu credi."

(23, 81–83)

[She spoke, so angry to see that she made me tremble within that stone, hearing: "I am not perhaps who you think I am!"]

Far from revealing her identity to either poet or reader, her words function instead to call it radically into question. Thus she establishes her distance both from the poet and from the reader, a distance to be maintained throughout the collection in the various and partially contradictory indices of her affective postures and her role.

61. See Vickers, "Diana Described," 109. For Laura as "at once the *voice of the interdict* and the *object of the interdict,*" see John Brenkman, "Writing, Desire, Dialectic in Petrarch's *Rime* 23," *Pacific Coast Philology* 9 (1974): 18.

Following these two highly dramatic and provocative utterances, Laura will not speak again directly in the *Rime sparse.* Yet we must listen closely, for Petrarch's Laura is characterized not only by her beauty but by her expressiveness. Her speech, depicted most often as that *dolce parlar* or *dolce favella* celebrated by earlier poets as an attribute of the favored lady,[62] is identified in the *Rime* as a principal agent of the poet's *innamoramento* (206). Here again Petrarch works a personal variation: the sweetness of Laura's speech is largely vested in its sound, favored by the homonymous relation to "l'aura" as it re-presents her sighs and her voice to his enchanted memory.[63] Like her beauty, these identify Laura as unique among women. Just as he who has not seen her glances "looks in vain for divine beauty," the poet tells us, so too he is ignorant of Love's awesome power:

> non sa come Amor sana et come ancide,
> chi non sa come dolce ella sospira
> et come dolce parla et dolce ride.
>
> (159, 12–14)

[he does not know how Love heals and how he kills, who does not know how sweetly she sighs and how sweetly she speaks and sweetly laughs.]

These verses, it has often been observed, are a major instance of Petrarch's classical *imitatio:* they derive directly from Horace's praise of his own mistress, "Dulce ridentem Lalagen amabo / Dulce loquentem" (*Odes* I,

62. For examples, see Paolo Trovato, *Dante in Petrarca: Per un inventario dei dantismi nei "Rerum vulgarium fragmenta"* (Florence, 1979), 135. The poet insists on this attribute, which aligns Laura's speech with others in terms of their effect on their audience; cf. sonnet 205: "dolce parlare et dolcemente inteso, / or di dolce òra, or pien di dolci faci!" [sweet speech and sweetly understood, now a soothing breeze, now full of sweet flame!].

63. This identification, fundamental to the aesthetics of the *Rime*, is fully realized in a sonnet late in the collection:

> L'aura mia sacra al mio stanco riposo
> spira sì spesso ch' i' prendo ardimento
> di dirle il mal ch' i' ò sentito et sento,
> che vivendo ella non sarei stat' oso.
>
> (356, 1–4)

[My sacred breeze breathes so often for my repose in weariness that I become bold to tell her the ills I have felt and feel, which I would not have dared to do while she was alive.]

22, vv. 23–24), and Laura's sweet laughter, her "dolce riso," is repeatedly coupled with her sweet speech in the poems of the *Rime sparse*. The Italian poet not only doubles the adverbial "dulce" with an adjective apt to represent all the various forms of verbal expression, but also expands the Horatian enumeration: the description of sweet speech and sweet laughter becomes peculiarly his own, as Foscolo long ago remarked, through the addition of equally sweet sighs to the lady's audible expressive repertoire.[64]

While both utterances attributed to the "possente Donna" of canzone 23 are controlled by the context of metamorphoses that distances them from the feminine figure encountered in Valchiusa in the dominant fiction of the collection, making them dramatic and ultimately undecipherable, elsewhere Laura's speech is integrated into a familiar descriptive system in which a limited number of conventional elements are interrelated and recombined. The shore listens to her sweet words just as it retains the imprint of her lovely foot (162). "Et co l'andar et col soave sguardo / s'accordan le dolcissime parole / et l'atto mansueto umile et tardo," affirms her poet [and with her walk and her gentle glance her most sweet words accord, and her mild, humble, slow gestures] (165): verbs are stilled to assume substantive presence, speech takes shape to accord with the modeling of action. Laura's words are given concrete form as Love's own *écriture*, rendered both visible and permanent just as the lady herself is immobilized and fixed in the images of numerous poems of the collection:

> Quel dolce pianto mi depinse Amore,
> anzi scolpio, et que' detti soavi
> mi scrisse entro un diamante in mezzo 'l core.
>
> (155, 9–11)[65]

[That sweet weeping Love drew, nay sculpted, and those gentle words he wrote, on a diamond in the midst of my heart.]

Again the plastic images recur in astonishing transmutations as the poet recalls the spectacle of Laura weeping:

64. Ugo Foscolo, *Opere*, II; cited in Dotti, "Petrarca: Il mito dafneo," 13.

65. The relation of this process to that described in sestina 30, where the laurel becomes "l'idolo mio scolpito in verde lauro" [my idol carved in living laurel] and diamonds figure the hardness of the lady herself, is particularly suggestive. For its implications, see Durling, "Petrarch's 'Giovene donna'," 11–12.

>perle et rose vermiglie ove l'accolto
>dolor formava ardenti voci et belle,
>fiamma i sospir, le lagrime cristallo.
>
>   (157, 12–14)[66]

[pearls and crimson roses, where gathered sorrow formed ardent beautiful words, her sighs flame, her tears crystal.]

Laura's voice itself is suppressed in such depictions, which subject her speech to a process of reification similar to that informing the fragmented and often iconic description of her body.[67] Yet in Part I of the *Rime*, the very absence of her recorded speech creates a void in the text that insistently draws the reader's attention. Laura's discourse, like Laura herself, is singular, its extraordinary nature repeatedly proclaimed even as its tenor and content are withheld.[68] Following the lead of Dante in the *Vita Nuova*, he affirms that her voice, "pleasing even in Heaven, utters words so gracious and dear, that he could not conceive it who has not heard it" (193); still following Dante's lead, he insists that her words make the listener tremble with wonder, "tremar di meraviglia" (200).

What, then, do we know of Laura's words, and the circumstances of their utterance? Let us reconsider for a moment the speech of the poet himself. In *Rime* 23 it is his verbal or written manifestation of desire that provokes as punishment his transformation into a stone, unable even to cry out except through his rhymes.[69] His voice, however, is not silenced by this or any of the other obstacles repeatedly opposed to his speaking. If he is not to speak Laura's name, other "names" will serve as subterfuge: "l'auro," "l'aura," even the *lauro* itself.[70] His poems may be charged to utter his message; less conventionally, the river Rhône receives a commission to address his words to a distant Laura:

---

66. For Petrarch's treatment of Laura's tears evoked together with her sighs or her words, see Natascia Tonelli, " 'Piangea Madonna' (Da *Vita Nuova* XXII a *Rerum vulgarium fragmenta* CLV–CLVIII)," *Studi Danteschi* 57 (1985): esp. 43–44.

67. Vickers remarks that "bodies fetishized by a poetic voice logically do not have a voice of their own" ("Diana Described," 107).

68. For her "parolette accorte" (37, 183, 253), see Emilia Chirilli, "Di alcuni dantismi nella poesia di Francesco Petrarca," *L'Alighieri* 16 (1975): 55–59. See also poems 156, 158.

69. Santagata observes that the metamorphoses to which the poem alludes are chosen to highlight a distorted or sinful use of speech ("La canzone XXIII," 59–60).

70. See François Rigolot, "Nature and Function of Paronomasia in the *Canzoniere*," *Italian Quarterly* 18 (1974): 31: it enables the poet to "dire sans dire."

> Basciale 'l piede o la man bella et bianca;
> dille (e 'l basciar sie 'n vece di parole):
> "Lo spirto è pronto, ma la carne è stanca."
>
> (208, 12–14)

[Kiss her foot or her lovely white hand; tell her (let your kiss be heard as words): "The spirit is ready, but the flesh is weary."]

In other ways too the poet, conditioned not only by interdiction and transformation but also by fear, humility, or the physical obstacle of distance, nonetheless manages to speak, and not only with pen, ink, and *rime*, as he hopes still for comprehension for the pain that he cries out in silence, "la qual tacendo i' grido" (71).[71]

And so Laura also speaks, in silence. Again and again in the *Rime*, it is for Laura as for the poet himself: when words are suppressed, it is only to find new channels of expression, as in her apparent sympathy for his suffering: "Sometimes her tongue is silent but her heart cries out with a loud voice" (150). In this transposition of expressive function actions often speak louder than words, as her lowered gaze speaks eloquently on an occasion of his departure:

> Chinava a terra il bel guardo gentile
> et tacendo dicea, come a me parve:
> "Chi m'allontana il mio fedele amico?"
>
> (123, 12–14)

[She bent to earth her lovely noble glance and in her silence said, as it seemed to me: "Who sends away from me my faithful friend?"]

These are but two examples of a displacement that repeatedly renders Laura's words not as spoken but as recollected or imagined, words pronounced in fantasy or in a dream. Her speech appears with the conventional markers of direct discourse only when its source is problematized. In one of a series of poems apparently written in response to a report of her illness, she appears in a dream to calm the poet's fears: "et parea dir: "Perché tuo valor perde? / Veder quest'occhi ancor non ti si tolle" [and she seemed to say: "Why does your worth languish? Seeing

---

71. Here Petrarch reproduces almost exactly the formulation in Ovid's *Ars amandi* I, 574: "Saepe tacens vocem verbaque vultus habet;" see Ettore Bonora, "Le 'Canzoni degli occhi' (LXXI-LXXII-LXXIII)," *Lectura Petrarce, IV, 1984* (Padova, 1985), p. 301.

these eyes is not yet taken from you"] (33). The Laura who had witnessed the outward signs of his suffering occasioned by Love's violence must, he is certain, have commented to herself on their meaning:

> et certo son che voi diceste allora:
> "Misero amante! a che vaghezza il mena?
> Ecco lo strale onde Amor vol ch' e' mora."
>
> (87, 9–11)

[and I am certain that you said then: "Miserable lover! where does his desire lead him? Here is the arrow by which Love wishes him to die."]

The frequent occurrence of the verb "to seem," *parere*, to introduce these utterances inscribes them within the visionary mode of the poet's meditation, much like the attribution of words to her veil that "seems to speak" its acknowledgment of his loss as it hides her eyes (38).[72] When such a marker is absent from a direct citation of Laura's speech, that Laura herself is part of a vision, as in her appearance late in Part I to warn the fearful poet that their separation is soon to be definitive:

> "Non ti soven di quella ultima sera,"
> dice ella, "ch' i' lasciai li occhi tuoi molli
> et sforzata dal tempo me n'andai?
> "I' non tel potei dir allor, né volli;
> or tel dico per cosa esperta et vera:
> non sperar di vedermi in terra mai."
>
> (250, 9–14)

["Do you not remember that last evening," she says, "when, leaving your eyes moist, I departed forced by time? I could not nor did I wish to tell you then; now I tell you as something tested and true: do not hope ever to see me on earth."]

Parere returns in the counterpart to this imagined discourse in Part II *in morte*, where the message is conveyed not by dream-words, but by her glance:

72. This attribution of speech to personified entities and in particular the introductory locution "par che" is frequent in the lyrics of Cavalcanti; see Maria Corti's introduction to Guido Cavalcanti, *Rime*, ed. Marcello Ciccuto (Milan, 1987²), 20.

Quel vago, dolce, caro, onesto sguardo
dir parea: "To' di me quel che tu poi,
che mai più non mi vedrai da poi
ch'avrai quinci il pe' mosso a mover tardo,"

(330, 1–4)

[That sweet, dear, virtuous, yearning glance seemed to say: "Take
what you can from me, for you will never see me here again, once
you have moved your unwilling foot away,"]

an admonition followed by a more elaborate explanation "spoken" by
her eyes:

Taciti, sfavillando oltra lor modo,
dicean: "O lumi amici che gran tempo
con tal dolcezza feste di noi specchi,
il Ciel n'aspetta; a voi parrà per tempo,
ma chi ne strinse qui dissolve il nodo,
e 'l vostro, per farv'ira, vuol che 'nvecchi."

(9–14)[73]

[Silently, sparkling beyond their wont, they were saying: "O
friendly lights, who for a great time with such sweetness have
made us your mirrors, Heaven awaits us; to you it will seem early,
but He who bound us here dissolves the knot and in order to
cause you sorrow ordains that the knot of your life shall grow
old."]

The most poignant summary of this silent communication is found in
another recall of that final encounter, in the poem that contains the first
notice of Laura's death:

di speranza m'empieste et di desire
quand'io parti' dal sommo piacer vivo,
ma 'l vento ne portava le parole.

(267, 12–14)

73. Cf. *Rime* 328 and 331 for the words that he might have read on that occasion in
Laura's face, "ne la fronte a Madonna." For this insertion of direct discourse within a
secondary system or "subsystem" of temporal reference, see Edoardo Taddeo, "Petrarca e
il tempo," *Studi e problemi di critica testuale* 27 (1983): 103–4.

[with hope you filled me and with desire, when I left still alive
that highest pleasure, but the wind carried off the words.]

Thus despite the fact that the story of the speaker's love for Laura
remains largely devoid of external event, and despite the absence of direct
exchange between poet and lady, an illusion of dialogue is established
between the poet of the collection, whose speech is silenced by interdic-
tion, and the lady, whose direct response to his amorous urgings is
equally denied. Nor does Laura's death put an end to the illusory
dialogue. On the contrary: following her death, the report of her speech
becomes more frequent. He imagines her responding both lovingly and
piously from Heaven to his sighs, or assuring him that she awaits him in
the third circle of Paradise (279, 341, 342, 302); within his mind she
appears with such immediacy that he begs her for her sweet speech,
reporting that "sometimes she replies and sometimes she does not say a
word" (336). She both comforts and rebukes him in a long imagined
dialogue (359); leading him at last to God in a prayerful fantasy, she
commends his changed *costumi* that now prompt her love for the aging
poet (362).[74]

In this generally edifying vein, Petrarch's reader draws inferences
concerning the content of Laura's speech. The characterization of her
words as holy, *sante*, is frequent, but in most instances devoid of any
precise meaning: the "alte parole sante," high holy words, of 204 are not
unlike her speech filled with "sweet high insights" (213), her sweet words
"chaste and strange" (220), or the "holy word" that a tranquil old age
might have led her to use in response to the account of his ancient burden
of love (317). Nonetheless, as if in confirmation of the saintly quality of
her discourse, we are assured that her "ragionar cortese," her courteous
speech, if properly understood could transform a soul from baseness to
nobility (270), and that her angelic words are better understood in Heaven
than among mortals (275). More than once the poet gratefully recalls her
faithful counsel that had made him think of his salvation even as he
burned with love, her "fedel consiglio" that urges him toward Heaven
(285, 289). Her speech, he recalls, was not only sweet but wise and
humble (297). In the *Trionfo della Morte* her wise and chaste speech is
cited as one of her weapons in overcoming Cupid (I, 7–9), and in the
Rime too, reflecting on her chastity, he will recollect:

> Dolci durezze et placide repulse
> piene di casto amore et di pietate . . .

74. For Foster this womanly, communicative Laura is arguably Petrarch's finest creation;
see *Petrarch, Poet and Humanist*, 44–45.

gentil parlar in cui chiaro refulse
con somma cortesia somma onestate. . . .

(351, 1–2, 5–6)

[Sweet rigors and placid repulses full of chaste love and pity . . .
noble speech in which highest chastity brightly shone with highest
courtesy. . . .]

The lady speaks of chastity, then, and of honor, assimilating her
speech both *in vita* and *in morte* to an exemplary, morally edifying
vein.[75] Yet while Laura may be praised as a fountain of eloquence, it is
not the wisdom of her words to which the poet is primarily attentive, but
rather the sweetness of her speech and her sighs, the sound of a voice that
takes away every other care (105, 258). Her words, whose sound is
silence, induce forgetfulness of all other concerns; it is from them, the
poet reminds Amor, that he learns what love is, "che cosa è amore"
(270).

Laura's speech, moreover, does not exhaust her expressive repertory.
Generally unobserved by critics, the lady also sings.[76] The record of her
singing appears frequently in the series of nouns and conventional
modifiers that characterize her vocal expression: "l'angelico canto et le
parole" (133); " 'l riso e 'l canto e 'l parlar dolce umano" (249); "un
mover d'occhi, un ragionar, un canto" (264). In the *Trionfo della Morte*
the poet demands of his reader: "chi udirà il parlar di saver pieno / e 'l
canto pien d'angelico diletto?" [Who now will hear the wisdom of her
words, or the angelic sweetness of her song?] (I, 149–50). In a poem of
the *Rime* that illustrates the close affinities between the *Trionfi* and the
lyric collection, a vision of Laura in the company of other ladies captures
her in the act of singing:

Poi le vidi in un carro triunfale,
Laurea mia con suoi santi atti schifi
sedersi in parte et cantar dolcemente.

(225, 9–11)

75. A very unusual sonnet in dialogue, *Rime* 262, consists entirely of a conversation
between a woman, presumably Laura, and her mother on the subject of chastity.

76. Laura's singing was, however, to be noted by later poets. Her many literary
descendants in the Petrarchan tradition were much admired for their musical ability; as
Forster observes, "almost all petrarchistic ladies can sing or play an instrument or both"
(*The Icy Fire*, 11–12). For a recent notation, see Adelia Noferi, "*Voluptas canendi, voluptas
scribendi:* Divagazioni sulla vocalità in Petrarca," *Paradigma* 7 (1986): 6–7.

[Then I saw them in a triumphal chariot, and my Laurel with her holy, retiring manner sitting to the side and sweetly singing.]

In a less visionary mode, the poet represents her on the shady, flowering hillside typical of her appearances in the *Rime,* where she sits sometimes thoughtful, sometimes singing (243).

> Qui cantò dolcemente, et qui s'assise . . .
> qui disse una parola, et qui sorrise,
> qui cangiò il viso . . . ;
>
> (112, 9, 12–13)

[Here she sang sweetly and here sat down . . . here she said a word, here she smiled, here she frowned . . .]

Like her glances, her greeting granted or withheld, and even her weeping, this representation of the lady belongs not to a realism in which concrete event intrudes upon the lyric mode, but rather to the transformation of Laura's presence into spectacle.[77]

The adjectives that characterize Laura's song corroborate its association with her speech: it too is *dolce,* angelic, heavenly. Yet with regard to both its content and the effect on its audience, in particular the privileged audience who is the poet-lover of the *Rime,* the significance of that "singing that is felt in the soul" (213) is not fully accounted for by this apparent assimilation. Its direct association with amorous expression, implicit in the *Rime,* is explicitly acknowledged in the retelling of the poet's story in the *Trionfi,* where it is Laura herself who evokes it. Here, as Petrarch attributes to her the revision of that presumption of unrequited love lamented throughout the lyric collection, the burden of the song is love and its concealment, the song as subterfuge replacing direct avowal. Its function is to reveal what words cannot say, and its concern is precisely the words of love that may not be spoken:

> "Ma non si ruppe almen ogni vel, quando
> soli i tuo' detti, te presente, accolsi,
> 'Dir più non osa il nostro amor' cantando?"
>
> (*Trionfo della Morte* II, 148–50)

["But was not every veil between us rent, when in thy presence I received thy verse, and sang, 'Our love dares not say more than this'?"]

77. See Umberto Bosco, *Francesco Petrarca* (Bari, 1968), 30–32.

In the absence of such avowals in the *Rime,* the allure of Laura's song is suggested through a set of textual affinities. The first of these, like the echo of Horace that founds the description of her sweet speech and sweet laughter, exemplifies again Petrarch's recourse to classical models:

> . . . così avolge et spiega
> lo stame de la vita che m'è data
> questa sola fra noi del ciel sirena.
>
> (167, 12–14)

[thus she both threads and unwinds the spool of my appointed life, this only heavenly siren among us.]

This unusual representation, it has been suggested, is the single direct derivation in the *Rime* of Platonic doctrine, alluding to the celestial harmony resulting from the singing of seven sirens in a movement governed by the Fates.[78] In Petrarch's poem, however, Laura's manipulation of the thread of his life makes of her a Fate as well as a siren; and while the allusion to the Fates renders her powerful, mention of the siren renders her seductive: when Love looses her breath in a voice described as "clear, soft, angelic, divine," the poet confides, the sound that he hears is one whose hypnotic sweetness binds the senses. In this lies its peril: the seductive sweetness of music itself is repeatedly acknowledged in Petrarch's meditations on the appeal to the senses in earthly experience.[79]

In one of his *Epistole metriche* closely linked to the thematic concerns of the *Rime,* Petrarch describes his fear of Amor's renewed attack in terms of the sweet melodies carried by a nymph's angelic voice.[80] His preamble to the identification of Laura as siren initiates more precise literary associations: with that most famous of sirens in whose unbearably sweet song lay the peril of shipwreck for the mariner. The relevance of Ulysses' adventure to the poet-lover's story in the *Rime* is confirmed in another, later mention of sirens in the collection:

> Così di ben amar porto tormento,
> et del peccato altrui cheggio perdono—

---

78. See Robert V. Merrill, "Platonism in Petrarch's *Canzoniere,*" *Modern Philology* 27 (1929): 162. The account of the myth of Er is found in the tenth book of the *Republic.*

79. For these meditations, frequent in Petrarch's letters and in the *De remidiis utriusque fortune,* see Noferi, "*Voluptas canendi, voluptas scribendi,*" 4–5.

80. I, 8, "Ad Lelium suum": "carmina quid dulcesque modos, quos nocte serena, / quos oriente die vel quos moriente decora / concinit angelico trans rivum murmure Nimpha"; cited from *Opere di Francesco Petrarca,* ed. Emilio Bigi (Milan, 1968⁴), 426.

anzi del mio, che devea torcer li occhi
dal troppo lume, et di sirene al suono
chiudere li orecchi, et ancor non men pento
che di dolce veleno il cor trabocchi.

(207, 79–84)[81]

[Thus from loving well I gain torments, and I ask to be pardoned
for another's crime; rather for my own, for I should have turned
my eyes away from the excessive light, closed my ears to the siren
song; and still I do not repent that my heart is overflowing with
sweet poison.]

Here his inability to turn away from the brilliant light that overwhelms
him is coupled with the failure to seal his ears against the siren's song,
and both light and song are subsumed under the rubric of "dolce veleno,"
the sweetness strikingly transposed from the light and song to the poison
that destroys him. Like the light of Laura, which, as we shall see, not
only attracts but dazzles and ultimately blinds, the siren's song both
attracts and threatens with destruction, lending special force to the
depiction of Laura's singing in *Rime* 220 as that which undoes him, "quel
cantar celeste che mi disface."

While Petrarch had not read Homer, other classical accounts of Ulys-
ses' passage before the sirens were available to him, as well as a number
of allegorical readings. But he did not have to look so far: the immediate
subtext of the poet's self-reproach in *Rime* 207 is the reproach delivered
by Beatrice in the *Commedia* to the pilgrim Dante on the occasion of
their reunion in the Earthly Paradise. Beatrice insists in this reproach,
she tells the now-repentant Dante,

". . . perché mo vergogna porte
del tuo errore, e perché altra volta,
udendo le sirene, sie più forte."

(*Purg.* XXXI, 43–45)

["that you may now bear shame for your error, and another time,
hearing the Sirens, may be stronger."]

81. Similarly, in one of the *rime disperse* Petrarch represents the peril of amorous
entanglement in terms of the sirens' song, to which he claims to have been at last rendered
deaf by the death of Laura; see "Responsio ad Iacobum da Imola" in Durling, *Petrarch's
Lyric Poems*, 593.

This rebuke does not, of course, accurately reflect the famed adventure of Ulysses, a voyager who, forewarned by Circe and securely lashed to the mast, was piloted past the perilous rocks of the sirens by a crew whose ears were literally sealed. That Dante might be cast as a new, errant Ulysses has already been suggested, however, in a yet more famous passage of the *Commedia* in which a siren figures not allusively, but dramatically. The pilgrim dreams of a hideous female figure who is transformed under his gaze into a beautiful woman, and that woman immediately sings, proclaiming her identity:

> "Io son," cantava, "io son dolce serena,
> che' marinari in mezzo mar dismago;
> tanto son di piacere a sentir piena!
> Io volsi Ulisse del suo cammin vago
> al canto mio; e qual meco s'ausa,
> rado sen parte; sì tutto l'appago!"
>
> (*Purg.* XIX, 19–24)

["I am," she sang, "I am the sweet Siren who leads mariners astray in mid-sea, so full am I of pleasantness to hear. Ulysses, eager to journey on, I turned to my song; and whosoever abides with me rarely departs, so fully do I satisfy him."]

While this boastful claim to have seduced Ulysses from his course has prompted a wealth of commentary,[82] its significance as subtext in the *Rime* lies in Petrarch's inscription into his own text of the siren as she appears to the sleeping pilgrim of the *Commedia*. That inscription has three essential elements: (1) she is a beautiful, seductive female figure; (2) she is transformed by the observer's attentive gaze, which "com' amor vuol, così le colorava" [colored her pallid face even as love requires]; (3) she boasts of the capacity not only to attract men but to detain them, so great is her ability to satisfy the desires of any who fall under her spell. In the record of his own dream experience the pilgrim offers confirmation of her claim: "cominciava a cantar sì, che con pena / da lei avrei mio intento rivolto" [she began to sing so that it would have been hard for me to turn my attention from her] (XIX, 17–18).

The first characteristic of this siren, that of her seductive beauty, is

---

82. Among numerous readings see Marianne Shapiro, *Woman Earthly and Divine in the Comedy of Dante* (Lexington, Ky., 1975), 93; Joseph Mazzeo, *Medieval Cultural Tradition in Dante's Comedy* (Ithaca, 1960), 209–11; David Thompson, *Dante's Epic Journeys* (Baltimore and London, 1974), 40–49.

only too evident in Petrarch's depiction of his Laura, and no subtext is required for its full understanding. The second and third, however—the dependence of the image on the lover's creative participation and the satisfaction afforded by the apparition—are exemplified in a poem recording an experience comparable to that of the dreaming pilgrim:

> Ma mentre tener fiso
> posso al primo pensier la mente vaga,
> et mirar lei et obliar me stesso,
> sento Amor sì da presso
> che del suo proprio error l'alma s'appaga;
> in tante parti et sì bella la veggio
> che se l'error durasse, altro non cheggio.
>
> (129, 33–39)

[But as long as I can hold my yearning mind fixed on the first thought, and look at her and forget myself, I feel Love so close by that my soul is satisfied by its own deception; in so many places and so beautiful I see her, that, if the deception should last, I ask for no more.]

Here the similarity is underscored by Petrarch's adoption of Dante's rhymes; other occurrences of the rhyme series *dismago: vago: appago* in the collection confirm Dante's rendering of the siren's song as one of the passages of the *Commedia* whose traces are particularly prominent in the *Rime sparse*.[83] The element of fascination and of spellbound gratification is most evident in the first of these, as the lover-as-Acteon in the metamorphosis canzone gazes transfixed on the forbidden nakedness of the lady:

> in una fonte ignuda
> si stava, quando 'l sol più forte ardea.
> Io perché d'altra vista non m'appago
> stetti a mirarla . . .
> et in un cervo solitario et vago
> di selva in selva ratto mi trasformo.
>
> (23, 150–53, 158–59)

[. . . in a spring naked when the sun burned most strongly. I, who am not appeased by any other sight, stood to gaze on her

---

83. There are no fewer than seven occurrences, in whole or in part with negligible variations, listed by Trovato, *Dante in Petrarca*, 93.

. . . and into a solitary wandering stag from wood to wood quickly I am transformed.]

It is the association of this effect with the "dolcezza" or sweetness characteristic of the siren's appearance that informs the poet's longing for an absent Laura who alone can still the desire of his eyes, a desire that shows forth his cares:

> et la fera dolcezza ch'è nel core
> per gli occhi, che di sempre pianger vaghi
> cercan dì et notte pur chi glie n'appaghi.
>
> (37, 62–64)

[the cares and the savage sweetness that are in my heart, my eyes that, always eager to weep, seek day and night only for her who will still their desire.]

The siren's song of *Purgatorio* XIX functions as a supplement to the Petrarchan text, affording an evaluatory perspective for the poet's description of his obsessive (re)creation of Laura's image in inanimate nature.

In Dante's *poema sacro*, Ulysses is but the single, boastfully cited example of a more general principle, as the siren's attraction illustrates the larger lesson of choice that runs through the *Commedia* as a whole.[84] The "mezzo mar" where her tempting song is to be heard recalls that other metaphor of life's voyage that located the pilgrim Dante "nel mezzo del cammin di nostra vita" [midway in the journey of our life] in the opening verse of the *Inferno*,[85] and the effect of that song recalls also another locus of the *Commedia* that enjoys a privileged status as subtext in the *Rime:* the definition of the lustful as those "who subject reason to desire" in *Inferno* V. Already before Dante the Christian mythographers had allegorized the siren who tempts Ulysses as lust, as the embodiment

84. See Robert Hollander, *Allegory in Dante's Commedia* (Princeton, 1969), esp. 136, 140–41; Glyn P. Norton, "Retrospection and Prefiguration in the Dreams of *Purgatorio*," *Italica* 47 (1970): 351–65.

85. The commentary of Pietro di Dante explains: "By her deceiving delight, the Siren would submerge us in the three vices in the middle of the sea, i.e., midway through life's course"; cited from the paraphrase by John Paul Bowden in Bernard Stambler, *Dante's Other World: A Reading of the Purgatorio* (New York, 1957), 349. For the relation of the siren to the metaphors of choice, see W. B. Stanford, "The 'Maggior Fortuna' and the Siren in *Purgatorio* XIX," in *Dante Commentaries*, ed. D. Nolan (Dublin, 1977), 85–91.

of sensual pleasure.[86] When the pilgrim at last offers to Beatrice the shamed confession that "present things, with their false pleasure" had turned his steps astray following her death (*Purg.* XXXI, 34–35), she begins a general admonition concerning sirens with a reminder of the supreme beauty once present to him in her own beautiful body, then continues in terms highly reminiscent of his recent dream:

> "e se 'l sommo piacer sì ti fallio
> per la mia morte, qual cosa mortale
> dovea poi trarre te nel suo disio?"
>
> (52–54)[87]

[and if the highest beauty thus failed you by my death, what mortal thing should then have drawn you into desire for it?]

Vulnerability to the siren's song and its impact upon moral choice is one of the major points of intersection between the experience of the poet-lover of the *Rime sparse* and that of the pilgrim of the *Commedia*. Yet that relation itself confronts the reader who recognizes the presence of the Dantean subtext with a fundamental difference. In the intertextual strategy that relates the *Rime* to both the *Vita Nuova* and the *Commedia*, it is Beatrice who affords the pervasive prototype for Petrarch's Laura, and among the female incarnations of desire in Dante's poems, Beatrice, like the "holy and alert" lady who alerts Virgil to the present peril for the pilgrim, is the opposite of the siren, and her adversary;[88] thus she can

---

86. See D. W. Robertson, Jr., *A Preface to Chaucer* (Princeton, 1962), 143: "the sirens represent lust on the rock of the flesh"; Pierre Courcelle, "Quelques symboles funéraires du Neo-Platonism latin," *Revue des Etudes Anciennes* 46 (1944): 90; O. Beigbeder, *Lexique des Symboles* (Paris, 1969), 144, 181–182; Giorgio Padoan, *voce* "sirene," *Enciclopedia Dantesca* 5 (Rome, 1976): 268–69. The bestiary tradition, well known to Petrarch as to Dante, exploits this reading of the siren as signifying the temptations of the flesh; see Jean Maurice, "Lectures du Bestiaire d'Amour de Richard de Fournival" (Thèse pour le doctorat de 3e cycle: Faculté des Lettres et Sciences humaines de Rouen, 1983), II, 349.

87. This "mortal thing" of course anticipates the "pargoletta" evoked by Beatrice in her rebuke, and thus suggests a relation to the lady who figures in two of Dante's own *Rime* (87, 89) and in one of the *petrose*. See Colin Hardie, "Dante's 'Mirabile Visione' (*Vita Nuova* xlii)," in *The World of Dante: Essays in Dante and His Times*, ed. C. Grayson (Oxford, 1980), 135–36; Sara Sturm-Maddox, "The *rime petrose* and the Purgatorial Palinode," *Studies in Philology* 84 (1987): 119–33.

88. See Shapiro, *Woman Earthly and Divine*, 93. Robert Hollander suggests that Beatrice is Dante's "antisiren" and the siren a false Beatrice; see *"Purgatorio* XIX: Dante's Siren/ Harpy,"* in *Dante, Petrarch, Boccaccio: Studies in the Italian Trecento in Honor of Charles S. Singleton*, ed. Aldo S. Bernardo and Anthony L. Pellegrini (Binghamton, N.Y., 1983), 79–80; *Allegory in Dante's Commedia*, 136–44.

chide Dante for having listened to the siren's song and at the same time
exemplify the opposing principle of love rightly directed that may protect
him from the seduction of the siren's deceptive pleasure. In the Laura of
the *Rime* the roles of Beatrice and the siren, the positive and the negative,
the desired and the feared aspects of female attraction are combined.
They suggest over and over again, as Cambon observes, the obsessive
preoccupation in the collection with the erotic image "sacralizzato e
demonizzato insieme," rendered at once both sacred and demonic.[89]

Not so, says Amor. Very near the end of the *Rime sparse*, the god
assures the poet that Laura should indeed have been for him a "scala al
Fattor," and his enumeration of her exceptional qualities includes her
speech and her song:

> ". . . et sì dolce idioma
> le diedi et un cantar tanto soave
> che penser basso o grave
> non potè mai durar dinanzi a lei."
>
> (360, 101–4)

> [". . . and I gave her such sweet speech and such soft singing, that
> no low or heavy thought could ever endure in her presence."]

Are we—or is the poet—to believe him? Here Amor advances his defense
against the poet's accusation that the amorous servitude to which he has
been subjected has imperiled his soul, distracting him from the love of
God and the proper attention to his ultimate salvation. In this poem, cast
in the form of a debate to be adjudicated by Reason, the question remains
unresolved for both reader and poet: Reason declines to pronounce,
deferring the final verdict. Amor's argument, however, is rendered sus-
pect by the associations of "dolce" and "soave" throughout the collec-
tion: it affords a final recall of that *dulcedo* and *suavitas* whose semantic
field, as Noferi points out, is repeatedly identified not only in the *Rime*
but frequently elsewhere in Petrarch's reflections on the nature of music,
of poetry, and of feminine beauty as a peril and a deception—a form of
seduction.[90]

---

89. Cambon, "L'eterno femminino petrarchesco," 15. For Petrarch's fusion of two
distinct entities, the angelic and the erotic, formerly separated both by the myth and by the
stilnovist tradition, see Pierre Blanc, "La poétique de la métamorphose chez Pétrarque," in
Poétiques de la Métamorphose, ed. Guy Demerson (Publications de l'Université de Saint-
Etienne, 1981), esp. 47–49.

90. See Adelia Noferi, "*Voluptas canendi, voluptas scribendi:* divagazioni sulla vocalità in
Petrarca," *Paradigma* 7 (1986): esp. 3–19.

In the final canzone, addressed not to the earthly lady but to the Virgin, another name sounds instead as agent of the poet's ills:

> Medusa et l'error mio m'àn fatto un sasso
> d'umor vano stillante.
>
> (366, 111–12)

> [Medusa and my error have made me a stone dripping vain moisture.]

This final metamorphosis of the collection, concealing the name of Laura, once again conceals too—in the simple conjunction "e" and the present perfect of the verb—the role to be assigned to the Laura of both Part I and Part II of the *Rime sparse*. And it is yet another name that sounds now as the source of a possible resolution of his anguish and his spiritual dilemma: that of the Virgin, to whom he addresses his plea for a positive reordering of his love.[91] The final canzone refers directly to Laura only in the extraordinarily compact and final phrase "tale è terra," one now turned to dust. She had left him nothing of herself but her name, he had lamented early in Part II of the collection (291); even the name of Laura is absent from the closing poem.

---

91. In this canzone, suggests Cambon, Petrarch attempts to separate two aspects of dominant femininity, projecting in Laura the demonic, nocturnal, paralyzing aspect and in the Virgin the salvific, solar, and maternal ("L'eterno femminino petrarchesco," 9); see also Kenelm Foster, "Beatrice or Medusa," in *Italian Studies Presented to E. R. Vincent*, ed. C. P. Brand, K. Foster, and U. Limentani (Cambridge, 1962), 41.

2

LANDSCAPES

The elusive lady of the *Rime* is known to the reader in part through her association with place. She determines place for the poet: it is she for whom he has exchanged the river Arno for the Sorga (308). This apparent autobiographical candor, however, is uncommon in the collection, and for more precise information Petrarch's commentators and biographers regularly turn to the brief obituary entered on the flyleaf of his treasured Virgil manuscript. The inscription concerns both Laura's death and the *innamoramento:*

> Laura . . . first appeared to my eyes in my youth, in the year of our Lord 1327, on the sixth day of April, in the church of St. Clare in Avignon, at matins. . . .[1]

The coordination of day and date is identical with that recorded in the *Rime* to mark the poet's entry into the labyrinth of love. In the lyric collection, however, it is further correlated insistently with Good Friday, revealing a degree of adaptation and consequently of fiction suggestive of the nature of Petrarch's personal mythmaking.[2] The setting of the initial encounter has in contrast provoked little comment; Petrarch was in residence principally in Avignon in 1327, and certainly it is plausible that

1. Translated by E. H. Wilkins, *Life of Petrarch* (Chicago, 1961), 77.
2. It was not Good Friday, the occasion repeatedly advanced in the *Rime* as that of the *innamoramento*, on 6 April 1327; for a careful review of the question, see Bortolo Martinelli, " 'Feria sexta aprilis': La data sacra nel canzoniere del Petrarca," *Rivista di storia e letteratura religiosa* 8 (1972): 449–84; now in *Petrarca e il Ventoso* (Bari, 1977), 103–48.

both the young cleric and numerous ladies of the city would have attended the early morning service during Holy Week.[3]

Thus Petrarch's biographers and commentators routinely record that "Petrarch saw Laura for the first time in the Church of St. Clare in Avignon."[4] In his letters from and about Valchiusa, moreover, including the well-known *metrica* to Giacomo Colonna and the depiction of his "Clausa Vallis" in *Fam.* VIII, 3, Petrarch represents his retreat to the country as an attempt to escape Laura and her image, and Avignon as the place of danger—implicitly or explicitly the "place of Laura."[5] It is striking, then, that not one of the many poems in the *Rime* recalling the *innamoramento*, including those specifying its occurrence on Good Friday or on April 6, mentions its setting as either a city or a place of worship.[6] The fact is particularly significant with regard to the *innamoramento* because in the collection, that event is frequently "set"—and it is set in nature. It is landscape that serves as catalyst for Laura's image whether in memory or in fantasy, and it is in nature that he will seek her traces both *in vita* and *in morte*.

What then constitutes nature in the *Rime sparse?* While a number of Petrarch's works testify to his keen observation of nature,[7] the landscape of the lyric collection is frequently generic. Spare, unmodified catalogues of natural elements suggest the world through which the poet wanders

3. The further indication that Laura was buried at vespers in the Church of the Brothers Minor adds to the correlation of calendrical circumstance the further symmetry of two settings for her "chaste and lovely form," as well as a note of sincerity that is furthered by his recall of his sojourn in Verona at the time and that "the sad tidings reached me in Parma, in the same year, on the morning of the 19th day of May, in a letter from my Ludovicus."

4. The apparent contradiction between the obituary note concerning a Laura *avignonese* and the Laura of the *Rime* oriented many of the attempts to identify the historical personage who inspired the lyrics; see Enrico Carrara, "La leggenda di Laura," in his *Studi Petrarcheschi e altri scritti* (Turin, 1959), esp. 80–81, 97–98. Hugo Friedrichs, however, suggests that Petrarch's record of the story's initiation in a church may itself have a literary dimension, as in the introduction to Boccaccio's *Decameron;* see *Epochen der italienischen Lyrik* (Frankfurt, 1964), 196 n. 1.

5. This identification is also in keeping with the warning in the *Secretum* against a return to Avignon; see *Petrarch's Secret*, esp. 146.

6. In fact, as Durling points out, "there is no mention of any encounter with Laura taking place indoors (the inference is possible in several cases but not imposed by the text)" (*Petrarch's Lyric Poems*, 6). Thus the question, as Durling puts it: "Did he first see her in Avignon and later fall in love with her in Vaucluse? That is possible, but for the purposes of the *Rime sparse* it is assumed that the first encounter and the decisive encounter are the same."

7. "Après l'étude," summarized Pierre de Nolhac, "c'est la nature que Pétrarque a le mieux aimé"; see "Pétrarque et son jardin, d'après ses notes inédites," *Giornale storico della letteratura italiana* 9 (1887); 404.

compelled by Amor, or function as spatial markers to measure the distance that separates him from Laura:

> Quante montagne et acque,
> quanto mar, quanti fiumi
> m'ascondon que' duo lumi. . . .

$$(37, 41-43)^8$$

[How many mountains and waters, how much ocean, how many rivers hide from me those two lights. . . .]

Modifiers too are frequently generic, conventional: leafy fronds and grass are green; hills are high, green, or white; stars are shining; the day is bright, and the night shadowy. As readers have observed, the elements of this nature, even when including proper names such as Sorga or Po, are emblematic rather than naturalistic; all of these substantives appear to convey an equal measure of "reality."[9] In its general outline, moreover, it is fully in keeping with the practices of medieval nature description, which, as inherited from late Antiquity, offered an "ideal" landscape largely determined not by observation, but by rhetoric. In the classical literary tradition in which Virgil affords a direct mediation for Petrarch, the depiction of landscape is a major topic, and its requisite elements are quickly enumerated, as by Curtius: "Above all, shade. . . . A tree, then, or a group of trees; a spring or brook for refreshment; a grassy bank for a seat."[10] In this assortment Petrarch's reader at once recognizes the characteristic landscape of the *Rime sparse*.

Yet for all its conventionality, that landscape has a particular set of spatial coordinates: it renders the rivers, hills, plains, and forests, occasionally of Italy, but generally of Provence. Not merely hills, but *those*

---

8. Petrarch's penchant for this type of expansive catalogue is best illustrated in sonnet 148:

> Non Tesin, Po, Varo, Arno, Adige et Tebro,
> Eufrate, Tigre, Nilo, Ermo, Indo et Gange,
> Tana, Istro, Alfeo, Garona, e 'l mar che frange,
> Rodano, Ibero, Ren, Sena, Albia, Era, Ebro—
> non edra, abete, pin, faggio o genebro—
> poria 'l foco allentar che 'l cor tristo ange. . . .

$$(1-6)$$

9. See especially G. Contini, "Preliminari sulla lingua del Petrarca," in *Varianti e altra linguistica*, 180–81.

10. E. R. Curtius, *European Literature and the Latin Middle Ages*, trans. Willard Trask (New York, 1953), 186–87.

hills; not merely a river and a fountain, but *that* river, *that* fountain; not merely a grassy bank, but *that* grassy bank, the one that bears the record of Laura's passage. Not merely a tree, but a laurel. Each of these natural objects may be not only *bello*, beautiful, but *dolce* and *gentile*, sweet and noble. *Dolce ghiaccio, gentil ramo, leggiadri rami, tenera neve, aere sereno*—these are both a part of Laura's beauty and its reflection, acquiring an affective coloration from the adjectives used repeatedly to describe her.[11] And this, of course, is Laura's landscape, a place invested with value by her presence, the fixed point in all the poet's wanderings and that to which he desires and attempts to return.[12] To this landscape, to these witnesses of his weary life (71), he flees to escape the curious gaze of the public. And in it, like the Romantic poets of a later century, he finds a compensation for his alienation from his fellow men, a sort of complicity:

> Sì ch'io mi credo omai che monti et piagge
> et fiumi et selve sappian di che tempre
> sia la mia vita, ch'è celata altrui.
>
> (35, 9–11)[13]

[So that I believe by now that mountains and shores and rivers and woods know the temper of my life, which is hidden from other persons.]

This is the "riposato porto," the restful port in which he hopes to be buried (126), the only place in which he finds comfort and repose:

> . . . 'l bel paese e 'l dilettoso fiume
> con serena accoglienza rassecura
> il cor già vòlto ov'abita il suo lume.
>
> (177, 12–14)

11. See Kenneth Cool, "The Petrarchan Landscape as Palimpsest," *Journal of Medieval and Renaissance Studies* 11 (1981): 86. Nature in the *Rime*, Francesco De Sanctis observes, is frequently "come l'ornamento e la veste di Laura"; see *Saggio critico sul Petrarca* (Turin, 1983), 90. Jennifer Petrie suggests a precedent in the Sicilian poets for Petrarch's usage; *The Augustan Poets, the Italian Tradition, and the "Canzoniere"* (Dublin, 1983), 63.

12. Here are "i dolci colli ov'io lasciai me stesso, / partendo onde partir giamai non posso" (209). On Laura's function in the *Rime* "to embody the vitality of the paradisiac place," see Terry Comito, *The Idea of the Garden in the Renaissance* (New Brunswick, N.J., 1978), 60.

13. For Petrarch's development of the theme of sympathetic nature in the context of its classical and vernacular antecedents, see Petrie, *The Augustan Poets, the Italian Tradition, and the "Canzoniere,"* esp. 92–96.

[. . . the lovely country and the delightful river with serene welcome reassure my heart, already turned toward where his light dwells.]

The use of the definite article here in conjunction with "paese" and "fiume" is reassuring, contrasting with the generic and collective nouns— the "thousand slopes and thousand rivers"—evoked earlier in the poem.[14] The definite or demonstrative article again and again identifies this landscape, as he will recall it following the death of Laura:

> Amor, che meco al buon tempo ti stavi
> fra queste rive a' pensier nostri amiche,
> et per saldar le ragion nostre antiche
> meco et col fiume ragionando andavi. . . .
>
> (303, 1–4)

[Love, who in the happy times stayed with me along these banks so friendly to our thoughts, and used to walk talking with me and with the river, to settle our old accounts. . . .]

The strong affective value of this setting is founded in a specific association: it evokes not only the repeated appearances of Laura but more specifically a single appearance, the primordial experience of the *innamoramento:*

> Io amai sempre, et amo forte ancora,
> et son per amar più di giorno in giorno
> quel dolce loco . . .
> et son fermo d'amare il tempo et l'ora
> ch'ogni vil cura mi levar dintorno,
> et più colei . . .
>
> (85, 1–3, 5–7)

[I have always loved and I still love and I shall day by day love even more that sweet place . . . and I am fixed in loving the time and the hour that removed every low care from around me, and above all her . . .]

14. See Paola Mastrocola, "Gli 'errori' del Petrarca," in *L'Arte dell'Interpretare: Studi critici offerti a Giovanni Getto* (Cuneo, 1984), 100.

On that occasion, determinate for all future occasions, nature is "signed" by Laura, as he reminds the green shore where she had appeared to him:

> Ben sai che sì bel piede
> non toccò terra unquanco
> come quel dì che già segnata fosti.
>
> (125, 53–55)

[You know well that so beautiful a foot never touched the earth as on that day when you were marked by hers.]

A later poet, recording such an epiphanic experience, will sacrifice the sight of nature to the lady's image: "Une femme est plus belle que le monde où je vis," writes Paul Eluard, "Et je ferme les yeux" [A woman is more beautiful than the world in which I live, and I close my eyes].[15] Petrarch's poet too experiences the temptation of that renunciatory gesture, recalling Laura's first appearance to his eyes "on that day when I would gladly have closed them so as never to look on any lesser beauties" (116), in an encounter that is determinate for his seeing:

> . . . ò sì avezza
> la mente a contemplar sola costei
> ch'altro non vede, et ciò che non è lei
> già per antica usanza odia et disprezza.
>
> (116, 5–8)

[I have so accustomed my mind to contemplate her alone that it sees nothing else, and whatever is not she, already by ancient habit it hates and scorns.]

Yet he does not close his eyes upon this inner image of the lady; instead he projects it obsessively onto the world around him, as he will affirm over and over again: "although I gaze intent and fixed on a thousand different things, I see only one lady and her lovely face" (127). And indeed from among those "thousand things" that make up the external world there emerge certain elements, those privileged by their association with Laura and forever indelibly etched in memory like the day itself,

---

15. Cited in Leon-Gabriel Gros, "A miracol mostrare," *Cahiers du Sud* 30 (1953): 36; what the movement pursues, he adds, is the *coup de foudre*.

which will form a new natural world for the enamored poet. Thus it is that he arrives, "alone with Love," in Valchiusa:

> ivi non donne ma fontane et sassi
> et l'imagine trovo di quel giorno
> che 'l pensier mio figura ovunque io sguardo.
>
> (116, 12–14)

[there I find not ladies but fountains and rocks and the image of that day which my thoughts image forth wherever I may glance.]

In the seclusion of this privileged place, he will not exclude the world but recreate it in the image of his lady.

And indeed, for all their apparent generality, the descriptive terms that depict the locus of Petrarch's vision of Laura in nature collectively figure not a fictive but a determinate place, one with a name: Valchiusa.[16] Its geographical coordinates are set out in the tenth of the *Bucolicum carmen*, as the Petrarchan persona begins the account of his misfortunes where the Sorga and the Durenza rivers mingle their waters in the Rhône:

> There . . . in the midst of the stones and the gnarled trunks of oak trees there had grown, on the bank of the river, a most beautiful laurel [pulcherrima laurus].[17]

"Then let this lovely laurel grow on the fresh bank," Petrarch writes to commemorate the planting of a laurel on the bank of the river Sorga (148);[18] the confluence of the two rivers affords the coordinates of the protagonist's captivity in the love of one "who between two rivers closed me in lovely green and sweet ice" (66).

16. Petrarch, in retreat from Avignon, spent (cumulatively) several years in the French Vaucluse, to which this study will refer with his designation of Valchiusa. Divided between Avignon and Valchiusa, he was in residence in Provence between 1326 and 1341, and thereafter he alternated between Italy and Provence until 1353. Boccaccio, apparently echoing Petrarch himself, identifies his compatriot's retreat from Avignon as "Valchiusa, solitudine famosa della Francia, dove sgorga la Sorga, regina delle fonti" (*Genealogia Deorum Gentilium*, XIV, xix); see W. H. Herendeen, "Castara's Smiles . . . Sabrina's Tears: Nature and Setting in Renaissance River Poems," *Comparative Literature* 39 (1987): 299.

17. The text is in Guido Martellotti, ed., "*Laurea uccidens: Bucolicum carmen X* (Rome, 1968), 16; translation mine.

18. "Riva" is a constituent lexeme in the depiction of Laura's landscape in the *Rime*. For the variety of senses suggested by its adjectival characterization—"fresca," "amata," "sinistra," "toscana," "verde"—see Vincenzo Dolla, "Il 'ciclo' dei Madrigali e la struttura del Canzoniere petrarchesco," *Esperienze letterarie* 4 (1979): 72–73.

As representations of reality these poems do not differ from other depictions of landscape in the *Rime;* it is evident that even when overtly evoking Valchiusa Petrarch's tendency is to obliterate realistic detail.[19] The suggestiveness of the place-name, however, lends them a symbolic concreteness.[20] The changing seasons in this setting assume an emblematic quality that transposes natural surroundings into an inner landscape.[21]

> Et io nel cor via più freddo che ghiaccio
> ò di gravi pensier tal una nebbia
> qual si leva talor di queste valli,
> serrate incontra a gli amorosi venti
> et circundate di stagnanti fiumi,
> quando cade dal ciel più lenta pioggia.

(66, 7–12)

[And I have in my heart, much colder than ice, heavy thoughts in such a cloud as rises sometimes from these valleys, closed around about against the loving winds and surrounded by stagnating rivers, when there falls from the sky the gentlest rain.]

At the same time, the implications of confinement and captivity confirm that this setting of the poet's love experience has not only a geographic but a literary dimension, relating it once again to that of the *rime petrose.*[22] The suffering lover of Dante's "Al poco giorno," constrained by Amor "among little hills," imagines his lady "in a fine meadow of grass . . . closed in all around with high hills." Only allusively present in some poems of the *Rime,* the suggestiveness of name and place initiates a full development in others, as when the poet describes his seclusion amid the hills of Provence:

19. See the comments of W. Th. Elwert, "A Valchiusa o dell'utilità dei sopralluoghi letterari," in his *Saggi di Letteratura Italiana* (Studien zu den Romanischen Sprachen und Literaturen, III) (Wiesbaden, 1970), 92–99.

20. For the "sense of the encompassing" that relates Petrarch's references, see Comito, *The Idea of the Garden in the Renaissance,* 60–61.

21. On these "metaphors of interiority," see the discussion of Luigi Blasucci, "La sestina LXVI," *Lectura Petrarce, II, 1982* (Padua, 1983), esp. 55–59, who contrasts this development with Dante's sestina "Io son venuto al punto de la rota," which also relates the poet's affective life to the inclement season.

22. See Domenico De Robertis, "Petrarca petroso," *Revue des Etudes Italiennes* 29 (1983): 33; for the many echoes in the *Rime* of Dante's depictions of landscape and in particular of atmospheric phenomena see esp. 29–30. Marianne Shapiro observes that "Dante's claustrophobic situation is the prior content, the immovable given" of Petrarch's sestina; see *Hieroglyph of Time: The Petrarchan Sestina* (Minneapolis, 1980), 111.

In una valle chiusa d'ogn'intorno,
ch'è refrigerio de' sospir miei lassi,
giunsi sol con Amor, pensoso et tardo.

(116, 9–11)[23]

[In a valley closed on all sides, which cools my weary sighs, I
arrived alone with Love, full of care, and late.]

Petrarch's adaptation of the "valle chiusa," however, is unmistakably
marked as his own. If the essential traits of a landscape—the stones, the
closed valley itself, its great waters from the source of the river Sorga—
are still generic in sonnet 116 cited above, its identity is exploited and
confirmed in the following poem in the explicit indication of Valchiusa as
proper name, pointing to ". . . 'l sasso ond' è più chiusa questa valle / (di
che 'l suo proprio nome si deriva) . . ." [the rock that mainly closes this
valley, from which its name is derived] (117, 1–2). Dante's "canzone
montanina" too, in its *congedo*, briefly identifies a specific place, the city
of Florence, but this new perspective is alien to the geographic setting of
the lover's experience among the hills.[24] In Petrarch's poem, as elsewhere
in the *Rime*, story and place are inseparably blended in a process of
symbolization through which not only Laura herself but elements of her
landscape inspire a mythical elaboration prompted by onomastic sugges-
tion.

In the *Rime* Valchiusa is called insistently to the attention of the reader
in a poem of early composition that marks a thematic pivot in the
collection through its focus on the "strangeness" of the love experience
and of the protagonist's consequent alienation.[25] Canzone 135 evokes a
series of marvels with exotic settings: a phoenix renascent that flies "there
whence the day comes forth," a fabulous magnetic stone that induces
shipwrecks "out there on the Indian Sea," a gentle wild creature that
bears pain and death in its eyes "in the farthest west," an alternately cold
and boiling fountain "in the south," another wondrous spring that
kindles and extinguishes fire "at Epirus," yet two more springs with

---

23. In his "ivi non donne ma fontane et sassi . . . trovo" we may hear again the echo of
Dante's frustrated lover, who in the "canzone montanina" protests his captivity by Love
within a valley: "Lasso, non donne qui, non genti accorte / veggio, a cui mi lamenti del
mio male" ("Amor, da che convien," 67–68).

24. See J. C. Barnes and Z. G. Baranski, "Dante's 'Canzone montanina'," *Modern
Language Review* 73 (1978): esp. 298–99.

25. See Kenelm Foster, *Petrarch, Poet and Humanist* (Edinburgh, 1984), 70–71; Claudia
Berra, "L'Arte della similitudine nella canzone CXXXV dei 'Rerum vulgarium fragmenta',"
Giornale storico della letteratura italiana 163 (1986): 161–99.

powers of life and death "in the famous islands of Fortune." These phenomena are all relevant to the poet's cruel fate because in the measure of their strangeness they are like his own enamored condition. The final marvel, however, is of a different order: it is "this spring, which we see always full but with largest vein when the sun is united with Taurus." The periodic fluctuations of the source of the river Sorga in Valchiusa, to which Petrarch here alludes, are a phenomenon that is marvelous but not remote, and open to general observation. It is evoked as an immediate analogy to his suffering, to the flux of his tears: "thus my eyes weep at all times, but most at the season when I saw my lady."[26] In contrast to the earlier images, this one is marked as private: "Taceremo," he tells Amor, "We will not speak of it." His poem, however, may speak of this place in response to those who might inquire concerning his state:

> Chi spiasse, canzone,
> quel ch' i' fo, tu poi dir: "Sotto un gran sasso
> in una chiusa valle ond'esce Sorga
> si sta; né chi lo scorga
> v'è se no Amor, che mai nol lascia un passo,
> et l'imagine d'una che lo strugge,
> ch'e' per sé fugge tutt'altre persone."
>
> (91–97)[27]

[If anyone should wish to know, Song, what I am doing, you can say: "Beside a great stone in a closed valley, whence Sorgue comes forth, he is; nor is there anyone to see him save Love, who never leaves him even for a step, and the image of one who destroys him: he, for his part, flees all other persons."]

The compelling complement to this *congedo* is found in a poem *in morte*, where he implores Laura in Heaven not only to attend to his sighs but to "see" him in this landscape familiar to them both:

> Mira 'l gran sasso donde Sorga nasce,
> et vedra'vi un che sol tra l'erbe et l'acque
> di tua memoria et di dolor si pasce;

---

26. In sonnet 301 the connection between the waters of the Sorga and the poet's tears is complete: "Valle che de' lamenti miei se' piena, / fiume che spesso del mio pianger cresci. . . ."

27. On this passage that invests Petrarch's retreat in Valchiusa with a particular symbolic value, see Berra, "L'Arte della similitudine," 195.

ove giace il tuo albergo et dove nacque
il nostro amor. . . .

(305, 9–13)

[Gaze at the great rock from which Sorgue is born, and you will
see there one who among the grass and the waters feeds only on
your memory and on sorrow. . . .]

This passage, it should be noted, is the single affirmation in the collection
of the *innamoramento* as a mutual experience.

Around these suggestive images Petrarch organized entire segments of
the *Rime sparse*. A series of poems *in vita* is set off by two sonnets (107,
118) marking the fifteenth and the sixteenth anniversaries of the *innamo-
ramento*, both written during Petrarch's second residence in Valchiusa.[28]
The dominant theme of the series is identified in *Rime* 108 as Valchiusa
"aventuroso più d'altro terreno" [luckier than any other ground], and
the following poems recall Laura present in that place or describe the
greeting proffered by her there. A poem addressed to Petrarch's friend
Sennuccio (112) fixes with nine occurrences of the adverbial "qui" the
association of that landscape with Laura. The paired sonnets 113 and
114, enlarging the autobiographical context in the opposition of Valchiusa
to Avignon, again stress the adverbial designation: "Qui dove mezzo son,
Sennuccio mio . . . Qui son securo . . . ;" "Qui mi sto solo" [Here where
I only half am, my Sennuccio . . . Here I am safe . . . ; Here I am alone].
The series concludes with the pair of poems cited above (116 and 117)
that play upon the name of Valchiusa.

A second sequence, in Part II, confirms that after the death of Laura
this landscape remains the catalyst for the poet's memory and the setting
for his lament. Within the span of components between the commemo-
ration of the third anniversary of her death (278) and the affirmation that
he goes searching through every region where he has seen her (306), no
fewer than nine poems clustered into two groups evoke the landscape of
Valchiusa. In 279–82 it is the setting of Laura's imagined reappearance;
in 301 and 303–5, it witnesses the poet's grief. Positioned among the
intervening poems, sonnet 288 affords an unusually detailed listing of the
components of the landscape:

Non è sterpo né sasso in questi monti,
non ramo o fronda verde in queste piagge,

28. See E. H. Wilkins, *The Making of the "Canzoniere" and Other Petrarchan Studies*
(Rome, 1951), 349–59.

> non fiore in queste valli o foglia d'erba,
> stilla d'acqua non ven di queste fonti,
> né fiere àn questi boschi sì selvagge,
> che non sappian quanto è mia pena acerba.
>
> (288, 9–14)

[There is no shrub or stone in these mountains, no branch or green leaf on these slopes, no flower in these valleys, or blade of grass, no trickle of water comes from these springs, nor do these woods have beasts so savage that they do not know how bitter my sorrow is.]

One of the sonnets of the following group, calling upon the elements that had witnessed his happy time to witness now his desolate state, catalogs these elements in a stark enumeration that achieves, not descriptive realism, but the force of an incantation:

> fior, frondi, erbe, ombre, antri, onde, aure soavi,
> valli chiuse, alti colli, et piagge apriche,
> porto de l'amorose mie fatiche,
> de le fortune mie tante et sì gravi . . .
>
> (303, 5–8)

[flowers, leaves, grass, shadows, waves, gentle breezes, closed valleys, high hills, and open slopes, harbor of my amorous laborings, of my so frequent and so heavy storms . . .]

This, then, is Laura's landscape. That it is familiar to even occasional readers of the *Rime*, however, is due primarily to a series of frequently anthologized poems that detail the intimate connection between the lady and nature. To nature the poet turns in search of vestiges of her presence:

> Così avestu riposti
> de' be' vestigi sparsi
> ancor tra' fiori et l'erba,
> che la mia vita acerba
> lagrimando trovasse ove acquetarsi!
>
> (125, 59–63)

[Would you had hidden away some lovely footprints still among the flowers and grass, that my bitter life might weeping find a place to become calm! but my fearful, yearning soul satisfies itself as best it can.]

Not only does he confirm the finding of those vestiges, traces both visible and invisible; the memory traces are themselves vestiges of Laura.[29] The entire last stanza of this well-known canzone strikingly defines the closed cycle in which nature and memory conjoin to compensate for the absence of the lady herself:

> Ovunque gli occhi volgo
> trovo un dolce sereno
> pensando: "Qui percosse il vago lume."
> Qualunque erba o fior colgo,
> credo che nel terreno
> aggia radice ov'ella ebbe in costume
> gir fra le piagge e 'l fiume
> et talor farsi un seggio
> fresco fiorito et verde.
>
> (125, 66–74)

[Wherever I turn my eyes, I find a sweet brightness, thinking: "Here fell the bright light of her eyes." Whatever grass or flower I gather, I believe that it is rooted in the ground where she was wont to walk through the meadows beside the river, and sometimes to make herself a seat, fresh, flowering, and green.]

The following canzone lovingly reinscribes Laura among the elements of this same landscape, valorized now in terms of her physical presence:

> Chiare fresche et dolci acque
> ove le belle membra
> pose colei che sola a me par donna,
>   gentil ramo ove piacque
> (con sospir mi rimembra)
> a lei di fare al bel fianco colonna,
>   erba et fior che la gonna

---

29. Cool discusses the figural use of nature as a "memory locus" in the *Rime:* "nature becomes a mnemonic system which suggests to the reader the presence of something that is really not there except by means of the poet's rhetorical persuasion"; see "The Petrarchan landscape," 92–94.

> leggiadra ricoverse
> co l'angelico seno . . .

$$(126, 1-9)^{30}$$

[Clear, fresh, sweet waters, where she who alone seems lady to me rested her lovely body, gentle branch where it pleased her (with sighing I remember) to make a column for her lovely side, grass and flowers that her rich garment covered along with her angelic breast . . .]

These verses do not represent Laura *in* nature; the discrete physical elements of lady and landscape are so blended as to form a single phantasmagoric scene.[31]

This blending of the lady with her natural setting recalls the extraordinary intimate relation between animate and inanimate, human and vegetal forms in the metamorphosis of the nymph Daphne into the evergreen laurel.[32] A tableau of Laura seated barefoot amid the grass and flowers "in treccie e 'n gonna" [in a mere robe with loose hair] (121) is followed by her integration into that same landscape: "Qual miracolo è quel, quando tra l'erba / quasì un fior siede" [What a miracle it is, when on the grass she sits like a flower!] (160).[33] The poet's substance too is one with its substance, the vanishing of his illusion of Laura's presence

30. The "insistent adverb, 'ove' (2, 4, 11), seeks to define, within the contracted perimeter of the natural enclosure, the marks left behind by Laura's body"; see Giuseppe Mazzotta, "Petrarch's Song 126," in *Textual Analysis: Some Readers Reading*, ed. Mary Ann Caws (New York, 1986), 126. The sensuality of this scene, in which a rain of blossoms will fall about Laura, contrasts sharply with its model, the appearance of Beatrice to Dante in the Earthly Paradise; Durling draws its erotic implications in *Petrarch's Lyric Poems*, 23–24.

31. André Pézard comments of this poem that "la vertu de sa poésie nous fait sentir *comme une création irréelle* ce qui fut à coup sûr un spectacle parfaitement naturel: une belle jeune fille au bord d'une belle rivière"; see "Le sens du magique chez Pétrarque," *Cahiers du Sud* 38 (1953): 19.

32. For the "sistema di universale compenetrazione della natura" elaborated from the mythological model, see Gianfranco Contini, "Saggio d'un commento alle correzioni del Petrarca volgare," in *Varianti e altra linguistica* (Turin, 1970), esp. 13, 22–23. For subjective experience externalized in terms of the natural environment, see Marga Cottino-Jones, "The Myth of Apollo and Daphne in Petrarch's *Canzoniere*: The Dynamics and Literary Function of Transformation," in *Francis Petrarch, Six Centuries Later: A Symposium*, ed. Aldo Scaglione (Chapel Hill and Chicago, 1975), p. 152.

33. Raffaele Amaturo cites the "almost synonymic" substantives "fiori" and "erba" in illustration of Petrarch's "lessico identico e mutevole, questo mobile universo di *signa*," which, emptied of their habitual connotations, are free to assume "una carica allusiva ed evocativa di remote esperienze"; see *Petrarca* (Bari, 1971), 357–58.

leaving him "pietra morta in pietra viva" [a dead stone on the living rock] (129). In contrast to this ominous still life, the elements of this landscape are animated and transfigured by their physical contact with Laura:

> Lieti fiori et felici, et ben nate erbe
> che Madonna pensando premer sòle . . .
> o soave contrada, o puro fiume
> che bagni il suo bel viso et gli occhi chiari
> et prendi qualità dal vivo lume . . .
>
> (162, 1–2, 9–11)

[Happy and fortunate flowers and well-born grass, whereon my lady is wont to walk in thought . . . O lovely countryside, O pure river that bathe her lovely face and bright eyes and take your nature from that living light . . .]

This too is a process of metamorphosis, one not complete until the natural elements become animated as Laura has become a natural element:

> L'erbetta verde e i fior di color mille
> sparsi sotto quell'elce antiqua et negra
> pregan pur che 'l bel pe' li prema o tocchi.
>
> (192, 9–11)[34]

[The young green grass and the flowers of a thousand colors scattered under that ancient black oak beg that her lovely foot touch or press them.]

Thus the sight of this landscape calls forth and revivifies Laura's presence in the poet's memory, as natural beauty evokes in turn her beauty.[35] The cycle of the seasons is remarkably correlated with that of Laura's life:

> Amor col rimembrar sol mi mantene:
> onde s'io veggio in giovenil figura
> incominciarsi il mondo a vestir d'erba,

---

34. Antonio Lanza observes that in this final verse "la venustà di Laura appare contemplata e sottolineata con un compiacimento sensuale insolito in quasi tutta la lirica italica precedente"; see *Studi sulla lirica del Trecento* (Rome, 1978), 60.

35. Gordon Poole discusses Petrarch's ability to "infondere Laura in un *locus amoenus* ed esso in lei" in "Il topos del 'effictio' e un sonetto del Petrarca," *Lettere Italiane* 32 (1980): 18.

parmi veder in quella etate acerba
la bella giovenetta ch' ora è donna;
poi che sormonta riscandando il sole,
parmi qual esser sòle
fiamma d'amor che 'n cor alto s'endonna;
ma quando il dì si dole
di lui che passo passo a dietro torni,
veggio lei giunta a' suoi perfetti giorni.

(127, 18–28)

[Love maintains me solely with memory: wherefore if I see the world begin to clothe itself in green in youthful guise, I seem to see at that same unripe age the beautiful young girl who is now a lady; after the sun has mounted on high, making all things warm, it seems to be like the flame of love that masters the deep heart; but when the shorter day laments that the sun turns back step by step, I see her arrived at her fullest days.]

The following stanzas of this poem identify one by one elements of nature—"leaves on a branch or violets on the ground," "new snow on the hills struck by the sun," "white and crimson roses in a vase of gold," the movement of wandering stars through a clear sky following a nocturnal rain, the rising of the sun and its decline, the movement of white and yellow flowers in the breeze—all to recall equally specific attributes of Laura, as the two series of elements, those of Laura and those of nature, tend toward convergence.[36] So fully are natural elements identified with the recall or the projection of her presence that other sites through which the poet may pass are immediately assimilated to that first landscape, becoming full objective correlatives of his thought as he progresses from thought to thought and from mountain to mountain, "di pensier in pensier, di monte in monte" (129).

In this affective economy, which unites the inner and outer worlds as memory reinvests nature and nature catalyzes memory, nothing is lost: "così nulla sen perde" (125). There is also an imaginary *surplus*, as Laura invests nature not only with her own plenitude but with a superabundance. Thus it is she who vivifies nature:

Come 'l candido pie' per l'erba fresca
i dolci passi onestamente move,

36. Adelia Noferi, "La canzone CXXVII," *Lectura Petrarce, II, 1982* (Padua, 1983), 14–15: the elements of the two series "tendono a slittare l'uno sull'altro, l'uno nell'altro, a confluire insieme verso qualcosa che non è né l'uno né l'altro, ma la compenetrazione emblematica e reversibile dell'uno e dell'altro."

vertù che 'ntorno i fiori apre et rinove
de le tenere piante sue par ch'esca.

(165, 1–4)[37]

[As her white foot through the green grass virtuously moves its sweet steps, a power that all around her opens and renews the flowers seems to issue from her tender soles.]

In her presence nature not only flourishes but rejoices:

e 'l ciel di vaghe et lucide faville
s'accende intorno e 'n vista si rallegra
d'esser fatto seren da sì belli occhi.

(192, 12–14)

[and the sky takes fire with shining sparks all around and visibly rejoices to be made clear by eyes so lovely.]

Urging the Rhône to speak to her on his behalf, the poet identifies Laura as "quel nostro vivo et dolce sole / ch' adorna e 'nfiora la tua riva manca" [that living, sweet sun of ours, who adorns and beflowers your left bank] (208).

Animated and adorned by Laura, this setting assumes for the poet the status of a paradise on earth. Returning here after Laura's death he will acknowledge its particular nature:

né giamai vidi valle aver sì spessi
luoghi da sospirar riposti et fidi,
né credo già ch'Amore in Cipro avessi
o in altra riva sì soavi nidi.
L'acque parlan d'amore, et l'òra e i rami,
et gli augelletti e i pesci et l'erba,
tutti inseme pregando ch'i' sempre ami.

(280, 5–11)

[nor have I ever seen a valley with so many hidden, trusty places for sighing; nor do I believe that Love ever had, in Cyprus or on any other shore, such sweet nests. The waters speak of love and

---

37. The apparently spontaneous images of Laura in these poems "della loda" are rich in literary reminiscences. For sonnet 165 they include several classical poets and, as Carducci noted, popular poetry; see Raffaele Amaturo, *Petrarca* (Bari, 1971), 310–11.

the breeze and the branches and the little birds and the fish and the flowers and the grass, all together begging me always to love.]

The allusion to the isle of Venus is not simple poetic hyperbole: at the end of this sonnet Laura herself is imagined to admonish the poet from Heaven to renounce the world and its sweet hooks, "i suoi dolci ami" (280).

Thus the seductive beauty of this landscape is seen in a new light. In the *Trionfi*, where the island of Venus is represented in some detail, the narrator interrupts the account of his dream vision to give us his newly enlightened interpretation of the place: "In così tenebrosa et stretta gabbia / rinchiusi fummo . . ." [It was within this dark and narrow cage that we were shut] (*Tr. Cup.* IV, 158–59). Is the Valchiusa of the lyric collection also a place of captivity? Let us return to an earlier poem in which a literal snare for the poet's capture is deployed in the green grass of the shore:

> Nova angeletta sovra l'ale accorta
> scese dal cielo in su la fresca riva
> là 'nd' io passava sol per mio destino.
> Poi che senza compagna et senza scorta
> mi vide, un laccio che di seta ordiva
> tese fra l'erba ond' è verde il camino.
> Allor fui preso, et non mi spiacque poi,
> sì dolce lume uscia degli occhi suoi.

(106)

[A new little angel on agile wings came down from Heaven to the fresh shore where I was walking alone by my destiny. Since she saw me without companion and without guide, a silken snare which she was making she stretched in the grass wherewith the way is green. Then I was captured, and it did not displease me later, so sweet a light came from her eyes!]

Here the familiar scene of the *innamoramento* is once again recreated, but with new figures and a highly suggestive variation: while the lover once again assumes the role of prey, of innocent victim, his capture is effected by the lady. The new rendering is shaded into the familiar version of Amor's vengeful attack through the portrayal of the lady as a winged heavenly creature and the depiction of the poet as apparently defenseless and unsuspecting. Here, however, the setting is brought into focus as an essential component of the event. The elements of its landscape, no longer neutral, are the markers of the poet's itinerary in its metaphorical configuration as a journey, and they conceal the snares laid by the "nova angeletta" in which he finds himself inextricably bound.

This new version of the *innamoramento*, with its renewed emphasis on the poet's captivity, immediately precedes a sonnet commemorating its fifteenth anniversary. Here we find, for the first time in the collection, a dense figural setting:

> Solo d'un lauro tal selva verdeggia
> che 'l mio avversario con mirabil arte
> vago fra i rami ovunque vuol m'adduce.
>
> (107, 12–14)

[From only one laurel tree such a wood grows green that my adversary, with marvelous art, leads me wherever he wishes, desirous and wandering among the branches.]

With these two poems we pass directly from a scene, fixed in time and space, set in the familiar landscape of the grassy riverbank, to a landscape filled with trees, all related to the laurel, amid whose branches Amor as the poet's adversary leads him at will. The "nova angeletta" lays her silken snares in the landscape of Valchiusa; other poems will locate the snares of Amor in the laurel's limed branches, its "invescati rami" (142, 195). The dense forest in which the poet is perennially Love's prey is not the "mixed forest," with its wide variety of trees, bequeathed by late Antiquity to medieval poets as one of the varieties of ideal landscape;[38] nor is it the forest of myrtle to which Love's victims fall in the *Aeneid*, to which Petrarch alludes in his own *Africa* and the *Trionfo d'Amore*.[39] This forest is entirely generated by the unique laurel, "solo d'un lauro." Just as the image of Laura is substituted for all other images—"I see only one lady and her lovely face" (127)—so too the laurel, only emblematically representative of natural landscape, proliferates to fill the landscape of the poet's story.

While numerous lyrics among the *Rime sparse* have rendered the grassy riverbank of Valchiusa familiar to Petrarch's readers, this second setting is no less suggestive as locus of the poet's experience of love. One of the great canzoni cited above celebrating Laura in nature and evoking the

38. See Curtius, *European Literature and the Latin Middle Ages*, 190ff.

39. *Aeneid* VI, 442ff.; *Africa* VI, 41ff.; *Tr. Cup.* I, 150. See the comments of Enrico Fenzi, "Per un sonetto del Petrarca: R.V.F. XCIII," *Giornale storico della letteratura italiana* 151 (1974): 505 hr n. 15.

familiar elements of her landscape closes with a *congedo* in which the occurrence of another nature term, "bosco," stands out in sharp relief:

> Se tu avessi ornamenti quant' ài voglia,
> poresti arditamente
> uscir del bosco et gir infra la gente.
>
> (126, 66–68)

[If you had as many branches as you have desire, you could boldly leave the wood and go among people.]

Unexpectedly substituted here for the images of Valchiusa, this forest has already been evoked as a setting for the representations of desire. It is here that Petrarch locates the fugitive object of desire in the first sestina of the collection—"Non credo che pascesse mai per selva / sì aspra fera" [I do not believe that there ever grazed in any wood so cruel a beast]— here that he would wish to spend an endless night with his lady, here that he figures the reenactment of her evasion:

> et non se transformasse in verde selva
> per uscirmi di braccia, come il giorno
> ch'Apollo la seguia qua giù per terra!
>
> (22, 19–20, 34–36)

[and let her not be transformed into a green wood to escape from my arms, as the day when Apollo pursued her down here on earth!]

These verses remind us of the literary affinities of this forested land-scape: if Valchiusa is the landscape of Laura, the forest is that of the Ovidian nymph, the place where she flees to elude Apollo.[40] Ovid, moreover, had associated Daphne in her rejection of her suitors with the huntress Diana, in emulation of whom the nymph frequented the pathless woods; in the *Rime* Diana as well as Daphne figures in the association of

---

40. P.R.J. Hainsworth finds in the prominence of the "selve" or "boschi" in which Petrarch's poet seeks an elusive Laura "a defining feature of his use of Ovid's myth of Daphne"; see "The Myth of Daphne in the *Rerum vulgarium fragmenta*," *Italian Studies* 34 (1979): 30–31.

the forest setting with myths of both erotic desire and erotic fulfillment.[41]
It is as hunter that the protagonist of the metamorphosis canzone
encounters the goddess, cast like the Laura of sestina 22 as a "fera"
suggestive of his prey:

> I' segui' tanto avanti il mio desire
> ch' un dì, cacciando sì com' io solea,
> mi mossi, e quella fera bella et cruda
> in una fonte ignuda
> si stava, quando 'l sol più forte ardea.
>
> (23, 147–51)

[I followed so far my desire that one day, hunting as I was wont,
I went forth, and that lovely cruel wild creature was in a spring
naked when the sun burned most strongly.]

It is through the forest too that the lover, transformed into a stag, flees
pursued by the hounds that represent his own desire: "di selva in selva
ratto mi trasformo, / et ancor de' miei can fuggo lo stormo" [from wood
to wood quickly I am transformed and still I flee the belling of my
hounds] (159–60).[42] While the protagonist cast as Acteon, rejected and
punished by the object of his desire cast as Diana, is threatened with
dismemberment in this forest, a wooded setting is also the locus of a
fantasy in which he recalls a nocturnal visit by that same goddess,
enamored, to another mortal, Endymion:

> Deh, or foss' io col vago de la luna
> adormentato in qua' che verdi boschi,
> et questa ch' anzi vespro a me fa sera
> con essa et con Amor in quella piaggia
> sola venisse a starsi ivi una notte,
> e 'l dì si stesse e 'l sol sempre ne l'onde!
>
> (237, 31–36)

41. Charles Segal writes suggestively of the settings of the *Metamorphoses* that "the
landscape symbolized by virginity may . . . suddenly become the landscape of lustful
sensuality; images of sanctity may become images of desire." See *Landscape in Ovid's
Metamorphoses: A Study in the Transformations of a Literary Symbol* (Weisbaden, 1969),
25. Mary Barnard attributes the dark Petrarchan setting to a projection upon the landscape
of the *Rime* of his "darker, remorseful side"; see *The Myth of Apollo and Daphne from
Ovid to Quevedo: Love, Agon, and the Grotesque* (Durham, 1987), 102–3.

42. See the discussion of this flight in Luigi Vanossi, "Petrarca e il mito di Atteone,"
Romanistische Zeitschrift für Literaturgeschichte 10 (1986): 11–12.

[Ah, would that with the lover of the moon I had fallen asleep in some green wood, and that she who before vespers gives me evening with the moon and with Love to that shore might come alone to stay there one night, and that the day might stay, and the sun, forever under the waves!]

The union with the beloved figured here again through mythological allusion remains only a fantasy; when the protagonist retreats again and again to the woods it is in solitude, to seek the vestiges of Laura.

This setting of the *bosco* or its near-analogue *selva* enlarges the horizons of the poet's world, to accommodate a new set of meanings. Medieval commentators on classical texts read the *silva* as a locus not only of physical but of psychic activity: Servius explains of the *silva* in which the Golden Bough is to be found in the *Aeneid* that "silvas, tenebras, et lustra" signify "those things where wild animal nature and the passions dominate."[43] In the vernacular romance, where it was frequently in the forest that the knight pursued his quest or confronted his adventure, quest and adventure suggest not only physical movement in space but moral movement within the psyche as well;[44] the forest as symbol of the unconscious was particularly favored by the poets of the *matière de Bretagne*.[45] In Petrarch's immediate vernacular context, Dante had already adapted this typology in the opening verses of the *Commedia:*

> Nel mezzo del cammin di nostra vita
> mi ritrovai per una selva oscura,
> che la diritta via era smarrita.
>
> (*Inf.* I, 1–3)[46]

[Midway in the journey of our life I found myself in a dark wood, for the straight way was lost.]

43. See Paul Piehler, *The Visionary Landscape: A Study in Medieval Allegory* (Montreal, 1971), 75–76.

44. For an overview, see Marianne Stauffer, "Die Wanderung," in *Der Wald* (Bern, 1959), 127–39.

45. See, for example, Antoinette Knapton, *Mythe et psychologie chez Marie de France* (Chapel Hill, 1975), 49.

46. See Michelangelo Picone, "Dante e la tradizione arturiana," *Romanische Forschungen* 94 (1982): 7–8: "Ritrovare la via smarrita, e al tempo stesso riuscire ad imporsi in tutta una serie di prove che mettono in pericolo l'incolumità morale prima che fisica del protagonista: questi gli scopi immediati dell'*aventure*."

This pathless dark wood, suggestive of a life dominated by the passions without the governance of reason and virtue,[47] has another anticipatory analogue in Augustine's recall in the *Confessions* of the "immensa silva" full of snares and dangers through which men struggle to find a path toward their spiritual goal.[48] Thus a Christian orientation is given to the moral reading, which is itself furthered by a typological tradition of long standing based on the Latin rendering of the Greek *hyle*, unformed matter, as *silva*.[49]

In one of his Penitential Psalms Petrarch describes his entry into such a forest: "Of my own volition I abandoned the straight way; and I was led far and wide through pathless places. I penetrated into every harsh and inaccessible place. . . ."[50] The passage inescapably recalls Dante's evocation of an entry into that "selva" described as "aspra." So too the forest of the *Rime sparse*: Dante's protagonist finds himself in a "selva selvaggia e aspra" and confronts a "piaggia deserta," Petrarch's proceeds "per selve aspre," again in a setting suggestive of chaos both physical and moral. That the initial situation of Dante's pilgrim in the *Commedia* was decisive for Petrarch's conception of his own spiritual itinerary is confirmed by other Petrarchan texts, not all of them components of the *Rime*: a close echo of the phrasing of Dante's opening canto is found in *Seniles* IV, 5, which explicates not the *Commedia*, but the *Aeneid*.[51]

Once again, however, closer attention to the affinity discloses not likeness but difference. Finding himself in the dark wood, Dante's poet is uncertain how he arrived there:

> Io non so ben ridir com' i' v'intrai,
> tant'era pien di sonno a quel punto
> che la verace via abbandonai.
>
> (*Inf.* I, 10–12)

47. See Barbara Zandrino, "La divina foresta spessa e viva," *Letture classensi* 8 (Ravenna, 1979): 60.

48. *Confessions* X, 35. See John Freccero, "Dante's Prologue Scene," *Dante Studies* 84 (1966): 9.

49. See Piehler, *The Visionary Landscape*, 75, and for a discussion of the philosophical origins of Dante's use of this imagery, Ann H. Hallock, "Dante's 'selva oscura' and other obscure 'selvas'," *Forum Italicum* 6 (1972): esp. 63.

50. *Les Psaumes Pénitentiaux publiés d'après le manuscrit de la Bibliothèque de Lucerne*, ed. Henri Cochin (Paris, 1929), I, 2; translation mine.

51. For the citation and discussion of the interpretation, see Michele Feo, "Petrarca e Dante," *Enciclopedia Dantesca* 4 (1973): 453. Most telling of Dante's impact, as Feo points out, is the interpretation of Virgil's "media silva" as "circa tempus vitae medium," founding the analogy of the geographic extension of the "selva" and the journey of a human life that Dante had figured in his "nel mezzo del cammin di nostra vita."

[I cannot rightly say how I entered it, I was so full of sleep at the moment I left the true way.]

Petrarch's poet, in significant contrast, clearly recalls that occasion. An allegorical recasting of his youthful experience affirms his entrance into the wood: "sola pensando pargoletta et sciolta, / [l'alma] intrò di prima-vera in un bel bosco" [alone, thoughtful, young, and free, [a soul] in springtime entered a lovely wood] (214). The adjective "bel" in itself sets the wood apart from that of the opening of the *Commedia*,[52] but the "bosco" here differs yet more significantly from Dante's "selva" in that it is not merely the locus of error; it is the place in which the fateful action occurs.[53] Petrarch's delicate depiction of the soul "pargoletta et sciolta" recalls Dante's own representation of the infant soul:

> Esce di mano a lui che la vagheggia
> prima che sia, a guisa di fanciulla
> che piangendo e ridendo pargoleggia,
> l'anima semplicetta che sa nulla . . .
>
> *(Purg.* XVI, 85–88)

[From His hands, who fondly loves it before it exists, comes forth after the fashion of a child that sports, now weeping, now laugh-ing, the simple little soul, which knows nothing . . .]

It is in the "bosco," however, that the unsuspecting soul of Petrarch's poem encounters the fatal snares that leave it bound and deprive it of freedom:

> Era un tenero fior nato in quel bosco
> il giorno avanti, et la radice in parte
> ch'appressar nol poteva anima sciolta;
> ché v'eran di lacciuo' forme sì nove,
> et tal piacer precipitava al corso,
> che perder libertate ivi era in pregio.
>
> (214, 7–12)

52. Significantly, Petrarch's exegesis of the wood of *Aeneid* I cited above also adds to the forbidding depiction the fascination of its beauty; "anche qui," comments Feo, "risuona la corda più vera dell'anima petrarchesca" ("Petrarca e Dante," 453).

53. Here, Vanossi observes, "bosco" is "lo scenario, il luogo dell'erranza, su cui si situa il dramma esistenziale"; see "Identità e mutazione nella sestina petrarchesca," *Cultura Neolatina* 40 (1980): 293.

[A tender flower had been born in that wood the day before, with its root in a place that could not be approached by a soul still free; for there were snares there of form so new and such pleasure hastened one's course that to lose liberty was there a prize.]

The implied contrast is decisive: the infant soul in Dante's *Purgatorio* is evoked to initiate a discussion of free will; the soul in Petrarch's poem suffers what appears to be a definitive loss of liberty that it gladly embraces. The following stanzas offer a retrospective reassessment of this wood initially described only as "bel" and as "quel bosco"; throughout the poem, it identifies the locus both of the initial entrapment and of the victim's continuing captivity.[54] The poem ends inconclusively:

> Or ecco in parte le question mie nove:
> s'alcun pregio in me vive o 'n tutto è corso,
> o l'anima sciolta o ritenuta al bosco.
>
> (37–39)

[Now behold in part my strange doubts: if any worth is alive in me or all run out, if my soul is free or captive in the wood.]

In the *Commedia*, the protagonist's fear concerning the impossibility of escape from this dark and perilous place is soon assuaged; the very mention of the "diritta via" lost to him implies that the wood need not be a closed space, a place of no issue. Like the forest of the romance tradition, Dante's wood as a place of chaos owes much of its meaning to the order to which it is opposed.[55] Perhaps the most significant contrast between the dark, chaotic forest of *Inferno* I and that of the *Rime sparse* is that the Dante-pilgrim's experience of the "selva oscura" is recalled in the retrospective account that is the *Commedia* precisely because it is there that the escape begins:

54. See Shapiro, *Hieroglyph of Time,* 122, on the relation of "bosco" in this poem to the terms "corso" and "sciolta." In sestina 142 the possibility of leaving the wood is raised over and over again only to be denied; the poet who sends canzone 126 on its way does not project his own departure. See Nancy Vickers, "Re-membering Dante: Petrarch's 'Chiare, fresche, e dolci acque'," *MLN* 96 (1981): 11: "Petrarch seems unwilling to abandon the woods of his erotic fantasy and step into the city beyond."

55. For the chivalric hero this is the worldly perfection and glory of the court, from which he departs for a necessary period of self-realization; for the pilgrim of the *Commedia* it is the City of God. See Picone, "Dante e la tradizione arturiana," 8.

Tant' è amara che poco è più morte;
ma per trattar del ben ch'i' vi trovai,
dirò de l'altre cose ch'i' v'ho scorte.

(*Inf.* I, 7–9)

[It is so bitter that death is hardly more so. But, to treat of the
good that I found in it, I will tell of the other things that I found
there.]

The fearful wood that stands as symbolic locus for the errant Dante
undergoes a series of transformations in the course of the *Commedia*, to
figure finally both the "divine forest" of the Earthly Paradise (*Purg.*
XXVIII, 2) and the *selva antica* of innocence that replaces the dark wood
of the soul's waywardness.[56] The Earthly Paradise itself, however, is only
an intermediate stage of the pilgrim's journey, the prelude to his salva-
tion, as Beatrice affirms:

"Qui sarai tu poco tempo silvano;
e sarai meco sanza fine cive
di quella Roma onde Cristo è romano."

(*Purg.* XXXII, 100–102)[57]

["Here shall you be a short time a forester, and you shall be with
me forever a citizen of that Rome whereof Christ is Roman."]

Petrarch's identification of his own poet as "abitador d'ombroso bosco"
[dweller in a shady wood] in *Rime* 214 recalls Dante's "silvano," but
within a wood, as Shapiro observes, whose larger meanings are reduced
to that of his enamorment.[58]

That reduction is fraught with consequences. The poet of the *Rime*,
despite protesting that he is Amor's unwitting victim, proclaims again
and again his acceptance of his condition. While Dante's pilgrim is
encouraged by the rays of the sun "che mena dritto altrui per ogne calle"
(*Inf.* I, 17–18), Petrarch's poet flees "ogni segnato calle," choosing
instead to follow paths unmarked and unsigned:

56. On this relation, see Piehler, *The Visionary Landscape*, 130.
57. See the chapter devoted to "Dante 'Poco Tempo Silvano': A Pastoral Oasis in the
Commedia" in Renato Poggioli, *The Oaten Flute* (Cambridge, Mass., 1975), 135–52.
58. Shapiro, *Hieroglyph of Time*, 127–28: "It is not, this *bosco*, the universe of human
existence, but specifically a piece of it enlarged to a whole—the experience of fatal love.
And this is only one part cut from D's plan. Petrarch acknowledges these parts to be in
turn a part of his store of content-forms."

et quanto in più selvaggio
loco mi trovo e 'n più deserto lido,
tanto più bella il mio pensier l'adombra.

(129, 46–48)[59]

[and whatever wildest place and most deserted shore I find myself,
so much the more beautiful does my thought shadow her forth.]

Or consider *Rime* 176, "Per mezz' i boschi inospiti et selvaggi."[60] While
the poet's situation here as he sings of his lady in the forest contains a
probable echo of an ode by Horace,[61] the sonnet emphasizes that the
forest is a place of danger. Yet the poet celebrates his condition, and the
sonnet merits citation in full for its revelation of his state of mind and the
hallucinatory nature of the experience:

Per mezz' i boschi inospiti et selvaggi
onde vanno a gran rischio uomini et arme,
vo securo io, ché non po spaventarme
altri che 'l sol ch' à d'Amor vivo i raggi.

E vo cantando (o penser miei non saggi!)
lei che 'l ciel non poria lontana farme,
ch' i' l'ò negli occhi, et veder seco parme
donne et donzelle, et sono abeti et faggi.

Parmi d'udirla, udendo i rami et l'ore
et le frondi, et gli augei lagnarsi, et l'acque
mormorando fuggir per l'erba verde.

Raro un silenzio, un solitario orrore
d'ombrosa selva mai tanto mi piacque,
se non che dal mio sol troppo si perde.

59. See Timothy Bahti, "Petrarch and the Scene of Writing: A Reading of *Rime*
CXXIX," *Yale Italian Studies* 1 (1980): 57–58, who argues that the whole of canzone 129
is "an obvious perversion of the first canto of the *Inferno*."

60. For the relation of this rude landscape to a Valchiusa transformed into a comfortless
place by Laura's absence, see Eugenio Battisti, "Non chiare acque," in *Francis Petrarch, Six
Centuries Later: A Symposium*, ed. Aldo Scaglione (Chapel Hill and Chicago, 1975), 330–
31.

61. Ode I, 22: "Integer vitae," its presence suggested by the adjective "inhospiti," a
hapax in the *Rime*. See F. Maggini, "Un ode di Orazio nella poesia del Petrarca," *Studi
Petrarcheschi*, 3 (1950): 7–12; B. König, "Petrarcas Landschaften," *Romanische Forschungen*
92 (1980); 272–73; and *Fam.* XXIV, 10, where Petrarch describes a passage "per inhospitas
silvarum latebras." E. H. Wilkins suggests a source in Propertius's elegy, "Haec certe
deserta loca"; see *The Making of the "Canzoniere,"* 331–32.

[Through the midst of the inhospitable savage woods, where even armed men go at great risk, I go without fear, nor can anything terrify me except the sun that has Love's living rays. And I go singing (oh my unwise thoughts!) of her whom the heavens could not make far from me, for she is before my eyes and with her I seem to see ladies and damsels, but they are firs and beeches. I seem to hear her, when I hear the branches and the breeze and the leaves, and birds lamenting, and the waters fleeing with a murmur across the green grass. Rarely has the silence, the solitary chill of a shady wood pleased me so much; except that I lose too much of my sun.]

This poem reveals, exceptionally, a historical stratum, that of Petrarch's voyage through the forest of the Ardennes.[62] Nonetheless, as De Robertis comments, the persona travels here *sui generis;* his situation is exemplary rather than particular, that of the enamored traveler who goes through the perilous forest not only secure but singing because he is oblivious to everything except the images of his absent love.[63]

Petrarch's depiction of his lyric protagonist lost in this forest contrasts with the positive evaluation of the "forest dweller" that he found in the bucolic tradition and reiterated in other works, both poetic and epistolary.[64] Early in the *Rime* his categorization suggests not a fruitful choice, but a fate constrained by Love: "maledico il dì ch'i' vidi 'l sole / che mi fa in vista un uom nudrito in selva" [I curse the day on which I saw the sun, for it makes me seem a man raised in the woods] (22, 17–18). This forest dweller's affinities are with a mythical type familiar in folklore and widely represented in the *selvaggio* tradition, the wild or savage man who is a solitary outcast from society, uninhibited by social or moral con-

---

62. It is confirmed in the companion poem that follows and attested in three letters among the *Familiares*. See Domenico De Robertis, "La traversata delle Ardenne: Sonetti CLXXXVI and CLXXXVII," *Lectura Petrarce VI, 1986* (Padua, 1987), 209–31.

63. See "La traversata delle Ardenne," 217–20. In one of the letters that records this same voyage, he points out, Petrarch explicitly recalls Virgil's tenth eclogue, which relates the separation of Lycoris and Gallus and the latter's "insanus amor"; the passage concludes, with obvious relevance for Petrarch's sonnet, "Omnia vincit Amor: et nos cedamus Amori." Nicolae Iliescu identifies in this poem "lo stupendo miraggio da cui il poeta è preso"; see *Il Canzoniere Petrarchesco e sant'Agostino* (Rome, 1962), 118–19.

64. In the tenth of his *Bucolicum carmen*, the name of the Petrarchan persona himself is Silvius; Petrarch explains to his brother Gherardo that the rustic protagonist is so called because he not only has spent his life in the woods, but hates the city and loves the forest. "That," Petrarch adds, "is why many of our friends call me Silvanus rather than Franciscus"; and indeed in the *De Genealogia Deorum* Boccaccio refers to the poet as "silvanus" (*Familiares* X, 4).

straints.[65] In courtly literature the type often suggests a form of erotic mania, as romance heroes denied the favors or the love of their ladies retreat into the wilderness.[66] So too the poet of Petrarch's sestina cited above is alienated, not only from his fellow creatures, but even from man's natural state: the pattern of his nights and days is unlike that of other earthly creatures because it is governed not by natural rhythms of light and darkness, but by his constant weeping for Laura, "she whom I weep for in the shadow and in the sun" (22).[67]

A yet more succinct formulation of the nature of the fatal experience in the forest defines it as "le piaghe ch'i' presi in quel bosco" [the wounds I received in that wood] (214). The reader is not startled: the representation of the *innamoramento* as wounding is conventional in medieval literature, which works numerous variations both on the theme of love as warfare[68] and on the Ovidian model of Cupid as archer. Long monologues in early vernacular romances are devoted to the physiology of this wounding.[69] Marie de France gives us its definition: "Amur est

65. See the comments of Shapiro, *Hieroglyph of Time*, 104–5. In the literary and artistic incarnations of this type, Richard Berkheimer observes, he is "a reminder that there are basic and primitive impulses clamoring for satisfaction"; see *Wild Men in the Middle Ages: A Study in Art, Sentiment, and Demonology* (Cambridge, Mass., 1952), 2.

66. This is "the only environment congenial to their sense of disorientation" (Berkheimer, *Wild Men*, 14). See also Roger Boase, *The Origin and Meaning of Courtly Love: A Critical Study of European Scholarship* (Manchester, 1977), 67, 95–96.

67. Here the recall may well be more specific, suggestive of the mythic figure of the "uomo selvaggio" whose relation to nature is apparently contrary to logic, laughing in the rain and weeping in fair weather; vernacular poets before Petrarch had adopted this figure as a sign of hope for a more favorable amorous season. See Roger Boase, "The 'Penitents of Love' and the Wildman in the Storm: A Passage of *The Knight of La Tour-Landry*," *MLR* 84 (1989): 817–33, and, for its pertinence to the *Rime*, Antonio Daniele, "Il sonetto CCXLV," *Lectura Petrarce VI, 1986* (Padua, 1987), 239–45.

68. This imagery is often associated with a negative philosophical assessment of passion, whether in act or in desire. Three Virgilian texts well known to Petrarch, the *Eclogues*, the *Georgics*, and *Aeneid* IV, represent love as a wound, or as an aggressor that ambushes and binds in chains. See John O'Meara, "Virgil and Saint Augustine: The Roman Background to Christian Sexuality," *Augustinus* 13 (1968): 307–26.

69. Examples are numerous; see, for example, the fate of Lavinia in the Old French *Eneas*, ed. J.-J. Salverda de Grave (Paris, 1968), II, 8066–67, and esp. 8159–62:

> Il me navra an un esgart,
> en l'oil me feri de son dart,
> de celui d'or, qui fet amer;
> tot lo me fist el cuel coler.

Chrétien de Troyes offers in a single romance the case histories of Alexandre and of Cligès (*Cligès*, ed. Alexandra Micha [Paris, 1965], vv. 439–40, 445–55, 694–96, 762–92), and again that of Yvain (*Le chevalier au lion*, ed. Mario Roques [Paris, 1965], vv. 1366–78).

plaie dedenz cors, / e si ne piert nient defors" [Love is a wound within the heart, which is not visible without].[70] Petrarch's more immediate precursors, the poets of the *dolce stil novo*, frequently depict Amor in the act of wounding or killing his victim.[71] In its most conventional and most obvious guise, the poet's wounding in the *Rime* recalls both this general scenario and the specific Ovidian narrative that dominates the mythic substructure of the collection, evoking Daphne's flight and Apollo's pursuit provoked by Love's vengeful blows (6). The numerous mentions of the poet's *piaghe* invariably refer back to the initial scene of the *innamoramento,* one obsessively replayed with both Laura and Amor as its dramatis personae: the stirring of the breeze in the green leaves, he confides, "makes me remember when Love gave me the first deep sweet wounds" (196); it is the *antiche piaghe* of the first fatal encounter that are renewed again and again with the commemoration of its anniversaries.

The Amor who inflicts the fatal wound upon the poet is not a mischievous juvenile Cupid but a full-grown adversary, one who in the initial scene of the *Rime* awaits a moment of vulnerability to strike without warning: "celatamente Amor l'arco riprese, / come uom ch'a nocer luogo e tempo aspetta" [Love took up his bow again secretly, like one who waits for the time and place to hurt] (2, 3–4). The paradigm informs another metaphor for the lover's condition familiar from the courtly tradition, that of Amor as jailer. Every effort to escape from amorous captivity, warns Augustinus in the *Secretum* in counseling Franciscus against a return to Avignon, meets with renewed determination on the part of the captor-adversary.[72] Two closely related sonnets in Part I offer a dramatization of this analysis, as well as an equally suggestive characterization of Amor as traitor:

> Amor con sue promesse lusingando
> mi ricondusse a la prigione antica,
> et die' le chiavi a quella mia nemica
> ch'ancor me di me stesso tene in bando.
>
> (76, 1–4)

Striking elaborations are found in the *Roman de la Rose,* where several of Amor's arrows are individually identified, and in Cavalcanti's "O tu, che porti nelli occhi sovente / Amor tenendo tre saette in mano."

70. "Guigemar," vv. 483–84; in Marie de France, *Lais,* ed. A. Ewert (Oxford, 1965).

71. See the entries "Amore uccide," "Amore ferisce," in Eugenio Savona, *Repertorio tematico del Dolce Stil Nuovo* (Bari, 1973), 54–63.

72. Thus, he advises, it is "not wise for the prisoner who has broken his chains to go wandering round the prison gates, ever ready to take him in again, before which the jailer is ever on guard, laying his traps with special care to recapture those whose escape he regrets" (*Petrarch's Secret,* 146).

[Alluring me with his promises, Love led me back to my former prison and gave the keys to that enemy of mine who still keeps me banished from myself.]

> Fuggendo la pregione ove Amor m'ebbe
> molt'anni a far di me quel ch'a lui parve . . .
> . . . tra via m'apparve
> quel traditore in sì mentite larve
> che più saggio di me ingannato avrebbe.

$$(89, 1-2, 6-8)$$

[Fleeing the prison where Love had kept me for many years to do what he willed with me . . . along the way appeared to me that traitor, in such disguising garments that he would have fooled a wiser man than I.]

The account of Amor's assault, augmented in the *Rime* by other elements common to the tradition of amatory poetry in the Middle Ages such as the snares, hooks, and traps laid for the unsuspecting or reluctant prey,[73] is complemented by peculiarly Petrarchan variants. Amor arms himself with the beauty of Laura's eyes, in them too he gilds and sharpens his arrows (127, 151), and numerous other poems identify her eyes themselves as the wounding agents.[74] The interchangeability of Amor and lady, eyes and arrows in the scenario of the assault leads the poet to compare Laura to the capable archer who assesses the accuracy of his shot; "Here is the arrow by which Love wishes him to die," she is imagined to reply (87).[75] In a poem excluded from the *Rime* Petrarch gives us a striking depiction of Laura as archer, girding herself with bow and quiver.[76] A less colorful scenario in the *Rime* represents an armed Laura as the

73. For this tradition deriving from Ovid's *Ars Amatoria*, see Marcelle Thiébaux, *The Stag of Love* (Ithaca and London, 1974), 96–102.

74. For the implications of a similar "demythologizing" in the troubadour lyric, see Thomas Hyde, *The Poetic Theology of Love: Cupid in Renaissance Literature* (London and Toronto, 1986), 33–34. The metaphor of the eye as archer and the "aggressive eye topos" are traced by Lance K. Donaldson-Evans, *Love's Fatal Glance: A Study of Eye Imagery in the Poets of the "Ecole Lyonnaise"* (University, Mississippi, 1980), chap. I: "The Eyes' Role in Love Literature since Antiquity" (9–49). Cf. the angels' presentation of Beatrice to the pilgrim in Purgatory: "posto t'avem dinanzi a li smeraldi / ond'Amor già ti trasse le sue armi" (*Purg.* XXXI, 116–17).

75. Petrarch may here again recall the scene of wounding in Dante's "canzone montanina," where upon approaching the lady he hears the words, "Vie via vedrai morir costui" (v. 42). See also poems 75; 95; 105; 133.

76. See Joseph A. Barber, "Il sonetto CXIII e gli altri sonetti a Sennuccio," *Lectura Petrarce II, 1982* (Padua, 1983), 33–34.

> . . . fera donna che con gli occhi suoi
> et con l'arco a cui sol per segno piacqui
> fe' la piaga onde, Amor, teco non tacqui.
>
> (174, 5–7)

[. . . cruel lady who with her eyes, and with the bow whom I pleased only as a target, made the wound about which, Love, I have not been silent to you.]

In a sonnet late in Part I, the description of the poet's condition assumes a baroque extravagance as Petrarch doubles the wound of the *innamoramento* with a second one, that of *pietate*, also inflicted by Amor: fire and smoke pour from the first wound, tears from the other (241). In one of the few poems of Part II to return to the motif, the victim will remind Amor that his weapons had been the arrows lit with invisible fire that issued from the lady's eyes (270).[77]

Petrarch's depiction of armed assault reveals once again his indebtedness to his great lyric precursor. Dante's poem known as the "canzone montanina," entirely devoted to the lover's torment, contains an original and striking formulation of a wound inflicted as the prospective victim turns fearfully toward the lady:

> Allor mi volgo per vedere a cui
> mi raccomandi; e 'ntanto sono scorto
> da li occhi che m'ancidono a gran torto . . .
> E mostra poi la faccia scolorita
> qual fu quel trono che mi giunse a dosso;
> che se con dolce riso è stato mosso,
> lunga fiata poi rimane oscura,
> perché lo spirto non si rassicura.
>
> (43–45, 56–60)

---

77. It is noteworthy that the other recall of this attack in Part II recasts it in a ceremonial allegory whose dignity contrasts sharply with the depictions of Love's crafty violence in Part I: the poet recalls Laura's human form as a "bella pregion" of alabaster, gold, ivory, and sapphire,

> inde i messi d'Amor armati usciro
> di saette et di foco, ond'io di loro
> coronati d'alloro,
> pur come or fusse, ripensando tremo.
>
> (325, 20–23)

[Then I turn about to find someone to appeal to, and at that instant she catches sight of me with the eyes that kill me wrongfully . . . And my face, all pale, shows what thunderbolt landed on me, for though it was sent with a sweet smile, my face long stays dark, for my spirit has no confidence.]

In its devastating effect this "dolce riso" is related to another Dantean phenomenon, the "salute" of Beatrice in the *Vita Nuova*, and Petrarch's version effects a characteristic synthesis of the two Dantean passages, including the lady's greeting along with her eyes:

> Perseguendomi Amor al luogo usato,
> ristretto in guisa d'uom ch'aspetta guerra,
> che si provede e i passi intorno serra,
> de' miei antichi pensier mi stava armato;
> volsimi et vidi . . .
> come col balenar tona in un punto,
> così fu' io de' begli occhi lucenti
> et d'un dolce saluto inseme aggiunto.
>
> (110, 1–5, 12–14)[78]

[Since Love was pursuing me to my accustomed place, I, drawn up like one who expects war and who prepares and closes the passes round about, was armed with my own thoughts. I turned and saw . . . as with lightning the thunder comes at the same instant, so I was overtaken by those beautiful shining eyes together with a sweet greeting.]

Drawing again upon the *petrose* to depict the lady's invulnerability to Love, he pleads for a vendetta that has its direct antecedent in the *congedo* of "Così nel mio parlar." Dante writes:

> Canzon, vattene dritto a quella donna
> che m'ha ferito il core e che m'invola
> quello ond'io ho più gola,

---

78. For this effect of Laura's beauty that distances Petrarch's praise of the lady from that of the stilnovists and in particular from the *Vita Nuova*, see Bernhard König, "*Dolci rime leggiadre:* Zur Verwendung und Verwandlung stilnovisticher Elemente in Petrarcas *Canzoniere*," in *Petrarca 1304–1374: Beiträge zu Werk und Wirkung*, ed. F. Schalk (Frankfurt, 1975), 136–38.

> e dàlle per lo cor d'una saetta:
> ché bell'onor s'acquista in far vendetta.
>
> (79–83)

[Song, go straight to that lady who has wounded my heart but steals away from me what I am most greedy for: strike her through the heart with an arrow, for to take vengeance is a lovely honor.]

Petrarch's plea, however, is addressed to Amor:

> I' son pregion, ma se pietà ancor serba
> l'arco tuo saldo et qualcuna saetta,
> fa di te et di me, signor, vendetta.
>
> (121, 7–9)[79]

[I am a prisoner, but if mercy has kept your bow whole and an arrow or two, take vengeance, lord, for yourself and for me.]

In the *Trionfi* the hypothetical scene of vengeance exacted is rewritten with the opposite consequence, as Laura and her few chaste companions aggressively disarm the archer, shattering his weapons and stripping the feathers from his wings (*Triumph of Chastity* II, 133ff.).

Elaborating upon the metaphors of aggression, the scene of amorous wounding acquires further dramatic force in the *Rime* from the location of the topos within a broader scenario of violence. The physical violence attributed to Laura in canzone 23—"she opened my breast and took my heart with her hand"[80]—recurs in the identification of her active role in his wounding, resulting in a torment he will endure "fin che mi sani 'l cor colei che 'l morse" [until she who wounded my heart makes him whole again] (29). His complaint to a pitiless Laura that "mi vedete straziare a mille morti" [you see me torn asunder by a thousand deaths] (144) recalls again the dismemberment central to the Acteon myth evoked as the last of the poet's transformations in the metamorphosis canzone.[81] Lamenting his fate attributed to a "cruel star," a "cruel cradle," and

---

79. See the discussion of G. Capovilla, "I Madrigali (LII, LIV, CVI, CXXI)," *Lectura Petrarce, III, 1983* (Padua, 1984), 23–24.

80. Marco Santagata discusses the critical reception of this passage and calls attention to the particular violence of the image; see "La canzone XXIII," *Lectura Petrarce, I, 1981* (Padua, 1982), 62–63.

81. For the implications of myths of dismemberment in the collection, see Nancy J. Vickers, "Diana Described: Scattered Woman and Scattered Rhyme," in *Writing and Sexual Difference,* ed. Elizabeth Abel (Chicago, 1982), 95–109.

"cruel ground where I later set my foot," he focuses then on Laura as the "cruel lady" who

> fe' la piaga onde, Amor, teco non tacqui,
> ché con quell'arme risaldar la poi.
> Ma tu prendi a diletto i dolor miei;
> ella non già, perché non son più duri,
> e 'l colpo è di saetta et non di spiedo.
>
> (174, 7–11)

[made the wound about which, Love, I have been silent to you, for with those same weapons you can heal it. But you are pleased with my pain; not she, for it is not harsh enough, and the blow is from an arrow, not a spear.]

Even the celebration of the beauty of Laura's hand suggests physical cruelty: apostrophizing the "bella man che mi destringe 'l core / e 'n poco spazio la mia vita chiudi" [beautiful hand that grasps my heart and encloses in a little space all my life], the poet will describe her soft fingers as "sol ne le mie piaghe acerbi et crudi" [only bitter and cruel to wound me] (199).[82]

Earlier poets, departing from a romance tradition in which a "courtly" god of Love inflicts his wounds gently and without physical suffering,[83] had sporadically suggested a more aggressive *battaglia d'amore*. Guido Cavalcanti was among them;[84] the association between Love and Death is revealed, Guittone d'Arezzo ingeniously affirms, by the very name of Amor, in which "MOR" indicates death, *morte*.[85] It is Dante's "Così nel

---

82. See the discussion of this representation in James Mirollo, "In Praise of *La bella mano:* Aspects of Late Renaissance Lyricism," *Comparative Literature Studies* 9 (1972): 34.

83. The God of Love in the *Roman de la Rose* carries the banner of courtliness; Guittone d'Arezzo writes of Amor "ch'usando cortesia po l'om dar morte . . . or siate donque me nemica forte, / e m'auzidete, amor, cortesemente." See Joan Ferrante, "*Cortes'Amor* in Medieval Texts," *Speculum* 55 (1980): 693–94.

84. See the remarks of Paolo Possiedi in "Con quella spada ond'elli ancise Dido," *MLN* 89 (1974): 31–32, and on the threatening aspect of Amor in Cavalcanti's corpus, see Corrado Calenda, *Per altezza d'ingegno: Saggio su Guido Cavalcanti* (Naples, 1976), 18–20. For the Amore-Morte topos in Cavalcanti's poems, see Maria Corti, Introduction to the *Rime*, ed. M. Ciccuto (Milan, 1987²), 14–19. Other examples are cited in Christopher Kleinhenz, *The Early Italian Sonnet: The First Century (1220–1321)* (Lecce, 1986), 137–43.

85. Cited in Guglielmo Gorni, "Il segreto del nome: Beatrice," *Versants* 2 (1981–82): hr n. 11. Santagata summarizes: "l'accoppiata amore-morte è tra le più frequenti nella poesia cortese"; see "Il giovane Petrarca e la tradizione poetica romanza: modelli ideologici e letterari," *Rivista di letteratura italiana* 1 (1983): 48.

mio parlar," however, that radicalizes this representation of violence, and once again we find the precursor of Petrarch's poet as victim in the suffering lover of the *rime petrose*. Dante shows us the god standing above his helpless victim, armed not with arrows but with "quella spada ond'elli ancise Dido":[86]

> Elli mi fiede sotto il braccio manco
> sì forte che 'l dolor nel cor rimbalza;
> allor dico: "S'elli alza
> un'altra volta, Morte m'avrà chiuso
> prima che 'l colpo sia disceso guiso."
>
> (48–52)

[He strikes me under the left arm so fiercely that the pain rebounds into my heart; then I say: "If he lifts his arm another time, Death will have shut me up before the blow can descend."]

In the *Rime* another blow is anticipated, one sometimes fervently invoked as the death that would put an end to the poet's suffering, sometimes deplored and feared;[87] the specter of death is raised in his warning to his lady that his heart might fail in its natural course (21). Laura's eyes too, agents of his wounding, may bear his death. Her casting as a "fera" or wild creature that bears weeping and sorrow and death in her eyes (135) suggests the basilisk of the bestiaries, a creature already associated in the lyric tradition with the lady who kills with her gaze.[88]

If death lies at one extreme of this scenario of wounding, at the opposite end of its logical spectrum is the possibility of healing. The Amor of the romance tradition not only possesses but regularly exercises curative powers.[89] The paradox of a god who both wounds and heals, who gives life as well as death, is developed as part of the iconography of Amor by the mother of innocent Lavinia in the Old French *Eneas* already cited, as she explains to her daughter the two arrows in his right hand and the small box in his left: the former indicates his power to wound,

86. See Bruce Comens, "Stages of Love, Steps to Hell: Dante's *Rime petrose*," *MLN* 99 (1986): 183, and on the savagery of this description and the violent eroticism to which it leads in Dante's canzone, 182–85.

87. See especially poems 36; 202; 207.

88. For the motif of the lady "che porta morte negli occhi," see Berra, "L'arte della similitudine," 182–83.

89. See Knapton, *Mythe et psychologie*, 98; she discusses also the related motif of the lady healing a wound of a different origin, as in the *Tristan* and the *Guigemar* of Marie de France.

the latter his power to heal.[90] "Il resane quant a navré," he heals as much as he has wounded: this optimistic and occasionally playful view of "l'amour-médecin," however, has little relevance for the prospects of the protagonist of the *Rime sparse*. While Petrarch acknowledges the topos— he who does not know Laura's sweet speech, sighs, and laughter "does not know how Love heals and how he kills" (159)—the doubling of the destructive and curative powers is invested in Laura herself. "There are no herbs to cure love," Apollo laments as he pursues Daphne (*Met.* I, 521–24); now Petrarch's mortal poet:

> I begli occhi ond' i' fui percosso in guisa
> ch' e' medesmi porian saldar la piaga,
> et non già vertù d'erbe o d'arte maga
> o di pietra dal mar nostro divisa.
>
> (75, 1–4)

[The lovely eyes that struck me in such a way that they themselves could heal the wound, but not the power of herbs or of magic art or of any stone distant from our sea.]

The hand that wounds and the hand that heals are one and the same (164)[91]—within the conventional matrix of the *innamoramento* as wounding, Petrarch's poet repeatedly insists in the poems *in vita* that Laura alone has the power to heal the wound that she and Amor have inflicted.[92]

This healing of Love's wound, however, would imply reciprocity, and it is precisely this prospect that is denied the poet of the *Rime*. In Marie's *Guigemar* cited above, the physical and amorous wounds are to be healed together: the wounded hunter's suffering can only be ended by a lady who will suffer great pain and sorrow for his love. Later, afflicted by the

---

90. *Eneas*, II, vv. 7985–90. The mother's advice is offered to encourage Lavinia to entrust herself to Love, because despite the initial suffering, good will follow:

> sanz herbe boivre et sanz racine
> a chascun mal fet sa mecine;
> n'e estuet oignement n'entrait,
> la plaie sane qui il fait;
> se il te velt un po navrer,
> bien te savra anprés saner.
>
> (7969–74)

91. For the "fall into oxymoron" in this poem, see Thomas M. Greene, *The Light in Troy: Imitation and Discovery in Renaissance Poetry* (New Haven and London, 1982), 116–18, who notes that this verse echoes Ovid's *Remedia amoris*.

92. See also poems 105; 161; 195.

beauty of a lady, Love's victim will recognize that death is sure if he is not healed by her. Again and again in the *Rime* the poet confides his sorrowful awareness that his wound, his "piaga amorosa," will never be healed:

> Esser po in prima ogni impossibil cosa
> ch'altri che Morte od ella sani 'l colpo
> ch'Amor co' suoi belli occhi al cor m'impresse.
>
> (195, 12–14)

[Every impossible thing will happen before another than she or Death heals the wound that Love made in my heart with her lovely eyes.]

Whether the denial of remedy be attributed to positive or negative motives, to the lady's resolute chastity or to her disdainful cruelty, for the wound received in the wood there is no medicine, ancient or new:

> Ma, lasso, or veggio che la carne sciolta
> fia di quel nodo ond' è 'l suo maggior pregio
> prima che medicine antiche o nove
> saldin le piaghe ch' i' presi in quel bosco. . . .
>
> (214, 19–22)

[But now, alas, I see that my flesh shall be free from that knot for which it is most greatly prized, before medicines old or new can heal the wounds I received in that wood. . . .]

Soon the possibility of healing is to be definitively precluded (or so it seems) by Laura's death; the poet will be left to wander, disconsolate, through a world disconsolate, a world bereft of sense and value because bereft of Laura.

3

CHIAROSCURO

As the enamored protagonist of the *Rime* pursues his elusive lady through landscape, whether that landscape be the flowering hills and grassy riverbank of Valchiusa or the forest in which he wanders amid the branches seeking traces of her presence, he moves in shade and through shadow: "Se 'nfra duo poggi siede ombrosa valle, / ivi s'acqueta l'alma sbigottita," he confides in the great canzone "Di pensier in pensier" in which inner and outer landscape are ultimately fused [If between two peaks (there is) a shady valley, there my frightened soul is quieted]; and again: "ove porge ombra un pino alto od un colle / talor m'arresto" [where a tall pine or a hillside extends shade, there I sometimes stop] (129). It is thus that he experiences the familiar landscape of Valchiusa, thus that he experiences the forest, the "ombrose selve ove percote il sole" [shady woods where strikes the sun . . .] (162). Laura too moves through shadow, the "ombrosa chiostra" of the hills, in this, her landscape (192, 194); and following her death, this is the landscape to which he will return to seek her with his thoughts, "per luoghi ombrosi et foschi . . . cercando col penser" (281). As constants of the descriptive system of the *Rime sparse,* these shadows and this shade add a play of chiaroscuro, a softening of contour to the various yet constant settings of the poet's story.[1]

Cumulatively, however, the many designations of shade and shadow in the *Rime* far exceed that chromatic nuance. Indeed, *ombra* defines not only the poet's amorous experience but the project of the *Rime sparse:* in his recall that as a consequence of his love for Laura "i' depinsi poi per mille valli / l'ombra ov' io fui" [I depicted then through a thousand

---

1. On this play of the connotations of "ombra," see Fredi Chiappelli, *Studi sul linguaggio del Petrarca: La canzone delle Visioni* (Florence, 1971), 65.

valleys the shade where I had been] (66), the shadow painted across a vast range of symbolic landscape corresponds remarkably to his amorous lament resounding, as he records in other poems, through the landscape of his life.[2] What happens to the poet within that shade? To attempt to reply to that question, fundamental to the reading of the collection as a whole, one must consider not only shadow but light: for just as shadow marks the passage of the poet and his lady through landscape in its contrast to the light that ranges across the hills and riverbank of Valchiusa or penetrates into the recesses of the forest, the figural shadow play of *ombra* is inextricably interrelated with the play of light. Together light and shadow define sets of oppositions that bring into relation not only time and atemporality, vision and blindness, but also the psychic tensions of self-awareness and illusion, and ultimately spiritual darkness and illumination. These oppositions are interwoven in a dense figural network, one that is enriched with each new occurence for which it in turn affords the resonances of earlier contextualizations. In order to explore their implications for the major thematic concerns of the collection, however, we may attempt first to disentangle these threads and consider each in turn.

Once again we may begin with Petrarch's adaptation of the primary mythological model and the earliest forms of the collection. Here we find at once that the blending of anthropomorphic and natural elements in the Ovidian paradigm is doubled: whereas in the Ovidian story only Daphne appears in two guises, human and arboreal, in the *Rime* Petrarch exploits also the mythic identity of Apollo with the sun. It is this identity that generates the triad of sonnets based on meteorologic conceits in which Laura's presence or absence, provoking a serene or a disconsolate response on the part of the enamored deity, determines fair or inclement weather (41–43). Yet already in other poems among those in the early forms of the collection a more suggestive and complex adaptation is evident. In *Rime* 34, in the poet's appeal for clement weather to protect the beloved laurel, the solar body is substituted for the solar deity, but the sun is figured as the face of Apollo:

> dal pigro gelo et dal tempo aspro et rio
> che dura quanto 'l tuo viso s'asconde
> difendi or l'onorata et sacra fronde
> ove tu prima et poi fu' invescato io. . . .
>
> (34, 5–8)

2. Tassoni in his commentary attributes to the verb here the technical, painterly sense of "ombreggiare"; cited in Marianne Shapiro, *Hieroglyph of Time: The Petrarchan Sestina* (Minneapolis, 1980), 113.

[against the slow frost and the harsh and cruel time that lasts as long as your face is hidden, now defend the honored and holy leaves where you first and then I were limed. . . .]

In *Rime* 188, which opens with an invocation of Apollo as "Almo Sol," the zone of shadow created by the passage of the sun through the heavens deprives the poet of the sight of Laura's birthplace:

> Stiamo a mirarla, i' ti pur prego et chiamo,
> o sole; et tu pur fuggi et fai dintorno
> ombrare i poggi et te ne porti il giorno,
> et fuggendo mi tòi quel ch' i' più bramo.
>
> (188, 5–8)

[Let us stay to gaze at her, I beg and call on you, O sun, and you still run away and shadow the hillsides all around and carry off the day, and fleeing you take from me what I most desire.]

As readers have pointed out, these lengthening shadows have ample poetic precedent; they suggest a probable assimilation of the *petrose*, where in "Al poco giorno" Dante had recorded himself "closed in all around with high hills" and their dark shadow, with the pastoral Virgil, whose verse "maioresque cadunt altis de montibus umbrae" (*Buc.* I, 83) is closely translated by Petrarch in another poem as "onde discende / dagli altissimi colli maggior l'ombra" [the shadows descend most widely from the highest mountains] (50).[3] In Petrarch's sonnet, however, the emphasis falls on the progressive present of the verb:

> L'ombra che cade da quell'umil colle . . .
> crescendo mentr'io parlo, agli occhi tolle
> la dolce vista del beato loco . . .
>
> (188, 9, 12–13)

[The shadow that falls from that low hill . . . growing as I speak, takes from my eyes the sweet sight of the blessed place . . .]

3. Domenico De Robertis, "Petrarca petroso," *Revue des Etudes Italiennes* 29 (1983): 24–25. For the deviation of Petrarch's sonnet from the affirmative natural rhythms evoked in both this Virgilian text and Horace's "Carmen saeculare" echoed in the opening apostrophe of *Rime* 188, see Thomas Greene, *The Light in Troy: Imitation and Discovery in Renaissance Poetry* (New Haven and London, 1982), 135–43.

Here the phrase "crescendo mentr'io parlo," a revision of the earlier formulation "crescendo a poco a poco," achieves a new immediacy through the shadow falling across the hills at the moment of enunciation by the watching poet.[4] In its daring fusion of natural and mythological time, this poem also subverts the adequation of the mythological paradigm to the poet's story, the sun's departure leaving the lady's abode in deepening shadow observed only by her latter-day poet-lover;[5] it affords an admonitory reminder that the two kinds of time here represented— mythical time that eludes temporality, and "historical" and linear time— are incompatible.[6]

The evocation of Apollo as sun-god serves only as introduction to this drama of time's passing.[7] Acknowledged in many other Petrarchan texts, this theme achieves singular prominence in the *Rime* in the proemial poem in the closing affirmation that "quanto piace al mondo è breve sogno" [whatever pleases in the world is a brief dream], although it is only much later that the reader will relate the "vain hopes" of this sonnet to particular causes—Laura's inaccessibility *in vita*, and definitively her death—and to universal causes—the inevitability of death that conditions the characterization of *speranza* elsewhere in the collection as *fallace*.[8] In the disappearance of Laura herself, in the perception of the transience of earthly beauty, it finds a dramatic example: "Questo nostro caduco et fragil bene, / ch' è vento et ombra et à nome beltate," Petrarch will define it near the end of the collection [This brittle, frail good of ours, which is wind and shadow and is called beauty] (350). Yet it is not only beauty that is evanescent: Laura and her beauty become the measure of the transience of all mortal life, and in this the primary vehicle for a fundamental theme of the collection.[9] The situation in which the lover

4. On this rapid disappearance of Laura as one of the most effective expressions of Petrarch's drama, see Ugo Dotti, "Petrarca: Il mito dafneo," *Convivium* 37 (1969): 21.

5. As Cesare Galimberti suggests, we find here a demythification of the creature beloved of the sun and now abandoned by her celestial lover; see "Amate dal sole: R.V.F. XXXIV, CLXXXVIII, CCCLXVI," in *Miscellanea di Studi in onore di Vittore Branca*, I (Florence, 1983), 431.

6. Cf. Shapiro, *Hieroglyph of Time*, on the embodiment in this representation of "conflicting dreams that are ultimately irreconcilable" (66). Ricardo J. Quinones comments on the reversion of the sun in this poem "to its more terrifying physical being" in *The Renaissance Discovery of Time* (Cambridge, Mass., 1972), 126.

7. See for example Gianfranco Folena, "L'orologio del Petrarca," *Libri e Documenti* 3 (1979): 1–12.

8. Armando Balduino notes that "fallace" is little less than a constant epithet for "speranza," as in *Rime* 31, 32, 99, 290, and esp. 294. See "Il sonetto XXXII," *Lectura Petrarce, I, 1981* (Padua, 1982), 32.

9. See the chapter "Il senso della labilità" in Umberto Bosco, *Francesco Petrarca* (Bari,

finds himself in *Rime* 188, as the fading of the light "agli occhi tolle la dolce vista del beato loco," will be reinterpreted in an absolute key in a sonnet *in morte di Laura* in which her light is occulted, not by Time, but by Death:

> L'aura et l'odore e 'l refrigerio et l'ombra
> del dolce lauro et sua vista fiorita,
> lume et riposo di mia stanca vita,
> tolto à colei che tutto il mondo sgombra.
>
> (327, 1–4)

[The breath and the fragrance and the coolness and the shade of the sweet laurel and its flourishing sight, the light and repose of my weary life, have been taken away by her who empties the whole world.]

In a suggestive analogue in the *Trionfo del Tempo* the sun declaims a mission, to eradicate all traces of mortal fame, and at the conclusion of his speech he hastens his course into a vertiginous passage recalled by the awestruck mortal observer as the acceleration of the seasons.[10] In a poem near the end of Part II of the *Rime* the poet rewrites his reproach to Apollo as an apostrophe to Time: "O tempo, O ciel volubil che fuggendo / inganni i ciechi e miseri mortali . . ." [O time, O revolving heavens that fleeing deceive us blind and wretched mortals] (355). The theme of the *fuga temporis* attests to the lasting impact of Petrarch's reading of the Roman philosophers and Cicero in particular,[11] but in Augustine he found dramatized the paradox of our *vita mortalis*, life leading to death. An oration by Augustinus in the *Secretum*, which like the *De otio religioso* and the *De vita solitaria* stresses the theme of mortality, reminds us that Petrarch's most suggestive variations on the theme again associate his sense of loss with *ombra*: "As often as you behold at sunset the

---

1973), especially 52–54. Balduino identifies a sequence early in the collection (*Rime* 31–34) in which an apparent meditation on Laura's illness initiates a meditation on time and death ("Il sonetto XXXII," 39–43).

10. *Tr. Tem.* 67–69, 76, 86; for this hostile time indicated by bellicose metaphors, see Edoardo Taddeo, "Petrarca e il tempo," *Studi e problemi di critica testuale* 27 (1983): 70. Cf. the great patriotic canzone "Italia mia" (128): ". . . mirate come 'l tempo vola, / et sì come la vita / fugge et la Morte n'è sovra le spalle" [see how time flies and how life flees, and how Death is at our backs].

11. As Balduino notes, Petrarch's lengthy evocation of his early reading and of excerpts on this theme in *Fam.* XXIV, 1 closes with a recall of Cicero; see "Il sonetto XXXII," 31.

shadows of the mountains lengthening on the plain, say to yourself: 'Now life is sinking fast; the shadow of death begins to overspread the scene . . .' " ["Nunc vita fugiente umbra mortis extenditur"].[12] Dante had provided the formula of our "vivere ch'è un corso alla morte" [life that is a race to death] (*Purg.* XXXIII, 54), but in the *Rime* it is as a shadowed course that the poet dramatizes his own race toward death:[13]

> Lasso, che pur da l'un a l'altro sole
> et da l'una ombra a l'altra ò già 'l più corso
> di questa morte che si chiama vita!
>
> (216, 9–11)

[Alas! for from one sun to the next, and from one night to the next, I have already run through most of this death which is called life!]

Here the recurring daily cycle of *ombra* that in sestina 22 evokes the inexorable sequence of the poet's days and nights is suddenly unrolled into the linearity of a passage never to be repeated in which the two shadows define the span of a human life.[14] "I dì miei più leggier che nesun cervo / fuggir come ombra" [My days, swifter than any deer, have fled like a shadow] (319): the resonance, of course, is no longer primarily mythological but Biblical, the same as that of the affirmation of one of Petrarch's Penitential Psalms that "Limus et umbra tenuis sum, et fumus ante impetum ventorum."[15]

Yet even as time casts its shadow over the poet of the *Rime sparse*, *ombra*, figure of time's passing and the ephemeral nature of earthly experience, figures also, in a more pervasive network of imagery, to suggest the annihilation of time: the marvelous epiphanic escape from time in the experience of the *innamoramento* and its recall. Again it

---

12. *Petrarch's Secret*, 185. The same sentiment is present in the opening letter of the last book of the *Familiares:* "We are continuously dying. . . ." For its relevance to *Rime* 188, see Nicholas Mann, *Petrarch* (Oxford and New York, 1984), 83; Dotti, "Petrarca: Il mito dafneo," 21.

13. See esp. *Rime* 37. Other examples, from both the *Rime* and other Petrarchan texts, are cited in Bosco, *Francesco Petrarca*, 60–61.

14. Jill Tilden comments acutely on the poet's "lightless time"; see "Spiritual Conflict in Petrarch's Canzoniere," in *Petrarca 1304–1374: Beiträge zu Werk und Wirkung*, ed. F. Schalk (Frankfurt, 1975), 296–97.

15. Psalms 7:16; in *Opere di Francesco Petrarca*, ed. Emilio Bigi (Milan, 1963), 506. Here biblical echoes blend with an echo of Horace: "pulvis et umbra sumus" (*Odes* IV, 7, 16). For the prominence of shade and shadows, see Marino Casali, "Petrarca 'penitenziale': Dai *Salmi* alle *Rime*," *Lettere Italiane* 20 (1968): esp. 373–82.

represents a fundamental imaginative adaptation of the Ovidian paradigm, and it too is present in the early sonnet 34. That poem, as we have seen, moves from an initial address in which Apollo as sun-god is urged to recall the lost Daphne, to the blending of human and arboreal forms as the beloved assumes a posture evocative of her transformation, to "far de le sue braccia a se stessa ombra" [with her arms making a shade for herself]; here Laura in full sunlight sits within the shadow of her own making, and that shadow, through its association with the "onorata et sacra fronde" for which Apollo's protection is invoked in the preceding verses, is at the same time the shadow of the laurel.

In the definitive ordering of the collection, in which the development of the mythological paradigm is deferred, the initial occurrences of *ombra* are punctual and occasional, all evoking the familiar natural phenomenon that we designate as shadow or shade: the nightingale sings in the shade (10), Laura's veil is not set aside in either sunlight or shade (11), the dawn chases away the shadows while the poet weeps for Laura in both sunlight and shade (22). In the recapitulation of the *innamoramento* and its consequences in the metamorphosis canzone 23, however, shadow is attributed to both the lady and the laurel, anticipating the dual nature of its associations with Laura throughout the collection. First it stands for her physical presence:

> ch' a quei preghi il mio lume era sparito,
> ed io non ritrovando intorno intorno
> ombra di lei né pur de' suoi piedi orma . . .
>
> (23, 107–9)

[for at those prayers my light had disappeared, and I, not finding anywhere a shadow of her, or even a trace of her feet . . .]

At the close of the poem, in a stunning affirmation of timelessness and simultaneity in relation to the mythological model, the poet proclaims his fidelity to the laurel that had figured his initial transformation on the occasion of the *innamoramento* and attributes that fidelity to the plant's sweet shade:

> né per nova figura il primo alloro
> seppi lassar, ché pur la sua dolce ombra
> ogni men bel piacer del cor mi sgombra.
>
> (23, 167–69)[16]

16. Petrarch's tenth eclogue, where the laurel stands for Laura, again affirms the exclusive nature of that fascination: "Quickly I made my way towards it and shortly reaching its fragrant shadow I held myself by it, forsaking all other pleasures"; see *Petrarch's Bucolicum Carmen*, trans. and annotated by Thomas G. Bergin (New Haven and London, 1974).

[nor for any new shape could I leave the first laurel, for still its sweet shade turns away from my heart any less beautiful pleasure.]

The play on shade or shadow, absent from Ovid's account, is grafted carefully onto the original Ovidian stock in poems such as 23 and 34, its intelligibility guaranteed by the explicit or covert allusion to Daphne's transformation. But like the image of the lady beneath the tree, it also has vernacular subtexts, primarily (once again) Dante's *rime petrose*. The final verses of *Rime* 23 cited above are closely related, not only through content but through the rhyme scheme "ombra" / "disgombra," to Dante's "Io son venuto."[17] Another of the best-known poems of the *Rime sparse*, "Giovene donna sotto un verde lauro" (30), opens with a recall of a verse from "Al poco giorno," "sotto un bel verde la giovane donna" [under a lovely green the youthful lady] and has as a whole been termed a "tissue of allusions" to Dante's poem.[18] The recurrence of "ombra" as one of the six rhyme words of Dante's sestina, where affective states are related to natural phenomena to render the contradictions of the experience of love,[19] suggests representational possibilities whose traces are found throughout Petrarch's collection. In particular, its system of correspondences promotes the substitution of shadow for lady as love object, to proclaim "l'amor ch'io porto pur a la sua ombra" [the love that I feel for her very shadow]; Petrarch in his turn will love and fear the shadow of his lady / laurel: "Senz'acqua il mare et senza stelle il cielo / fia innanzi ch'io non sempre tema et brami / la sua bell'ombra" [The sea will be without water and the sky without stars when I no longer fear and desire her lovely shadow] (195).[20]

Dante's protagonist, however, follows the moving shadow of his lady Petra; Petrarch's poet in *Rime* 30 follows that of an immobile tree.[21] While he is unrelenting in the fixity of his love, like the speaker of

17. See Marco Santagata, "Il giovane Petrarca e la tradizione poetica romanza: Modelli ideologici e letterari," *Rivista di letteratura italiana* 1 (1983): 19–20.

18. Robert M. Durling, "Petrarch's 'Giovene donna sotto un verde lauro'," *MLN* 86 (1971): 5. For a stylistic and thematic analysis of the two poems, see also Werner von Koppenfels, "Dantes 'Al poco giorno' und Petrarcas 'Giovene donna': Ein Interpretationsvergleich zweier Sestinen," *Deutsches Dante-Jahrbuch* 44–45 (1967): 150–89.

19. For this polarization as a given in the poetics of *fin'amor*, see Pierre Bec, "L'antithèse poétique chez Bernard de Ventadour," in *Mélanges J. Boutière* (Liège, 1971), 107–37.

20. See the comments of De Robertis, "Petrarca petroso," 21.

21. Thus, John Freccero points out, the symbolic search turns in a circle, and the exterior quest becomes an internal obsession, a form of idolatry; see "The Fig Tree and the Laurel: Petrarch's Poetics," *Diacritics* (Spring 1975): 38. See also the comments of De Robertis, "Petrarca petroso," 33.

Dante's "Al poco giorno," his own proclamation substitutes the shadow
of the laurel for that of the lady:

> Ma perché vola il tempo et fuggon gli anni
> sì ch'a la morte in un punto s'arriva
> o colle brune o colle bianche chiome,
> seguirò l'ombra di quel dolce lauro . . .
>
> (30, 13–16)

[But because time flies and the years flee and one arrives quickly
at death either with dark or with white locks, I shall follow the
shadow of that sweet laurel . . .]

Seeking shelter from a violent light like his Dantean precursor, he flees
to the shade of the "belle frondi" that are the branches of the laurel, the
"pianta più gradita in cielo," most favored in Heaven (142).[22] The free
movement between laurel and Laura is the nucleus of numerous poems
in which *ombra*, common to both, effects their identity.

Many of these occurrences have an additional resonance because they
participate in one of the major thematic clusters detailed in the preceding
chapters. Laura's body—though it cannot be integrally identified—marks
and signs the landscape in which she is present and through which she
passes; her body—but it cannot be directly looked upon—is recognized
by the shadow it casts:

> . . . con quanti luoghi sua bella persona
> coprì mai d'ombra o disegnò col piede . . .
>
> (100, 7–8)

[with however many places her lovely body ever covered with its
shadow or marked with a foot . . .]

> volsimi et vidi un'ombra che da lato
> stampava il sole, et riconobbi in terra
> quella . . .
>
> (110, 5–7)

---

22. In the Coronation Oration it is in the shade of the laurel, "arbor haec umbrifera,"
that the poet finds rest, a mythological allusion suggestive not only of Apollo's favor but of
the protection afforded the tree by Jove; see Sara Sturm-Maddox, *Petrarch's Metamorphoses:
Text and Subtext in the Rime sparse* (Columbia, Mo., 1985), 25–32.

[I turned and saw a shadow on the ground to one side, cast by the sun, and I recognized her . . .]

This *ombra*, which may be (like Laura herself) not only *dolce* but *bella* and *lieta*,[23] figures in the *Rime* as one of the several surrogate images of Laura and as one of her many displacements. Throughout the collection, moreover, the shade or shadow of lady and laurel retain a privileged status as markers of a zone where other events, visionary or magical, may occur. The shade of Laura's eyes, a locus that invites the presence of Amor (125), is interchangeable with the shade of the laurel, in which Amor may sit along with the lady (337).[24] A singular poem unites Laura's iconography with that of her landscape in a visionary tableau set in the laurel's shade, creating a symbolic identity in which the human form vanishes entirely:

> Una candida cerva sopra l'erba
> verde m'apparve con duo corna d'oro,
> fra due riviere all'ombra d'un alloro.
>
> (190, 1–3)

[A white doe on the green grass appeared to me, with two golden horns, between two rivers, in the shade of a laurel.]

The evocative potential of this shade receives its final realization in a vision of the young, straight laurel, "giovenetto e schietto," late in the collection:

> . . . di sua ombra uscian sì dolci canti
> di vari augelli et tant' altro diletto
> che dal mondo m'avean tutto diviso.
>
> (323, 28–30)

[from its shade came forth such sweet songs of diverse birds and so much other delight that it had rapt me from the world.]

23. In a poem that situates the *innamoramento* in the shade of the laurel, love's snares are spread in its "ombre più triste che liete" (181). For an inventory of the occurrences of *ombra* in the collection and its associations with *dolce*, see Chiappelli, *Studi sul linguaggio del Petrarca*, 64.

24. Again there is a precedent in the *rime petrose*, as Dante describes the shade of the garland worn by the cold but beautiful lady of "Al poco giorno": "sì bel, ch'Amor li viene a stare a l'ombra" [so beautifully that Love comes to stay in the shade there].

While Petrarch's implementation of the Ovidian association of Daphne and the laurel evolves toward differentiation rather than identity, as we have seen in Chapter 1, in the elaboration of his concept of *ombra* the two remain mutually suggestive: the lady's *ombra* and that of the laurel are integrated in the suggestion of a magical force-field generated by a singular and compelling presence, in an attraction whose cumulative implications remain to be explored.

"Stiamo a mirarla," the poet urges his Ovidian counterpart in sonnet 188, that they may preserve their simultaneous vision of Laura's birthplace, but in vain: "fleeing you take from me what I most desire," he complains to Apollo. Shadows figure in the preoccupation evident throughout the *Rime* with modes of seeing, and in particular modes of seeing Laura. Here the association of *ombra* with *velo* [veil] is particularly suggestive among the vehicles for her presence-in-absence. In combination with *ombra*, the latter term may designate the mortal body, or render the opposition of body and spirit;[25] like *ombra* and its synonymic counterparts *tenebre* and *nebbia*, it may also designate obstacles to understanding.[26] More frequently, however, it renders presence, and it evokes in particular the body of Laura, as in one of the first poems announcing her death that had separated her soul, her "invisible form," from "quel velo / che qui fece ombra al fior degli anni suoi" [the veil that here shadowed the flower of her years] (268).[27] As a term in substitution for her body, its characterization is suggestive of her grace and beauty: "quel soave velo / che per alto destin ti venne in sorte" [that soft veil that was allotted to you by high destiny], the poet recalls it in addressing her *in morte* (352).

In the poems *in vita* the veil that frequently not only shades Laura's eyes but covers her hair calls attention also to the poet's desire, to which

25. "Ciò ne fa l'ombra ria del grave velo" [the bitter shadow of the heavy veil does that to us] (122). The poet voices his wish that he had preceded Laura in death, "dolcemente sciolto / in sua presenza del mortal mio velo" [sweetly shaking off in her presence my mortal veil] (331); see also poems 70, 77, 264, 313, 362.

26. See 28; 277; 329. For the veil image in discussions of Christian hermeneutics, see D. W. Robertson, Jr., *A Preface to Chaucer* (Princeton, 1962), 51. Paul Colilli assesses the veil as hermeneutic metaphor in "Petrarch's Theology of the Veil" (Ph.D. dissertation, University of Toronto, 1983), 31–42. Freccero suggests that the "velo" of madrigal 52 may be read in terms of medieval discussions of allegory ("The Fig Tree and the Laurel", 39); on canzone 125, see Giuseppe Mazzotta, "The *Canzoniere* and the Language of the Self," *Studies in Philology* 75 (1978): 285, 291–92.

27. See the comments of Nicolas J. Perella, *Midday in Italian Literature: Variations on an Archetypal Theme* (Princeton, 1979), 44–46. Analogous is the use of "vesta" to evoke Laura's body in *Rime* 8; see Kenneth Cool, "The Petrarchan Landscape as Palimpsest," *Journal of Medieval and Renaissance Studies* 11 (1981): 98–99.

it imposes an obstacle.[28] While he may celebrate Laura's eyes seen in the shadow of her veil on the occasion of the *innamoramento* (127), more frequently he complains that the veil occults the fullness of his vision. "What I most desired in you has been taken from me," he complains to Laura:

> sì mi governa il velo
> che per mia morte et al caldo et al gielo
> de' be' vost' occhi il dolce lume adombra.
>
> (11, 11–14)[29]

[thus the veil controls me and to cause my death shades the sweet light of your lovely eyes in both warm and icy weather.]

Like the glove shaped to her adored hand, her veil assumes the status of a fetish object;[30] exulting in his temporary possession of her glove, the poet exclaims, "Would I had again as much of that lovely veil!" (199).

Thus it is that Laura's veil is the subject of the madrigal that contains the most explicit recall of the myth of Acteon in the *Rime sparse:*

> Non al suo amante più Diana piacque
> quando per tal ventura tutta ignuda
> la vide in mezzo de le gelide acque,
> ch'a me la pastorella alpestra et cruda
> posta a bagnar un leggiadretto velo
> ch' a l'aura il vago et biondo capel chiuda;
> tal che mi fece, or quand' egli arde 'l cielo,
> tutto tremar d'un amoroso gielo.
>
> (52)

[Not so much did Diana please her lover when, by a similar chance, he saw her all naked amid the icy waters, as did the cruel

---

28. The "problématique du diaphragme" relating the various obstacles to the sight of Laura is discussed by Fredi Chiappelli in "Le Thème de la *defectio solis* dans le *Canzoniere: Variatio intus*," in *Il legame musaico*, ed. Pier Massimo Forni (Rome, 1984), 169–70. Luigi Vanossi, who identifies the motif of the veil and associated emblems as a fundamental symbolic nexus in the *Rime*, discusses also that of the *nebbia* or mist that often surrounds Laura's body; see "Petrarca e il mito di Atteone," *Romanistische Zeitschrift für Literaturgeschichte* 10 (1986): 12, 15–16.

29. In a suggestive variation, Laura shields her eyes with her hand as well as her veil; the poet complains of it and "un vel che due begli occhi adombra / et par che dica: 'Or ti consuma et piagni' " [a veil that shades two lovely eyes and seems to say: "Now suffer and weep"] (38).

30. See Vanossi, "Petrarca e il mito di Atteone," 14–15.

mountain shepherdess please me, set to wash a pretty veil that keeps her lovely blond head from the breeze; so that she made me, even now when the sky is burning, all tremble with a chill of love.]

Suggesting the seeing of that which is not to be seen, this veil reminds us that the Ovidian Diana transforms Acteon into a stag because he has seen her "unveiled" ("posito velamine"). Some of Petrarch's readers have preferred to identify the "pastorella" of the madrigal as a servant charged with the washing of Laura's veil, a reading through which the myth is eluded.[31] Yet Petrarch's scene strongly suggests not an encounter with a shepherdess unique to this poem but the observation of Laura herself, in a willed ambiguity comparable to the opening scene of *Rime* 126 where the evocation of the "acque / ove le bella membra / pose colei che sola a me par donna" [waters where she who alone seems lady to me rested her lovely body] permits the reading of Laura either *beside* or *in* the waters of the river.[32] Here again the phrase "a l'aura" can be read as "a Laura"— "Erano i capei d'oro a l'aura sparsi" [her golden hair was loosed to the breeze] opens sonnet 90, which is closely related to the madrigal in its account of a visionary experience—and in other poems it is Laura who is "cruda," as in the allusion to the Acteon myth in canzone 23 where she is "that lovely cruel wild creature" who was found bathing naked in a spring. The potential for this reading makes madrigal 52 one of the most erotically suggestive poems of the collection: the water is a veil for Laura's body, as it is a veil for the body of the goddess of Ovid's myth and Petrarch's canzone 23, with the difference that the implication of nudity is here attenuated to that of the freeing of Laura's hair from the veil that frequently conceals it.[33]

31. See Mazzotta, "The *Canzoniere* and the Language of the Self," 282–83. See also Freccero: "Laura's name, hidden in the pun . . . is her only presence in these verses, just as her veil is her only presence in the charming anecdote" ("The Fig Tree and the Laurel," 39); Nancy Vickers, "Diana Described: Scattered Woman and Scattered Rhyme," in *Writing and Sexual Difference,* ed. Elizabeth Abel (Chicago, 1982), 101–2.

32. For the relation of these three poems, see Raffaele Amaturo, *Petrarca* (Bari, 1971), 261, 269, and for the erotic implications of the connection of Laura with Diana, see Nancy Vickers, "Re-membering Dante: 'Chiare, fresche et dolci acque'," *MLN* 96 (1981): 8–9. Vanossi notes controversy concerning the critical history of the opening verses of *Rime* 126 ("Petrarca e il mito di Atteone," 10). These verses are related through rhyme schemes to madrigal 52; see Guido Capovilla, "I madrigali (LII, LIV, CVI, CXXI)," *Lectura Petrarce, III, 1983* (Padua, 1984), 29.

33. The two depictions are further related through the ardent light of the sun (23, 52). For a similar reading of the madrigal, see Vanossi, "Petrarca e il mito di Atteone," esp. 9–11; see also Vincenzo Dolla, "Il 'ciclo' dei madrigali e la struttura del Canzoniere petrarchesco," *Esperienze letterarie* 4 (1979): 64–66; Norbert Jonard, "I miti dell'Eros nel *Canzoniere* del Petrarca," *Lettere Italiane* 34 (1982): 461–62.

In this preoccupation with modes of seeing Laura, the *ombra* that frequently signals Laura's presence in absence characterizes also the poet's projection of her image into nature, softening and blurring the conventional categories of perception just as it softens and blurs the categories of landscape:

> Ove porge ombra un pino alto od un colle
> talor m'arresto, et pur nel primo sasso
> disegno co la mente il suo bel viso . . .
> et quanto in più selvaggio
> loco mi trovo e 'n più deserto lido,
> tanto più bella il mio pensier l'adombra.
>
> (129, 27–29, 46–48)

[Where a tall pine or a hillside extends shade, there I sometimes stop, and in the first stone I see I portray her lovely face with my mind . . . and in whatever wildest place and most deserted shore I find myself, so much the more beautiful does my thought shadow her forth.]

The aporetical character of the verb "adombrare," which may suggest both to represent and to conceal, is central to this declaration.[34] If the poet cannot "paint" the lady, he can shadow forth her image:

> Le lode, mai non d'altra et proprie sue,
> che 'n lei fur come stelle in cielo sparte,
> pur ardisco ombreggiare, or una or due.
>
> (308, 9–11)

[Still now and again I dare to adumbrate one or two of the praises that were always hers, never any other's, that were as many as the stars spread across the sky.]

This stunning imagery relating Laura's pluralized "high beauties" and the corresponding praises offered in homage further conveys the inevitable inadequation between what the enamored poet observes and his shadowy capturing of that image through the medium of words. Verbs built upon *ombra*, repeatedly suggestive of the shadowy nature of his

---

34. See Timothy Bahti, "Petrarch and the Scene of Writing: A Reading of *Rime* CXXIX," *Yale Italian Studies* 1 (1980): 49, with discussion of other mentions of shade or shadows in the poem.

word pictures of Laura, suggest too the nuance, the imprecision of his mental images of the lady.[35]

Yet in these multiple adaptations that suggest time or its stoppage, Laura's presence or her absence, vision or its occultation, *ombra* is of course but one term of a fundamental dichotomy: the pervasive presence of shade or shadow heightens by contrast the insistence throughout the collection on the light that is their necessary condition. As with shadow, the phenomenon is not limited to natural sources. Not only does Apollo figure as sun-god, as we have seen; Laura herself, source of shadow, is also a source of light. The light that emanates from the lady, a commonplace of amatory lyric from the poets of Provence and their Sicilian successors to the stilnovisti and the Dante of the *rime petrose*,[36] is celebrated in many of the best-known poems of Petrarch's collection. An early sonnet, enlarging upon the compliments with which his lyric precursors attributed to their ladies a radiance like that of the sun, opens with the effect of the natural sun on the revival, flowering, and fecundation of nature in the spring season, then turns to Laura:

> Così costei, ch' è tra le donne un sole,
> in me movendo de' begli occhi i rai
> cria d'amor penseri atti et parole. . . .

> (9, 10–12)

[Thus she who among ladies is a sun, moving the rays of her lovely eyes, in me creates thoughts, acts, and words of love. . . .]

The status suggested here is repeatedly confirmed in other poems where she appears as "a living sun," the sun that alone shines to his eyes.[37]

35. Oscar Büdel identifies "a semantically close-knit word group which, in its various configurations, points in the direction of imagination and illusion, such as *adombrare, contemplare, depingere, disegnare, figurare, imaginare, imagine, pensare, pensiero, ritrarre*," almost all of which appear in the first part of the collection; see "Illusion Disabused: A Novel Mode in Petrarch's Canzoniere," in Aldo Scaglione, ed., *Francis Petrarch, Six Centuries Later: A Symposium* (Chapel Hill and Chicago, 1975), 135.

36. Among the *petrose* both "Al poco giorno" and "Amor, tu vedi ben" feature the light emanating from the lady; for points of evident contact, see De Robertis, "Petrarca petroso," 26. On the early development of the *topos* of *donna / sole*, see W. Pagani, *Repertorio tematico della scuola poetica siciliana* (Bari, 1968), 338–39.

37. Thus Laura's landscape to which he returns after her death is that "dove li occhi tuoi solean far giorno" [where your eyes used to make day] (321). For the massive adoption of the *topos* of the sun in the collection, see Chiappelli, "Le thème de la *Defectio solis*," 167–68. Petrarch engages in constant word play with the term "sole"; see Shapiro, *Hieroglyph of Time*, 82–83.

Laura's usurpation of the functions of celestial bodies creates a fusion of the imaginative and the natural cosmos in which her image is exploded to fill the heavens as well as the thoughts of the lover:

> et sì come di lor bellezze il cielo
> splendea quel dì, così bagnati ancora
> li veggio sfavillare, ond' io sempre ardo.
> Se 'l sol levarsi sguardo,
> sento il lume apparir che m'innamora;
> se tramontarsi al tardo,
> parmel veder quando si volge altrove,
> lassando tenebroso onde si move.

(127, 63–70)

[and as the sky shone with their beauty that day so I see them still sparkle, bathed in tears, whence I ever burn. If I see the sun rise, I sense the approach of the light that enamors me; if setting at evening, I seem to see her when she departs, leaving all in darkness behind her.]

Here the contrast between sunlit open space and heavily shadowed forest, frequently exploited as a setting both for the poet and for Laura, yields to a contrast within the psyche. *In vita* her eyes are "que' duo lumi / che quasi un bel sereno a mezzo 'l die / fer le tenebre mie" [those two lights, which made my darkness into a clear sky at noon] (37); he flees from his dark and turbid thoughts toward their "divine light" (151, 194); following her death, the natural shadow that had once occulted the poet's vision is replaced by a different darkness, such that he entertains thoughts of Death (327). Both *in vita* and *in morte*, the correlative of the plenitude of Laura's light is that in its absence all is darkness.

Yet the full radiance of that light, in the phenomenology of vision established by the fundamental opposition of light to darkness, is also a cause of darkness. Already in the *Vita Nuova* Dante had described his lady's greeting as so radiant that eyes do not dare to look upon it (XXVI, 1–4);[38] in "Al poco giorno," writing of another lady, he emphasizes the potentially destructive nature of her light, protesting that "dal suo lume non mi può far ombra / poggio né muro mai né fronda verde" [and yet

---

38. See the observations of Antonio Lanza, *Studi sulla lirica del Trecento* (Rome, 1978), 70, and for the nonverbal communication in which the recipient is simultaneously ravaged and renewed, see Gérard Genot, "Pétrarque et la scène du regard," *Journal of Medieval and Renaissance Studies* 2 (1972): 1–2.

from her face there is no shade, not of a hill, or a wall ever, or a green branch].[39] Petrarch insists on the consequences of the experience of this dazzling light: just as Acteon was not to look with impunity on the unveiled Diana, so the lover of the *Rime* is not to look with impunity upon the light of Laura. Early in the collection he acknowledges that her light extinguishes his own, addressing his weary eyes turned to the "bel viso di quella che v'à morti . . ." [the lovely face that has slain you] (14).[40] Another poem in the initial section elaborates this peril in a long and complicated play on "luce":

> Quand' io son tutto volto in quella parte
> ove 'l bel viso di Madonna luce,
> et m'è rimasa nel pensier la luce
> che m'arde et strugge dentro a parte a parte,
> i' che temo del cor che mi si parte,
> et veggio presso il fin de la mia luce,
> vommene in guisa d'orbo, senza luce,
> che non sa ove si vada et pur si parte.
>
> (18, 1–8)

[When I am all turned toward the place where shines my lady's lovely face, and in my thought the light remains that burns and melts me within bit by bit, since I fear for my heart, which is breaking, and see my days near their end, I go without light like a blind man who does not know where to go and still departs.]

Blindness is also the subject of the following sonnet, which reduces the metaphorical distancing by comparing the lover's state to that of other creatures in terms of visual acuity. Some animals, he explains, can bear to look at the sun; others, because its light harms them, are nocturnal; but there is yet a third category, those moved by a "folle desio," a mad desire to fly into the fire and be consumed, and he is among their number:

> lasso, e 'l mio loco è 'n questa ultima schera.
> Ch' i' non son forte ad aspettar la luce

---

39. For the *stilemi* common to this sestina and Dante's *rime petrose*, see G. Gorni, "Metamorfosi e redenzione in Petrarca: Il senso della forma Coreggio del *Canzoniere*," *Lettere Italiane* 30 (1978): 6; see also Luigi Vanossi, "Identità e mutazione nella sestina petrarchesca," *Cultura Neolatina* 40 (1980): 294.

40. For a convincing interpretation of this ballata as an early statement of the theme of the lover's inability to sustain the sight of the lady, see F. Figurelli, "Note su dieci rime del Petrarca," *Studi petrarcheschi* 6 (1956): 201–21.

di questa donna, et non so fare schermi
di luoghi tenebrosi o d'ore tarde.

(19, 8–11)

[alas, and my place is in this last band. For I am not strong enough
to look on the light of this lady, and I do not know how to make
a shield of shadowy places and late hours.]

Nor is this consequence limited to the poems of the opening section of
the *Rime*. In the sonnet marking the fifteenth anniversary of the *inna-
moramento* he affirms that the dazzling effect of Laura's eyes has but
intensified with the passing of the years and that now they dazzle him,
"m'abbaglian," much more than on the occasion of their first encounter
(107); at the risk of his own destruction he returns again and again to
Laura, to his "fated sun" from whose eyes he receives such sweetness
(141). Led forcibly back to her by Amor, he is both dazzled and blinded:
"perir mi dà 'l ciel per questa luce, / ché da lunge mi struggo et da presso
ardo" [the heavens give me death in this light, for when I am afar I am
tormented, and when I am close by I burn] (194). He commemorates the
twentieth anniversary of the *innamoramento* by gazing at the sun whose
brightness extinguishes his power of sight, leaving him blind and weary
"ad ogni altro ch' al mio danno" [to everything except my harm] (212).

In the lexical interdependence of the poems of the *Rime*, blindness is
associated repeatedly with the love experience itself. Desire is blind: the
poems variously but repeatedly identify the lover's "cieco desir" (56), his
"engordo / voler ch'è cieco et sordo" [greedy desire, which is blind and
deaf] (135); "veramente la voglia [è] cieca e 'ngorda" [truly, desire is
blind and greedy], he reaffirms wearily in Part II (294). Amor himself is
once depicted as blind, suggestive (as in the *Ovide moralisé*) of the
consequences of his influence:

Ma 'l cieco Amor et la mia sorda mente
mi traviavan sì ch'andar per viva
forza mi convenia dove Morte era.

(290, 9–11)[41]

[But blind Love and my deaf mind led me so astray that by their
lively force I had to go where Death was.]

41. On this "fallen Amor," see Erwin Panofsky, *Studies in Iconology* (1939; repr. New
York, 1967), 109, and the observations of Mary Barnard, *The Myth of Apollo and Daphne
from Ovid to Quevedo* (Durham, 1987), 87. In an earlier poem (151) Petrarch had denied
the god's blindness: "cieco non già. . . ."

Blindness characterizes an action, *errare:* the poet records that "chiuso gran tempo in questo cieco legno / errai" [shut up a long time in this blind ship I wandered] (80). It characterizes also a place, the labyrinth: "our blind and treacherous guide," he will term Amor in the poem in which the *innamoramento* is rendered as the entrance into a labyrinth (211). He will describe his amorous captivity as a "lungo errar in cieco labirinto" [a long wandering in a blind labyrinth] (224).[42] It is in the labyrinth, to which we shall return, that the images of darkness converge to define the lover's itinerary in desire.

The fatal light of Laura participates in another of the great myths invoked in the telling of the poet's story. It threatens him not only with blindness but with petrification, a metamorphosis like that effected by the "Possente donna" of canzone 23:

> Poco era ad appressarsi agli occhi miei
> la luce che da lunge gli abbarbaglia,
> che, come vide lei cangiar Tesaglia,
> così cangiato ogni mia forma avrei.
>
> (51, 1–4)[43]

[Had it come any closer to my eyes, the light that dazzles them from afar, then, just as Thessaly saw her change, I would have changed my every form.]

This, then, is one virtuality of the power that likens Laura to Medusa. The comparison, introduced in the ending of *Rime* 51 with the allusion to Atlas as victim of her gaze, is later made explicit as the poet confides that a posture of perfect humility is his only defense:

> E ciò non fusse, andrei non altramente
> a veder lei che 'l volto di Medusa,
> che facea marmo diventar la gente.
>
> (179, 9–11)[44]

---

42. On the relation between the labyrinth and darkness, see Colilli, "Petrarch's Theology of the Veil," 54–55. In the *Secretum* Augustinus couples blindness with another of Petrarch's favored metaphors for "erring": "And when you had been struck blind by this meeting, if you chose the left-hand path it was because to you it seemed more broad and easy; for that to the right is steep and narrow, and of its hardship you were afraid" (*Petrarch's Secret*, 129).

43. The term appears with similar force in sonnet 194: "cerco 'l mio sole et spero vederlo oggi . . . poi si m'abbaglia che 'l fuggir m'è tardo" [I seek my sun and hope to see it today . . . then he dazzles me so that my fleeing is slow].

44. For the relation of Laura's beauty to the awesome destructive power of Medusa, see the comments of Jonard, "I miti dell'Eros," 454–55.

[And if that were not so, I would not go to see her otherwise than to see the face of Medusa, which made people become marble.]

A further allusion to Medusa leads to the assertion of a yet more formidable force, one of cosmic proportions that rules spirit as well as matter:

> . . . que' belli occhi che i cor fanno smalti,
> possenti a rischiarar abisso et notti
> et torre l'alme a' corpi et darle altrui.
>
> (213, 9–11)

[. . . those lovely eyes that turn hearts to stone, powerful enough to brighten the abyss and night and to take souls from their bodies and give them to others.]

In these poems the affirmation of the beauty of Laura's eyes yields to the fearful effect of that beauty on the poet who beholds them. Other poems, however, celebrate the positive guidance of her light that illumines his world. Her eyes light his course like the stars that guide the mariner (73, 189, 299), they are the beacons that light the voyage of his life:

> Or con sì chiara luce et con tai segni
> errar non dèsi in quel breve viaggio
> che ne po far d'eterno albergo degni.
>
> (204, 9–11)

[Now with so clear a light and such signs, we must not lose our way in that brief journey which can make us worthy of an eternal dwelling.]

Is Laura then to be likened, not to the Medusa, but to the lady whose eyes are celebrated by Dante in the *Commedia*? A fundamental distinction subverts the analogy. Beatrice is not herself a source of light in the redemptive itinerary of her own poet-pilgrim; instead, her eyes function as mirrors, and they reflect a higher order.[45] It is in them that the pilgrim, reunited at last with her in the Earthly Paradise, sees the griffin that figures Christ:

45. Of the several studies of this function, see especially Genot, "Pétrarque et la scène du regard," 4–8.

Mille disiri più che fiamma caldi
strinsermi li occhi a li occhi rilucenti,
che pur sopra 'l grifone stavan saldi.
Come in lo specchio il sol, non altrimenti
la doppia fiera dentro vi raggiava . . .

(*Purg.* XXXI, 118–22)

[A thousand desires hotter than flame held my eyes on the shining
eyes that remained ever fixed on the griffin. As the sun in a mirror,
so was the twofold animal gleaming therewithin . . .]

Beatrice's eyes will further mediate for him the "mirabili cose" of
Paradise as she guides him through the celestial spheres, but it will be
another guide, Saint Bernard, who will direct Dante's eyes to the final
vision of its glory;[46] it will be not the eyes of Beatrice but those of the
Virgin that will serve as intermediary to his ultimate vision, as he follows
her gaze turned toward the "eternal light" (*Par.* XXXIII, 40–45).

"Come in lo specchio il sol," like the sun in a mirror: Dante's simile
for the mediated vision of Christ made possible by the eyes of Beatrice is
highly suggestive for Petrarch's praise of Laura's eyes. It defines in terms
of visual perception a transaction that presupposes a hierarchy, as one
participant explicitly mediates for another that which, in differing de-
grees, transcends them both. In the *Rime,* as Genot observes, the vertical
orientation of this communication is replaced by a system of horizontal
exchange.[47] Laura's eyes are the mirror of the poet's own eyes: she is the
one who alone was "light and mirror" to his eyes" (312), and he will
imagine her eyes addressing his as "lumi amici che gran tempo / con tal
dolcezza feste di noi specchi . . ." [friendly lights, who for a great time
with such sweetness have made us your mirrors] (330). The poet, more-
over, proposes himself to Laura as a surface in which she may see herself
reflected and measure the beauty of her own eyes:

luci beate et liete
se non che 'l veder voi stesse v'è tolto,

46. Saint Bernard instructs the pilgrim:

e drizzeremo li occhi al Primo Amore,
sì che, guardando verso lui, penetri
quant'è possibil per lo suo fulgore.

(*Par.* 32, 142–44)

[and we will turn our eyes to the Primal Love, so that, gazing toward Him, you may
penetrate, as far as that can be, into His effulgence.]

47. See Genot's observations in "Pétrarque et la scène du regard," 8.

ma quante volte a me vi rivolgete
conoscete in altrui quel che voi siete.

(71, 57–60)[48]

[happy and carefree lights—except that to see yourselves is denied
you, but whenever you turn to me you know in another what you
are.]

This, then, is not only a horizontal transaction but a closed one, whose
suggestion of an ideal of reciprocity must be read in its contrast to
Laura's gazing into her own mirror, in two poems already examined,
with a self-absorption that prompts a warning about the fate of Narcis-
sus.[49] The identification of Laura as the poet's mirror intensifies the
shadow of narcissism that hovers over the collection as a whole: if her
literal mirrors, excluding him from her attention, are termed murderous,
"micidiali specchi," her eyes as mirrors threaten him in turn with
narcissism, just as his obsessive projection of Laura's image onto nature
frequently mirrors not Laura, but himself.[50]

The multiple evocations of *ombra* in the *Rime sparse*, Thomas Greene
observes, "seem to circle around all that is problematic in the poet's
experience and in his art."[51] And indeed, as we have seen, the poet
himself circles around the laurel, following its shadow, in a pursuit that
is one with the flight of time, while refusing time. In his pursuit of Laura
and her image through a world made over in the image of Laura, the

48. These verses may be suggested by Ovid's Narcissus. A long life had been prophesied
for the beautiful youth unless he should come to know himself. "For a long time this
pronouncement seemed to be nothing but empty words," Ovid tells us, until "the strange
madness which afflicted the boy and the nature of his death proved its truth" (*Met.* III,
349–50).

49. Genot relates the infernal connotation of the term "specchio" in *Rime* 45 and 46 to
the mirrors in the negative erotic discourse of sonnet 136 depicting Avignon as a new
Babylon ("Pétrarque et la scène du regard," 15–16). Ambivalence marked medieval versions
of the Narcissus story; see Frederick Goldin, *The Mirror of Narcissus in the Courtly Love
Lyric* (Ithaca, 1967), 37, and the discussion of stilnovist images of the lady, 256–257.

50. On this Laura as "a brilliant surface, a pure signifier whose momentary exteriority
to the poet serves as an Archimedean point from which he can create himself," see Freccero,
"The Fig Tree and the Laurel," 39. On his declaration in 129 that he is content to "mirar
lei et obliar me stesso" [look at her and forget myself], see Bahti, "Petrarch and the Scene
of Writing," who notes also the ironic relevance of the Senecan text following that
concerning mirrors cited in the *Secretum* (48).

51. "Even when the shadow is hospitable and nourishing, we are aware of its dangerous
duplicities, if only because the tree that casts the shadow is a locus of tenebrous power and
ontological insecurity"; see *The Light in Troy,* chap. 7, "Petrarch: Falling into Shadow"
(citation, 134).

fundamental conditions of existence are altered. Not only are the conventional orders of reality and illusion inverted, the vision of Laura rendering all other sights less substantial and less convincing to the point that in contrast all else appears "dreams, shadows, and smoke" (156). Very early in the collection Amor explains that the separation of the lover's body from his spirit, which is thus freed to remain with the beloved on his departure, is due to the privilege of lovers, "released from all human qualities" (15). Augustinus in the *Secretum* undertakes to define that *amantum infame privilegium*, the sorry privilege of lovers: "In whatever place you are, to whatever side you turn you will behold the face, you will hear the voice of her whom you have left. By that sad enchantment that belongs to lovers, you will have the power to see her though you are absent, and to hear her though she is far away."[52] A passage from the widely known *De Amore* of Andreas Capellanus is startlingly pertinent to the conduct of Petrarch's enamored poet:

Quando vi veggio, nessuna pena mi potrebbe toccare, né perturbare
malavoglienza d'alcuno; e più, che pure vedere lo luogo nel quale
voi state e l'aura che viene dall'aere vostro, nudrimento mi danno
di vita e prestanmi molti diletti. Ma quando corporalmente isguardare
non vi posso, né vedere l'aere vostro, tutti si conturbano verso
di me gli elementi, e a strignere mi cominciano generazioni di
pene diverse, né d'alcuno sollazzo posso godere, se non che tal
volta per dimostrazione falsa, per l'imaginare passato, vi veggio
dormendo. E avegna cio che tale dimostrazione per sogno sia
falsa, nondimeno molte grandissime grazie al sonno ne rendo, che
tal volta mi vuole ingannare d'inganno sì dolce![53]

[When I see you, no pain can touch me, nor anyone's ill-will; and moreover, just to see the place where you are and the breeze that come from your air gives me vital nourishment and great delight. But when I cannot look upon you physically, nor see your air, all the elements distress me, and all sorts of pains begin to afflict me, not can I enjoy any solace, except for those times when in my

52. *Petrarch's Secret*, III, 143. Büdel, who notes this passage, observes that this aspect is prominent too in Petrarch's letters, for example in *Fam.* VII, 12, 5 which also contains the citation from Virgil's eighth eclogue that appears in the *Secretum:* "An qui amant ipsi sibi somnia fingunt?" See "Illusion Disabused," 133, 139, 142.

53. Cited from the vernacular version of Riccardiano 2318 dating probably from the first half of the fourteenth century as published by Salvatore Battaglia: Andrea Capellano, *Trattato d'Amore*, testo latino del secolo XII con due traduzioni toscane inedite del secolo XIV (Rome, 1947).

sleep I see you through a false, imagined appearing. And although such an appearance in my dreams is false, nonetheless I thank Heaven greatly for it, that it sometimes deceives me with such a sweet deception!]

Could this not be the poet of the *Rime,* enraptured in Laura's presence, turning longingly in absence to receive the breeze that blows from her familiar surroundings, welcoming with sleep a "falsa dimonstrazione"?

Thus while the poet repeatedly protests that he has been the victim of his illusions—like the Dante of the "canzone montanina" cited above who indicts his own reception of the obsessive image of his lady as "l'anima folle, che al suo mal s'ingegna" [my crazy soul, clever and busy to its own hurt]—he is a victim not only willing but willful, one who consciously retains and cultivates his illusion.[54] "Beato in sogno et di languir contento, / d'abbracciar l'ombre et seguir l'aura estiva" [blessed in sleep and satisfied to languish, to embrace shadows, and to pursue the summer breeze], is how he defines his state (212), and verbal constructions whose radical is *ombra* indicate the opposition of truth to self-deception:

> tanto più bella il mio pensier l'adombra.
> Poi quando il vero sgombra
> quel dolce error . . .
>
> (129, 48–50)

[so much the more beautiful does my thought shadow her forth. Then, when the truth dispels that sweet deception . . .]

The gesture by which the poet embraces his illusion finds its pertinent commentary in medieval explanations of the Narcissus myth, as for example in the fourteenth-century *Ovide moralisé:*

> C'est la fontaine decevable
> Qui fet l'ombre fainte et muable
> Cuidier vrai bien et parmanent . . .

[It is the deceiving fountain that makes one believe a faint and changing shadow to be true and enduring . . .]

---

54. For illusion raised to the status of a new mode of existence for the poet, see Büdel, "Illusion Disabused," esp. 128–30, 135–44.

the text explains, going on to characterize the actions of one who takes delight in "la faulse ombre":

> Adez cuide prendre et haper
> Ce qui ne fine d'eschaper,
> D'escalorgier et de foir,
> Et dont nulz ne puet bien joir. . . .[55]

[He thinks to capture and possess that which never ceases to escape, flee, and elude him, which no one can fully enjoy. . . .]

These verses, in an analysis not very different from the Augustinian argument concerning illusion, self-deception, and error,[56] aptly characterize the poet's movement through the *Rime sparse*, as he pursues the elusive shadow of an elusive Laura.

The "moralized Ovid" draws a moral, and it is unambiguous:

> Pour fol tieng et pour esperdu
> Qui pert la pardurable gloire
> Pour tel faulse ombre transitoire.

[I consider him a fool, and lost, who loses enduring glory for such a false, fleeing shadow.]

So too is its exegetical counterpart: Hugh of St. Victor writes that man as Adam, having lost the "straight way," hides from the truth within the shadow of his ignorance.[57] The shadowed course through which the poet of the *Rime* pursues his Laura has the Biblical precedent of *vias tenebrosas*, as we read in a passage from Proverbs translated by Dante in the *Convivio*: "via impiorum tenebrosa: nescient ubi corruant."[58] While engaged in the *vie tenebrose* of his pursuit of Laura, however, he is not unaware of the implications of the darkness in which he finds himself, nor those of having entrusted to a mortal creature the illumination of his

---

55. *Ovide moralisé*, III, cited in Louise Vinge, *The Narcissus Theme in European Literature up to the Early Nineteenth Century* (Lund, 1967), 95, with other examples of this reading of the myth stressing illusion.

56. Petrarch found the argument in Augustine's *De vera religione* XX–XXIII; for a concise summary, see Kenelm Foster, *Petrarch, Poet and Humanist* (Edinburgh, 1984), 77.

57. *In Ecclesiasten Homiliae*, cited in F. Mazzoni, *Saggio di un nuovo commento alla Divina Commedia* (Florence, 1967), 44. The consequences too describe Petrarch's poet: "cadis et ruis et impelleris; appetis nec consequeris . . . quarens veritate ubi non est."

58. *Convivio* IV, vii, 9; cited by Mazzoni, p. 44.

enamored cosmos. In the great penitential poem "Padre del Ciel," the divine light is directly invoked against the dazzling light of Laura as a remedy for the poet's spiritual dilemma: "piacciati omai col tuo lume ch'io torni / ad altra vita et a più belle imprese . . ." [let it please you at last that with your light I may return to a different life and to more beautiful undertakings . . .] (62).[59] This is the light that may overcome the shadows that surround him:

> Ma tu, Signor, ch'ài di pietate il pregio,
> porgimi la man destra in questo bosco,
> vinca 'l tuo sol le mie tenebre nove.
>
> (214, 28–30)

[But you, Lord, who have all pity's praise, reach me your right hand in this wood: let your sun vanquish this my strange shadow.]

As the opposition of darkness to light resolves itself into a spiritual polarity,[60] the recurrent motif of the poet's blindness occasioned by the dazzling light of Laura recurs to characterize his spiritual dilemma. In the *Secretum* it is thus that Augustinus defines the *innamoramento*, in reply to Franciscus's admission that his turning from the right course had coincided with his first sight of Laura: "The unwonted dazzle [fulgor] blinded your eyes, so I believe. For they say the first effect of love is blindness."[61] It is in similar terms of vision that the poet's dilemma is defined in a canzone devoted to the contradictions and the dubious outcome of the lover's unhappy state. Among the probable Augustinian sources of the opposition in this poem between the love inspired by the beauty of earthly creatures and the love of God himself as its creator, a passage from the *Confessions* is particularly suggestive: "The eyes delight in beautiful shapes of different sorts and bright and attractive colors. I would not have these things take possession of my soul. Let God possess

59. See E. Williamson, "A Consideration of 'Vergine bella'," *Italica* 29 (1952): esp. 219, 225, 227.

60. In addition to its long biblical and exegetical history, for Petrarch it may also have classical authority. In the first poem of the collection not directly concerned with the poet's love for Laura (7), a "benign light" represents the positive pole in human life; Foster identifies this moral norm as "the 'kindly divine light' (Cicero's *igniculi*, 'sparks') gleaming in the depths of human nature" (*Petrarch, Poet and Humanist*, 56).

61. *Petrarch's Secret*, 129. Augustinus goes on to cite Virgil's example of Dido, blinded at the first sight of Aeneas.

it, He who made them all. He made them all very good, but it is he who is my Good, not they."[62] Now Petrarch:

> Tutte le cose di che 'l mondo è adorno
> uscir buone de man del mastro eterno,
> ma me che così a dentro non discerno
> abbaglia il bel che mi si mostra intorno;
> et s'al vero splendor giamai ritorno
> l'occhio non po star fermo . . .

(70, 41–46)

[All things with which the world is beauteous came forth good from the hand of the eternal Workman: but I, who do not discern so far within, am dazzled by the beauty that I see about me, and if I ever return to the true splendor, my eye cannot stay still . . .]

While the record of the effect of Laura's eyes throughout the collection is fraught with ambiguity, as we have seen, this is clear enough: the dazzling light of earthly beauty, the beauty of Laura, here is placed in opposition to the true splendor of the divine light.[63] But the compulsion of that beauty does not end with this piece of self-analysis. On the contrary: the light of Laura's eyes dazzles more with the passing of the years, as the poet confesses: "che volver non mi posso ov'io non veggia / o quella o simil indi accesa luce" [I cannot turn without seeing either that light or a similar one lit from it] (107).

The opening component of Part II of the *Rime*, a poem that both reflects and recapitulates the tensions of Part I and projects into Part II the alternatives invoked for a different course, evokes the two fundamental connotations of *ombra* in the collection, that of time—with its reminder of the ephemeral nature of earthly existence—and that of obscurity, to complete the spiritual definition of the term:

62. *Confessions* X 34, cited by Adelia Noferi in *L'esperienza poetica del Petrarca* (Florence, 1962), 273, and by Nicolae Iliescu, *Il Canzoniere petrarchesco e sant'Agostino* (Rome, 1962), 119, both noting also the *De vera religione* XX 40; Francisco Rico cites in addition *De civitate Dei* XX 22; *Vida u obra de Petrarca: I. Lectura del "Secretum"* (Padua, 1974), 298, 302.

63. See the reading of this poem by Francisco Rico in *Vida u obra*, 301–2. Santagata proposes on the contrary that the opposition is between two ways of seeing the beloved lady, one in terms of her dazzling beauty, the other in recognition of the "vero splendore" that is hers as a creature of God; see "Il giovane Petrarca e la tradizione poetica romanza," 43.

> . . . ond'io, perché pavento
> adunar sempre quel ch' un'ora sgombre,
> vorre' 'l ver abbracciar, lassando l'ombre.

(264, 70–72)[64]

[therefore, since I fear to be always gathering what one hour will scatter, I wish to embrace the truth, to abandon shadows.]

To *see* the truth, to *desire to embrace* the truth: will seeing and desiring result in the loss or the renunciation of illusion? In the *Trionfo del Tempo*, in an intervention that interrupts the past-tense account of the narrator's vision to affirm a present awareness, Petrarch replies in the affirmative:

> Segui' già le speranze e 'l van desio;
> or ho dinanzi agli occhi un chiaro specchio
> ov'io veggio me stesso e 'l fallir mio.

(55–57)

[I followed then my hopes and vain desires, but now with mine own eyes I see myself as in a mirror, and my wanderings.]

This "chiaro specchio" that enables clear sight reminds us that Petrarch had mirrors other than Laura. In reading the *Confessions,* he acknowledges, he found in Augustine a reflection of his own inner self,[65] and it is the Augustinus of the *Secretum* who observes pointedly, citing Seneca, that "mirrors were invented that men might know themselves. Much profit comes thereby. First, knowledge of self; second, wise counsel."[66]

Augustinus urges Franciscus to consult his mirror because he has need of its counsel: he has failed to meditate on the significance of his own graying hair.[67] Late in the *Rime* the poet finds himself gazing into his mirror, and what he finds recorded there is the consequence of time's

---

64. These verses, notes Iliescu, render the principal theme of Augustine's *De Soliloquia,* in the light of which the early commentator Bernardino Daniello suggested that the poem be read (*Il Canzoniere Petrarchesco e sant'Agostino,* 107–8). In the *Confessions* Augustine writes: "Let truth, the light of my heart, speak to me and not my own darkness [tenebrae meae]" (XII, 10, 10).

65. See the discussion of Elio Gianturco, "The Double Gift: Inner Vision and Pictorial Sense in Petrarch," *Renaissance and Reformation* 8 (1972): 101.

66. *Petrarch's Secret,* 161.

67. *Petrarch's Secret,* 161. Augustinus cites Seneca's *Naturales Quaestiones,* I, 17, 4, 67. On the faithful mirror in Petrarch's iconography of time in relation to his insistence on clear sight, see Quinones, *The Renaissance Discovery of Time,* 141.

passing: " 'Non ti nasconder più, tu se' pur veglio' " ["Do not pretend anymore, you are old"]. Now the mirror offers what Augustinus would surely regard as wise counsel: " 'obedir a Natura in tutto è 'l meglio, / ch' a contender con lei 'l tempo ne sforza' " ["to obey Nature in all is best, for time takes from us the power to oppose her"]. As if waking from a long sleep, in a paroxysm of self-awareness the poet acknowledges its evidence: "veggio ben che 'l nostro viver vola / et ch'esser non si po più d'una volta" [I see well that our life flies and that one cannot be alive more than once] (361). We are reminded of the retrospective summation of the *Rime sparse* contained in its proemial sonnet, of both the "vain hopes" that recur with insistent frequency throughout the collection and the clear vision confided at the conclusion of that poem "that whatever pleases in the world is a brief dream." At intervals in the *Rime* this awareness punctuates the poet's story. It is this that he invokes early in the collection against his "speranza / che ne fe' vaneggiar sì lungamente" [the hope that made us rave so long]:

> "sì vedrem chiaro poi come sovente
> per le cose dubbiose altri s'avanza,
> et come spesso indarno si sospira;"
>
> (32, 9–10, 12–14)

[we shall see clearly then how often people put themselves forward for uncertain things and how often they sigh in vain;]

It is in this that his experience, for all his proclamations of its uniqueness, is one with that of mankind:

> Veramente siam noi polvere et ombra,
> veramente la voglia cieca e 'ngorda,
> veramente fallace è la speranza.
>
> (294, 12–14)[68]

[Truly, we are dust and shadow; truly, desire is blind and greedy; truly, hope deceives.]

68. The connection of all mortal "speranza" with an insubstantial term to denote the human body—here "polvere et ombra"—is anticipated in other poems, especially in *Rime* 32, "Quanto più m'avicino al giorno estremo" [The more I approach that last day]: ". . . 'l duro et greve / terreno incarco come fresca neve / si va struggendo . . ." [this hard and heavy earthly burden, like new snow, is melting . . .].

In the last of the anniversary components of the *Rime* the poet offers a stark affirmation of unabused vision much like that of the narrator of the *Trionfi*: "ch' i' conosco 'l mio fallo et non lo scuso" [for I recognize my fault and I do not excuse it] (364).

This uncompromising declaration of clear sight and self-awareness, however, is found very near the end of the *Rime sparse*; between it and the occurrence of Laura's death there remains a major portion of the poet's itinerary. As Death definitively hides the light of the earthly Laura the shadows close around the poet, leaving his sorrowing soul in "tene-broso orrore" (276). Despite Laura's death, the quest and the obsession defined early in the collection through the polysemous investments of light and shadow continue to characterize the poet's journey; but as the succession of hours, days, seasons, and years draws him nearer that "final day" and the succession of poems draws us nearer the end of the collection of *rime sparse*, other perspectives emerge in terms of which they must be reread, and redefined.

PART II

4

CHOICES

In the thirteenth-century French romance known as the *Quête du Saint Graal* we find the following dramatic account:

> The enemy, who first caused man to sin and led him to his fall, saw you so armed and well-protected on every side that he feared he might find no means to seduce and take you. . . . He entered then into the heart of Queen Guenevere. . . . When you saw that she looked upon you, you were attentive; and immediately the enemy wounded you openly with one of his arrows, so grievously that he made you falter. He made you falter, so much that he caused you to stray from the straight way and to enter into that which you had hitherto never known: into the way of *luxure*. . . .[1]

This passage retells the "fall" of a well-known literary *innamorato*, the knight Lancelot, for Guenevere, Arthur's queen. This *innamoramento* will be retold again by Dante in a celebrated passage of the *Inferno*, where it is indicted by his Francesca da Rimini as the story-*galeotto* of her own sinful love.[2] It is the account in the Old French prose romance, however, that is the more powerfully suggestive for the poet's *innamoramento* in the early poems of Petrarch's *Rime sparse*. Despite the obvious differences, principal among them the reader's presumed awareness of the love of Lancelot and Guenevere in relation to an entire Arthurian

---

1. See *La Queste del Saint Graal*, ed. A. Pauphilet (Paris, 1965), 125–26.
2. *Inferno* V, 115–38. It was after reading of the kiss exchanged by Lancelot and Guenevere that Francesca and Paolo, imitating the example of the celebrated lovers, "read no further"; "Galeotto fu il libro e chi lo scrisse!" [a Gallehault was the book and he who wrote it], accuses Francesca (v. 137).

order that it places in jeopardy, many of the details in the passage in the *Quête* strikingly anticipate the record of the event in Petrarch's lyric collection. Here we find the conventional triangle of archer, victim, and lady; the apparent invulnerability of the intended victim; and the beginnings of love represented by the shooting of the fatal arrows. Less a matter of convention, and therefore more striking, is the identical strategy of recourse to the intended object of love to overcome the victim's resistance: Guenevere is induced to look upon the hitherto invulnerable Lancelot, and Amor's efforts in *Rime* 23 are vain without a "powerful Lady."[3] The dramatic difference, of course, is the investment of the role of archer and aggressor: here "the Enemy"—a common medieval designation of the devil—replaces the familiar figure of Cupid.

While the image of the devil assuming both the role and the iconography of the conventional Cupid, shooting the arrows that inflict the wounds of love, may seem uncharacteristic and perhaps somewhat incongruous to the modern reader, the synthesis of the two figures would not have seemed so to Petrarch. Consider his identification of Amor in one of his *epistolae metricae*, as he laments that even in his retreat to Valchiusa the image of Laura pursues him:

> Such snares Love spreads for me, nor have I hope
> Save in the mercy of almighty God
> That from this tempest he may rescue me,
> Defeat the wiles of the enemy.[4]

Here the conventional "enemy" Cupid, who had wounded Apollo and now continues to torment Laura's poet, is assimilated through this new, prayerful contextualization to the Biblical Enemy. It is this Enemy whose power is wearily acknowledged in one of the great penitential poems of the lyric collection:

> Io son sì stanco sotto 'l fascio antico
> de le mie colpe et de l'usanza ria,

3. In the *Quête*, where the devil appears generally in a mask or disguise, this recourse is exceptional; see Edina Bozoky, "Les masques de l' 'Ennemi' et les faux chemins du Graal," in *Masques et déguisements dans la littérature médiévale*, ed. Marie-Louise Ollier (Montreal and Paris, 1988), 85–95. On this episode, see Jean-Charles Payen, "Pour en finir avec le diable médiéval," in *Le diable au Moyen Age* (*Senefiance* 6) (Aix-en-Provence, 1979), 409.

4. *Ep. met.* I, 6; cited in translation in E. H. Wilkins, *Petrarch at Vaucluse* (Chicago, 1958), 8. For discussion of the letter, see Aldo Bernardo, *Petrarch, Laura, and the "Triumphs"* (Albany, N. Y., 1974), 69–72. The fearful indictment of female attraction echoes the danger of cupidinous love evoked in biblical texts, for example *Ecclesiastes* 7:27: "I find woman more bitter than death: she is a snare, her heart a net, her arms are chains."

ch' i' temo forte di mancar tra via
et di cader in man del mio nemico.

(81, 1–4)

[I am so weary under the ancient burden of my sins and bitter
habit that I am much afraid I shall fail on the way and fall into the
hands of my enemy.]

In another of the penitential components the poet implores God's aid
against the snares laid by his "adversary":

piacciati omai col tuo lume ch'io torni
ad altra vita et a più belle imprese,
sì ch'avendo le reti indarno tese
il mio duro avversario se ne scorni.

(62, 5–8)

[let it please you at last that with your light I may return to a
different life and to more beautiful undertakings, so that, having
spread his nets in vain, my harsh adversary may be disarmed.]

This stage set for a deliberate act of entrapment anticipates and conditions
the identification, in the poem that commemorates the fifteenth anniver-
sary of the *innamoramento*, of Amor as the poet's "avversario" who
leads him at will among the branches of the forest (107).

This scenario that finds the poet bent beneath the burden of his sins
and fearful of the snares laid for his soul has implications that far exceed
the immediate drama of his love for Laura. In another metaphor of
unmistakable Biblical resonance Petrarch gives us its universal definition:

Questa vita terrena è quasi un prato
che 'l serpente tra' fiori et l'erba giace,
et s'alcuna sua vista agli occhi piace
è per lassar più l'animo invescato.

(99, 5–8)

[This mortal life is like a meadow where the serpent lies among
the flowers and the grass, and if anything we see there pleases our
eyes, the result is to enlime our souls more deeply.]

While the serpent frequently appears in medieval texts and iconography as a figure of temptation,[5] this version of the vulnerability of man's earthly state is doubly suggestive. Its immediate resonance is with the serpent's appearance in Dante's *Purgatorio,* where it symbolically reenacts the drama of the temptation in Eden:

> Da quella parte onde non ha riparo
> la picciola vallea, era una biscia,
> forse qual diede ad Eva il cibo amaro.
> Tra l'erba e' fior venìa la mala striscia.

(VIII, 97–100)

[At that part where the little valley has no rampart was a snake, perhaps such as gave to Eve the bitter food. Through the grass and the flowers came the evil streak.]

In Petrarch's poem, moreover, the characterization of the soul as "invescato" recalls a tradition of Patristic commentary that identifies the bird-snare figure with the temptation of man by Satan.[6]

Other Petrarchan texts redeploy these same metaphors. His canon, Greene observes, "abounds with evocations of the Christian journey's harshness: 'all of the roads are full of snares; the branches of the trees are viscous with lime; the ground is everywhere strewn with brambles and thorns; the foot finds no place to step without danger'."[7] The appropriateness of this imagery to the poet's amorous adventure in the *Rime sparse* is only too apparent, but in the *Rime* the universal drama retains the highly particular coloration of the love of this poet for this Laura. While in the *Roman de la Rose* well known to Petrarch Cupid places his "las" and "engins" within the beautiful garden to capture young ladies and young men, "por prendre demoiseilles e demoisiaus,"[8] in the *Rime*

---

5. See L. Réau, *Iconographie de l'Art Chrétien,* II (Paris, 1956), 84–85. Jennifer Petrie suggests as Petrarch's probable source Virgil, *Eclogues* III, 92–93: "Qui legitis flores et humi nascentia fraga, / frigidus, o pueri (fugite hinc!), latet anguis in herba," a passage that might readily suggest a moral interpretation in an allegorical reading; see *The Augustan Poets, The Italian Tradition, and the "Canzoniere"* (Dublin, 1983), 98–99.

6. For this tropological reading, see B. G. Koonce, "Satan the Fowler," *Medieval Studies* 21 (1959): 178.

7. Thomas Greene, citing *Familiares* XVI, 6, in "Petrarch's *Viator:* The Displacements of Heroism," *Yearbook of English Studies* 12 (1982): 38.

8. *Le Roman de la Rose,* ed. Felix Lecoy, I (Paris, 1965), vv. 1586–92. For the strategy of entrapment, see Carol F. Heffernan, "The Bird-snare Figure and the Love Quest in the *Roman de la Rose,*" in *The Spirit of the Court,* ed. Glyn S. Burgess and Robert A. Taylor (Cambridge, 1985), esp. 182–84.

the calculated strategy is more specific. Not only does Amor lay his snares in her landscape; all of Laura's various attributes may be represented as "lacci," "rete," "ami," and "esca," and the laurel's branches too, "invescati," render the soul "invescato."⁹ Allusions to Adam's first sight of a beautiful Eve appear in several components of the collection to identify Adam as a prototype for Petrarch's enamored poet, whose fall into the snares of Amor is reminiscent of the Fall in Eden.¹⁰

Despite the inclusive nature of its formulation, the reader recognizes in the pessimistic pronouncement concerning "this mortal life" of *Rime* 99 its relevance to the poet's experience of love. From the poems that precede this sonnet in the ordering of the *rime sparse*, Petrarch's reader knows well what is pleasing to the eyes of the poet-lover: from the time of the *innamoramento* it is the sight of Laura, and it alone.¹¹ The next poem again recalls the *innamoramento* as his forcible subjection to Amor:

> 'l fiero passo ove m'agiunse Amore,
> et la nova stagion che d'anno in anno
> mi rinfresca in quel dì l'antiche piaghe.
>
> (100, 9–11)

[. . . the cruel pass where Love struck me, and the new season that year by year renews on that day my ancient wounds.]

Here contiguity gives prominence to the complementarity of the two scenes of entrapment, reminding us that wounding is a common and well-known definition of sin; "vulnus est peccatum" is the confident gloss to the afflictions or *vulnere* of Job in a commentary attributed to Rabanus Maurus.¹² Dante in the *Purgatorio* makes dramatic use of the

9. Cf. poems 55, 59, 142, 181, 195, 270, and esp. 214:

> ché v'eran di lacciuo' forme sì nove,
> et tal piacer precipitava al corso,
> che perder libertate ivi era in pregio.

[for there were snares there of form so new and such pleasure hastened one's course that to lose liberty was there a prize.]

10. For a detailed examination of this pattern, see Sara Sturm-Maddox, "Petrarch's Serpent in the Grass: The Fall as Subtext in the *Rime sparse*," *Journal of Medieval and Renaissance Studies* 13 (1983): 213–26.

11. This, the cumulative implicit burden of most of the preceding poems, is also explicit: see poems 37, 97.

12. *Allegoriae in Sacram Scripturam* (*Patrologiae* 112: 1084), cited in Paul F. Reichardt, "Gawain and the Image of the Wound," *PMLA* 99 (1984): 156.

topos of the *vulnera naturae* that from the early Christian centuries indicates the primordial wound suffered by the soul.[13] Near the end of the *Paradiso* original sin is "la piaga che Maria richiuse e unse" [the wound which Mary closed and anointed] (XXXII, 4).[14] In bringing the drama of the Fall to bear on the record of his protagonist's amorous experience, moreover, Petrarch had ample patristic authority. In their multiple analyses of original sin and its circumstances, the Church Fathers had not neglected its sexual reading: in Augustine's well-known version, the temptation by the serpent represents the senses or the concupiscence of the flesh.[15]

For the full significance of this matrix in the *Rime sparse* we must turn again to the opening sonnets of the collection. While Petrarch's poet, like Apollo, is taken by surprise by Love's vengeful assault, he differs from his mythological prototype in his extended reflection on the nature and causes of his injury. In this initial depiction as much attention is directed to his flawed defenses as to the enactment of Love's project. At the time of the attack, he tells us, his "virtue" or vital power was concentrated in his heart and eyes. This strategic deployment was well motivated: heretofore it had always proved successful, such that his defense remained confidently concentrated there "where every previous arrow had been blunted."[16] Taken unawares on this new occasion, however, this "virtue" was not able to take up its arms; nor, fatally, could it effect the appropriate defense of last resort, withdrawal to the "poggio faticoso et alto" [weary high mountain] (2). This identification of parts of the body

13. See the discussion of John Freccero, "The Firm Foot on a Journey without a Guide," in *Dante: The Poetics of Conversion*, ed. Rachel Jacoff (Cambridge, Mass., 1986), esp. 50–51; Reichardt, "Gawain and the Image of the Wound," 156.

14. "Piaghe" are the marks traced on the pilgrim's forehead to be cleansed on his journey through Purgatory (IX, 112–14); it is only in passing through the wall of purgatorial fire "che la piaga da sezzo si ricuscia" [must the last wound of all be healed] (XXV, 138–39). See Luigi Blasucci, *voce* "piaga," *Enciclopedia Dantesca*, IV (Rome, 1973).

15. For this and other patristic readings of the serpent as the "animal nature," see A. Kent Hieatt, "Eve as Reason in a Tradition of Allegorical Interpretation of the Fall," *Journal of the Warburg and Courtauld Institutes* 44 (1980): 221–23.

16. This defense concentrated in the heart is described again in the metamorphosis canzone:

> e d'intorno al mio cor pensier gelati
> fatto avean quasi adamantino smalto
> ch'allentar non lassava 'l duro affetto.

(23, 24–26)

[and around my heart frozen thoughts had made almost an adamantine hardness which my hard affect did not allow to slacken.]

as loci of the various faculties, commonplace in the philosophical tradition, was not unknown to earlier poets: within Petrarch's immediate vernacular context Dante represents his own *innamoramento* in the *Vita Nuova* as the disordering of the various "spirits" that govern his physical state, each personified to cry out its own portentous message (*VN* I, 2).[17] Yet whereas an occasional reader may be inclined to smile at the high allegorical style in which Dante depicts the palpitations and digestive disturbances of a love-struck youth, Petrarch presents us with a scene whose spiritual implications are at once apparent by drawing our attention to the faculty that is cut off by the attack: the "poggio faticoso et alto" to which he is unable to retreat is commonly glossed as the mountain of Reason.[18] Augustinus in the *Secretum* uses a similar metaphor in urging the unrepentant lover of earthly beauty to turn to his reason, "the true source of all remedies," to reevaluate his love. "Remember," he warns, "what you are now called to is that citadel wherein alone you can be quite safe against the incursions of passion and by which alone you will deserve the name of Man."[19]

In the final poem of the introductory sequence this preeminence of passion over reason recurs in more dramatic form. *Rime* 6 renders the poet's reenactment of Apollo's pursuit of a fugitive object of desire and suggests a new frame for its evaluation: "sì traviato è 'l folle mi' desio" [so far astray is my mad desire] is its opening statement, and the subsequent verses elaborate metaphorically his inability to dominate that desire, to call it back to the safe path. It is desire out of control, the poem tells us, but its victim retains sufficient lucidity to recognize and proclaim its peril: this desire, he acknowledges, carries him off to death against his will. Where indeed does it carry him? His destination is not only, abstractly, death; it is concretely the laurel, where his precipitous course at last ends. The laurel here has none of the evergreen splendor with which it was honored by Apollo; it is rather a plant "onde si coglie / acerbo frutto, che le piaghe altrui / gustando affligge più che non conforta" [whence one gathers bitter fruit that, being tasted, afflicts one's wounds more than it comforts them].

The depiction of the poet's plight in these early poems, deflecting our attention from the "blows of Love" whether mythological or courtly,

---

17. For a careful review of the extensive critical discussion of these "spiritelli," see Robert Klein, "Spirto peregrino," in *La forme et l'intelligible* (Paris, 1970), esp. III: "La couche médicale et la psycho-physiologie" (44–48).

18. In the *Vita Nuova*, in significant contrast, Dante specifies that the nobility of the object of his love never permitted Love's dominion without "the faithful counsel of reason" (*VN* I, 2). See Domenico De Robertis, *Il Libro della Vita Nuova* (Florence, 1970), 35–36.

19. *Petrarch's Secret*, 162.

attributes to the wound that he suffers a value that exceeds the conventional metaphors of Love's assault. And it will recur with the implicit or explicit identification of the incapacitation of reason, as in the poet's admission that it is not only Laura's inaccessibility but also the impotence of his reason that forecloses on the possibility of healing that "piaga ond' io non guerrò mai" [the wound of which I shall never be cured]. On that initial occasion, "gli occhi invaghiro allor sì de' lor guai / che 'l fren de la ragione ivi non vale . . ." [my eyes so fell in love with their woes then that the rein of reason no longer avails] (97). This phenomenon is one already familiar to medieval readers, through careful explanations such as that of Aquinas: the consequence of original sin, that "wounding of nature," was that reason lost its perfect control over the lower part of the soul.[20] "Reason overcome by desire," Petrarch defines his poet's condition in sonnet 240; "reason which wanders after my senses," he decries its helplessness again in the great pivotal canzone 264.[21]

Thus the *innamoramento* both results in the incapacitation of the poet's reason and inflicts a wound.[22] That wound renders him lame, he confesses, "debile et zoppo / da l'un de' lati ove 'l desir mi à storto . . ." [weak and lame on one side where desire has twisted me] (88). He will despair of all earthly remedies for his injuries, to redefine them as

> . . . le piaghe ch'i' presi in quel bosco
> folto di spine, ond' i' ò ben tal parte
> che zoppo n'esco, e 'ntravi a sì gran corso!
>
> (214, 22–24)

[the wounds I received in that wood thick with thorns; on account of them it is my lot to come out lame, and I entered with so swift a course!]

This protestation of lameness once again likens Petrarch's enamored protagonist to the pilgrim of the opening of the *Commedia*. John Freccero marshals extensive evidence to explicate the enigmatic verse that

20. Cited in Reichardt, "Gawain and the Image of the Wound," 156.

21. For the central importance of the opposition of reason and desire in the *Rime*, which reflects both medieval definitions of *cupiditas* and the usage of Petrarch's vernacular precursors, see Sara Sturm-Maddox, *Petrarch's Metamorphoses: Text and Subtext in the Rime sparse* (Columbia, Mo., 1985), 79–86.

22. In a reading of another well-known literary wound, that inflicted upon the hero of *Sir Gawain and the Green Knight*, Paul Reichardt observes that as an incapacitation of reason it suggests the failure of human desire apart from divine aid; see "Gawain and the Image of the Wound," *PMLA* 99 (1984): 159.

recounts that pilgrim's halting progress as he attempts unsuccessfully to scale the mountain perceived as his goal, "sì che 'l piè fermo era 'l più basso" [so that the firm foot was always the lower] (*Inf.* I, 30): Dante's pilgrim limps, and his limp is to be attributed to an infirmity in his left leg or foot—one suggestive of the wound of concupiscence incurred as the consequence of original sin.[23] Late in Part II of the *Rime*, Petrarch's poet opens the plaint against Love that he submits to the adjudication of Reason by recalling the time in his youth when "il manco piedo / giovenetto pos'io nel costui regno" [when I was young I placed my left foot in his kingdom] (360), and elsewhere Petrarch's allusions are less enigmatic than Dante's: the wound is identified and located on the left side in poems distributed throughout the *Rime*. Early in the collection, he evokes the arrow wounds inflicted on his left side and relates them to his desire (29); he compares himself to a wounded stag "con quello stral nel lato manco" [with that arrow in my left side] (209).[24]

Thus the plight of the poet in Petrarch's lyric collection is not unlike that of Lancelot in the *Quête du Saint Graal*. That comparison, however, while fertile in suggestive analogies, requires also an essential distinction. The Old French grail romance is explicitly attentive to the intersection of two domains, material and spiritual, in which the devil is a principal manipulator of the destinies of the chivalric heroes;[25] and Lancelot's *innamoramento* defines his destiny: the point of the story in the Old French romance is that Lancelot's adulterous love for Guenevere has definitively precluded his achievement of the quest of the Holy Grail, an experience reserved for the purest among men. The abandonment of the straight path or "droite voie" is in the *Quête* the usual consequence of the devil's successful interventions in the itineraries of chivalric heroes. While we have seen that both the poet of the *Rime* and Augustinus in the *Secretum* similarly define the *innamoramento* in terms of deviation from the proper course, Petrarch's protagonist does not stand accused of sinful

---

23. The analogy drawn between sides of the body and faculties of the soul affirmed that the higher faculty, or *intellectus*, was subject to the wound of ignorance, and that of *affectus*, the left side, to that of concupiscence. In the philosophical tradition, Freccero observes, the wound "was so firmly linked to the doctrine of original sin as to be considered by many of the scholastics both the sin and its consequence" ("The Firm Foot," 45).

24. In the *Secretum* the Petrarchan persona Franciscus similarly likens himself, bearing the wound of love wherever he goes, to a stag, adapting Virgil's metaphorical casting of Dido as a fatally wounded hind (*Aeneid* IV, 69–73) to the consequences of his own wounding (*Petrarch's Secret*, 141). Petrarch was also no doubt familiar with the medieval allegories of the love chase featuring the stag as love's quarry; for this tradition, see Marcelle Thiebaux, *The Stag of Love* (Ithaca and London, 1977), especially chap. 4.

25. See Robert Deschaux, "Le Diable dans la *Queste del Saint Graal:* Masques et Méfaits," *Perspectives Médiévales* 2 (1976): 56–60.

conduct; he is inculpated instead by the deficiency of his will to effect his escape from Love's bondage. A change thus remains possible, and it is the possibility of change that defines the gravity of the recognition: the awakening to the peril of his course is both disclosed and complemented by the insistent postulation of alternatives. For the elements that anticipate and constrain that preoccupation we must turn from the more celebrated components to the *innamoramento* and its consequences. *Rime* 25–28 have attracted critical comment largely in terms of negative definition that calls into question their inclusion in the collection: they are not, we are reminded, about the love of Laura. On the other hand, their occurrence in sequence merits further attention;[26] among what have been termed the "non-love poems" of the *Rime* they represent an exceptional concentration, the longest series of this type in the collection.[27] The strategic placement of this block of poems assumes particular interest, moreover, in that it follows closely upon the metamorphosis canzone 23, the "prima vera cesura del romanzo" that recapitulates the story told in fragments in the opening section of the *Rime sparse;* as Santagata observes, it is only with *Rime* 29 that the poet's story will take up its interrupted thread.[28]

What, then, is the nature and the point of this apparent interruption? A casual reading discloses that poems 25–28 share an obvious common element in that each is addressed to an unnamed *destinatorio*. Sonnet 25 addresses an unidentified individual who chooses a path in relation to love, and that choice is celebrated again in sonnet 26. Sonnet 27 encourages an unidentified addressee to take up arms in support of the abortive crusade proclaimed by John XXII against the Moslems in 1334;[29] it introduces in turn the better-known canzone 28, also addressed to an

---

26. If Petrarch's placement of his poems had been motivated primarily by a concern for variety, Adolfo Jenni observes, we might expect to find such components singly distributed among the overwhelming majority of poems celebrating or lamenting the poet's love for Laura; see "Un sistema del Petrarca nell'ordinamento del *Canzoniere*," in *Studi in onore di Alberto Chiari*, II (Brescia, 1973), esp. 722.

27. For the designation, see Also Bernardo, "The Importance of the Non-Love Poems of Petrarch's *Canzoniere*," *Italica* 27 (1950): 302–12.

28. Marco Santagata, "La canzone XXIII," *Lectura Petrarce, I, 1981* (Padua, 1982), 56. In general, he notes elsewhere, poems of the allocutionary type appear to counter the general tendency of the components of the *Rime* to articulate themselves in terms of a sustained narrative dimension; see "Connessioni intertestuali nel *Canzoniere* del Petrarca," *Strumenti critici* 9 (1975): 93–94.

29. Petrarch's optimism concerning both the crusading venture and the return of the papacy to Italy at this time proved ill founded. "Il successor di Carlo" evoked in this poem is Philip VI of France, who was to lead the crusade. Pope John XXII died in 1334 and was followed by Benedict XII, the "vicario di Cristo" of v. 5.

unnamed recipient, "O aspettata in ciel beata e bella / anima" [O soul awaited in Heaven, blessed and beautiful], and exhorting to zeal in that same Christian enterprise. Thus an initial thematic reading yields two pairs of poems: 25 and 26, characterized by Aldo Bernardo as "friendship poems," that celebrate a return to the poetry of love, and 27 and 28, both "patronage poems," concerned with a crusading venture.[30]

The inclusion of the anonymous addressees would seem a priori to suggest the occasional nature of these poems, and in fact *Rime* 27 and 28 have close affinities with depictions of the Colonna family that appear frequently in Petrarch's correspondence of this period.[31] Relations between the four components, however, are readily divulged, and a number of internal linkages subvert both the particularity of the single texts and their bipartite thematic distinction. Sonnets 25 and 26, whose mutual theme is bondage to Love, both contain pronounced, traditional religious imagery:

> col cor levando al cielo ambe le mani
> ringrazio lui che' giusti preghi umani
> benignamente sua mercede ascolta.
>
> (25, 6–8)

[in my heart lifting both hands to Heaven I thank Him who in His mercy listens kindly to just human prayers.]

> ché più gloria è nel regno degli eletti
> d'un spirito converso, et più s'estima,
> che di novantanove altri perfetti.
>
> (26, 12–14)

[for there is more glory in the realm of the elect for one converted spirit, and he is more esteemed, than for ninety and nine others who are just.]

---

30. See Bernardo, "The Non-Love Poems," 304; Jenni, "Un sistema del Petrarca," 731.

31. Giacomo Colonna is frequently proposed as the likely recipient of canzone 28; in *Familiares* IV, 2, Petrarch laments his untimely death in terms highly reminiscent of that poem. Marco Santagata, however, argues persuasively in favor of the Domenican Giovanni Colonna di Gallicano; see "Sul destinatario della canzone petrarchesca 'O aspectata in ciel beata et bella' (*R.V.F.*, 28)," *Rivista di Letteratura Italiana* 3 (1985): 368–80. The obscure reference to the "gentil agna," the "noble lamb" to be consoled in sonnet 27 may suggest Agnese Colonna, the sister of Giovanni and Giacomo, and evoke the struggle of her family against rival Roman nobility; see Arnaldo Foresti, *Aneddoti della vita di Francesco Petrarca* (Brescia, 1928), 29–34. The "gloriosa Columna" of the opening verse of *Rime* 10 is Petrarch's tribute to Stefano Colonna the Elder; to Orso dell'Anguillara, husband of Agnese Colonna, he addresses sonnets 38 and 98.

And both the poems with overt politico-religious content, exhorting to participation in the Crusade, specifically note varieties of love, canzone 28 in some detail:

> a l'alta impresa caritate sprona.
> Deh qual amor sì lecito o sì degno,
> qua' figli mai, qua' donne
> furon materia a sì giusto disdegno?
>
> (42–45)

[charity spurs all to the high undertaking. Ah! what love, however legitimate or worthy, what sons, what ladies ever were the cause of so just an anger?]

This interconnection strongly suggests that these poems should be read in conjunction, in the manner proposed by their sequential arrangement.

Closer examination discloses a closer connection between the two pairs of poems. Whereas sonnet 25 refers to a friend's recent liberation from Love's bonds as "l'anima vostra da' suoi nodi sciolta" [your soul . . . freed from his knot] and affirms of the soul's course that "al dritto camin l'à Dio rivolta" [God has turned it back to the right path], canzone 28 promises its lauded addressee that a favorable western wind will assist his voyage:

> la condurrà de' lacci antichi sciolta
> per drittissimo calle
> al verace oriente ov'ella è volta.
>
> (13–15)

[will lead it, freed from its former bonds . . . by a straight course to the true Orient toward which it is turned.]

This second evocation of a liberation from bondage retrospectively confirms a negative evaluation of the bonds with which the protagonist of sonnet 25 had been held captive by Amor. In *Rime* 27, moreover, the sword as image of the struggle with Amor in sonnet 26—"veggendo quella spada scinta / che fece al segnor mio sì lunga guerra" [I see put back in its sheath that sword which made so long war on my lord]—recurs as the sword heroically raised against the Infidel, replacing servitude in one cause with service to another: "per Jhesù cingete omai la spada" [gird on your sword for Jesus now].

In the explicit identification of both Amor and God as agents acting upon the protagonist, *Rime* 25 presents an opposition drawn with a directness uncommon in the collection. The Amor whose name opens the poem, whose weeping is the subject of the initial verse and from whom the poet's own steps have never strayed far, is clearly that god of Love whose assault is recounted in the metamorphosis canzone 23. The opening scene records the escape of the sonnet's addressee from amorous bondage, and the poet himself, *solidaire* (at least partially: "tal volta") with his own master Amor, had wept at the loss. This escape, however, is but a first, anterior moment of the poem; the second stanza opens with the relational phrase "or ch'al dritto camin l'à Dio rivolta" [now that God has turned it back to the right path] to characterize the new course undertaken, and the poet, again *solidaire* with a powerful deity who is now not Amor but God, acknowledges the difficulty of the escape for which the addressee and protagonist of the sonnet is congratulated in terms of unmistakable Biblical resonance:

> fu per mostrar quanto è spinoso calle
> et quanto alpestra et dura la salita
> onde al vero valor conven ch'uom poggi.
>
> (25, 12–14)[32]

[it was to show how thorny the path is, how mountainous and hard the ascent by which one must rise to true worth.]

His gesture of gratitude raised to heaven in this poem is reenacted in *Rime* 28 for the new course that will lead another to the better port, "al miglior porto":

> Per che inchinare a Dio molto convene
> le ginocchia et la mente
> che gli anni tuoi riserva a tanto bene
>
> (103–5)

[Wherefore it is most necessary to bend your knees and heart to God, who has reserved your years for so much good.]

---

32. Commentaries to this and the following poem sometimes propose that their addressee is congratulated for his return to Love's bonds after a prolonged absence; see *Rime, Trionfi, e poesie latine*, ed. F. Neri (Milan and Naples, 1951); *Il Canzoniere*, ed. G. Contini, notes by D. Ponchiroli (Turin, 1964); *Il Canzoniere*, annotated by N. Vianello (Basiano, 1966). The assumption that God has redirected the steps of the anonymous protagonist to Love's "nodi," however, presses beyond credence even that ambiguous and ironic use of the religious lexicon found in numerous components of the *Rime sparse*.

The two crusade poems, then, are related to the sonnets depicting bondage to Amor as positive examples following negative ones.

Attention to the rhetorical strategies of these poems reveals a further relational feature, in that the choice between opposing courses is repeatedly cast in metaphors of voyage. This recurrence prompts the reader to consider a set of related questions: what is the nature of the journey, and what its goal? What is the criterion for the choice of a course, and what is the merit of the anonymous addressee that in each instance occasions the poet's admiration and praise? A preliminary answer leads us well beyond the immediate concerns of this series of poems. The particular resonance of the first mention of the choice of roads in the series, however, leads to another text and another journey already repeatedly evoked: the "dritto camin" to which God has returned the errant soul in sonnet 25 awakens the echo of another *diritta via*, that lost in the dark wood of *Inferno* I.[33]

The present echo lays particular claim to our attention because it initiates a complex recall of the *Commedia* in these four components of the *Rime;* here the rhythms of Petrarch's verses, their timbric quality, and their semantic features all repeatedly demonstrate his memory of Dante's *poema sacro*.[34] Santagata notes in particular the "sapore dantesco" of the opening stanza of canzone 28, whose images relate it to the opening *canti* of each of the three canticles of the *Commedia*. In each case the identical symbolic act, that of abandoning a negative reality, is performed; the "barca / ch'al cieco mondo à già volte le spalle / per gire al miglior porto" [ship which has already turned away from the blind world to go to the better port] of Petrarch's canzone recalls in particular the "navicella" of *Purgatorio* I, the little craft that to "correr miglior acqua / lascia dietro a sè mar sì crudele" [course over better waters . . . leaving behind her a sea so cruel].[35]

What associations does this multivocal evocation of the *Commedia* bring to bear on poems 25–28 of the *Rime sparse*? In Dante's poem the negative reality that the protagonist is led to reject takes a rather precise form. It is characterized in a sharp rebuke addressed to him by Beatrice:

---

33. For the classical, Biblical, and romance antecedents of Dante's readings of the opposing "vie," see F. Mazzoni, *Saggio di un nuovo commento alla Divina Commedia* (Florence, 1967), 32–45.

34. See the notations for each poem in Paolo Trovato, *Dante in Petrarca: Per un inventario dei dantismi nei "Rerum vulgarium fragmenta"* (Florence, 1979).

35. Marco Santagata, "Presenze di Dante 'comico' nel *Canzoniere* del Petrarca," *Giornale Storico della Letteratura Italiana* 146 (1969): 194. While considering Petrarch's conscious recall of these Dantean *loci* improbable, Santagata calls our attention also to the pilgrim Dante's description of his own voyage (*Inferno* XV, 49–54), which both recapitulates *Inferno* I and anticipates Petrarch's later formulations (195).

> ". . . Per entro i mie' disiri,
> che ti menavano ad amar lo bene
> di là dal qual non è a che s'aspiri,
> quai fossi attraversati o quai catene
> trovasti, per che del passare innanzi
> dovessiti così spogliar la spene?"
>
> (*Purg.* XXXI, 22–27)

[". . . Within your desires of me that were leading you to love God beyond which there is nothing to which man may aspire, what pits did you find athwart your path, or what chains, that you had thus to strip you of the hope of passing onward?]

This phrasing is the probable direct source of Petrarch's address to his friend in *Rime* 25:

> Et se tornando a l'amorosa vita
> per farvi al bel desio volger le spalle
> trovaste per la via fossati o poggi . . .
>
> (9–11)[36]

[And if, returning to the life of love, you have found in your way ditches or hills that try to make you abandon your lovely desire . . .]

From the further detail of Beatrice's reprimand and the pilgrim's subsequent confession, it is clear that as he sought to "amar lo bene," to direct his love aright, his journey was impeded by temptations of an amorous nature, by "falso piacere" of a quite earthly variety: the confrontation between two types of love that is precisely the subject of Petrarch's sonnets 25 and 26.

Echoes of the pilgrim's journey in Dante's *poema* occur in both the first and second pairs of poems under consideration in the *Rime*. The temptations to which the errant Dante had succumbed, and from whose consequences he escapes only through the arduous journey narrated from the beginning of the *Commedia* to its triumphant conclusion, are those from which the exemplary addressee of Petrarch's sonnets 25 and 26 escapes through his own effort aided by "just human prayers." The liberated soul of canzone 28, setting sail in a new and divinely favored

---

36. See Enzo di Poppa Vòlture, "Dante e Petrarca," in *Il Padre e i Figli* (Naples, 1970), 138; Santagata, "Presenze," 185–86.

enterprise, in turn recalls the positive journey of Dante's pilgrim, whose course had been painstakingly corrected: the "miglior acque" of the opening verse of the *Purgatorio* and the angelic crossing of souls to that shore, and at last the poet's "legno che cantando varca" [ship that singing makes her way] of *Paradiso* II,[37] all anticipate the boat of the addressee of canzone 28, moved by the "sweet comfort" of a favorable wind toward its heavenly goal.[38]

In the sequence of *Rime* 25–28 the metaphors of choice central to the *Commedia* become central to Petrarch's lyric collection as well. In the *Commedia* the entire drama of the soul, as Virgil and others expound it to the pilgrim in Purgatory, is to be understood in terms of the choice between two types of love, earthbound and divine; the principle of merit that determines the ultimate fate of the soul operates "secondo / che buoni e rei amori accoglie e viglia" [according as it garners and winnows good and evil loves] (XVIII, 65–66). In each of the three canticles of the *Commedia*, the references to *buon amor* and *mal amor* are interrelated with those to the *via diritta* and *via torta* through the metaphor of the journey. In the *Secretum* it is in terms of a parting of the ways that Franciscus is led by Augustinus to identify the beginning of his turmoil and then, reluctantly, to acknowledge that his turning from the right road coincided with the inception of his love for Laura.[39] To recognize the importance of this opposition in the overall structure of the *Rime* we need recall only two moments: the opening of Part II of the collection, which finds the poet "ripensando ov' io lassai 'l viaggio / da la man destra ch' a buon porto aggiunge" [I go thinking back where I left the journey to the right, which reaches a good port] (264), and the final poem, where he will implore the Virgin that "la mia torta via drizzi a buon fine" [direct my twisted path to a good end] (366).

The traces of the *Commedia* in these poems exemplify a phenomenon

---

37. In the secondary prologue of *Purgatorio* II, 7–9, we find the conjunction of Minerva, Apollo, and the Muses to which Petrarch's disavowal alludes. Santagata notes the reminiscence of Dante's "legno che cantando varca" in *Rime* 28, "onde al suo regno di qua giù si varca" [by which from down here one crosses over into His kingdom] ("Presenze," 195).

38. Repeatedly in the *Rime* the marine metaphor and the designation of ports of arrival suggest the perils of the poet's own enterprise; see Sara Sturm-Maddox, "Eaux troubles: la navigation de l'âme dans les *Rime sparse* de Pétrarque," in *L'Eau au Moyen Age (Senefiance* 15) (Aix-en-Provence, 1985), 337–47. On the "thematic of the port and of peace," see Bortolo Martinelli, *Petrarca e il Ventoso* (Bari, 1977), 231.

39. *Petrarch's Secret*, 128. For a version familiar to Petrarch of the choice at a fork in the road of life, see Theodor E. Mommsen, "Petrarch and the Story of the Choice of Hercules," *Journal of the Warburg and Courtauld Institutes* 16 (1953): esp. 178, 182–84. The "secura strada" or safe path is abandoned in *Rime* 6; see Adelia Noferi, "Note ad un sonetto del Petrarca," *Forum Italicum* 2 (1968): 199–200.

that is far from unique in the organization of Petrarch's collection: like many others later in the *Rime*, they identify its lyric protagonist in relation to the pilgrim and protagonist of the *Commedia*. Here, as that relation is first established through the metaphors of choice, it is revealed to be fundamentally negative. In both pairs of components the choice made by the unidentified addressee casts a strong negative light on the condition of the speaker of the poems, who remains a bondsman to earthly attachments; he whose steps have never strayed far from Love in sonnet 25 is he who in canzone 28 still inhabits that "oscura valle / ove piangiamo il nostro et l'altrui torto" [dark valley where we bewail our own and others' faults].

This sequence of poems, then, takes the measure of the distance between amorous servitude and service to God. Nor is it an isolated demonstration: its programmatic status is confirmed by its integration into its immediate textual environment. It is preceded by another ostensibly non-love poem to an unnamed but readily identified addressee: poem 24 is a reply *per le rime* to a sonnet addressed to Petrarch by Stramazzo da Perugia, who asks that he too be brought to participate in the benefits of that fount of Helicon from which he assumes Petrarch's poetic inspiration to flow.[40] Petrarch's response is both apologetic and strangely pessimistic:

> Se l'onorata fronde che prescrive
> l'ira del ciel quando 'l gran Giove tona
> non m'avesse disdetta la corona
> che suole ornar chi poetando scrive,
> i' era amico a queste vostre dive
> le qua' vilmente il secolo abandona;
> ma quella ingiuria già lunge mi sprona
> da l'inventrice de le prime olive. . . .
>
>   (24, 1–8)

[If the honored branch that protects one from the anger of heaven when great Jove thunders had not refused me the crown that decorates those who write poetry, I would be a friend to those goddesses of yours, whom the world so basely abandons; but that injury drives me far away from the inventor of the first olives. . . .]

Through these mythological allusions, whose function has been clearly established in the preceding poems, he thus replies (obscurely enough)

40. For Stramazzo's poem, see Durling, *Petrarch's Lyric Poems*, 603.

that his love for Laura has prevented him from being a friend of Wisdom. His poetic correspondent is advised therefore to seek a more tranquil fountain; his own fount, alas, is not that of Helicon, and it is dry except for the constant distillation of his tears.

Not only does this portrait of the poet as Love's unhappy servant anticipate the applause that accompanies the escape of another from amorous bondage in sonnets 25 and 26; it also anticipates canzone 28, which will posit the rectification of love and the use of inspired eloquence. The sacred waters of Helicon, denied to the poet in Petrarch's reply to Stramazzo, become the "dottrina del santissimo Elicona" [knowledge of sacred Helicon] of canzone 28, and the addressee of that poem is urged to take up not only his sword but his pen and devote his gift of eloquence to the promotion of the crusading Christian cause:

> et che 'l nobile ingegno che dal cielo
> per grazia tien de l'immortale Apollo
> et l'eloquentia sua vertù qui mostri
> or con la lingua, or co' laudati inconstri.

> (28, 64–67)

> [let your noble mind, which you hold from Heaven by grace of the immortal Apollo, and your eloquence now show their power both through speech and through praiseworthy writings.]

Extending the interconnections forward in the lyric sequence, the injury that causes the poet to weep in sonnet 24 acquires added precision in *Rime* 29 as the wound inflicted to his left side. The image of the sword, resheathed following the struggle with Love in sonnet 26 but raised by another in a righteous cause in both the Crusade poems, recurs here with heightened dramatic impact in the allusion to the death of a passion-driven Dido, "tal già qual io mi stanco / l'amata spada in se stessa contorse" [one driven like me once turned the beloved sword upon herself]. Finally the metaphor of the choice of course recurs, complete with the image of the boat that undertakes its voyage toward Heaven:

> ché men son dritte al ciel tutt' altre strade
> et non s'aspira al glorioso regno
> certo in più salda nave.

> (29, 40–42)

> [for all other paths to Heaven are less straight, and certainly one cannot aspire to the glorious realm in any stronger ship.]

While the inclusion of this allocutionary sequence appears on a first reading to interrupt the narrative thrust of the *enchaînement* of poems, substituting an authentic historical moment for the fictive *durée* of the poet's story, it is now evident that these apparently anomalous components are neither non-love poems nor a digression in the ordering of the *rime sparse*. Framed by two components that focus on the poet and declare his bondage to love, *Rime* 25–28 dramatize the choice between that bondage and freedom through the celebration of others who have chosen between opposing courses.[41] This larger group is framed in turn by two of the most suggestive summary characterizations of the poet's experience of love: it is preceded by *Rime* 23, the first canzone of the collection, in which are dramatized the lover's vulnerability, his alienation, and his loss of speech, all inculpated in the pessimistic disavowal of sonnet 24;[42] and it is followed by sestina 30, "Giovene donna sotto un verde lauro," in which the idolatrous nature of the poet's passion is defined. The latter poem, the first of the anniversary components of the collection, commemorates the seventh anniversary of the *innamoramento*—thus locating itself, in terms of the internal chronology of the *Rime*, in 1334, the year of those events that inspired the Crusade poems 27 and 28. And it is the second of the anniversary poems, "Padre del ciel" (62), that will redefine the poet's bondage in penitential terms. Its sorrowful avowal of the "dispietato giogo" [pitiless yoke] to which he has been subjected recalls both the admission in *Rime* 29 that he bears no yoke less heavy, no "giogo men grave," than his love for Laura, and the movement of liberation urged upon the addressee of canzone 28:

> Dunque ora è 'l tempo da ritrare il collo
> dal giogo antico, et da squarciare il velo
> ch' è stato avolto intorno agli occhi nostri.

(61–63)

[Therefore it is time to withdraw our neck from the ancient yoke and to rend the veil that has been wrapped over our eyes.]

It is also "Padre del ciel," in the verses considered early in this chapter, that redefines in Christian terms the opposition between alternative

41. The series is anticipated in this respect only by *Rime* 7, "La gola e 'l sonno e l'oziose piume," again to an unidentified recipient who has chosen an "altra via" and is exhorted not to abandon a "magnanima impresa."

42. For the close relation between canzone 23 and the following sonnet to Andrea Stramazzo, see Santagata, "La canzone XXIII," 68–70.

courses: pursuing the wrong path in *Rime* 25–28, the poet would turn now "ad altra vita et a più belle impresse" [to a different life and to more beautiful undertakings].

While the question of choice will seldom be thematized again in the *rime sparse* as explicitly as in this sequence, the penitential components will continue to cast a sharp light on the love for Laura celebrated joyfully or sorrowfully in the vast majority of the poems of the collection, reminders both to the poet and to the reader of that other light in which it is differently read. And they are not alone: frequently the overt thematics of a component are conditioned by strategies, linguistic and intertextual, that orient the reading of the poet's story. That orientation begins with the opening verse of the proemial sonnet, where we are convoked as "listeners." We are not only to hear in the poet's sighs the record of his love experience; while later in the poem he will hope to find a reception "ove sia chi per prova intenda amore" [where there is anyone who understands love through experience], the absolute vocative construction "Voi che ascoltate," unique in the *Rime*, designates a virtual public that is the human race, recalling the "O vos omnes qui transitis per viam" of Jeremiah.[43] The audience thus constituted will find the pervasive Biblical lesson of the vanity of earthly things blended with classical echoes in the celebrated closing verse of this poem, "che quanto piace al mondo è breve sogno" [that whatever pleases in the world is a brief dream];[44] it will find in the *rime* to follow a language and an imagery that are not circumscribed by the conventions of amorous lyric.

A language closely akin and frequently indebted to that of religious devotion was already a common feature in the love lyric; Santagata suggests that the presence of a *certificazione sacra* may well have been one of the criteria orienting Petrarch's choices from among the vast repertory of *luoghi communi* afforded by the vernacular tradition.[45] Petrarch himself sketches a history of that orientation in the *De Otio Religioso* of 1347, where he reviews his early reading and attributes to Augustine the decisive impetus in a turn from secular to sacred poetry.[46] This record,

43. See Gianfranco Contini, *Letteratura italiana delle origini* (Florence, 1970), 580. On the difference between this opening and the other allocutionary poems of the collection, see Alfred Noyer-Weidner, "Il Sonetto I," *Lectura Petrarce, IV, 1984* (Padua, 1985), 330–35.

44. See Marino Casali, "Petrarca 'penitenziale': Dai *Salmi* alle *Rime*," *Lettere Italiane* 20 (1968): esp. 373ff. For the contrast between the complex syntax of the quatrains with their allusions to the amorous lyric tradition and the syntactical simplicity and directness of the tercets with their Biblical echoes, see Noyer-Weidner, "Il Sonetto I," 346–49.

45. Marco Santagata, "Prestilnovisti in Petrarca," *Studi Petrarcheschi*, n.s., 2 (1985): 94.

46. The same attribution concerning his reading of the *Confessions* is made in *Sen.* VIII, 6 and XVI, 1; see the comments of R. Fubini, "Intendimenti umanistici e riferimenti patristici dal Petrarca al Valla," *Giornale Storico della Letteratura Italiana* 151 (1974): esp. 537–38.

less than accurate in its indication that he had only lately sought the "wholesome nourishment" of Scripture, is an element of Petrarch's self-fashioning patterned on the *Confessions* in which Augustine appears as exemplary reader-protagonist.[47] In another way, however, Augustine demonstrably motivated his new experience of sacred poetry: the Psalter is the single Scriptural text cited in the *De Otio* passage for special attention, and Petrarch lists Augustine's commentary on the Psalms among his favorite books.[48] Of the impact of this reading he left an eloquent record in the seven Penitential Psalms that he himself composed, poems inspired by the Biblical psalms that in the liturgical tradition appear frequently in penitential rituals and during Holy Week, those same poems that had been favored by Augustine as relevant to the lament for his own early sinfulness.[49] These penitential poems are characterized by the frequency and extraordinary vigor of figures and emblems that are the common currency of the lyric collection as well: the ship in tempest, the deficient will, the prominent use of shade and shadows to suggest the refuge as well as the lability of human life and the vanity of mortal hope.[50] With regard to Petrarch's forging of his vernacular poetic idiom, moreover, this experience appears to have been decisive; while the impact of Scripture on the language of the *Rime* is particularly evident in its penitential poems, the imitation of the "simple" and "humble" language of Scripture in the intimate, dense Latin verses of Petrarch's Penitential Psalms anticipates the style of many of the most characteristic poems of the lyric collection.

Against this background in the *Rime* there emerges a more evident

---

47. His early and assiduous frequentation of certain Biblical texts and of several works of Augustine is well documented; see Kenelm Foster, *Petrarch, Poet and Humanist* (Edinburgh, 1984), 157–58. Augustine records that the language of Scripture "seemed to me unworthy of comparison with the nobility of Cicero's writings. My swelling pride turned away from its humble style, and my sharp gaze did not penetrate into its inner meaning" (*Confessions* III, V, 9); cited in Eugene Vance, "Augustine's *Confessions* and the Grammar of Selfhood," *Genre* 6 (1973): 21.

48. Petrarch added the Augustinian *Enarrationes in Psalmos* to his "favorite books," which by his own indication already included four works by Augustine, in 1337; see the discussion of his professed early disdain for "sacred writings" in Foster, *Petrarch, Poet and Humanist*, 3.

49. The date, on some evidence 1347, is disputed. Petrarch describes their composition in a letter (*Sen.* X, 1) accompanying a copy of the Psalms; see Casali, "Petrarca 'penitenziale'," 366–68.

50. Casali, "Petrarca 'penitenziale'," especially 373–82. Many of these are the common currency too of the *Secretum*, where the language and favored metaphors of the Petrarchan persona's dialogue with Augustinus appear to be filtered through Petrarch's reading of Augustinian texts; see Casali, 370–73; Nicolae Iliescu, *Il Canzoniere Petrarchesco e sant'Agostino* (Rome, 1962), 58, 74–79.

type of Scriptural presence, that of allusion or near-citation. Here it functions as what Michael Riffaterre terms an interpretant, "a sign that translates the text's surface signs and explains what else the text suggests."[51] In Petrarch's lyric collection the strategy of Scriptural citation and the introduction of Biblical exemplars, examined less frequently than his use of mythological allusion, is like the latter in that it demands the reader's complicity not only in recognizing the source but in analyzing the connection.[52] The most resounding example is the invective series of "Babylonian sonnets" (136–38) in which Avignon is characterized as greedy, false, and wicked Babilonia;[53] here only the dramatic allusion to the Whore of Babylon in Apocalypse 17 guarantees the full intelligibility of the divine wrath invoked upon a corrupt papal court in the famous sonnet "Fiamma dal ciel su le tue treccia piova, malvagia" [May fire from Heaven rain down on your tresses, wicked one] (136).[54]

Other poems, however, more numerous and more insistent, bring the "other voices" of Scripture directly to bear on the experience of the protagonist of the collection.[55] In the *Rime* this citation or near-citation locates the poet's experience in relation to a particularly rich patrimony for which centuries of authoritative exegesis had already afforded both precepts and examples of interpretation. Frequently, as Calhoun observes, Scriptural allusion or paraphrase establishes a perspective from which the speaker's character is redefined; it is a means through which Petrarch "can compile in a sequence of lyrics a vision of personal history and at the same time invoke a structure to evaluate that history."[56] Here

---

51. Michael Riffaterre, *Semiotics of Poetry* (Bloomington, Ind., 1978), 81; texts either quoted or alluded to are among the signs that mediate between two signifying systems.

52. For this process generally, see Carmela Perri, "On Alluding," *Poetics* 7 (1978): 299–301; for its pertinence to Petrarch's practice of *imitatio*, see Giuseppe Velli, "La memoria poetica del Petrarca," *Italia medioevale e umanistica* 19 (1976): esp. 182, and for the *Rime*, see Sturm-Maddox, *Petrarch's Metamorphoses*, chap. 1: "Reading the Poet's Story" (1–8).

53. This type of Biblical allusion, anticipated in Dante's vehement denunciation of the corrupt Church in the *Commedia* (*Inferno* XIX, 106–11), appears in other denunciations of the Papal Court among Petrarch's writings, notably in the *Epistolae sine nomine;* see the comments of E. H. Wilkins, *Studies in the Life and Works of Petrarch* (Cambridge, Mass., 1955), 113.

54. On the echoes of the Book of Revelations in these poems and on Petrarch's repeated opposition of Babylon, the earthly city, to the heavenly Jerusalem, see Ann H. Hallock, "The Pre-Eminent Role of *Babilonia* in Petrarch's Theme of the Two Cities," *Italica* 54 (1977): 290–97.

55. See Angelo Jacomuzzi's commentary on the literary function of citation, which becomes an instrument of interpretation through evocation of antecedent tradition, in "La citazione come procedimento letterario," in *L'Arte dell'interpretare: studi critici offerti a Giovanni Getto* (Cuneo, 1984), 11.

56. Thomas Calhoun, "*De Vita Solitaria,* Alieniloquium, and Petrarch's *Canzoniere,*" *Italian Quarterly* 23 (1982): 28–29.

Petrarch requires the active participation of his reader because the allusion may be significantly deflected, the citation altered in ways that force its reorientation; in many instances it invites evaluation, not through contextual appropriateness, but through contextual inversion.

This strategy is readily illustrated by poems examined in other contexts in the preceding chapters. The sestina in which images of Laura and the laurel are elaborated from the initial scene of a "Giovene donna sotto un verde lauro" ends as follows:

> L'auro e i topacii al sol sopra la neve
> vincon le bionde chiome presso a gli occhi
> che menan gli anni miei sì tosto a riva.
>
> (30, 37–39)

[Gold and topaz in the sun above the snow are vanquished by the golden locks next to those eyes that lead my years so quickly to shore.]

These verses, Durling suggests, provide the key to the significance of the whole poem: while the precious stones were associated in the commentary tradition with the contemplative life and the beatific vision, Petrarch's depiction of his vision of Laura echoes Psalm 118, "I have loved thy commandments above gold and topaz," with the idolatrous inversion that "where the psalmist places God's commandments, the lover places Laura's beauty."[57] In another poem the river Rhône is instructed to carry the poet's message to a distant Laura: " 'Lo spirto è pronto, ma la carne è stanca' " [The spirit is ready, but the flesh is weary] (208). While it was conventional in the lyric tradition, as exemplified in the *commiato* with which many poems closed, that the poem be directed to carry the lover's words to their destination, to speak eloquently of his devotion and to plead his case, the words with which Petrarch's poet formulates an apology for his involuntary absence are appropriated, in an immediately transparent paraphrase, from Scripture, where their context is the night spent by Christ and his disciples in the garden of Gethsemane. If their inclusion here is profane—the river is to convey its message through the kiss of its waters on Laura's foot or her white hand—it is not disingenuous: their reinscription in an amatory sonnet demands an ironic reading

57. Robert Durling, "Petrarch's 'Giovene donna sotto un verde lauro'," *MLN* 86 (1971): 13–15.

of the poet's plight.[58] While the speaker of the poem remains unaware of this perspective, it is not lost on the reader, for whom its relevance is further heightened by recall of its Scriptural significance in Christ's admonition to his disciples: "Watch ye; and pray that ye enter not into temptation."[59]

Again: the poet's lament for Laura's death in sonnet 276, as we have seen, ends with a redirected paraphrase of Psalm 38:10: "'l dolce amoroso et piano / lume degli occhi miei non è più meco" [the sweet loving mild light of my eyes is no longer with me]. Here the implied contrast with the Biblical text conditions the reading of the poet's dilemma: the psalmist, enumerating his physical afflictions brought on by God's wrath at his sinfulness, confesses his sins and prays for healing, imploring God not to forsake him; the poet of the *Rime*, lamenting the loss of his beloved lady, acknowledges neither the threat of idolatry in his love, nor any relief possible beyond the lost Laura.[60] Another lament concludes an enumeration of Laura's physical beauties now lost to his sight with a verse appropriated and translated from Job: "secca è la vena de l'usato ingegno, / et la cetera mia rivolta in pianto" [dry is the vein of my accustomed wit, and my lyre is turned to weeping] (292).[61]

Petrarch himself identifies as *alieniloquium* an "other" discourse that invokes through its language a perspective alien to the poem in which it occurs.[62] In these echoes of Scriptural voices, that perspective forces a recasting of the amorous experience recorded by the poet, and at the same time it urgently suggests the adoption of an alternative course. To effect such a change, however, would require a decisive movement like that of the "blessed and beautiful soul" of canzone 28, the noble soul

58. The citation recalls both Matthew 26:41 and Mark 14:38: "The spirit indeed is willing, but the flesh is weak." On its revelation of the "moral problems hovering in the background" of the poem and of the collection as a whole, see William J. Kennedy, *Rhetorical Norms in Renaissance Literature* (New Haven and London, 1978), 34–35; Calhoun, *"De Vita Solitaria,"* 27–29.

59. Another example from an amatory sonnet in Part I is the beautiful opening of *Rime* 226, "Passer mai solitario in alcun tetto / non fu quant'io" [no sparrow was ever so alone on any roof as I am] that echoes the well-known verse of Psalm 101, "I have watched, and have become as a sparrow all alone on a house-top." The implicit comparison measures a revealing distance: in the Psalm the image occurs in an impassioned plea to God, whereas in Petrarch's poem it introduces his solitude when separated from Laura.

60. See Calhoun, *"De vita solitaria,"* 26–27.

61. See Thomas Greene, *The Light in Troy: Imitation and Discovery in Renaissance Poetry* (New Haven and London, 1982), 144–45. In such appropriations, Greene points out, in the "counterpoint of subtexts" in relation to their new contexts "the provenience of the voices in dialogue forces itself into the reader's mind. Each side is *ticketed.*"

62. *Familiares* X, 4; see the comments of Noferi, *L'esperienza poetica del Petrarca,* 19–21.

that escapes from the "ancient snares" to turn toward a more noble enterprise and set sail for a better port. The fortunate pilgrim of the *Commedia*, whose journey is implicitly recalled here, will be launched upon more favorable waters; the less fortunate poet of the *Rime* avows that he is incapable of that redirection. In the *Commedia*, we recall, it is in terms of liberation that Dante defines the role of Beatrice in the itinerary of her devoted poet: "Tu m'hai di servo tratto a libertate," he will affirm in the final grateful tribute that he addresses to her in the *Paradiso* ["It is you who have drawn me from bondage into liberty"] (XXXI, 85). What then of Laura? In the first stanza of canzone 29, and precisely in terms of the road denied the poet by his love, she is identified as "questa che mi spoglia / d'arbitrio et dal camin de libertade / seco mi tira" [this one who deprives me of choice and draws me with her from the path of freedom].

Concluding the sequence 25–28, and specifically at the end of the canzone in which the adoption of a better path is both urged and celebrated, Petrarch returns rather surprisingly in the *commiato* to the theme of Love:

> Tu vedrai Italia et l'onorata riva,
> canzon, ch'agli occhi miei cela et contende
> non mar non poggio o fiume
> ma solo Amor, che del suo altero lume
> più m'invaghisce dove più m'incende,
> né natura può star contra 'l costume.
> Or movi, non smarrir l'altre compagne,
> che non pur sotto bende
> alberga Amor, per cui si ride et piagne.
>
> (28, 106–14)

[Song, you will see Italy and the honored shore that is hidden from my eyes not by sea, mountain, or river, but only by Love, who with his noble light makes me desirous where he most enflames me: nor can nature resist habit.]

While the brief self-portrayal in the principal movement of this passage is constructed of the familiar terms that will remain central to the love story of the *Rime*, with Amor in the role of adversary, the final verses acknowledge that there is love other than that devoted to ladies. They acknowledge too, however, that Petrarch, who sends on its way this vigorous poem marked by the crusading spirit, is still bound by love for his lady: the canzone will set out just as its addressee will set out, but the poet is to remain impeded by Amor alone.[63]

In a pivotal canzone later in Part I Petrarch's poet will "reread" his own experience. Now he attributes the blame for his suffering not to Laura's compelling beauty nor to the stars, but to his own infirmity:

> l'occhio non po star fermo,
> così l'à fatto infermo
> pur la sua propria colpa, et non quel giorno
> ch'i' volsi in ver l'angelica beltade
> "Nel dolce tempo de la prima etade."
>
> (70, 46–50)

[my eye cannot stay still, it is so weakened by its very own fault, and not by that day when I turned toward her angelic beauty: "In the sweet time of my first age."]

This affirmation would appear to stand as a palinode with regard to the version of the *innamoramento* in *Rime* 23, whose opening verse is appropriated here to close the final stanza.[64] Yet despite the apparent lucidity of the poet's self-analysis, his bondage to Amor is soon to be reasserted in another sequence of components. *Rime* 83–97, whose major thematic preoccupation is the futility of his attempts at flight from that bondage, constitute a fundamental nexus of the collection: they confirm that the effects of the *innamoramento* will continue to define his condition—that "piaga per allentar d'arco non sana" [a wound is not healed by the loosening of the bow] (90).[65] Like the addressee of *Rime* 25, the poet himself had effected a difficult liberation, but only to lament it, to exclaim "quanto la nova libertà m'increbbe" [how much my new liberty was irksome to me] (89); his flight, Amor intimates, will be resolved in a new bondage: "di man mi ti tolse altro lavoro, / ma già ti raggiuns'io mentre fuggivi" [another work took you out of my hand, but I caught

---

63. Santagata notes that the Stoic doctrine relating nature and custom is found also in sonnet 7, a poem that again represents the poet in contrast to the addressee as bound still by his habitual attachments ("Sul destinatario," 373–74).

64. See Marco Santagata, "Il giovane Petrarca e la tradizione poetica romanza: Modelli ideologici e letterari," *Rivista di letteratura italiana* 1 (1983): 40–41.

65. See Enrico Fenzi, "Per un sonetto del Petrarca: R.V.F. XCIII," *Giornale storico della letteratura italiana* 151 (1974): esp. 510–12. For a reading in a biographical key, see Arnaldo Foresti, "Dalle prime alle 'seconde lagrime': Un capitolo della storia dell'amore di Francesco Petrarca," *Convivium* 12 (1940): 8–35.

up with you as you were fleeing] (93).[66] At the end of the sequence he reaffirms his loss of liberty, the "piaga ond'io non guerrò mai" [the wound of which I shall never be cured]:

> Amor in altra parte non mi sprona,
> né i pie' sanno altra via, né le man come
> lodar si possa in carte altra persona.
>
> (97, 12–14)

[Love does not spur me anywhere else, nor do my feet know any other road, nor do my hands know how on paper any other person can be praised.]

The alternatives to the love and celebration of Laura thematized in *Rime* 25–28 and evoked here once again through their denial are insistently redefined in a poem to which Petrarch evidently attributed particular importance. The sestina "A la dolce ombra de le belle frondi" [To the sweet shade of those beautiful leaves] (142) is a recapitulatory poem whose appropriateness as epilogue has been disclosed by recent studies; according to Wilkins's conjecture, it closed Part I of the so-called "Correggio" form of the collection.[67] Here the story of the poet's love for Laura is identified in the rhyme words of the six stanzas: "frondi" and "rami" invite associations with Laura and the mediation of the mythological paradigm; "poggi" recalls the hills among which Laura was seen or encountered; and "lume," "cielo," and "tempo" combine to identify the poet's guide, his goal, and his motivation. The *tornada* of *Rime* 142 may then be read as the epilogue to the epilogue, and as such it is particularly suggestive that, rather than affording a conclusion, these verses consist of an urgent statement of alternatives:

> Altr' amor, altre frondi, et altro lume,
> altro salir al ciel per altri poggi
> cerco (che n'è ben tempo), et altri rami.
>
> (142, 37–39)

66. See Fenzi, esp. 512–13. The poet's recapture intimated here is anticipated in *Rime* 69 addressed to Amor.

67. Guglielmo Gorni, "Metamorfosi e redenzione in Petrarca: Il senso della forma Correggio del Canzoniere," *Lettere Italiane* 30 (1978): 3–13; Luigi Vanossi, "Identità e mutazione nella sestina petrarchesca," *Cultura Neolatina* 40 (1980): 283–84. On the collection prepared for Azzo da Correggio, see E. H. Wilkins, *The Making of the "Canzoniere" and Other Petrarchan Studies* (Rome, 1951), 150–53.

[Another love, other leaves, and another light, another climbing to Heaven by other hills I seek (for it is indeed time), and other branches.]

In this dense recapitulation, two new elements are added to the six nouns that define the alternatives: "another love" and "another climbing to Heaven." While the markers of Laura's image and of her landscape participate in a complex play of combination and recombination throughout the collection, these new elements are closely related to the sequence of *Rime* 25–28 in their postulation of alternatives. We have seen that those poems, disclosing an opposition between earthly and heavenly love, set out also an opposition between two courses: to the clearly marked ascent charted for the blessed soul of canzone 28 is contrasted the equally symbolic immobility of the poet in "this dark valley."

In a text much frequented by Petrarch, Augustine comments on the words of the Psalmist: "Quis dabit mihi pennas sicut columbae ut volabo et requiescam?" This is echoed in the *Rime* in a weary closing:

> Qual grazia, qual amore, o qual destino
> mi darà penne in guisa di colomba,
> ch'i' mi riposi et levimi da terra?

(81, 12–14)

[What grace, what love, or what destiny will give me wings like a dove, that I may rest and lift myself up from earth?]

Augustine's commentary develops through an opposition of earthbound love or *concupiscentia* and divine love. Every love either ascends or descends, he continues, in accord with the interpretation of the *pondus amoris* that conveys the vectors of love through the metaphor of gravity; the soul sinks with earthly seductions, or it rises with spiritual aspiration.[68] In Petrarch's corpus this motif recurs with a particular insistence.[69]

---

68. *Ennarrationes in Psalmos*, 121 and 122. In a marginal note to the latter, Petrarch relates the passage to the doctrine of the *pondus amoris* in *Confessions* 13; see Pierre Courcelle, *Les Confessions de S. Augustin dans la tradition littéraire: Antécédents et Postérité* (Paris, 1963), 333. In the *Secretum* he attributes to Augustinus an explanation of the soul "uplifted on one side to heaven by its own nobility, and on the other dragged down to earth by the weight of the flesh and the seductions of the world, so that it both desires to rise and to sink at the same time" (*Petrarch's Secret*, 25).

69. Raffaele Amaturo, *Petrarca* (Bari, 1971), 279; Iliescu, *Il Canzoniere Petrarchesco e sant'Agostino*, 128–30. In *Ep. met.* I, 14, the letter *Ad seipsum* that closes Book I of this epistolary collection, it recurs following the report of an inner voice that warns him against earthly pleasures through a reminder of time's inexorable passing and the certainty of death; for discussion of the letter, see Aldo Bernardo, *Petrarch, Laura, and the "Triumphs"* (Binghamton, N.Y., 1974), 73–74.

The poet's love for Laura, present in the poem through the allusion to "l'usanza ria," is not otherwise mentioned. Yet the word "amore" is sounded—"qual amore"—and it is clearly related to that "altro amor" invoked in *Rime* 142: a love in opposition to that which renders him now fearful and in need of deliverance. In the opposition between courses postulated in the close of sestina 142, on the other hand, it is immediately evident that the alternative is not between immobility and ascent, but between two distinct avenues of ascent to Heaven. "Altro salir al ciel," its prominence singularly heightened here by the almost identical "altro sentier di gire al cielo" [another pathway to go to Heaven] in the preceding stanza, is the only element of the concluding oppositions to have a verb of its own.

This insistent "altro," this necessity to seek another course toward Heaven, invites us to attend more closely to that alternative and to its implications. It is anticipated not only by the sequence of poems 25–28. In a sonnet apparently inspired by a visit to Rome, Heaven and Laura appear as opposing destinations:

> L'aspetto sacro de la terra vostra
> mi fa del mal passato tragger guai
> gridando: "Sta' su, misero, che fai?";
> et la via de salir al ciel mi mostra.
> Ma con questo pensier un altro giostra
> et dice a me: "Perché fuggendo vai?
> Se ti rimembra, il tempo passa omai
> di tornar a veder la donna nostra."
>
> (68, 1–8)

[The holy sight of your city makes me bewail my evil past, crying: "Get up, wretch! what are you doing?" and shows me the way to mount to Heaven. But with this thought another jousts, and says to me: "Why do you flee? If you remember, the time is passing now when we should return to see our lady."]

To embark upon the course leading toward Heaven, or to return to Laura? The poet is torn between the alternatives: "Qual vincerà non so, ma 'nfino ad ora / combattuto ànno et non pur una volta" [which one will win, I do not know; but up to now they have been fighting, and not merely once.] Yet in a poem that comes shortly after, we find the following tribute to Laura:

> Gentil mia Donna, i' veggio
> nel mover de' vostr' occhi un dolce lume
> che mi mostra la via ch'al ciel conduce. . . .

(72, 1–3)

[My noble Lady, I see in the moving of your eyes a sweet light that shows me the way that leads to Heaven. . . .]

How are we to interpret this apparent contradiction? Are we to find in this second affirmation a resolution of the poet's dilemma, in which the love blinded by the false splendor of earthly beauty is sublimated through the attribution of a new role to Laura? Is this a new formulation in which salvation may be achieved through love, reconciling the two opposing "destinations" set out in *Rime* 68, Heaven and the lady?[70]

We must not be too hasty to conclude in favor of this positive resolution, one that would indeed cast Laura in the role of Beatrice. In one of the earliest poems of praise in the collection, the poet had assured his soul of the "uplifting" effect of his love for Laura:

> "Da lei ti ven l'amoroso pensero
> che mentre 'l segui al sommo ben t'invia,
> poco prezzando quel ch'ogni uom desia;
> da lei vien l'animosa leggiadria
> ch'al ciel ti scorge per destro sentero,
> sì ch'i' vo già de la speranza altero."

(13, 9–14)

["From her comes the amorous thought that, while you follow it, sends you toward the highest good, little valuing what other men desire; from her comes the courageous joy that leads you to Heaven along a straight path, so that already I go high with hope."]

This effect is rendered suspect not only by the "amoroso pensero" and "animosa leggiadria" by which it is engendered but by the admission of its immediate cause, the beauty of Laura. The praise of Laura in *Rime* 72

---

70. For Santagata, the shelter afforded the poet as he flees from a "burning light" in sestina 142 would confirm the new stilnovistic attributes of a Laura whose role is altered from that of canzone 23, to become a step toward virtue in a reformulation of the *innamoramento* as a conscious choice; see "Il giovane Petrarca," 58–61; see also "La canzone XXIII," 72–73.

cited above opens one of the celebrated *canzoni degli occhi* in which the
poet's adoration presses toward idolatry; rather than a new conception
of Laura's role, these verses may be read as a new confirmation of the
dazzling effect inculpated in *Rime* 70, to be reaffirmed in the comparison
of the lover to the firefly drawn irresistibly to the flame:

> . . . sì m'abbaglia Amor soavemente
> ch'i' piango l'altrui noia et no 'l mio danno,
> et cieca al suo morir l'alma consente.
>
> (141, 12–14)

[. . . so sweetly does Love dazzle me that I bewail another's pain
and not my own harm, and my soul, blind, consents to her own
death.]

Here Petrarch deepens and extends the proclamations of rapture char-
acteristic of the stilnovist poets' responses in the presence of the beloved,
and here again it is "oblio" that defines his poet's response:

> cominciai a mirar con tal desio
> che me stesso e 'l mio mal posi in oblio.
> I' era in terra e 'l cor in paradiso
> dolcemente obliando ogni altra cura. . . .
>
> (325, 44–47)

[I began to gaze at her with such desire that I forgot myself and
my misfortune. I was on earth and my heart in paradise, sweetly
forgetting every other concern. . . .]

In its negation of a rival reality, this state of rapt contemplation likens
the lyric protagonist to lovers in the vernacular romance tradition: the
heroes of courtly romance fall repeatedly into such raptures, losing
contact with the real world so that they are rendered oblivious, for
example, to the approach of enemies or to a fall into water. The
protagonist of the *Rime* is gazing at the sea when suddenly he sees "that
noble branch":

> Amor che dentro a l'anima bolliva
> per rimembranza de le treccie bionde
> mi spinse, onde in un rio che l'erba asconde
> caddi, non già come persona viva.
>
> (67, 5–8)

[Love, which boiled within my breast for memory of her blond tresses, pushed me forward, wherefore in a stream that the grass hides I fell, and not like a living person.]

In another sonnet already discussed, it is his rapt contemplation of a white doe that ends in his fall into the water:

> Et era 'l sol già vòlto al mezzo giorno,
> gli occhi miei stanchi di mirar, non sazi,
> quand'io caddi ne l'acqua et ella sparve.
>
> (190, 12–14)[71]

[And the sun had already turned at midday; my eyes were tired by looking but not sated, when I fell into the water, and she disappeared.]

The experience has its price, however gladly paid. It is recorded not only in his inadvertent immersion: the poet is repeatedly immobilized, deprived of his natural state by the sight of this lady. Late in the collection he will recall his response to Laura *in vita:* "et mia viva figura / far sentia un marmo e 'mpier di meraviglia . . ." [and I felt my living form become marble and full of wonder] (325). Here, of course, the lady is once again cast as Medusa, the Medusa of a tradition that attributed the transformation effected by the gorgon to an overwhelming beauty; Isidore of Seville explains that the Gorgons were three sisters of such beauty that they occasioned stupefaction in all who saw them (*Etym.* XI, 3, 29). Boccaccio, for whom Medusa is "spetiosissima mulierum," cites Fulgentius: "Medusa signifies oblivion. . . ."[72]

"Dolcemente obliando": the sweetness of this experience occults for the poet the imperative to reevaluate his course, to seek the "other way" that leads to Heaven. In this it is not unlike the nostalgia of Casella's song, rendering Dante's own amorous verses, that hinders the ascent of the souls newly arrived in Purgatory as they linger "sì contenti, / come a nessun toccasse altro la mente" [content as if naught else touched the

---

71. It has been suggested that the celebrated example of Lancelot, another "amante estatico," may illuminate the state of Petrarch's poet, who falls into water while rapt in contemplation of one of the surrogate images of Laura; see Ernesta Caldarini, "Da Lancillotto a Petrarca," *Lettere Italiane* 27 (1975): 373–80.

72. *De genealogie deorum gentilium,* X, 10. For discussion of the relevance of these definitions to the *abbagliamento* occasioned by Laura's beauty, see Martinelli, *Petrarca e il Ventoso,* 236–37.

mind of any].[73] "Oblio ne l'alma piove / d'ogni altro dolce, et Lete al fondo bibo" [oblivion rains into my heart of all other sweetness, and I drink Lethe to the bottom] (193): this is otherwise defined in the *Rime* as the loss of the self, as in the recall of the *innamoramento*—"Quando mi vene inanzi il tempo e 'l loco / ov' i' perdei me stesso" [When I remember the time and the place where I lost myself] (175)—and again in the curious poem "S'i' 'l dissi mai," "(che me stesso perdei / né più perder devrei)" [(when I lost myself, nor should I lose more)] (206). The same effect will be attributed to the laurel as the poet recalls the "first boughs" within his heart "per cui sempre altrui più che me stesso ami" [because of which I must always love another more than myself] (255).

As a description of the experience of earthly love, the "oblio" into which the poet falls repeatedly illustrates the perversion of desire from God to His creatures:

> [il] caldo desio
> che quando sospirando ella sorride
> m'infiamma sì che oblio
> niente aprezza, ma diventa eterno . . .
>
> (127, 52–55)

[the hot desire that, when she sighing smiles, inflames me so that my forgetfulness prizes nothing but becomes eternal . . .]

This is that God-forgetfulness and self-forgetfulness, "Dei suique oblivio," that Augustinus in the *Secretum* attributes to the obsessive love for Laura. Both are stressed in the poet's indictment of Amor in canzone 360 in the accusation that he had been made to "men amar Dio / ch'i' non deveva, et men curar me stesso" [love God less than I ought and be less concerned for myself].[74] In another poem of radically different imagery the peril of this "oblio" is again defined:

> Passa la nave mia colma d'oblio
> per aspro mare a mezza notte il verno
> enfra Scilla et Caribdi, et al governo
> siede 'l signore anzi 'l nemico mio.
>
> (189, 1–4)

73. *Purg.* II, 116–17. The peril of their absorption is revealed in Cato's prompt rebuke: "qual negligenza, quale stare è questo?" ["What negligence, what stay is this?"]

74. On this "Dei suique oblivio," see Kenelm Foster, "Beatrice or Medusa," in *Italian Studies presented to E. R. Vincent*, ed. C. P. Brand, K. Foster, U. Limentani (Cambridge, 1962), 48; *Petrarch, Poet and Humanist*, 74–75, 135.

[My ship laden with forgetfulness passes through a harsh sea, at midnight, in winter, between Scylla and Charybdis, and at the tiller sits my lord, rather my enemy.]

The rich and varied Biblical echoes in this sonnet support the staging of this existential drama in clearly Christian terms,[75] the adversary evoked here as "il mio nemico" standing once again for both Amor and the Biblical enemy.

While this designation of the poet's adversary reminds us once again of the exegetical rereading of Lancelot's *innamoramento*, there is yet another insight to be gleaned from the wonderfully direct account of that occasion in the *Quête du Saint Graal*. It concerns not only the thematic substance of the experience, summed up in the unself-conscious ease with which the figures of Cupid and the devil are merged, but also the nature of the utterance, of the hermit's rereading as a "reading back" of Lancelot's story. The addressee of the story is of course its protagonist, Lancelot himself. All too familiar with his own fall into love and its consequences, he now hears that story reread by a voice of authority, a saintly personage who interprets it both for him and for the reader. The account reflects the habitual interpretative contexts of both its utterer and its chivalric addressee: just as Dante's Francesca, recalling the reading of the first kiss exchanged by Lancelot and the Queen, casts the *innamoramento* read in the French romance in the likeness of her own, so here in the holy man's interpretation the naming of the diabolical Enemy unmasks an actor who in Lancelot's courtly context would more naturally appear in the guise of Amor. Thus the explanation, while retaining the familiar triad of actors associated in the *innamoramento*, exegetically recasts the amorous courtly episode.

The ubiquitous hermits who interpret not only the present but the past and future of the chivalric enterprise in the *Quête du Saint Graal* of course have no role in Petrarch's lyric collection, or in the experience of a poet who repeatedly flees the company of others; with few exceptions, his doubts and his queries are addressed to Amor, or to himself.[76] Yet

75. The words attributed to the "grande amico" are based on those of Christ in the Gospels: "Come unto me, all ye that labour and are heavy laden, and I will give you rest" (Matthew 11:28); "here is the way . . ." alludes to "I am the way, the truth, and the life" (John 14:6); the final tercet echoes Psalm 54: "Who will give me wings as of a dove, that I may fly away and rest?" (see Durling, *Petrarch's Lyric Poems*, 184).

76. A notable exception are the sonnets addressed to his friend Sennuccio del Bene which, along with three not included in the *Rime*, demonstrate a complex continuity; see Joseph Barber, "Il sonetto CXIII e gli altri sonetti a Senuccio," *Lectura Petrarce, II, 1982* (Padua, 1983), esp. 38–39.

despite the fact that in the *Rime* (almost) all the voices are those of the poet himself, other voices intrude, heard not only by the reader but by the poet as well, to establish an admonitory presence. Although the poems in which they are sounded constitute a very small minority in the collection as a whole, their dramatic content and veridical authority lend them a weight that far exceeds that suggested by their numbers.

The first is a warning voice, speaking in the second madrigal:[77]

> Perch' al viso d'Amor portava insegna,
> mosse una pellegrina il mio cor vano,
> ch' ogni altra mi parea d'onor men degna;
> et lei seguendo su per l'erbe verdi,
> udi' dir alta voce di lontano:
> "Ahi quanti passi per la selva perdi!"
>
> (54, 1–6)

[Because in her face she carried the ensign of Love, a foreign beauty moved my vain heart, for every other seemed to me less worthy of honor; and, as I followed her across the green grass, I heard a loud voice say from afar: "Ah, how many steps you are wasting through the wood!"]

In the opening of this poem, whose stilnovist affinities are marked at the outset by the echo of Dante's attempt in the *Vita Nuova* to explain his visibly enamored state in which he bore in his face the "insegne" of Amor (IV, 4),[78] we find a stylized reiteration of the poet's now-familiar pursuit of Laura through landscape. The irruption of the loud voice is thus unexpected, and it is dramatically brief. But it arrests the poet in midcourse, and his reaction to the admonition is remarkable for its allusive density:

> Allor mi strinsi a l'ombra d'un bel faggio
> tutto pensoso, e rimirando intorno
> vidi assai periglioso il mio viaggio;
> et tornai in dietro quasi a mezzo 'l giorno.
>
> (54, 7–10)

77. For the structural importance of the madrigals in the collection and of the crisis initiated by the voice in poem 54, see Vincenzo Dolla, "Il 'ciclo' dei Madrigali e la struttura del Canzoniere petrarchesco," *Esperienze letterarie*, 4 (1979): 59–76; citation, 68.

78. The "cor vano" of this poem may introduce also an early echo of the *Confessions*, in turn echoing Psalm 5:10, into this amorous rhetoric; see Pierre Courcelle, "Sonnets de Pétrarque et *Confessions* augustiniennes," *Latomus* 23 (1964): 346.

[Then I drew myself to the shadow of a handsome beech, all full
of care, and looking about me I saw my path to be most perilous;
and I turned back almost at midday.]

The midday occurrence prompts a relational reading with the first
madrigal of the collection, "Non al suo amante più Diana piacque" [Not
so much did Diana please her lover] (52), where the lover witnesses the
washing of a veil "or quand' egli arde 'l cielo" [now when the sky is
burning].[79] These equally dramatic representations appear at first to
oppose a spiritual drama in the second poem to the sensual, secular
concerns of the earlier lyric. More profoundly, the two madrigals are
related, in one of the richest allusive amalgams of the collection, to the
myth of Acteon, whose vision of Diana also occurs at midday.[80] The
forbidden sight of the naked Diana is the explicit subtext of madrigal 52,
but it is madrigal 54 that contains the most direct echo of Ovid's telling,
as the bathing goddess is surprised by the ill-fated hunter "wandering
with hesitant steps through this wood which he had never seen before"
(Met. III, 174–76). Thus the dramatic pronouncement of the distant voice
in madrigal 54—"Ahi quanti passi per la selva perdi!"—captures the poet
in his role as Acteon and brings the peril of that encounter to bear on his
spiritual dilemma.

That pronouncement also brings to bear on the moment of crisis
another set of associations as the setting of Rime 54, described before the
intervention of the voice as the green grass, alters suddenly and abruptly
to that of "selva." While equally generic, this new designation has, as we
have seen, an allegorical suggestiveness. Here the protagonist's sudden
awakening in midcourse to the perils of his journey combines with the
forest locus to evoke once again for the reader the early cantos of the
Inferno, and in particular its opening verses.[81] The lost or wasted steps to
which the poet is alerted in the madrigal, moreover, are not unlike those
in Petrarch's account of his ascent of Mount Ventoux, straying in search
of an easy path while his brother proceeds directly up the mountain.[82]

79. For the association of noontide with erotic passion in Petrarch's use of the Acteon
myth in madrigal 52, see Nicolas J. Perella, Midday in Italian Literature: Variations on an
Archetypal Theme (Princeton, 1979), 42.

80. Met. III, 144–45. S. Carrai relates the "mezzo giorno" that marks the end of the
poet's encounter with the cerva in Rime 190 to the Acteon myth as well; see "Il sonetto
'Una candida cerva' di F. Petrarca," Rivista di Letteratura Italiana 3 (1985): 238.

81. The reminiscence of the Inferno here is further confirmed in lexical correlations with
cantos IV, VIII, IX; see Guido Capovilla, "I Madrigali (LII, LIV, CVI, CXXI)," Lectura
Petrarce, III, 1983 (Padua, 1984), 19–22.

82. Martinelli terms it a clear reduplication of the scene of that ascent; see Petrarca e il
Ventoso, 276. See also E. Proto, "Per un madrigale del Petrarca," Rassegna critica della
letteratura italiana 16 (1911): 97–114.

Like the description of that ascent in Petrarch's letter to Dionigi da Borgo San Sepolcro (*Fam.* 4.1), the poem both signals a crisis and records an intervention. In the Ventoux letter, it is the reading of a passage of Augustine's *Confessions* that precipitates the "awakening," and a number of readings of the madrigal conclude that its "alta voce" is that of Augustine, if not that of God himself;[83] in either case, the Augustinian experience of an oracular utterance recorded in the *Confessions* is inscribed into the lyric text as well.[84]

In the *Rime*, however, this intervention is not conclusive. Madrigal 54 is immediately followed by another poem of anomalous metrical form, a ballata which records a new fall into the snares of Amor:

> Quel foco ch'i' pensai che fosse spento
> dal freddo tempo et da l'età men fresca
> fiamma et martir ne l'anima rinfresca.
>
> (55, 1–3)

[That fire which I thought had gone out because of the cold season and my age no longer fresh, now renews flames and suffering in my soul.]

This poem is a response to the madrigal in its negation of a positive consequence of the poet's awareness: although reaffirmed in the verses that follow, that awareness still is countered by Amor, whose appeal is now both different and very much the same: "mi rinvesca" [he enlimes me again]. In this poem the new bondage receives a new formulation as his "second error": "et temo no 'l secondo error sia peggio" [and I am afraid that my second error will be the worse]. The verse, while echoing the warning in the Gospel of Matthew "et erit novissimus error pejor priore,"[85] at the same time confirms the prolongation of the consequences of the *innamoramento* in its recall of the "primo giovenile errore" of *Rime* 1. The escape from the snares of Amor toward another life for

83. For readings of the poem, see Proto, "Per un madrigale del Petrarca," 100–129; Iliescu, *Il canzoniere Petrarchesco e sant'Agostino*, 51–53; Courcelle, "Sonnets de Pétrarque et *Confessions* augustiniennes," 345–47.

84. This coordination has prompted attempts to situate the poem within a larger evolution; for Martinelli it expresses Petrarch's first returning to God under the decisive influence of the *Confessions* (*Petrarca e il Ventoso*, 277). For an analysis of the Ventoux letter itself as measuring the distance between Petrarch's experience and that of Augustine, however, see Robert M. Durling, "The Ascent of Mt. Ventoux and the Crisis of Allegory," *Italian Quarterly* 18 (1974): 7–28.

85. See Martinelli, *Petrarca e il Ventoso*, 278.

which the poet prays in "Padre del ciel" is the escape that God has brought about for the addressee of sonnet 25, but not for the lyric protagonist: the warning heard in *Rime* 54 is echoed at the start of *Rime* 62 in the poet's acknowledgment of his lost days, his "perduti giorni." He invokes divine intervention to effect the change—"lead my wandering thoughts back to a better place"—but in a subsequent sonnet his steps are still lost, wasted, following Laura:

> . . . che' pie' miei non son fiaccati et lassi
> a seguir l'orme vostre in ogni parte,
> perdendo inutilmente tanti passi. . . .
>
> (74, 9–11)

[my feet are not worn and tired of following your footsteps everywhere, wasting in vain so many steps. . . .]

The admonitory voice is nonetheless not to be silenced. Sestina 80, "Chi è fermato di menar sua vita" [He who has decided to lead his life] superimposes the poet's voyage through life and the account of his amorous experience, both cast again in the traditional metaphors of navigation. The "aura soave" or soft breeze to which he had entrusted his craft has led him not to port but to "mille scogli," a thousand rocks. Then the divine voice:

> . . . piacque a lui che mi produsse in vita
> chiamarme tanto indietro da li scogli
> ch'almen da lunge m'apparisse il porto . . .
> così di su la gonfiata vela
> vid'io le 'nsegne di quell'altra vita;
> et allor sospirai verso 'l mio fine.
>
> (80, 16–18, 22–24)

[then it pleased Him who gave me life to call me back far enough from the rocks that at least from afar I might see the port. . . . thus above the swollen sail I saw the ensigns of that other life; and then I sighed toward my end.]

This account replicates the intervention of the voice in madrigal 54, and again the intervention provokes a crisis of self-awareness; again he is called to turn back, "indietro."[86] But the moment of crisis is followed by

---

86. For the lexical elements linking *Rime* 80 and 81 with madrigal 54, and with "Padre del ciel" as well, see Dolla, "Il 'ciclo' dei Madrigali," 68–69.

the admission that his course remains unsure, and the poem closes not with new resolution, but with a prayer:

> Se non ch'i' ardo come acceso legno,
> sì m'è duro a lassar l'usata vita.
> Signor de la mia fine et de la vita:
> prima ch'i' fiacchi il legno tra li scogli
> drizza a buon porto l'affannata vela.

(35–39)

[Except that I burn like kindled wood, it is so hard for me to leave my accustomed life. Lord of my death and of my life: before I shatter my ship on these rocks direct to a good port my weary sail.]

The immediately following sonnet, opening with a lament for that accustomed life, continues with yet another record of a divine intervention, once again with a direct citation of the distant voice:

> Ben venne a dilivrarmi un grande amico
> per somma et ineffabil cortesia;
> poi volò fuor de la veduta mia
> sì ch' a mirarlo indarno m'affatico.
> Ma la sua voce ancor qua giù rimbomba:
> "O voi che travagliate, ecco 'l camino;
> venite a me, se 'l passo altri non serra."

(81, 5–11)

[True, a great Friend did come to free me, in His highest and ineffable graciousness; then He flew out of my sight so that I strive in vain to see Him. But His voice still resounds down here: "O you who labor, here is the way; come to me, if the pass is not blocked by another."]

This dramatic record, concluding with a near-citation from Scripture that extends to the errant poet the invitation proffered by Christ to a weary mankind, is readily assimilated to the larger context of a promise of redemption, encouraging the reader to identify the source of the intervention as Christ himself.[87] Near the close of the *Secretum,* in terms whose

---

87. In his *De otio religioso* II, 76, Petrarch identifies this Scriptural passage in an enumeration of the many ways in which God calls to the soul. See Martinelli, *Petrarca e il Ventoso,* 280, for whom the "grande amico" who voices God's appeal in sonnet 81 is Giacomo Colonna: in *Fam.* V, Petrarch recounts that a dream of his friend calling to him and inviting him to follow had occurred on the day of Colonna's death.

relevance to the poet's course in the *Rime* are immediately evident, Augustinus appeals to Franciscus to heed that other voice: "Listen only to that Holy Spirit who is ever calling, and in urgent words saying, 'Here is the way to your native country, your true home.' You know what He would bring to mind; what paths for your feet, what dangers to avoid. If you would be safe and free obey His voice. There is no need for long deliberations. . . ." Franciscus responds with a prayerful assent that is nonetheless not a promise: "O may it indeed be as you have prayed! May God lead me safe and whole out of so many crooked ways; that I may follow the Voice that calls me. . . ."[88]

The positing of alternatives in *Rime* 142 is, as we have seen, recapitulatory: like the reader's recognition of the vicissitudes of the poet's love for Laura evoked through the several emblems of the sestina, the particular resonance of the *tornada* of this poem is conditioned by recall of the preceding components. The poet of sestina 142, it should be noted, has not exchanged one for the other: he is identified with the first, and if he seeks the alternatives identified in the insistent "altro" of the final tercet, the governing verb is simply that: "cerco." It is one thing to be shown the alternative, even to acknowledge its necessity; it is another entirely to enact it. Nonetheless the necessity for the poet to "far frutto" [bear fruit], substituting the poet for Laura in the arboreal metaphor, reorients the connotations of the rhyme word "frondi" that had stood for the leaves of the laurel itself—"frondi" in turn "belle," "verdi," "sparte," and finally, intimately, "queste"—throughout the preceding stanzas of the poem; it refocuses the reader's attention on the lyric protagonist himself.

If we accept Wilkins's conjecture, in the so-called "Correggio" form of the *Rime* the division between the two parts of the collection fell precisely between sestina 142 and canzone 264. In the definitive version, where the canzone still opens Part II, it is separated from the sestina by almost half the poems of Part I—almost one-third of the poems of the collection as a whole. Yet *Rime* 142 remains in the final form a perceptible marker of recapitulation and a temporary closure;[89] nor are the essential lines of conflict drawn in the sestina eradicated by the poems that follow in Part I, however profuse their praise of Laura's exceptional attributes and her virtue. Near the end of Part I the poet imagines the consequences of the possible loss of his lady, first for the world, then for himself:

88. *Petrarch's Secret*, 189, 192.

89. Foster, who divides Part I thematically, distinguishes the "first section" of the *Rime* as 1–142 to account for the penitential element of the sestina; his "second section," however, opens with canzone 135, to introduce the theme of the "strangeness" of the lover's condition (*Petrarch, Poet and Humanist*, 63–80).

sì ch'io non veggio il gran publico danno
e 'l mondo remaner senza 'l suo sole
né li occhi miei, che luce altra non ànno;
né l'alma, che pensar d'altro non vole,
né l'orecchie, ch'udir altro non sanno,
senza l'oneste sue dolci parole.

(246, 9–14)

[so that I may not see that great public loss, and the world left without its sun, nor my own eyes, which have no other light, nor my soul, which does not wish to think of anything else, nor my ears, which cannot hear anything else, left without her chaste sweet words.]

Here again as throughout Part I, the insistent coupling "non . . . altro," invested again and again with the various terms for Laura's beauty and the lover's response, structures the enumeration of alternatives excluded, alternatives denied.

The continued relevance of the dilemma defined in *Rime* 142 is evident in the recurrence of its principal terms in the dramatic images of canzone 264. The desire to seek the true "abandoning shadows" recalls the shade of the laurel and the desire to flee its enlimed branches; the inclination to "altro lagrimar," a different weeping, recalls the series of alternatives in the *tornada* of the sestina; the "other branches" of 142 are reflected now in the image of the crucified Christ: "quelle pietose braccia / in ch'io mi fido, veggio aperte ancora" [those merciful arms in which I trust I see still open].[90] Once again an admonitory voice speaks directly in the poem, but now it is internalized, a voice of conscience:

L'un penser parla co la mente, et dice:
"Che pur agogni? onde soccorso attendi?
Misera, non intendi
con quanto tuo disnore il tempo passa?"

(264, 19–22)

[One thought speaks to my mind, and says: "What are you yearning for still? whence do you expect help? Wretch, do you not understand with how much dishonor for you time is passing?]

This voice once again is an advocate of change, of an altered course, and its extended exhortation closes with the invocation of the joys of Heaven:

90. See Gorni, "Metamorfosi e redenzione," 12.

"or ti solleva a più beata spene
mirando 'l ciel che ti si volve intorno
immortal et adorno;
ché dove del mal suo qua giù sì lieta
vostra vaghezza acqueta
un mover d'occhi, un ragionar, un canto,
quanto fia quel piacer, se questo è tanto?"

(48–54)

["now raise yourself to a more blessed hope by gazing at the
heavens that revolve around you, immortal and adorned; for if
down here your desire, so happy in its ills, is satisfied by a glance,
a talk, a song, what will that pleasure be, if this is so great?"]

"There is no need for long deliberations": the insistence of Augustinus
in the *Secretum* was perhaps a warning. This persuasive stratagem, in its
reminder of the incomparable beauty of Laura, produces an effect
opposite to that in whose support it is adopted: immediately it gives way
to another thought, this one the bittersweet thought of fame; and that in
turn yields to "quell'altro voler di ch'i' son pieno" [that other desire of
which I am full], and finally to the direct evocation of Laura's eyes. In
earlier poems conflicting thoughts have represented, now a different
course, now a return to Laura, and sober reflection has frequently been
contrasted to the poet's "amoroso pensiero," his amorous thought.[91]
Now *Rime* 264, opening with "I' vo pensando," attributes argumentation
to one thought only, which thus assumes the function of the admonitory
voices heard intermittently in Part I. To its opponent is attributed not
argument, but demonstration: the "other" thought is one that "preme il
cor di desio, di speme il pasce" [oppresses my heart with desire and feeds
it with hope]; the "altro voler" overshadows all others.[92]

In *Rime* 264 the alternatives posited emblematically in sestina 142 are
drawn with a new clarity. They are the alternatives between earthly and
Heavenly love now set in lucid opposition, as the poet draws the
consequences of his love for Laura:

Ché mortal cosa amar con tanta fede
quanto a Dio sol per debito convensi
più si disdice a chi più pregio brama.

---

91. See for example *Rime* 68 and 72.

92. See the acute observations of Francesco De Sanctis, *Saggio critico sul Petrarca* (Turin,
ed. "Gli Struzzi" 1983), 128.

Et questo ad alta voce anco richiama
la ragione sviata dietro ai sensi.

(264, 99–103)

[For the more one desires honor, the more one is forbidden to love a mortal thing with the faith that belongs to God alone. And this with a loud voice calls back my reason, which wanders after my senses.]

This recall "ad alta voce" renews the drama of intervention by the "alta voce di lontano" of madrigal 54, and the moment of response, when the message is heard and the lover is poised in the act of turning, of altering his course, is captured here in its compelling immediacy. This passage contains an encapsulated recapitulation of all the poems in Part I in which a divine intervention erupts into the story of the poet's love for Laura, and that story, enchanted in the strong sense of the term, is momentarily cast into a strong external light. In the opening stanza of canzone 264, the terms of the opposition between earth and Heaven recall both the anguished question that closes *Rime* 81, in the poet's cry for wings to lift himself up from earth, and the course toward Heaven:

mille fiate ò chieste a Dio quell'ale
co le quai del mortale
carcere nostr'intelletto al Ciel si leva.

(264, 6–8)

[a thousand times I have asked God for those wings with which our intellect raises itself from this mortal prison to Heaven.]

Yet in the ordering of Part I, other poems postulating alternatives have been followed by relapses: both "Padre del Ciel" and sestina 142 itself distinguish a present awareness from a past state of error, and both are immediately followed by poems that reaffirm Laura's dominion over the poet, a sequencing whose possibility of coincidence is doubtful because of the depiction in both texts of the lady as holding the keys to the poet's heart and of the poet as delighting in his captivity.

Like the hermit's exegetical rereading of Lancelot's love for Guenevere in the *Quête*, the admonitory voices that speak in the *Rime sparse* urge upon the poet a rereading of his own story. The traces of that rereading, while seldom explicitly marked, are as pervasive as those of his solitary footsteps; they are revealed by the record of his thoughts as he proceeds "di pensier in pensier, di monte in monte" (129),[93] and they inform the opening verses of Part II of the collection:

> I' vo pensando, et nel penser m'assale
> una pietà sì forte di me stesso
> che mi conduce spesso
> ad altro lagrimar ch'i' non soleva.
>
> (264, 1–4)

[I go thinking and in thought pity for myself assails me, so strong that it often leads me to a weeping different from my accustomed one.]

Yet canzone 264 records once again, and repeatedly, the resurgence of the beloved image and the failure to effect the decisive change of direction:

> ma perch' ell' [la ragione] oda et pensi
> tornare, il mal costume oltre la spigne
> et agli occhi depigne
> quella che sol per farmi morir nacque,
> perch' a me troppo et a se stessa piacque.
>
> (264, 104–8)

[but although it [my reason] hears and thinks to come back, its bad habit drives it further and depicts for my eyes her who was born to make me die, since she pleased me and herself too much.]

Although "vergogna et duol" press for a change in course, they are opposed by "un piacer per usanza . . . sì forte / ch'a patteggiar n'ardisce co la Morte" [a pleasure so strong in me by habit that it dares to bargain with Death]. Thus the poet is immobilized in his conflicting desires, and it is not on a note of victory that the poem ends:

> che co la Morte a lato
> cerco del viver mio novo consiglio,
> et veggio 'l meglio et al peggior m'appiglio.
>
> (264, 134–36)

---

93. In the sonnet "Quanto più m'avicino al giorno extremo" Armando Balduino finds one of the earliest and most lucid demonstrations of Love as catalyst for self-knowledge and for a meditation on man's destiny; see "Il sonetto XXXII," *Lectura Petrarce, I, 1981* (Padua, 1982), 33. On solitude as a necessary condition for this meditation, see M. Pastore Stocchi, "Divagazione su due solitari: Bellerofonte e Petrarca," in *Da Dante al Novecento* (Milan, 1970), 63–83.

[for with Death at my side I seek new counsel for my life, and I see the better but I lay hold on the worse.]

This final verse, despite its apparent moral candor, echoes the anguished deliberations of Ovid's Medea, whose state is very much like that of Petrarch's poet.[94] And that poet has already proclaimed his condition in *Rime* 264 with an almost exact translation of Medea's words to Jason as she attempts in vain to master an ill-fated passion that she herself condemns: "Quel ch'i' fo veggio; et non m'inganna il vero / mal conosciuto, anzi mi sforza Amore . . ." [I see what I am doing, and I am not deceived by an imperfect knowledge of the truth; rather Love forces me].[95] Despite the passing of the years, the injury received on the occasion of the *innamoramento* still impedes his escape.

In the *Secretum,* when Franciscus attempts to defend his love for Laura, Augustinus remarks that "in all the passions, and most of all in this, every man interprets his own case favorably."[96] Here the stress falls, as Victoria Kahn observes, on the willfulness or eroticism of such self-interpretation.[97] In the fictive time of the *Secretum,* however, Laura is still very much *in vita,* as she is still *in vita* in *Rime* 264. In that canzone the death repeatedly evoked is that of the poet himself; the statement of his spiritual dilemma does not yet take into account the death of Laura. But that occurrence, of course, is the second decisive "event" of the collection, second only to the *innamoramento* in determining his fate. What then will be its impact on the precarious tension between the "meglio" and the "peggior," the better and the worse so defined in this poem that opens Part II of the *Rime sparse?*

Does the poet become, with the death of Laura, a reliable reader of his own experience of love, that experience that dominates the present of Part II of the collection as it had dominated its past? This is the question that will be addressed in the following chapter. It is a question rendered more insistent, in the context of the concerns of the present chapter, by

94. *Met.* VII, 20–21: "video meliora proboque / deteriora sequor" ["I see which is the better course, and I approve it; but still I follow the worse"]. With this near-quotation here in this position of extreme emphasis, Jill Tilden suggests that "Petrarch gives himself the exemplary status of a ritual victim, committed to a ritual guilt"; see "Spiritual Conflict in Petrarch's *Canzoniere,*" in *Petrarca 1304–1374: Beiträge zu Werk und Wirkung,* ed. F. Schalk (Frankfurt, 1975), 305. Petrarch's phrase suggests too the ascetic tradition of patristic commentaries on man's earthly nature; see Martinelli, *Petrarca e il Ventoso,* 268–69.

95. *Met.* VII, 92–93: "Quid faciam, video; non ignorantia veri / decipiet, sed Amor" [I see clearly what I am doing: love, not ignorance of the truth, will lead me astray"].

96. *Petrarch's Secret,* 120.

97. Victoria Kahn, "The Figure of the Reader in Petrarch's *Secretum,*" *PMLA* 100 (1985): 160–61.

the accusation leveled by the poet late in the collection against Amor, his longtime adversary: "Questi m'à fatto men amare Dio / ch' i' non deveva, et men curar me stesso" [He has made me love God less than I ought and be less concerned for myself] (360). This is precisely the accusation that Augustinus in the *Secretum* levels against Franciscus concerning his love for Laura: that it had deflected his love from the Creator to the creature, perverting its order.

5

DESTINATIONS

Laura *in vita*, like stilnovistic ladies before her, is repeatedly proclaimed to be a marvel of nature, a wondrous creature suggestive of divine creation:

> Non era l'andar suo cosa mortale
> ma d'angelica forma, et le parole
> sonavan altro che pur voce umana.
>
> (90, 9–11)

[Her walk was not like that of a mortal thing but of some angelic form, and her words sounded different from a merely human voice.]

After her death her poet at last understands the cause of that singularity, that "non . . . cosa mortale" of her terrestrial movement, that "sonavan altro" of her voice. Laura was a miracle:

> L'alto et novo miracol ch'a' dì nostri
> apparve al mondo et star seco non volse,
> che sol ne mostrò 'l Ciel, poi sel ritolse
> per adornarne i suoi stellanti chiostri. . . .
>
> (309, 1–4)

[The high new miracle that in our days appeared in the world and did not wish to stay in it, that Heaven merely showed to us and then took back to adorn its starry cloisters. . . .]

If we read this explanation as more than amorous hyperbole exacerbated by grief, the affirmation is surely daring. Yet like many other elements of

Petrarch's depiction of Laura already considered, it appropriates the authority of an illustrious literary model, the Beatrice of the *Vita Nuova* whose role will be fully realized in the *Commedia*.[1] It is after the death of Beatrice that the protagonist of Dante's *libello* explicates that which has been already intimated in visions and in signs: her persistent correlation with the number nine is indicative of her status as a miracle.[2] In the same chapter, however, Dante adds a highly significant remark: "Perhaps a more subtle mind could find a still more subtle reason for it; but this is the one which I perceive and which pleases me the most." So does it please Laura's poet, affording him an explanation of that presence that surpassed his understanding.

This proclamation of Laura's miraculous nature is particularly important because much of our reading of the *Rime sparse* ultimately depends upon our reading of the status of Laura. For a number of recent readers, that status is like to—and probably patterned on—that of Dante's Beatrice. For Martinelli, in the *Rime* and the *Trionfi* Petrarch juxtaposes to the Beatrice-Christ of the *Vita Nuova* and the *Commedia* the figure of Laura-Christ and Laura-Virgin.[3] Yet the role of Laura *in vita*, as we have seen, is more frequently contrasted to that of Beatrice, the recalls of the role of Beatrice repeatedly subverted by their context in the *Rime*. In the opening poem of Part II, moreover, closely preceding the revelation of Laura's death, Amor still spurs the poet along a course perceived as opposed to that of divine love:

> Quelle pietose braccia
> in ch'io mi fido veggio aperte ancora,
> ma temenza m'accora
> per gli altrui esempli, et del mio stato tremo,
> ch'altri mi sprona et son forse a l'estremo.
>
> (264, 14–18)

1. For the lady as "new" miracle, see especially the closing of Dante's sonnet "Ne li occhi" (*Vita Nuova* XXI): "sì è novo miracolo e gentile." For such claims in relation to vernacular antecedents, see Bernhard König, *"Dolci rime leggiadre": Zur Verwendung und Verwandlung stilnovistischer Elemente in Petrarcas* Canzoniere," in *Petrarca 1304–1374: Beiträge zu Werk und Wirkung*, ed. F. Schalk (Frankfurt, 1975), 113–38.

2. Thus Beatrice was by analogy a number nine, the number of miracles whose root is the Trinity (*VN* XXIX). Here and henceforth, the translation cited of the *Vita Nuova* is that of Barbara Reynolds (Harmondsworth, 1969). For the seriousness of Dante's affirmation, attested in the prose, that sets it apart from the hyperbolies of earlier love poets, see Charles S. Singleton, *An Essay on the "Vita Nuova"* (Cambridge, Mass., 1949; repr. Baltimore, 1977), 6–13.

3. Bortolo Martinelli, *Petrarca e il Ventoso* (Bari, 1977), 233.

[Those merciful arms in which I trust I see still open; but fear grasps my heart at the examples of others, and I tremble for my state; another spurs me and I am perhaps at the end.]

The casting of Laura as the poet's "beatrice," then, remains to be examined in a reading of the poems *in morte*.

In one sense, of course, Laura's death affords a new beginning to the poet's story, and some of Petrarch's most sensitive readers have concluded that, with her death, "everything changes." Based on diverse premises, their readings converge in the conviction that Laura's death initiates a radical if gradually effected change in the poet's response, from concupiscence to *caritas*. Thomas Roche, suggesting that the poems of the *Rime* are ordered according to a calendrical structure that sets the Nativity off against the crucifixion as Laura's death is set off against the *innamoramento*, concludes that "Petrarch indulges his longings without success, until he learns that Laura has died, when—deprived of the physical object of his desires—he learns to love her truly for her virtues by the end of the sequence."[4] Laura *in morte* thus comes to represent that "altro amor" perceived but unachieved in Part I of the collection; she will, like Beatrice, inspire a redirection of her poet's love toward Heaven. Kenelm Foster draws the lines of this reading with unusual precision, proposing that Part II of the collection gives us "Petrarch's liberation," in which two factors collaborate. The first of these is the removal by death of Laura's real body, which despite her virtue and innocence had remained *in vita* a source of temptation. The second is due to Laura herself *in morte:* "the liberation or purification proceeds, under Laura's influence, exerted through the apparitions, in three stages. Petrarch is first freed from despair, then from the carnal desire of Laura, finally from identifying his *summum bonum* with Laura whether carnally or spiritually considered."[5]

Proponents of this new appreciation of Laura, one that invites us to read Part II of the *Rime* "against" Part I, may well point out that within the collection the protagonist himself sets the example, for in the early section of the poems *in morte* we find him advancing a new conception of her response to him when yet *in vita:* "Or comincio a svegliarmi, et veggio . . ." [Now I begin to awaken, and I see . . .] (289); "or mi diletta

---

4. Thomas P. Roche, Jr., "The Calendrical Structure of Petrarch's *Canzoniere*," *Studies in Philology* 71 (1974): 166.

5. Kenelm Foster, *Petrarch, Poet and Humanist* (Edinburgh, 1984), 73, 77, 81. See also Fredi Chiappelli, "Le thème de la *defectio solis* dans le *Canzoniere: Variatio intus*," in *Il legame musaico*, ed. Pier Massimo Forni (Rome, 1984), 178–79.

et piace / quel che più mi dispiacque, or veggio . . ." [now I am pleased and delighted by what most displeased me . . .] (290). This avowed revision, moreover, has its literary precedent in Dante's *Convivio*, in his explanation that what he had once protested as the "disdainful and cruel acts" of his lady were instead the manifestations of her perfect chastity.[6] Such declarations in the *Rime*, consistent with poems at the end of Part I that identify chastity as Laura's principal virtue, presume a continuity between the influence attributed to her *in morte* and one which she deliberately exercised *in vita*, that benevolent manipulation of his emotional response whose modalities are explained in the *Trionfi*, as we have seen, by Laura herself.[7]

Yet the claim to credence of this affirmation of salutary new insight must be evaluated in the light of other poems that precede and follow it. Preceding is a series of poems that represent the immediate response to Laura's death, and here again comparison with the *Vita Nuova* is highly suggestive. Dante's bereaved poet-lover too had recorded the death of his lady. Following his notation of her death as "her departure from us," however, he explicitly denies it further comment (*VN* XXVIII, 1–2), turning instead to meditation on her spiritual significance. This minimal attention to the physical death of Beatrice, as Moleta observes, is not unlike his minimal attention to her physical person *in vita*, necessary to prevent the interference of a well-defined image or memory of her body in the spiritual influence that she exercises following her death.[8] It is the term Death, "Morte," conspicuously absent from this section of the *Vita Nuova*, that tolls insistently in each of the series of poems responding to Laura's death in the *Rime sparse* (267–78), and it is repeatedly coupled with an insistence on the physical beauty now lost: "Oimè il bel viso" [Alas the lovely face] (267); "Oimè, terra è fatto il suo bel viso" [Alas, her beautiful face has become clay] (268); "ritogli a Morte quel ch'ella n'à tolto / et ripon le tue insegne nel bel volto" [take back from Death what she has taken from us, and set up your standard again in that beautiful face], the poet defiantly challenges Amor (270). The thought of Heaven as Laura's new abode produces an intense recall of Laura on earth, and the place long associated with her physical presence, now the place of her burial, inspires a litany of striking physical immediacy: "Et

6. See Paolo Possiedi, "Con quella spada ond' elli ancise Dido," *MLN* 89 (1974): 34.

7. See Aldo Bernardo, *Petrarch, Laura and the "Triumphs"* (Albany, N.Y., 1974), 200: "By using chastity as his catalytic agent [Petrarch] finally appears to discover in the final Triumph how to convert earthly love into heavenly love without eliminating either."

8. See the comments of Vincent Moleta, " 'Oggi fa l'anno che nel ciel salisti': una rilettura della *Vita Nuova* XXVII–XXXIV," *Giornale storico della letteratura italiana* 161 (1984): 85.

tu che copri et guardi et ài or teco, / felice terra! quel bel viso umano"
[And you, happy earth, who cover and guard and have with you that
lovely human face] (276).[9]

The emphasis in these poems, following close upon the revelation of
Laura's death, results not in a meditation on her spiritual qualities but in
a lament for an apparently incontestable consequence: that the poet will
never see her again. "Her invisible form is in Paradise," he exclaims to
Amor in the first of these poems, and affirms that "mai veder lei /
di quà non spero" [I never hope to see her on this side] (268). There follow
several components that evoke Laura's beauty and grace only to empha-
size the chasm between the mortal world now empty of them and the
Heaven where they are henceforth to be found. The grieving poet
addresses his unappeased senses that have lost all they desired, "vederla,
udirla et ritrovarla in terra" [to see her, hear her, and find her on earth]
(275).

Laura is dead, he will not see her again. But the "story," of course,
does not end here. In the first poem *in morte* in which her continuing
influence over the poet is declared, it is from Heaven that she rules him—
but in terms that are startlingly reminiscent of her influence *in vita:*

> lasciando in terra la terrena scorza
> è l'aura mia vital da me partita
> et viva et bella et nuda al Ciel salita;
> indi mi signoreggia, indi mi sforza.
>
> (278, 3–6)

> [leaving her earthly vesture to earth, my vital breeze has departed
> from me and, alive and beautiful and naked, has risen to Heaven;
> from there she rules me, from there she forces me.]

The first two of these verses reinstate in a funereal key two of the
pervasive metaphors of Laura's presence *in vita*. The "scorza" evocative
of Daphne's metamorphosis, adapted earlier, as we have seen, to render
the simultaneity of lady and laurel as present objects of the poet's desire,
now finalizes the separation of body and spirit effected by death; the
departure of the poet's "aura," now qualified as "vitale," suggests not
only Laura's death but his own. Again, however, in "l'aura mia" we
recognize also Laura herself, and here, despite the clear acknowledgment
of her death, the verbs suggest not the spiritual admonitions of a soul in

9. So too in the *Trionfi:* "Felice sasso che 'l bel viso serra!" [Happy the stone that
covers her fair face!] (*Tr. Eter.* 142).

Paradise but the domination to which the poet had been subjected by Amor. The doctrinal plausibility of Laura's ascent to Heaven as "viva"— a living soul—is of course assured, and the Augustinian insistence on the paradox of earthly life as a living death set against life eternal is frequently echoed in Petrarch's corpus.[10] The coupling of "viva" with both "bella" and "nuda," however, betrays that the poet imagines her not as a disembodied soul in Heaven but as the beloved physical presence, confirmed in the recurrence of the term in the very next poem:

> là v'io seggia d'amor pensoso et scriva,
> lei che 'l Ciel ne mostrò, terra n'asconde
> veggio et odo et intendo, ch'ancor viva
> di sì lontano a' sospir miei risponde.
>
> (279, 5–8)

[where I am sitting in thoughts of love and writing, I see her whom Heaven showed us and the earth hides from us, I see and hear and understand her, for, still alive, from far away she replies to my sighs.]

The bereaved poet of the *Vita Nuova* finds comfort in the hopeful projection of a continued relationship that transcends death: "qual ch'io sia la mia donna il si vede, / et io ne spero ancor da lei merzede" [whatsoe'er I am, my lady sees and from her mercy still I hope for ease] (*VN* XXXI, "Li occhi dolenti per pietà del core," 69–70). Thus too Petrarch's poet: "sa ben Amor qual io divento, et (spero) / vede 'l colei ch'è or sì presso al vero" [Love knows well what I become, and, I hope, she sees it who is now so close to the truth] (268). The hope for Beatrice's "merzede," however, will only be fulfilled in the Otherworld of the *Commedia*, while in the *Rime* Laura returns to the poet's world to offer counsel and consolation. Finally Laura's poet finds himself once again in Valchiusa, where the landscape marked and once animated by her presence now serves as its enduring witness. The immediate consequence of this return is the rejection of a world from which Laura is absent:

> Ma tu, ben nata, che dal Ciel mi chiami,
> per la memoria di tua morte acerba
> preghi ch'i' sprezzi 'l mondo e i suoi dolci ami.
>
> (280, 12–14)

---

10. See poems 216, 324; *Tr. Mor.* 22.

[But you, born in a happy hour, who call me from Heaven: by the memory of your untimely death you beg me to scorn the world and its sweet hooks.]

The following sonnet, however, abruptly and dramatically reverses that denial. Retreating to his sweet hiding place, his "dolce ricetto," he declares that he has seen Laura again in that setting:

> Or in forma di ninfa o d'altra diva
> che del più chiaro fondo di Sorga esca
> et pongasi a sedere in su la riva,
> or l'ò veduto su per l'erba fresca
> calcare i fior com' una donna viva,
> mostrando in vista che di me le 'ncresca.
>
> (281, 9–14)

[Now in the form of a nymph or other goddess who comes forth from the deepest bed of Sorgue and sits on the bank, now I have seen her treading the fresh grass like a living woman, showing by her face that she is sorry for me.]

Once again Laura is alive, "viva," in an experience whose hallucinatory nature is underlined by the other forms of water sprite or goddess that she assumes, in clear resonance with the projections of her acknowledged *in vita:*

> I' l'ò più volte (or chi fia che mi l' creda?)
> ne l'acqua chiara et sopra l'erba verde
> veduto viva, et nel troncon d'un faggio
> e'n bianca nube . . .
>
> (129, 40–43)[11]

[I have many times (now who will believe me?) seen her alive in the clear water and on the green grass and in the trunk of a beech tree and in a white cloud . . .]

The difference is not in the status of the apparition but in the affective posture with which the poet now invests it. In the third of this series of

11. For the relation of these "reappearances" of Laura to *Rime* 176 *in vita*, see Domenico De Robertis, "La traversata della Ardenne (Sonetti CLXXVI e CLXXVII)," *Lectura Petrarce, VI, 1986* (Padua, 1987), 223–28.

poems on his return to Valchiusa he confirms triumphantly that she now comes there to console him:

> quanto gradisco ch' e' miei tristi giorni
> a rallegrar de tua vista consenti!
> così comincio a ritrovar presenti
> le tue bellezze a' suoi usati soggiorni.
>
> (282, 5–8)

[how I rejoice that you consent to make glad my sad days with the sight of you! Thus I begin to find your beauties present in their usual surroundings.]

In her return to this privileged setting, this Laura is not a heavenly spirit who offers pious counsel; she is the Laura of her "usual surroundings," the Laura of the *innamoramento* who sits on the bank and moves through the flowers, once again intimately familiar:

> Sol un riposo trovo in molti affanni,
> che quando torni te conosco e 'ntendo
> a l'andar, a la voce, al volto, a' panni.
>
> (282, 12–14)[12]

[I find but one repose in so much anguish, that when you return I know you, by your walk, by your voice, by your face, by your dress.]

To speak of this Laura, moreover, is still to speak of love:

> et se come ella parla et come luce
> ridir potessi, accenderei d'amore
> non dirò d'uom, un cor di tigro o d'orso.
>
> (283, 12–14)

[and if I could tell how she speaks and how she shines, I would inflame with love not only a man's but a tiger's or a bear's heart.]

---

12. For emphasis here on the illusion of Laura's physical presence in this poem, see Oscar Büdel, "*Parusia Redemtricis:* Lauras Traumbesuche in Petrarcas *Canzoniere*," in *Petrarca 1304–1374: Beiträge zu Werk und Wirkung*, ed. Fritz Schalk (Frankfurt, 1975), 40–41. Teodolinda Barolini notes "the literalization of the turning-back topos" in Part II of the collection; see "The Making of a Lyric Sequence: Time and Narrative in Petrarch's *Rerum vulgarium fragmenta*," *MLN* 104 (1989): 34.

In this sense, if with the death of Laura "everything is changed," with her return very little is changed:

> Amor, che m'à legato et tienmi in croce,
> trema quando la vede in su la porta
> de l'alma, ove m'ancide ancor sì scorta,
> sì dolce in vista, et sì soave in voce.
>
> (284, 5–8)

[Love, who has bound me and keeps me in torment, trembles when he sees her at the gate of the soul, where she still slays me, so alert, so sweet to see, and so gentle of voice.]

This is unmistakably the "old" Laura, she whose appearance is still under the sign, not of piety, but of Amor, and the poet's response is a benediction no less amorous and no less secular than that of the famous sonnet in Part I in which he celebrates the *innamoramento* ("Benedetto sia 'l giorno e 'l mese et l'anno" [Blessed be the day and the month and the year], 61), or of the later sonnet in which he celebrates the twentieth anniversary of its occurrence by declaring himself "beato in sogno et di languir contento" [blessed in sleep and satisfied to languish] (212). In the latter poem he has been blinded by the splendor of the lady's light; now she returns *in morte:*

> l'alma, che tanta luce non sostene,
> sospira et dice: "O benedette l'ore
> del dì che questa via con li occhi apristi!"
>
> (284, 12–14)

[my soul, who cannot bear so much light, sighs and says: "Oh, blessed the hours of the day when you opened this path with your eyes!"]

In the immediately following poem, the beautiful sonnet "Né mai pietosa madre al caro figlio" [Never did a pitying mother to her dear son] in which Laura's "new" role is defined, she offers him counsel prompted by a "doppia pietate . . . or di madre, or d'amante" [double pity . . . now that of a mother, now that of a lover]. Once cruel or indifferent, now affectionate and kind; once inaccessible, now intimately consolatory: the role assumed by this Laura contrasts sharply with that recorded and lamented in so many components of Part I. "This kind of spiritual intimacy between a man and a woman," Foster suggests, "is something new in Italian literature," one that effects "a sublimation of sensual desire, *amor concupiscentiae*, into friendship, *amor amicitiae*."[13] But this, of course, is also the favorable attitude and favorable response on the part of Laura fantasized by the poet in Part I of the collection:

> "forse a te stesso vile, altrui se' caro";
> et in questa trapasso sospirando:
> "Or porrebbe esser ver? or come? or quando?"
>
> (129, 24–26)

["perhaps, though vile to yourself, you are dear to someone else." And I go over to this thought, sighing: "Now could it be true? But how? but when?"]

and again:

> "Che sai tu, lasso? forse in quella parte
> or di tua lontananza si sospira."
> Et in questo penser l'anima respira.
>
> (63–65)[14]

["What do you know, wretch? perhaps off there someone is sighing now because of your absence."]

In much the same vein, during a separation from her still *in vita* he imagines her longing to be reunited with him: "forse (o che spero!) il mio tardar le dole" [perhaps (Oh what do I hope for!) my slowness pains her] (208).[15]

That "forse," never resolved in Part I of the *Rime*, is given a melancholy summation by the poet himself early in Part II:

> Soleano i miei penser soavemente
> di lor oggetto ragionare inseme:
> "Pietà s'appressa et del tardar si pente;
> forse or parla di noi, o spera o teme."
> Poi che l'ultimo giorno et l'ore estreme

---

13. Foster, *Petrarch, Poet and Humanist*, 45–46.

14. Of the "rhetorical economy of exchange" in this passage, see Timothy Bahti, "Petrarch and the Scene of Writing: A Reading of *Rime* CXXIX," *Yale Italian Studies* 1 (1980): 52.

15. On this Laura "pietosa e soccorrevole" *in morte* as a deception, see Domenico De Robertis, "Petrarca petroso," *Revue des Etudes Italiennes* 29 (1983): 37.

spogliar di lei questa vita presente,
nostro stato dal Ciel vede, ode et sente;
altra di lei non è rimaso speme.

(295, 1–8)

[My thoughts used to converse together gently about their object: "She will soon feel pity and be sorry for the delay; perhaps she now speaks of us, or hopes, or fears." Since the last day and the final hour have despoiled this present life of her, she sees, hears, and feels our state from Heaven: no other hope of her remains.]

Despite the apparent resignation of this avowal, there is that last widowed hope that remains, and it is one that opens new vistas. Laura's death, precluding a mutual avowal of love on earth, nurtures the hope of one in Heaven; the fantasy of her impatience for an anticipated reunion mirrors the earlier fantasy, identical except in the locus of its projected occurrence. It is not by chance that the first indication of her tender concern for the poet in Part II occurs in response to his desperate cry to Amor, "Che debb'io far? che mi consigli, Amore?" [What shall I do? What do you counsel me, Love?]. To his declaration of loss and the temptation to end his life Amor urges that he not be led by his intense sorrow to lose his hope of that Heaven

"dove è viva colei ch'altrui par morta
et di sue belle spoglie
seco sorride et sol di te sospira . . ."

(268, 70–72)

["where she is alive who seems dead, and she smiles to herself at her beautiful remains and sighs only for you . . ."]

With this return of Laura in dream, in fantasy, or in recollection return all the symptoms of the poet's love. In the *Secretum* Augustinus catalogs those symptoms in terms unmistakable to the reader of the *Rime:*

. . . how suddenly you fell to bemoaning, and came to such a pitch of wretchedness that you felt a morbid pleasure in feeding on tears and sighs. Passing sleepless nights, and murmuring ever the name of your beloved, scorning everything, hating life, desiring death, with a melancholy love for being alone, avoiding all your fellow-men . . . and the very sound of your words, indistinct and broken, with whatever other token can be imagined, of a heart distressed and in disorder? Do you call these the signs of good health? Was it not this lady with whom for you every day, whether feast or fast, began and ended? Was it not at her coming the sun shone forth, and when she left you, night returned? Every change of her countenance brought a change in your heart . . ."[16]

"In a word," Augustinus summarizes his analysis, "your life became totally dependent upon hers." Petrarch's interlocutor, of course, refers to Laura yet *in vita*, but his words apply as well to the poet's response to the Laura "refound" *in morte*, a dependence that is confirmed when for an interval he is deprived of her nocturnal visits:

> Dolce mio caro et prezioso pegno
> che Natura mi tolse e 'l Ciel mi guarda:
> deh, come è tua pietà ver me sì tarda,
> o usato di mia vita sostegno?
> Già suo' tu far il mio sonno almen degno
> de la tua vista, et or sostien ch'i' arda
> senz' alcun refrigerio, et chi 'l retarda?
> Pur lassù non alberga ira né sdegno. . . .
>
> (340, 1–8)

[Sweet, dear, and precious pledge of mine, whom Nature took from me and Heaven keeps for me: ah, how is it that your pity for me is so tardy, O accustomed sustainer of my life? You used to make my sleep at least worthy of the sight of you, and now you suffer me to burn without any relief, and who delays it? Surely up there no anger or scorn dwells. . . .]

It is reaffirmed, and gratefully, as she returns with advice and consolation:

> Deh, qual pietà, qual angel fu sì presto
> a portar sopra 'l cielo il mio cordoglio?
> ch'ancor sento tornar pur come soglio
> Madonna in quel suo atto dolce onesto
> ad acquetare il cor misero et mesto. . . .
>
> (341, 1–5)

---

16. *Petrarch's Secret*, 133–34.

[Ah, what pity, what angel was so swift to carry above the heavens my heartfelt sorrow? For again, as I am wont, I feel my lady return with that sweet chaste bearing of hers to quiet my wretched sad heart. . . .]

The "refound" Laura will speak to him again and again of the past that they had shared, remind him of their last encounter, and explicate the rigors of her conduct that had caused him pain. "Cotando i casi de la vita nostra" [telling over the events of our life]: this verse of sonnet 285 summarizes the continual retelling and reliving of that story in the poems *in morte di Laura*.[17]

It is uncontestable, and Petrarch's readers have often remarked, that this Laura of Part II seems more immediate, more concrete, and more "real" than the elusive lady *in vita*. Are we then to attribute to her *in morte* a status different from that of the Laura projected alternately by the poet's fearful or cherishing imagination in the poems of Part I of the collection? To accept this status without further scrutiny would be to forget that physical separation from Laura *in vita* is not an obstacle to vividly imagined contact. In a poem late in Part I the poet tells us that his soul, tormented at night by thoughts of Laura, abandons him, "et di tal nodo sciolta, / vassene pur a lei" [loosed from that knot goes off still to her]:

> Meravigliomi ben s'alcuna volta,
> mentre le parla et piange et poi l'abbraccia,
> non rompe il sonno suo, s'ella l'ascolta.
>
> (256, 12–14)

[I marvel if at some time, while my soul speaks to her and weeps and then embraces her, her sleep is not broken, if she is listening.]

In both its expression of intense desire and its physical immediacy, this nocturnal encounter anticipates the visits of Laura *in morte* to the poet's bedside; despite the appeal of this "new" Laura, there are compelling indications in the poems *in morte* that she is no less the creation of his deliberate imagining, no less a projection of his desires, than the "old" Laura.

In Part II as in Part I these are all, finally, fantasies, the cherished

---

17. Barolini calls attention to the heightened narrativity of Part II of the collection, the fashioning by the poet of a narrative regarding both their past and their present together; see "The Making of a Lyric Sequence," esp. 30–35.

projections of a cherishing imagination. This Laura enacts with the poet the scenes that were denied him *in vita*. Had she lived, he laments, with their advancing age when lovers may properly sit and speak together (315) he would have revealed to her the ancient burden of his thoughts of love (317); late in Part II the compassionate lady who returns to him in a dream emboldens him to tell her of the pain that he would not have dared to relate to her alive, a long story to which she listens silently and attentively (356). The compensatory relation in which this Laura *in morte* replaces the lost Laura adored *in vita*, moreover, is highly suggestive of the nature of the poet's attachment to the latter; it shows him constantly looking backward to a privileged moment of presence.[18] Part I found him looking back not only in time, nourishing his memory of moments spent in Laura's presence, but in space, toward her landscape:

> Io mi rivolgo indietro a ciascun passo
> col corpo stanco ch'a gran pena porto,
> et prendo allor del vostr'aere conforto
> che 'l fa gir oltra, dicendo: "Oimè, lasso."
>
> (15, 1–4)

[I turn back at each step with my weary body which with great effort I carry forward, and I take then some comfort from your sky, which enables my body to go onward, saying: "Alas, woe's me!"]

He would "turn back" time as well, if it were in his power (86). He laments its irreversible passage: "Né spero i dolci dì tornino indietro . . ." [nor do I hope that the sweet days will come back] (124). This tendency will be accentuated with the death of Laura, when all "happy" time is necessarily "past" time:

> Che fai? che pensi? chè pur dietro guardi
> nel tempo che tornar non pote omai?
> Anima sconsolata, ché pur vai
> giugnendo legno al foco ove tu ardi?
>
> (273, 1–4)

[What are you doing? What are you thinking? Why do you still look back to a time that can never return anymore?]

---

18. See De Robertis, "Petrarca petroso," 37. In the appearances of Laura *in morte*, he observes, "all'idolo . . . s'è sostituito il suo fantasma."

This backward looking is a backward longing—and it is precisely that against which Augustinus in the *Secretum* warns his disciple, who has acknowledged the spiritual peril inherent in his love and inquired as to the means by which to escape it: "You must . . . make your soul ready, and teach it to renounce the object of its love, never once to turn back, never to see that which it was wont to look for," the saint urges, and goes on to cite approvingly the words of Seneca: "If any man wishes to have done with love he must avoid all recollection of the beloved form. . . . For nothing is so easily rekindled to life again as love."[19] The poet of the *Rime* does not follow the prescription for a remedy urged upon the Franciscus of the *Secretum,* to avoid the familiar places that remind him of his captivity: we have seen that the series of poems which present the renewal of contact with Laura *in morte,* the initiation of her pious nocturnal visits or her imagined responses from Heaven to his sighs, are the same poems in which he recaptures her image in the familiar surroundings of Valchiusa.

We recall the transformation worked upon this privileged place by the presence of Laura *in vita.* The poet who exclaims of the lady seen there on the day of the *innamoramento,* "She was surely born in Paradise!" addresses its air as "holy" (126), and celebrates the landscape of Valchiusa as a "blessed place" (188). It is defined by Laura's presence, her beauty, and only that presence, that beauty, are necessary for its definition. Access is conferred by the sight of Laura: in her presence, the poet's soul is drawn from him toward its earthly paradise, "per gir nel paradiso suo terreno" (173). Enumerating his losses after her death, he will recall "gli occhi . . . et le braccia et le mani e i piedi e 'l viso . . . le crespe chiome d'or puro lucente / e 'l lampeggiar de l'angelico riso" [those eyes . . . and the arms and the hands and the feet and the face . . . the curling locks of pure shining gold, and the lightning of the angelic smile] as those attributes "che solean fare in terra un paradiso" [that used to make a paradise on earth] (292).

This designation of the locus of an amorous epiphany is of course not unprecedented in the lyric tradition.[20] In the *Rime,* however, it frequently acquires an additional resonance, as in "Chiare, fresche, et dolci acque" where the same experience is described:

> Quante volte diss'io
> allor, pien di spavento:

19. *Petrarch's Secret,* 144–45; Seneca, *Epist.,* lxiv.
20. See N. Scarano, "Fonti provenzali e italiane nella lirica petrarchesca," *Studi di filologia romanza* 8 (1901): 291; Antonio Daniele, "Il sonetto CCXLV," *Lectura Petrarce, VI, 1986* (Padua, 1987), 237–38.

"Costei per fermo nacque in paradiso!"
Così carco d'oblio
il divin portamento
e 'l volto e le parole e 'l dolce riso
m'aveano, et sì diviso
da l'imagine vera,
ch'i' dicea sospirando:
"Qui come venn'io o quando?"
credendo esser in ciel, non là dov'era.

(126, 53–63)

[How many times did I say to myself then, full of awe: "She was surely born in paradise!" Her divine bearing and her face and her words and her sweet smile had so laden me with forgetfulness and so divided me from the true image, that I was sighing: "How did I come here and when?" thinking I was in Heaven, not there where I was.]

The subtext of this depiction of Laura seated amid a rain of blossoms is the long-awaited appearance of Beatrice to Dante in the Earthly Paradise, and it proposes an immediate contrast because that scene prepares the pilgrim for his ascent to Heaven. Here Petrarch's poet, transfixed by his vision of Laura, is attentive to nothing else; here, as in moments recurring throughout the collection in which he contemplates or recalls Laura or projects her image, he confuses this paradise of his own making with that of Heaven.[21]

Not only does Laura's presence make this world a paradise; with far broader implications, the experience of Laura *in vita* is likened to that of Paradise. In the ecstatic absorption of Petrarch's poet in the beauty of the lady's eyes and of her smile, again Dante's voice is heard as a counterpoint to his own. The "double sweetness" of Laura's face (193) is a probable allusion to the angels' celebration of the eyes of Beatrice and of her mouth, her second beauty, "seconda bellezza" (*Purg.* XXXI, 122–38).[22] Even surrounded by the splendor of Paradise, so intense is the

21. See Nancy Vickers, "Re-Membering Dante: Petrarch's 'Chiare, fresche et dolci acque'," *MLN* 96 (1981): 5–7. The same effect is associated with paradise late in the collection, where the sweet bird-song emerging from a laurel that appeared "un delli arbor . . . di paradiso" is recalled, "che dal mondo m'avean tutto diviso" [one of the trees of Eden . . . that it had rapt me from the world] (323).

22. See Domenico De Robertis, "Contiguità e selezione nella costruzione del Canzoniere petrarchesco," *Studi di Filologia Italiana* 43 (1985): 53 hr n. 1. In the *Convivio* Dante explicates the "first and second beauties" in the allegory of Sapienza: the "occhi" are her *dimostrazioni,* the "riso" her *persuasioni* (III, xv, 12–13).

pleasure of the pilgrim Dante in this beauty that he, like the young poet-lover of the *Vita Nuova*, forgets all else in his response:

> ché dentro a li occhi suoi ardeva un riso
> tal, ch'io pensai co' miei toccar lo fondo
> de la mia grazia e del mio paradiso.
>
> (*Par.* XV, 34–36)

[for within her eyes was blazing such a smile that I thought with mine I had touched the limit both of my beatitude and of my paradise.]

But there is peril in this rapture: it is inadequate to the joy of Paradise, as Beatrice will herself remind him in a passage whose importance cannot be overstated as an explicit revision of the stilnovist poetics of love and light:

> Tanto poss'io di quel punto ridire,
> che, rimirando lei, lo mio affetto
> libero fu da ogne altro disire,
> fin che 'l piacere etterno, che diretto
> raggiava in Bëatrice, dal bel viso
> mi contentava col secondo aspetto.
> Vincendo me col lume d'un sorriso,
> ella mi disse: "Volgiti e ascolta;
> ché non pur ne' miei occhi è paradiso."
>
> (*Par.* XVIII, 13–21)

[This much of that moment can I retell, that as I gazed upon her my affection was freed from every other desire so long as the Eternal Joy that shone direct on Beatrice satisfied me from the fair eyes with its reflected aspect. Overcoming me with the light of a smile, she said to me, "Turn and listen, for not only in my eyes is Paradise."]

This is a lesson lost on the poet of the *Rime*. In the explicit proclamation of Laura's eyes as his guide toward Heaven cited above, that suggestion is subverted in the description of their effect that follows:

> Vaghe faville angeliche, beatrici
> de la mia vita, ove 'l piacer s'accende
> che dolcemente mi consuma et strugge;
> come sparisce et fugge
> ogni altro lume dove 'l vostro splende,

così de lo mio core,
quando tanta dolcezza in lui discende,
ogni altra cosa, ogni penser va fore
et solo ivi con voi rimanse Amore.

(72, 37–45)

[Lovely angelic sparks that make blessed my life, where the pleasure is lit that sweetly consumes and destroys me; just as every other light disappears and flees where yours shines, so from my heart, when so much sweetness descends into it, every other thing, every thought, goes out, and alone there with you remains Love.]

The qualification of these sparks as "angeliche," in apparent complement to the meaning of "beatrici" in the same verse, would affirm for Laura the role attributed to Beatrice in the literal reading of her name. It is apparent, however, that the beatitude of Petrarch's poet is of a different order, one dependent entirely on the sight of Laura's beauty, as in this record of the effect of an encounter:

I' mi riscossi, et ella oltra parlando
passò, ché la parola i' non soffersi
né 'l dolce sfavillar de gli occhi suoi.

(111, 9–11)

[I trembled, and she, conversing, passed onward, for I could not endure her speech or the sweet sparkling of her eyes.]

This, as Vanossi observes, is a sort of epiphany, "un evento sacrale";[23] it conditions our reading of the poet's paradise.

In a later century, a French poet was to capture the attitude implicit in these verses:

Car qui verroit de pres vostre celeste face
Feroit son Paradis en ceste terre basse,
Et ne voudroit jamais l'aller chercher aux Cieux.[24]

23. Luigi Vanossi, "Petrarca e il mito di Atteone," *Romanistische Zeitschrift für Literaturgeschichte* 10 (1986): 17.

24. Joachim Du Bellay, *Les Amours*, XVII, 12–14; in *Oeuvres poétiques*, ed. Henri Chamard, republished and updated by Henri Weber (Paris, 1970).

[For whoever would see from close by your heavenly face would make his Paradise in this low earth, and would never wish to seek it in Heaven.]

So is the poet of the *Rime* content to create his Earthly Paradise around Laura; but with her death that "heavenly face" is no longer to be seen on earth. It is almost as an afterthought that he seeks not to look back upon a time that can never return, and it is because of the finality of his loss that he resolves to seek Heaven: "cerchiamo 'l Ciel se qui nulla ne piace" (273). It was Valchiusa that during absences *in vita* had possessed the Laura from whom he was separated (226); so now it is Heaven that "possesses" Laura, there where the incomparably sweet sound of her speech is now heard: "l'angeliche parole / sonano in parte ove è chi meglio intende" [the angelic words are sounding in a place where there is someone who understands better] (275). Just as he had envied the Valchiusa that had heard her voice and received the imprint of her footsteps—"how much I envy you her virtuous and dear gestures!" (162)—so now he envies the souls who delight in her presence so much desired:

> Quanta [invidia] ne porto al Ciel che chiude et serra
> et sì cupidamente à in sé raccolto
> lo spirto da le belle membra sciolto,
> et per altrui sì rado si diserra!
> Quanta invidia a quell'anime che 'n sorte
> ànno or sua santa et dolce compagnia,
> la qual io cercai sempre con tal brama!
>
> (300, 5–11)

[How I envy Heaven, which encloses and locks in and has so eagerly gathered to itself the spirit freed from her beautiful members, but so rarely unlocks itself for others! How I envy those souls whose fate is now to have her sweet holy company, which (with what desire!) I have always sought!]

Even while evoking a disembodied spirit, this remarkable statement achieves an intensely physical coloration in its recall of the lady's "belle membra" and in the verbs "chiude" and "serra," intensified by the adverbial "cupidamente," that describe Heaven's reception of Laura. Even though Laura's body is now claimed by the earth—"poca terra il mio ben preme" [a little earth presses down all my wealth] (331)—it is in terms of her beauty that she is imagined in Heaven, and there it continues to occasion pleasure and delight: "fa 'l Ciel or di sue bellezze lieto" [with her beauties she now makes Heaven glad], the poet tells us (332); "or n'à diletto / il Re celeste, i suoi alati corrieri, / et io son qui rimaso ignudo e cieco" [now the heavenly King delights in them, and His winged couriers, and I have remained here naked and blind] (348).

Yet it may of course still be argued that if his love for Laura *in vita* leads him only to a terrestrial paradise that perilously occults his thought of Heaven, she may with her death become a creature of Heaven, to inhabit the Heavenly Paradise from which she descends to console and counsel the bereaved poet.[25] In fact an entire series of poems *in morte* is centered in the explicit or implicit opposition of *cielo* to *terra*, a series closely related, as verified by the manuscript tradition, to poems in Part I in which the "angelic" or "celestial" qualities of Laura are prominent.[26] Yet the poet of the *Rime* must remind himself again and again that *cielo* is now Laura's home, and that it is there that she is now to be imagined; an imagined guide directs his course because "la vera è sotterra; *anzi è nel Cielo*" [the true one is in the earth; rather she is in Heaven]. Despite an effort which is explicitly thematized in the poems, he never fully dissociates the heavenly from the earthly Laura, as he repeatedly recalls either her incomparable physical beauty or its remains that are now a bit of earth, "poca terra."[27]

Here again we may test Petrarch's conception against Dante's by considering a single scene found in both the *Rime* and the *Commedia*, that of the ascent of the beloved to Heaven. Both texts build upon a merging of personal and universal solar symbolism, first suggested in the *Rime* among the early poems *in morte:*

> Occhi miei, oscurato è 'l nostro sole,
> anzi è salito al Cielo et ivi splende,
> ivi il vedremo, ancora ivi n'attende
> et di nostro tardar forse il dole.
>
> (275, 1–4)

25. In the dream dialogue of canzone 359 the poet declares to Laura that he weeps only for himself, "certo sempre del tuo al Ciel salire / come di cosa ch'uom vede da presso" [for I have been as certain that you had risen to Heaven as a man is of a thing he sees close by].

26. See the observations of De Robertis, "Contiguità e selezione," 64.

27. Jill Tilden observes that this Laura remains "the earthly Laura placed against a painted backdrop of heaven—not the transformation of Laura into pure spirit"; see "Spiritual Conflict in Petrarch's Canzoniere," in *Petrarca 1304–1374: Beiträge zu Werk und Wirkung*, ed. F. Schalk (Frankfurt, 1975), 299–309 (citation, 308).

[My eyes, darkened is our sun, rather it has risen to Heaven and there shines, there we shall see it again, there it awaits us and perhaps is pained by our delay.]

Thus Laura, no longer a sun on earth, shines in Heaven, and Heaven, the poet affirms in a later sonnet, will rejoice in her superior radiance: "di sua chiaritate / quasi d'un più bel sol s'allegra et gloria" [rejoices and glories in its brightness as in a brighter sun] (326). Another poem goes far beyond this reorientation of the topos *donna / sole* to combine the secular metaphor with the yet more familiar religious one, rendering Laura's death as "quel sol . . . tornando al sommo Sole" [that sun . . . returning to the highest Sun] (306). These verses invite comparison with the scene in the *Commedia* in which the pilgrim Dante rises to the heaven of the sun in the company of Beatrice, the celestial lady confirming the completion of their passage with an effusion of gratitude:

> E Beatrice cominciò: "Ringrazia,
> ringrazia il Sol de li Angeli, ch'a questo
> sensibil t'ha levato per sua grazia."
>
> (*Par.* X, 52–54)

[And Beatrice began: "Give thanks, give thanks to the Sun of the Angels who of His grace has raised you to this visible one."]

The pilgrim in turn responds, not with his intellect, but with his love: "sì tutto il mio amore in lui si mise," Dante records, "che Beatrice eclissò ne l'oblio" [all my love was so set on Him that it eclipsed Beatrice in oblivion] (59–60).

Beatrice is not, of course, definitively forgotten; she will continue to lead and to interpret the experience of Paradise until confiding her charge to Saint Bernard for the final phase of his journey toward full vision. Nonetheless this "eclipse" of Beatrice marks a step in the light metaphysics of the lover's response, and his declaration of the plentitude of a love directed to Christ marks a major and necessary step in the pilgrim's itinerary from earthly to Heavenly love. Let us compare Petrarch's poet, in the verses that follow those cited above, revealing the extent to which he remains fixed in the habits of his love for Laura:

> ond' io son fatto un animal silvestro
> che co' pie vaghi, solitari et lassi
> porto 'l cor grave et gli occhi umidi et bassi
> al mondo, ch'è per me un deserto alpestro.

Così vo ricercando ogni contrada
ov'io la vidi; et sol tu che m'affligi,
Amor, vien meco et mostrimi ond'io vada;
lei non trov'io, ma suoi santi vestigi
tutti rivolti a la superna strada
veggio, lunge da' laghi averni et stigi.

(306, 9–14)

[so that I have become an animal of the woods, and with wander-
ing, solitary, and weary feet I carry about a heavy heart and eyes
wet and cast down in the world, which is for me a mountainous
desert. Thus I go searching through every region where I saw her,
and only you who afflict me, Love, come with me and show me
where to go; her I do not find, but I see her holy footprints all
turned toward the road to Heaven, far from the Avernian and the
Stygian lakes.]

In an earlier poem *in morte*, he had imagined Laura as a sun now shining
in Heaven and had lamented the loss of her presence on earth, of his
opportunity to see and hear her (275). Now, imagining Laura herself in
Heaven, he nonetheless seeks her vestiges on earth; imagining Laura with
God, he continues in the exclusive company of Amor. Here his protes-
tation of Laura's role as his guide to Heaven is radically subverted:
although the opening verse identifies her as "quel sol che mi mostrava il
cammin destro / di gire al Ciel con gloriosi passi" [that sun which showed
me the right way to go to Heaven with glorious steps], her departure
finds him still entrusting himself to the guidance of Amor, who shows
him the path he is to follow.

But what then of the many poems of Part II of the collection in which
Laura is explicitly postulated as the poet's guide to Heaven? Again a
number of Petrarch's readers have concluded that this Laura *in morte*
indicates to him the means to that "salire al cielo" whose urgency is
acknowledged in many poems of Part I. For Martinelli, this beloved
Laura is transformed in Petrarch's disenchanted eyes into a certain guide
toward Heaven, to whom he now fully entrusts himself; a study of the
anniversary poems concludes that "in death she becomes the model to
follow, a Christlike guide."[28] Yet we have seen that the poet's own
attributions of this function to Laura in Part I are subverted by his praise
of her sublime beauty, and it remains legitimate to question whether his

28. Martinelli, *Petrarca e il Ventoso*, 243; Dennis Dutschke, "The Anniversary Poems in
Petrarch's *Canzoniere*," *Italica* 58 (1981): 96.

eyes are indeed "disenchanted"—to question too whether his affirmations of her role in Part II are indeed radically different.

To effect this transformation would be to follow his own advice. In a poem in Part I concerning the death of the beloved of an unidentified recipient, a lady now surely in Heaven, Petrarch counsels the addressee to follow her "per via dritta espedita" [a straight and unimpeded road]— an undertaking made easier because the lady's departure leaves him free from the burden of earthly attachment (91). Confronted in turn with the death of Laura, Petrarch directs this same admonition to himself as he inscribes its record in his often-frequented Virgil manuscript: "that, now that the chief bond is broken, I may be warned by frequently looking at these words that it is time to flee from Babylon."[29] But this fragment of autobiographical evidence, the only direct testimony to Petrarch's reaction to Laura's death external to the lyric collection, does not describe the reaction of the poet of the *Rime:* just as he does not recover the keys to his heart, his avowed project to follow his lady "al cielo" is not unambiguous. Even when his destination is identified as Paradise rather than the Valchiusa where he seeks her traces, his motivation remains the presence of Laura. Now he wishes for an end to his own earthly life because of his desire to see her again (312). As he had desired life only because of Laura, so now he desires death:

> Mai questa mortal vita a me non piacque
> (sassel Amor con cui spesso ne parlo)
> se non per lei che fu 'l suo lume e 'l mio;
> poi che 'n terra morendo al Ciel rinacque
> quello spirto ond'io vissi, a seguitarlo
> licito fusse è 'l mi' sommo desio.

(331, 25–30)

> [Never did this mortal life please me (Love knows it, with whom I often speak of it) except for her who was his light and mine; since, dying on earth, that spirit by which I lived has been reborn in Heaven, my highest desire is to be permitted to follow her.]

This is the desire expressed in a poem already cited that immediately follows the notice of her death, whose second verse initiates an urging that will run through the following stanzas:

> Madonna è morta et à seco il mio core,
> et volendol seguire,

---

29. Cited in Morris Bishop, *Petrarch and His World* (Bloomington, Ind., 1963), 62–63.

> interromper conven quest'anni rei,
> perché mai veder lei
> di qua non spero, e l'aspettar m'è noia. . . .
>
> (268, 4–8)

[My lady is dead and has my heart with her, and if I wish to follow it I must break off these cruel years, for I never hope to see her this side, and waiting is painful to me. . . .]

Thus, he confides, he remains in the desolate state of a self divided:

> tal che s'altri mi serra
> lungo tempo il cammin da seguitarla,
> quel ch'Amor meco parla
> sol mi riten ch'io non recida il nodo.
>
> (268, 62–65)

[so that, if the way to follow her is long closed to me, only what Love says to me holds me back from cutting the knot.]

To go to Heaven to be with Laura. . . . Now his lament that, had he read correctly the omens of her impending death, he would have preferred to die before her culminates in a remarkable passage:

> Questo intendendo, dolcemente sciolto
> in sua presenzia del mortal mio velo
> et di questa noiosa et grave carne,
> potea inanzi lei andarne
> a veder preparar sua sedia in Cielo . . .
>
> (331, 55–59)

[Understanding that, and sweetly shaking off in her presence my mortal veil and this noisome heavy flesh, I could have gone on before her to watch her throne being prepared in Heaven . . .]

It is the attentiveness of this celestial Laura, her demonstration of affection and desire for the poet, that inspire the turning of his own desires and thoughts toward Heaven:

> et parte ad or ad or si volge a tergo,
> mirando s'io la seguo, et par ch'aspetti;

ond' io voglie et pensier tutti al Ciel ergo
perch' i' l'odo pregar pur ch' i' m'affretti.

(346, 11–14)[30]

[and still from time to time she turns back, looking to see if I am
following her, and seems to wait; and so I raise all of my desires
and thoughts toward Heaven, for I hear her even pray that I may
hasten.]

They are turned, of course, less toward Heaven than toward Laura *in*
Heaven. The "beatitude" that she affords is commensurate with the
illusion of the beloved presence, of her sight, of her voice, and it reveals
once again his desire for intimacy with Laura:

Beata s'è che po beare altrui
co la sua vista, o ver co le parole
intellette da noi soli ambedui. . . .

(341, 9–11)[31]

[She is indeed blessed who can make others blessed with her sight
or else with her words, understood only by us two. . . .]

As he had created his paradise on earth, he creates his celestial Paradise
around her presence. Already before her death he had imagined Heaven
in her image:

Io penso: se là suso,
onde 'l motor eterno de le stelle
degnò mostrar del suo lavoro in terra,
son l'altr'opre sì belle,
aprasi la pregione ov' io son chiuso
et che 'l camino a tal vita mi serra!

(72, 16–21)

[I think: if up there, whence the eternal Mover of the stars deigned
to show forth this work on earth, the other works are as beautiful,

---

30. For the "temporalizing of paradise" in the poems depicting Laura's arrival in heaven,
see Barolini, "The Making of a Lyric Sequence," 32–33.

31. For a different reading of this passage and its parallels with the reunion of Dante and
Beatrice, see Büdel, *"Parusia Redemtricis,"* 41–42.

let the prison open in which I am closed and which locks me from
the way to such a life.]

This infrequently noted passage again casts a strong light on the poet's
desire in Part II of the collection to leave behind his mortal "prison" in
order to go to Heaven—to be with Laura.

In the opening letter of Book XXIV of the *Familiares* Petrarch de-
scribes Heaven as he imagines it: it is there "where what once pleased
will be ever pleasing, whose unutterable and infinite charm can scarcely
be contained in the spirit, where there is no change and no reason to fear
its ending."[32] In the *Trionfi* Heaven is imagined as an Eternity from which
age, ugliness, and frailty are banished along with contingency and Death,
a place where the blessed will enjoy eternal fame with immortal beauty
in the flower of youth (*Tr. Eter.* 133–34). Unlike Dante, upon whose
rendering of Paradise he freely draws in this *capitolo*, Petrarch does not
present this "new world" as a vision: it is acknowledged as his own
imagining, inspired by his meditation on the contingency that governs
mortal existence. Laura, of course, is part of that Eternity, and the poet's
"imagining" concludes, as the text of the *Trionfi* itself concludes, with
the triumph of Laura's beauty in its heavenly transformation and the
anticipation of seeing her again in Heaven:

> chè, poi ch'avra ripreso 'l suo bel velo,
> se fu beato chi la vide in terra,
> or che fia dunque a rivederla in cielo?
>
> (*Tr. Eter.* 143–45)

[And now that she her beauty hath resumed, if he was blest who
saw her here on earth, what then will it be to see her again in
heaven!]

In the *Rime* Paradise is above all the setting for Laura's beauty, by
which it is illumined:

> Ma la forma miglior che vive ancora
> et vivrà sempre su ne l'alto cielo,
> di sue bellezze ogni or più m'innamora;

32. Aldo Bernardo, whose translation is cited, comments that "as in the last Triumph,
Petrarch cannot imagine an eternity that does not partake at least of the positive aspects of
earthly life"; see "Petrarch's Autobiography: Circularity Revisited," *Annali d'Italianistica*
4 (1986): 63.

et vo sol in pensar cangiando il pelo
quale ella è oggi e 'n qual parte dimora,
qual a vedere il suo leggiadro velo.

(319, 9–14)

[But her better form, which still lives and shall always live up in
the highest Heaven, makes me ever more in love with her beauties,
and I go with my hair turning, only thinking of what she is like
today and where she dwells, and what her lovely veil is to see.]

The first of these tercets makes of *Rime* 319 a companion poem to the
sonnet *in vita* evoked in the preceding chapter in which Laura's beauty
inspires in the poet amorous thoughts that lead him toward the "highest
good," toward Heaven (13). While he reports that Laura *in morte*
repeatedly counsels him to think of his salvation and prepare himself for
Heaven, his desire for Heaven is consistently expressed in terms of her
presence there; and that presence is intensely imagined, not as a disem-
bodied spirit, but in terms that recall the Laura adored *in vita:*

Morte m'à morto, et sola po far Morte
ch' i' torni a riveder quel viso lieto
che piacer mi facea i sospiri e 'l pianto.

(332, 43–45)

[Death has killed me, and only Death has the power to make me
see again that glad face that made sighs pleasing to me and
weeping.]

When Franciscus in the *Secretum* protests to Augustinus that he has
loved Laura for her soul more than for her body, his relentless mentor
demands to know whether he would have loved that soul with equal
fervor in an unlovely body, and Franciscus, although protesting, replies:
"I dare not say that. . . ."[33] Would he now—let us imagine Augustinus
again putting the direct question—so much desire Heaven without
Laura?[34]

As the emphasis in Part II of the *Rime sparse* falls over and over again

33. See *Petrarch's Secret,* 125–26.
34. Pertinent to this question is Giacomo da Lentino's often-cited sonnet "Io m'aggio
posto in core a Dio servire," in which he declares that he would not wish to go to Paradise,
the "santo loco," without his lady, because the sight of her beauty and grace are necessary
to his own contentment. For this poem as "a delightful spoof of the poet-lover's idolatry
masking itself as virtue," see Thomas P. Roche, Jr., *Petrarch and the English Sonnet
Sequences* (New York, 1989), 51–52.

on personal contact with Laura *in morte*, new scenes are invented to replace the cherished fantasies of a welcome extended by Laura *in vita*. The poet imagines his own passage to Heaven in terms of her welcoming reception:

> Piacciale al mio passar esser accorta,
> ch' è presso omai; siami a l'incontro, et quale
> ella è nel Cielo, a sé mi tiri et chiame;
>
> (333, 12–14)

[Let it please her to pay heed to my passing, which is nearby now; let her meet me, and let her draw and call me to herself, to be what she is in Heaven.]

> et spero ch' al por giù di questa spoglia
> venga per me con quella gente nostra,
> vera amica di Cristo et d'onestate.
>
> (334, 12–14)

[and I hope that when I put off these remains she will come for me with our people, the true friend of Christ and of virtue.]

Even in the more consistently pious poems late in Part II, where Christ also figures in this Heaven, the divine presence is accompanied by the presence of Laura: the poet attempts to console himself "vedendo tanto lei domesticarsi / con colui che vivendo in cor sempre ebbe" [seeing that she has come so near to Him whom in her life she had always in her heart], then imagines her among the angels at Christ's feet (345).[35] When he pleads for her intercession so that he too may be included among the blessed, the emphasis falls not on his repentance but on the reunion now possible only in Paradise. Thus, on rejoining the lost Laura:

> Dunque per amendar la lunga guerra
> per cui dal mondo a te sola mi volsi,
> prega ch' i' venga tosto a star con voi.
>
> (347, 12–14)

35. Robert Durling notes that this sonnet is of particular importance because it denounces the fantasies of Laura's visits to her lover "as dangerous nonsense," as "the fruit of self-pity and an obstacle to true repentance"; see *The Figure of the Poet in the Renaissance Epic* (Cambridge, Mass., 1965), 82–83.

[Therefore to make amends for the long war in which I turned away from the world toward you only, pray that I may soon come to be with you.]

Sol un conforto a le mie pene aspetto:
ch' ella che vede tutt' i miei penseri
m'impetre grazia ch'i' possa esser seco.

(348, 12–14)[36]

[Only one comfort for my suffering do I expect: that she who sees all of my thoughts will win grace for me that I may be with her.]

The presence of Dante is particularly strong in the dream appearances of Laura in this late section of the *Rime*, recalling not only several passages of the *Paradiso* but in particular the pilgrim's encounter with Beatrice in the Earthly Paradise of the *Purgatorio*, a locus whose impact on earlier poems in the collection has been documented in the preceding chapters.[37] Dante's otherworldly Beatrice, however, is transformed by her beatitude, as already in the *Vita Nuova* he had imagined her earthly beauty to become in Heaven a spiritual beauty, "spiral bellezza grande."[38] Compare the depiction of the otherworldly Laura, focusing simply and directly on the modalities of earthly existence: "or è in Cielo et ancor par qui sia / et viva et senta et vada et ami et spiri" [now she is in Heaven but seems to be here and to live and feel and walk and love and breathe] (286). It is in keeping with this difference that Dante's Beatrice encourages and rebukes her poet in the otherworldly context of the *Purgatorio*, while Petrarch's Laura frequently returns to *his* world, to sit at his bedside or reanimate for him her familiar landscape, encouraging and rebuking him in an obsessive alternate world of oneiric encounters.[39]

36. In such poems, as Jill Tilden observes, the reader feels that "repentance almost ceases, paradoxically, to be a religious experience where Petrarch turns in his search for a new life to a trans-humanised Laura"; see "Spiritual Conflict in Petrarch's Canzoniere," 297. In such poems "the balance of desire-motivation is always tipped towards Laura."

37. See Emilio Pasquini, "La Canzone CCCLIX," *Lectura Petrarce, V, 1985* (Padua, 1986), esp. 233–36, 241–47.

38. *Vita Nuova* XXXIII. For the contrast between Petrarch's representation of the lady in heaven and that of Dante, and for the protagonist's unrelenting preoccupation with the earthly image of Laura in the poems *in morte*, see Sara Sturm-Maddox, *Petrarch's Metamorphoses: Text and Subtext in the* Rime sparse (Columbia, Mo., 1985), 54–60.

39. As Pasquini notes, Petrarch's own annotation—"scribo enim non tamquam ego, sed quasi alius"—suggests a state of doubling, closed to the outside world and faithful to an oneiric inner reality ("La Canzone CCCLIX," 231).

Following a number of these records of Laura's reappearances *in morte* we find a poem that explicitly addresses their status:

> Tornami a mente (anzi v'è dentro quella
> ch'indi per Lete esser non po sbandita)
> qual io la vidi in su l'età fiorita
> tutta accesa de' raggi di sua stella;
>
> sì nel mio primo occorso onesta e bella
> veggiola in sè raccolta et sì romita,
> ch' i' grido: "Ell' è ben dessa, ancor è in vita!"
> e 'n don le cheggio sua dolce favella.
>
> Talor risponde et talor non fa motto;
> i' come uom ch'erra et poi più dritto estima
> dico a la mente mia: "Tu se' 'ngannata.
>
> "Sai che 'n mille trecento quarantotto,
> il dì sesto d'aprile, in l'ora prima
> del corpo uscio quell'alma beata."
>
> (336)

[She comes to mind (rather she is within my mind, for she cannot be banished thence by Lethe) just as I saw her in her flowering, all burning with the rays of her star; I see her in the first encounter so chaste and beautiful, so turned inward and shy, that I cry: "That is she, she is still alive!" and I beg her for the gift of her sweet speech. Sometimes she replies and sometimes she does not say a word; I, like one who errs and then esteems more justly, say to my mind: "You are deceived: you know that in 1348, on the sixth day of April, at the first hour, that blessed soul left the body."]

This poem, of capital importance to the fictive chronology of the *Rime* because it contains the full (and only) notation of the date of Laura's death, is hardly less important for its analysis of her reappearances *in morte*. The lucid response of the poet to his mind engrossed in its communion with this Laura, "tu se' ingannata," of course refers directly to the illusion that she is still alive, but the temporal identification that introduces this return of Laura tells us more; it confirms that this image is a reactivation of that primordial image of the first encounter, of the *innamoramento*. Thus the coordinates of the closing stanza bear a sad echo of the single other poem among the *Rime* in which they occur, where they lend singular temporal precision to the *innamoramento* itself:

> Mille trecento ventisette, a punto
> su l'ora prima, il dì sesto d'aprile,
> nel laberinto intrai, né veggio ond'esca.
>
> (211, 12–14)

[One thousand three hundred twenty-seven, exactly at the first hour of the sixth day of April, I entered the labyrinth, nor do I see where I may get out of it.]

Near the end of the collection, as the aging poet anticipates his own death, the affirmations of Laura's role as his heavenly guide become more frequent and more confident.[40] Now he finds reassurance in Christ's triumph over death, as well as that of Laura. Laura, however, is cast once again in the image of her physical beauty:

> [morte] or novellamente in ogni vena
> intrò di lei che m'era data in sorte,
> et non turbò la sua fronte serena.
>
> (357, 12–14)

[(death) recently entered into each vein of her who was allotted to me, and did not cloud her clear brow.]

> Non po far Morte il dolce viso amaro,
> ma 'l dolce viso dolce po far Morte:
> che bisogn' a morir ben altre scorte?
>
> (358, 1–3)

40.

> Ogni giorno mi par più di mill'anni
> ch' i' i' segua la mia fida et cara duce
> che mi condusse al mondo, or mi conduce
> per miglior via a vita senza affanni;
>
> (357, 1–4)
>
> quella mi scorge ond'ogni ben imparo. . . .
>
> (358, 4)

[Every day seems to me more than a thousand years, until I may follow my faithful, dear guide who led me in the world and now leads me by a better way to a life without troubles . . . She guides me from whom I learn every good. . . .]

[Death cannot make her sweet face bitter, but her sweet face can make Death sweet; what need is there of any other guides for my dying?]

Even in the *Trionfi*, where the emphasis falls more resoundingly than in the *Rime* on Laura's exemplary virtue and spiritual fortitude, her death is imagined in esthetic terms: "Morte bella parea nel suo bel viso" [even death seemed fair in her fair face].[41]

In a remarkable passage of the next poem Laura herself acknowledges that it is her physical beauty that renders the poet attentive to her pious and edifying message. To the beautiful apparition who comes once again to sit on his bedside he puts the question: "Son questi i capei biondi et l'aureo nodo . . . ch'ancor mi stringe, et quei belli occhi / che fur 'l mio sol?" ["Is this the golden hair and the golden knot . . . that still binds me, and those beautiful eyes that were my sun?"] No, she replies, she is instead a "spirito ignudo," a naked spirit, and she elaborates her reply into an explanation:

> "quel che tu cerchi è terra già molt' anni.
> Ma per trarti d'affanni
> m'è dato a parer tale, et ancor quella
> sarò più che mai bella,
> a te più cara. . . ."
>
> $\qquad\qquad\qquad\qquad\qquad\qquad$ (359, 61–65)

["what you seek has been dust for many years now. But to help you from your troubles it is given to me to seem such, and I shall be so again, more beautiful than ever, and more loving to you. . . ."]

Laura's declaration in fact subverts the pious counsel of renunciation that is the manifest content of this poem. It offers, along with the promise of yet greater love in Heaven, that of yet greater beauty, the culmination of promises already implied that the reunion anticipated in Heaven will entail also the reunion of Laura's spirit with her body. In the closing of the *Trionfi*, as we have seen, the resurrection of the body is invoked directly not only in that immortal beauty to be enjoyed by all the souls

---

41. See *Tr. Mor.* I, 151–72, evoking Laura's "bel seno" and "bel volto" and describing the latter: "Pallida no, ma più che neve bianca . . . Quasi un dolce dormir ne' suo' belli occhi . . ." [not pale, but whiter than the whitest snow . . . a sweet sleep upon her lovely eyes].

of the blessed but in the supreme beauty of Laura herself reunited with her "bel velo" (*Tr. Eter.* 143). In the *Rime* this anticipation retains its full physical suggestiveness; Amor, we recall, had encouraged the poet by invoking a Laura in Heaven who "smiles to herself at her beautiful remains and sighs only for you" (268), a doubly gratifying affirmation later confirmed by Laura herself—"I only wait for you and that which you loved so much and which remained down there, my lovely veil" (302). Nor does this final dream appearance end with a reflection on the spiritual import of her counsel, but rather with a scene of yet greater intimacy:

> I' piango; et ella il volto
> co le sue man m'asciuga, et poi sospira
> dolcemente, et s'adira
> con parole che i sassi romper ponno;
> et dopo questo si parte ella e 'l sonno.
>
> (359, 67–71)[42]

[I weep, and she dries my face with her hands and then sighs sweetly and grows angry with words that could break the stones; and after this she departs, as does my sleep.]

Thus it is not only through her appearance that this returning Laura comforts the poet; solace depends too upon her speech, as he confides: "sol quant' ella parla ò pace, o tregua" [only while she speaks do I have peace—or at least a truce] (285). And again, as for the Laura *in vita*, so for this Laura: it is not the edifying content of her speech but its sound, it sweetness, that enraptures and affords a momentary consolation. Let us consider his direct statement of her guidance toward Heaven:

> Ir dritto alto m'insegna, et io, che 'ntendo
> le sue caste lusinghe e i giusti preghi
> col dolce mormorar pietoso et basso,
> secondo lei conven mi regga et pieghi,
> per la dolcezza che del suo dir prendo,
> ch' avria vertù di far piangere un sasso.
>
> (286, 9–14)

42. Durling notes that this Laura sits on the left side of the poet's bed. "As a piece of self-analysis, the poem functions to identify the apparently sacrosanct figure of Laura as a sexual fantasy. The lover's interest is still—primarily or ultimately or also—in her body" (*The Figure of the Poet in the Renaissance Epic*, 80). For this poem as "the clearest summary of the constants in Petrarch's long, fragmentary dialogue with Dante over the problem of poetic transcendence," see Peter Hainsworth, *Petrarch the Poet* (London, 1988), 167–69.

[She teaches me to go straight up, and I, who understand her chaste allurements and her just prayers with their sweet, low, pitying murmur, I must rule and bend myself according to her because of the sweetness I take from her words, which would have the power to make a stone weep.]

The first of these verses, apparently unambiguous in its declaration of a salutary intervention, is totally isolated in this poem, which opens with his conviction that the "aura soave" [sweet breath] of the sighs with which she addresses him, could he but record it, would awaken "caldi desiri," hot desires, in his listener. In a closely related passage, reflecting back upon Laura's influence on his conduct when yet *in vita*, he will again characterize her action as "lusingare":

> benedetta colei ch' a miglior riva
> volse il mio corso et l'empia voglia ardente
> lusingando affrenò perch' io non pera!
>
> (290, 12–14)

[blessed be she who turned my course toward a better shore and, alluring my wicked ardent will, reined it in that I might not perish!]

The suggestiveness of the verb is immediate if we recall that in a poem *in vita* it rendered not the speech of Laura, but that of Love: "Amor con sue promesse lusingando / mi ricondusse a la prigione antica . . ." [Alluring me with his promises, Love led me back to my former prison] (76).

Here the question put to Franciscus in the *Secretum* concerning the beauty of Laura may be rephrased: would he attend to these edifying admonishments if they were not presented in the seductive blandishments of this much-beloved lady? What is the status of the affirmation that "I must rule and bend myself according to her" if it is due, not to his concern for his salvation, but to the compulsion of the sweetness of her speech? When Laura comes to sit at his bedside, her pious yet tender admonishment that he end his weeping is accompanied by an equally tender gesture whose reception is rendered ambiguous by a qualificatory phrase that reintroduces desire precisely when its sublimation is predicated:

> Con quella man che tanto desiai
> m'asciuga li occhi, et col suo dir m'apporta
> dolcezza ch'uom mortal non sentì mai.
>
> (342, 9–11)

[With that hand which I so much desired she dries my eyes and with her speech brings me sweetness that mortal man never felt.]

When instead of receiving her visits the poet imagines rejoining her in Heaven, she draws him toward Heaven as she had drawn him to her on earth: "E' mi par d'or in ora udire il messo / che Madonna mi mande a sé chiamando. . . ." [I seem at every moment to hear the messenger whom my lady sends calling me to her] (349). The representation of their fantasized reunion receives its fullest development in this late section of the *Rime sparse*.

"And then may it please Him who is the Lord of courtesy that my soul may go to see the glory of my lady, that is of the blessed Beatrice, who now in glory beholds the face of Him *qui est per omnia secula benedictus*."[43] These are of course Dante's words, and they bring the *Vita Nuova* to a pious close. Now Petrarch, in the well-known verses that close the poem cited above:

> O felice quel dì che del terreno
> carcere uscendo, lasci rotta et sparta
> questa mia grave et frale et mortal gonna
> et da sì folte tenebre mi parta,
> volando tanto su nel bel sereno
> ch' i' veggia il mio Signore et la mia donna!
>
> (349, 9–14)

[Oh happy that day when, going forth from my earthly prison, I may leave broken and scattered this heavy, frail, and mortal garment of mine, and may depart from such thick shadows, flying so far up into the beautiful clear sky that I may see my Lord and my lady!]

But this sonnet does not conclude the *Rime sparse*. Not only is the collection to end with a canzone addressed and dedicated to the Virgin in which Laura is evoked only in that sad phrase "tale è terra" and as Medusa; the desire expressed in *Rime* 349 itself invites a rereading in the ironic light of the next poem, which begins as a late tribute to Laura's sublime beauty:

43. Singleton remarks that this is Dante's fundamental innovation in his theory of love: "a troubadour's love would have seen only Beatrice, a saint's love would have sought only God"; see *An Essay on the "Vita Nuova,"* 77. Petrarch differs from Dante, we might say, in both the motivation and the manner of the seeing.

> Questo nostro caduco et fragil bene,
> ch' è vento et ombra et à nome beltate,
> non fu giamai se non in questa etate
> tutto in un corpo, et ciò fu per mie pene . . .
> Non fu simil bellezza antica o nova,
> né sarà, credo. . . .
>
> (350, 1–4, 9–10)

[This brittle, frail good of ours, which is wind and shadow and is called beauty, never was, except in this age, entirely in one body, and that was to my sorrow . . . There never was such beauty, old or new, nor will there be again, I believe. . . .]

It is the memory of this beauty that now inspires his thoughts of Heaven:

> Tosto disparve, onde 'l cangiar mi giova
> la poca vista a me dal Ciel offerta
> sol per piacer a le sue luci sante.
>
> (12–14)

[She disappeared quickly; and so I am glad to exchange the brief sight Heaven offers me, only to please her holy eyes.]

This movement culminates in the last direct evocation of Laura in the collection. It is like neither Dante's final experience of Beatrice in the *Vita Nuova* nor his renewed contact with his lady in the *Commedia*. In the former, Dante terms his sigh that ascends to Heaven a "spirito peregrino," which, although he knows that it speaks of Beatrice because her name is often repeated, cannot transmit in words its vision of the lady in glory; that vision, and the words to record it, are reserved for the Otherworld of the *poema sacro*.[44] Petrarch's poet, lifted to Heaven "with the wings of thought," engages there in a scene complete with speech attributed both to Laura and to Christ. First he hears Laura affirm the love that she now bears him: "Amico, or t'am'io et or t'onoro, / perch' à' i costumi variati e 'l pelo" [Friend, now I love you and now I honor you, because you have changed your habits and your hair] (362). Next he is led by his lady to Christ:

---

44. For the *arrière-plan* of *Vita Nuova* XLI, see Robert Klein, "Spirito peregrino," in *La forme et l'intelligible* (Paris, 1970), 31–64.

Menami al suo Signor; allor m'inchino,
pregando umilemente che consenta
ch' i' stia a veder et l'uno et l'altro volto.

(362, 9–11)

[She leads me to her Lord; then I incline myself, humbly begging
that He permit me to stay to see their two faces.]

There is a certain theological boldness in this representation, where
Christ responds to Laura's prayer with the assurance of her poet's eternal
salvation.[45] But there is also a different sort of audacity, in that even in
Christ's presence this poet attributes to Laura an equal status in the
motivation of his desire for Heaven. The immediate nature of his desire,
as the reply confirms—"per tardar ancor vent'anni o trenta / parrà a te
troppo, et non fia però molto" [a delay of twenty or thirty years will
seem much to you, but it will be little]—is that he remain now in this
imagined Heaven which, as we have seen throughout the poems of Part
II, is indistinguishable from his desire to be united—or reunited—with
Laura.[46]

To this prayer the best commentary is not a sacred text; it is the intense
fantasy of sonnet 302, "Levommi il mio penser in parte ov'era / quella
ch'io cerco et non ritrovo in terra" [My thought lifted me up to where
she was whom I seek and do not find on earth], in which he joins Laura
in the third circle, "fra lor che 'l terzo cerchio serra." This circle, of
course, is the traditional heaven of Venus to which Petrarch, in a poem
on the death of Sennuccio del Bene, has already assigned love poets, and
with them Laura:

. . . ben ti prego che 'n la terza spera
Guitton saluti, et messer Cino, et Dante,
Franceschin nostro et tutta quella schiera.
A la mia donna puoi ben dire. . . .

(287, 9–12)

[. . . I beg you to salute all in the third sphere: Guittone and
messer Cino and Dante, our Franceschino, and all that band. To
my lady you can well say. . . .]

45. See Foster, *Petrarch, Poet and Humanist*, 84.
46. On this "poetry of the happy dream," see Arnaud Tripet, *Pétrarque ou la connaiss-
ance de soi* (Geneva, 1967), 189–90.

The Paradise in which he later rejoins Laura in dream and imagination retains the coloration of this paradise of love poetry. When his thought raises him to this third circle she takes him by the hand with the assurance that " 'In questa spera / sarai ancor meco, se 'l desir non erra' " ["In this sphere you will be with me, if my desire is not deceived"].[47] And the poet:

> Deh, perché tacque et allargò la mano?
> ch'al suon de' detti sì pietosi et casti,
> poco mancò ch'io non rimasi in Cielo.
>
> (302, 12–14)

[Ah, why did she then become still and open her hand? for at the sound of words so kind and chaste, I almost remained in Heaven.]

We have but to compare these experiences of "Heaven" to that of the amorous vision of canzone 126, "credendo esser in ciel, non là dov'era" [thinking I was in Heaven, not there where I was], to recognize that the version of the Christian Heaven that emerges from many of the poems of Part II of the *Rime sparse* is not dissimilar to the secular earthly Paradise of the poet's creation in Part I: both are achieved via Laura, and in an important sense, both are "paradise" because of Laura.

Recapitulating once again the long story of a love that did not end with the death of Laura, Petrarch's poet interrupts his meditation on the hope to rejoin his lady in Heaven with an exclamation:

> Or avess'io un sì pietoso stile
> che Laura mia potesse torre a Morte
> come Euridice Orfeo sua senza rime,
> ch' i' viverei ancor più che mai lieto!
>
> (332, 49–52)

[Would that I had so sorrowful a style that I could win my Laura back from Death as Orpheus won his Eurydice without rhymes, for then I would live more glad than ever!]

---

47. See Francesco De Sanctis, *Saggio critico sul Petrarca*, ed. degli "Struzzi" (Turin, 1983), 224. While offering an acute reading of these poems *in morte*, he attributes the elaboration of this paradise centered on Laura not to a deliberate poetic strategy but to Petrarch's incapacity to render a paradise which without her does not appeal to his imagination (230). See also the observations of Benedetto Croce, "La poesia del Petrarca," in *Poesia popolare e Poesia d'arte* (Bari, 1946), 65–80.

Even with his certainty of Laura in Paradise, these verses tell us, he would choose to live with her, not in Heaven, but on earth. And repeatedly in the poems *in morte* the backward looking and backward turning that characterize his response to the "refound" Laura are of dubious compatibility with the expressed desire to "salire al cielo." On the contrary, the rapture occasioned now by that renewed sense of contact is very like the assimilation of the sight of Laura to the Beatific Vision in Part I:

> Sì breve è 'l tempo e 'l penser sì veloce
> che mi rendon Madonna così morta,
> ch'al gran dolor la medicina è corta:
> pur mentr'io veggio lei, nulla mi noce.
>
> (284, 1–4)

[So short is the time and the thought so swift which give my lady back to me though she is dead, that the remedy is close by for my great sorrow; as long as I see her, nothing pains me.]

The attraction, once again, is Laura, and its acknowledgment constrains our reading of the repeated—too often repeated?—protestations concerning the inspiration derived from her new heavenly state.

In the last of her dream visits to the poet Laura herself adopts the tone of the admonitory voices heard intermittently throughout the *Rime*, urging that he turn to God for aid in overcoming the power that has long bound him:

> "Or tu, s'altri ti sforza,
> a lui ti svolgi, a lui chiedi soccorso
> sì che siam seco al fine del tuo corso."
>
> (359, 53–55)

["Now you, if another is overpowering you, turn to Him, ask help from Him, so that we may be with Him at the end of your race."]

To be with Laura *and* with God: the alternative between loves and their direction urgently postulated in sestina 142 *in vita* would appear to be transcended in *Rime* 362 cited above, where Laura is associated with Christ in the poet's prayer to remain in Heaven to contemplate both faces, "et l'uno et l'altro volto." The collection closes, however, not on this conciliatory resolution but with a return to oppositions. In the great canzone that closes the *Rime sparse* the alternative to the poet's love for Laura is incarnated in another feminine figure, the "Vergine bella," the beautiful Virgin to whom the poem is addressed. While even a superficial reading of *Rime* 366 discloses its substantial conformity to the rhetoric and images of traditional Marianic poetry, in Petrarch's "Canzone alla Vergine" there appear also new and highly individual elements that converge in the systematic replacement of the image of Laura by that of the Virgin.

In the absence of Laura and of her name, the substitution of the Virgin for Laura in this canzone is a complex textual achievement. The proclamations of the Virgin's uniqueness—she is "sola . . . eletta," "sola al mondo," "senza essempio," "unica et sola," the only one chosen, alone of all the world, unexampled, single and unique—recall the earthly lady unique both *in vita* and *in morte;* the Virgin is "nostra Dea," our goddess, as Laura had been "diva."[48] Now the poet addresses to her many of the compliments that he had addressed to Laura.[49] While some of these had been offered to Laura *in vita,* others recall instead the Laura who comforts, guides, and consoles *in morte.* Now it is the Virgin whose ascent to Heaven is recalled, the Virgin who listens there to his pleas: "salisti al ciel, ond' e' miei preghi ascolti" [you mounted to Heaven whence you hear my prayers]. "Atti pietosi e casti" [merciful and chaste actions] are attributed to the Virgin, while in a poem not far distant Laura's acts were categorized as "piene di casto amore et di pietate" [full of chaste love and pity] (351). The Laura who came "pietosa" to sit at the poet's bedside was periphrastically identified as "chi né prima simil né seconda / ebbe al suo tempo" [she, whom no one surpassed or even approached in her time] (342); now the Virgin is identified as she "cui né prima fu simil né seconda" [whom no one ever surpassed or even approached]. An earnest appeal for Laura's "pietate" *in morte* has the tonality of the appeal later addressed to the Virgin:

> S'onesto amor po meritar mercede
> et se pietà ancor po quant'ella suole,

48. *Rime* 294, 366; Petrarch qualifies this attribution to the Virgin of a possibly unseemly term with pagan associations by adding parenthetically "se dir lice et convensi" [if it is permitted and fitting to say it]. Vernacular precedents of this and other terms now applied to the Virgin are noted in Franco Suitner, *Petrarca e la tradizione stilnovistica* (Florence, 1977), esp. 160–61.

49. Despite the argument of Martinelli (*Petrarca e il Ventoso,* 235), the fact that these compliments derive from a register traditionally employed in the praise of the Virgin does not enhance Laura's likeness to Mary. On the contrary: Tilden, who identifies several of these transferences, observes that "Vergine bella" "gives back to each of these virtues its full spiritual dimension, 'corrects' it, replaces it in its true context" ("Spiritual Conflict," 313–17; citation, 313).

mercede avrò, ché più chiara che 'l sole
a Madonna et al mondo è la mia fede.

(334, 1–4)

[If virtuous love can merit mercy and if pity still has all her wonted power, I shall find mercy, for brighter than the sun is my faithfulness to my lady and to the world.]

Laura's address to the poet in one of her dream appearances as "my faithful one," "fedel mio caro," suggests yet more strongly the double register of the stilnovist *fedeli d'Amore* and the liturgical designation *fideles*,[50] and his protestation of his "fede" to Laura anticipates the often-discussed verses of the final canzone with which he turns at last to the Virgin in an intimate declaration of love:

che se poca mortal terra caduca
amar con sì mirabil fede soglio,
che devrò far di te, cosa gentile?

(366, 121–23)

[for if I am wont to love with such marvelous faith a bit of deciduous mortal dust, how will I love you, a noble thing?]

Earlier poets had invoked the Virgin to replace the secular lady in their devotion. A sonnet by Guittone d'Arezzo affords an unusually explicit example:

Infondi in me di quel divino amore,
Che tira l'alma nostra al primo loco;
Si ch'io disciolga l'amoroso nodo.
Cotal rimedio ha questo aspro furore.
Tal' acqua suole spegner questo foco,
Come d'asse si trahe chiodo con chiodo.[51]

---

50. See Büdel, *"Parusia Redemtricis,"* 41.

51. Cited in E. Williamson, "A Consideration of 'Vergine bella'," *Italica* 29 (1952): 217, who notes that this poem is "an exemplar of the tradition from which Petrarch's poem separates itself." The homely images in Guittone's poem recall a remedy for love proposed by Augustinus (following Cicero and Ovid) but rejected by Franciscus in the *Secretum:* "Some think that an old love can best be driven out by a new, as one nail is by another," and again, "Old love affairs must always yield to new"; see *Petrarch's Secret,* 138.

[Instill in me that divine love that draws our soul back to its native place, so that I may untie the amorous knot. This savage madness has such a remedy. Such water is to put out this fire, as in a board one nail drives out another.]

Guittone pleads that the divine love inspired by the Virgin afford him a "rimedio," that, in terms of his concrete similes, it extinguish the flame of passion and drive out his earthly love; Petrarch's suppliant poet pleads rather than the Virgin replace Laura in all of those functions in which he had perceived and adored her. Invoked now as his guide, his "scorta," she can afford the guidance and protection for which he had long exalted Laura: she is the mariner's stable guide, "star of this tempestuous sea" as Laura had been identified over and over again as the guiding light for his perilous navigation.[52] Her designation as the "refrigerio al cieco ardor" [relief from the blind ardor] of foolish mortals recalls the shelter afforded by the laurel from an ardent and pitiless light in sestina 142, as well as the "refrigerio et l'ombra del dolce lauro" [the coolness and the shade of the sweet laurel] lost with the lost Laura (327) and the poet's complaint to Laura in Heaven that without her "pietà" he is burning "senz' alcun refrigerio," without any relief (340). The determination of the feminine roles assigned to Laura by implication throughout the *rime sparse* is at last explicitly formulated and resolved in the final canzone in the recognition of Mary as the second Eve, she who turns "the tears of Eve to rejoicing again."[53]

Laura is not directly inculpated in this redirection of the poet's love from its mortal to its divine object, for even the severe judgment of Augustinus in the *Secretum*, condemning as "insanias" the amorous disturbances that afflict and imperil his disciple, acknowledges that "ista innocens est"; even the Laura cast once again in this poem as Medusa would be only indirectly responsible.[54] The single direct reference to

52. The epithet of "stella maris" is common for the Virgin. For the motif of the lover as storm-tossed navigator and the beloved as his guide in the courtly tradition, see *Il Mare Amoroso*, ed. E. Vuolo (Rome, 1962), 220–23. Cf. *Rime* 73: "ne la tempesta / ch'i' sostengo d'amor, gli occhi lucenti / sono il mio segno e 'l mio conforto solo" [in the tempest I endure of love those shining eyes are my constellation and my only comfort].

53. As Williamson notes, according to a widespread typology, "the absence of concupiscence from Mary leads to pardon for the concupiscence of Eve" ("A Consideration of 'Vergine bella'," 219–20).

54. See Kenelm Foster, "Beatrice or Medusa," in *Italian Studies presented to E. R. Vincent*, ed. C. P. Brand, K. Foster, U. Limentani (Cambridge, 1962), 53, who observes that Laura remains "untouched by the penitential critique," and Williamson, "A Consideration of 'Vergine bella' ": "The sin is wholly in the cherishing mind of the beholder" (224). See also Martinelli, *Petrarca e il Ventoso*, 236: "non è coinvolta direttamente ma solo indirettamente, in quanto creatura mortale di stupefacente bellezza."

Laura in the final poem, however, evokes her failure to offer him comfort in terms that raise once again the interesting question of "what Laura knew":

> Vergine, tale è terra et posto à in doglia
> lo mio cor, che vivendo in pianto il tenne
> et de mille miei mali un non sapea;
> et per saperlo pur quel che n'avenne
> fora avvenuto, ch' ogni altra sua voglia
> era a me morte et a lei fama rea.
>
> (366, 92–97)

[Virgin, one is now dust and makes my soul grieve who kept it, while alive, in weeping and of my thousand sufferings did not know one; and though she had known them, what happened would still have happened, for any other desire in her would have been death to me and dishonor to her.]

In Part I, we recall, the poet repeatedly confessed his uncertainty concerning Laura's awareness of his suffering and the motivation of her failure to respond to his plaint:

> Et per far mie dolcezze amare et empie,
> o s'infinge o non cura o non s'accorge
> del fiorir queste inanzi tempo tempie.
>
> (210, 12–14)

[And to make the sweetness that I feel bitter and cruel, either she pretends or she does not care or she does not see how these temples are blossoming white before their time.]

But we recall too what is *not* included in his confession to the Virgin, the counsel and consolation offered by Laura in the poems of Part II *in morte*, invoked in terms very similar:

> Tu che dentro mi vedi e 'l mio mal senti
> et sola puoi finir tanto dolore,
> con la tua ombra acqueta i miei lamenti.
>
> (340, 12–14)

[You who see me within and know my suffering and are the only one who can end so much sorrow, with your image quiet my laments.]

This reflection, moreover, appears strikingly incongruent with the recall late in Part II of her "dolci durezze et placide repulse" [sweet rigors and placid repulses] and the tempering effect of her "leggiadri sdegni" [charming angers] while yet *in vita,* confirming the continuity of those postures with the role now assumed by Laura *in morte:*

> divino sguardo da far l'uom felice,
> or fiero in affrenar la mente ardita
> a quel che giustamente si disdice,
> or presto a confortar mia frale vita:
> questo bel variar fu la radice
> di mia salute, ch' altramente era ita.

(351, 9–14)

[a glance so divine as to make a man blessed, now fierce in reining in my daring mind from what is justly forbidden, now swift to comfort my frail life: this lovely variety was the root of my salvation, which otherwise was gone.]

In the last of her dream appearances Laura herself will assert this continuity, promising, as we have seen, to be for her poet in Heaven yet more beautiful and more loving, having been "sì selvaggia et pia, / salvando inseme tua salute et mia" [once so wild and kind, saving at once your salvation and my own] (359). This affirmation has a significant counterpoint in Petrarch's rewriting of the story in the dream vision of the *Trionfi,* where Laura herself, openly confessing her long-unavowed love, reminds the poet of the many ways in which she had governed his excessive ardor by modulating her responses, thereby safeguarding both his life and their honor (*Tr. Mor.* II, 100–108).[55] Foster, whose reading of the *Rime sparse* emphasizes "the great change . . . from the 'Laura-*object*' of Part I . . . to the Laura-*subject* of Part II," protests the final apparent denial to Laura of any intimate knowledge of the poet's suffering. Constrained by a reading that privileges her positive role in the poet's spiritual evolution following her death, he can conclude only that Petrarch, in order to close the collection with the Virgin replacing Laura, "sacrificed one side of his artist's nature to another, his instinct for unity and continuity to the claims of dramatic contrast."[56] The poet's evocation of his earthly love in "Vergine bella," however, in fact calls into question

---

55. For the close relation of the two episodes and their recall of Dantean *loci,* see Pasquini, "La canzone CCCLIX," 245–47.

56. Foster, *Petrarch, Poet and Humanist,* 83, 89.

the status of the Laura of Part II of the collection once again. Now he appeals to the Virgin to do what the earthly lady *in vita* both would not and could not: afford him consolation:[57]

> tu vedi il tutto, et quel che non potea
> far altri è nulla a la tua gran vertute:
> por fine al mio dolore . . .
>
> (101–3)

[you see all, and what another could not do is nothing to your great power, to put an end to my sorrow . . .]

The reciprocity impossible with Laura ("ogni altra sua voglia / era a me morte et a lei fama rea" [any other desire in her would have been death to me and dishonor to her]) is fully possible with the Virgin ("ch'a te onore et a me fia salute" [which to you would be honor and to me salvation]).[58] In the phrase "poca mortal terra caduca" [a bit of deciduous mortal dust] that now describes Laura, rendered more poignant through its bare simplicity, he renounces the attribution of transcendence to this extraordinary earthly creature in favor of the Virgin, whom he invokes to assist him "ben ch'i' sia terra et tu del Ciel regina" [though I am earth and you are queen of Heaven].

The poet who had loved and celebrated Laura now offers to the Virgin more than a newly redirected love and fidelity. The explicit rededication in *Rime* 366 promises to make of him her poet:

> Se dal mio stato assai misero et vile
> per le tu man resurgo,
> Vergine, i' sacro et purgo
> al tuo nome et pensieri e 'ngegno et stile . . .
>
> (124–27)

[If from my wretched and vile state I rise again at your hands, Virgin, I consecrate and cleanse in your name my thought and wit and style . . .]

---

57. For vernacular precedents for this statement of desired reward, see Valeria Bertolucci Pizzorusso, "Libri e canzonieri d'autore nel medioevo: Prospettive di ricerca," *Studi Mediolatini e Volgari* 30 (1984): 106.

58. Tilden, who notes this contrast, notes also that "however ill-defined it may be, the goal of all Petrarch's struggles is in some sort of positive relation, if not union, with the object of his desire"; see "Spiritual Conflict," 315, 316.

This is neither a daring nor an innovative gesture: from the early twelfth century Marianic lyric had exchanged both form and substance with vernacular poems in praise of earthly ladies.[59] The explicit thematization of an altered allegiance, in which the poet sets forth his new verse as concrete evidence of a change from secular love to spiritual devotion, also has precedents in earlier lyric. In the prologue to his collection of *Cantigas de Santa Maria*, Alfonso X el Sabio exalts the art of *trobar* as appropriate for the praise of his new Lady, whom he will henceforth serve exclusively as *trobador*;[60] the *canzoniere* of Lanfranco Cigala recants the earthly love celebrated in the lyrics in a concluding canzone dedicated to the Virgin.[61] A sequence of love poems by Guiraut Riquer, in which the *senhal* "Belh Deport" refers to both the earthly and the heavenly lady, affords suggestive analogies to the *Rime sparse* as a whole: it is following the death of the earthly lady that the Virgin replaces her as the object of the poet's love, and the collection closes with a brief epilogue in verse in the form of a prayer dedicated to the Virgin and to Christ.[62]

Yet while Petrarch is not the first to aspire to the role of the Virgin's troubadour, the terms of his rededication are particularly suggestive for the story of his love for Laura told in the lyric "fragments" of the *rime sparse*. This is not only a dedication but a consecration, "'i' sacro . . . al tuo nome,'" and as such it follows upon the gestures of consecration associated repeatedly with Laura and her name in poems late in the collection.[63] Now, in addition to his "pensieri e 'ngegno et stile," thought and wit and style, he will offer to his new Lady "la lingua e 'l cor, le lagrime e i sospiri," his tongue and heart, his tears and his sighs, the four terms together offering an extraordinarily concise evocation of his love for Laura. The poet of Part I of the collection weeps constantly, in fair and in foul weather, in apparent confirmation of the concise self-analysis that stands as self-definition in an early component: "Et io son un di quei che 'l pianger giova" [And I am one of those whom weeping pleases]

59. A well-known example is *Les Miracles de Nostre Dame par Gautier de Coinci*, ed. V. F. Koenig (Geneva, 1955–1970), 4 vols. For a suggestive study, see Bertolucci Pizzorusso, "Libri e canzonieri d'autore," 110–16.

60. Bertolucci Pizzorusso, "Libri e canzonieri d'autore," 104. Although no secular love lyrics appear among Alfonso's poems, their past production is assumed in the *fictio* as the prehistory of his "new" Marianic poetry (106).

61. See Giuseppe Ferrero, *I trovatori d'Italia* (Turin, 1967), I, 109.

62. The collection is described and analyzed in Bertolucci Pizzorusso's important study, 96–100.

63. See poems 297, 321, 327. Guglielmo Gorni observes that the entire canzone converges toward this final consecration of the Virgin as the true dedicatee; see "Petrarca Virgini (Lettura della canzone CCCLXVI 'Vergine bella')," *Lectura Petrarce, VII, 1987* (Padua, 1988), esp. 212.

(37).[64] It is weeping that testifies to the unchanged and unchanging nature of his desires as he marks the sixteenth anniversary of the *innamoramento:*

> et d'antichi desir lagrime nove
> provan com'io son pur quel ch'i' mi soglio,
> né per mille rivolte ancor son mosso.
>
> (118, 12–14)

[and new tears for old desires show me to be still what I used to be, nor for a thousand turnings about have I yet moved.]

In the opening of the great canzone that in turn opens Part II, a new weeping figures among the posited alternatives to his condition:

> I' vo pensando, et nel penser m'assale
> una pietà sì forte di me stesso
> che mi conduce spesso
> ad altro lagrimar ch' i' non soleva;
>
> (264, 1–4)

[I go thinking and in thought pity for myself assails me, so strong that it often leads me to a weeping different from my accustomed one]

But this soon gives way to another "altro lagrimar," that of his grief following the report of Laura's death. That weeping, initially the sign not only of mourning but of the finality of loss and separation—"si sbigottisce et si sconforta / mia vita in tutto, et notte et giorno piange . . ." [my life is terrified and unconsoled altogether, night and day it weeps] (277)— then takes on a different tonality through its reconnection with Laura, who returns in dreams and imagination to dry his tears. It is in terms of weeping that the last poem to mention Laura directly in the collection summarizes the poet's continued servitude to Amor since her death,

---

64. In the first group of poems in the collection, tears or weeping occur in 3; 15; 17; 18; 19; 22. See esp. 66: "piango al sereno et a la pioggia / et a' gelati et a' soavi venti" [I weep in clear weather and in rain, and in freezing and in warming winds]. Tears flow from the wound inflicted by Amor (87), and weeping is the tribute that Amor demands (107), figuring in his self-definition: "i' mi pasco di lagrime, et tu 'l sai" [I feed on tears, and you know it] (93). Tears define the poet's retreat in a poem addressed to his "cameretta" (234).

spent in "dieci altri anni piangendo" [ten more years of weeping] (364);[65] the following sonnet, the last poem preceding "Vergine bella," opens with the penitential declaration "I' vo piangendo i miei passati tempi / i quai posi in amar cosa mortale" [I go weeping for my past time, which I spent in loving a mortal thing] (365).

Now he implores the Virgin to alter the nature of his weeping:

> Vergine, tu di sante
> lagrime et pie adempi 'l meo cor lasso,
> ch'almen l'ultimo pianto sia devoto,
> senza terrestro limo,
> come fu 'l primo   non d'insania voto.
>
> (366, 113–17)

[Virgin, fill my weary heart with holy repentant tears, let at least my last weeping be devout and without earthly mud, as was my first vow, before my insanity.]

But weeping, like singing, has throughout the collection also suggested rhyming. In the proemial sonnet, the record promised the reader in scattered rhymes is to be recognized by the "vario stile in ch'io piango e ragiono" [the varied style in which I weep and speak]; in canzone 23, following the *innamoramento* before which he records that "lagrima ancor non mi bagnava il petto" [no tear yet bathed my breast], the verb suggests his attempted speech as he goes "lagrimando" in the guise of a swan, then with his own voice, then as a fountain, then as a disembodied spirit. The first poem to celebrate Laura's return to her accustomed places *in morte* finds him weeping, not singing:

> Là 've cantando andai di te molt'anni
> or, come vedi, vo di te piangendo—
> di te piangendo no, ma de' miei danni.
>
> (282, 9–11)

[Where I went singing of you many years, now, as you see, I go weeping for you—no, not weeping for you but for my loss.]

65. In two famous sonnets in which the poet likens his forlorn state to that of a solitary bird, the bird's song is "weeping"; see "Quel rosigniuol che sì soave piagne" [that nightingale that so sweetly weeps] (311) and the poem that before Petrarch's indication of reordering of the final lyrics was to precede "Vergine bella," "Vago augelletto, che cantando vai / o ver piangendo il tuo tempo passato" [Wandering bird that go singing or else weeping for past time] (353).

This weeping would seem to signal the end of his amorous rhymes: "or sia qui fine al mio amoroso canto," he announces, "et la cetera mia rivolta in pianto" [Now here let there be an end to my song of love . . . and my lyre is turned to weeping] (292). But it is only the transposition, the translation *in morte,* of that poetry; the rhymes continue, and he records a deliberate choice, "togliendo anzi per lei sempre trar guai / che cantar per qualunque" [(choosing) rather always to groan for her than to sing for anyone else] (296). Even as he confirms again that as a result of Laura's death his song is converted to weeping, "converso in pianto," she it is "che i' canto et piango in rime" [whom I sing and bewail in rhymes] (332).[66]

Tears and verses: both are promised to Christ as Petrarch invokes divine aid in the protasis of the *Africa:*

> Full many a reverent verse shall I bring back
> to Thee—if verses please Thee—from the crest
> of high Parnassus. If they please Thee not,
> then Thine shall be the guerdon of those tears
> which long since I might fittingly have shed.[67]

First poems, then tears are offered, with the suggestion that the latter may be the more welcome. At the conclusion of the *Rime,* both new tears and new love poetry are offered in return for the aid fervently solicited from the Virgin. Here is the culmination of the poet's project to "dire d'Amore," and its consecration.[68] "[I]l tempo fugge / che scrivendo d'altrui di me non calme" [time flies while I write of another, not caring about myself], he had acknowledged in the opening poem of Part II of the collection (264); no longer will his poetic celebration of his lady imperil his soul. The spiritual significance of this new allegiance is foregrounded when his idolatrous posture before the laurel—"et con

---

66. See also 344: "Piansi et cantai; non so più mutar verso, / ma dì et notte il duol ne l'alma accolto / per la lingua et per li occhi sfogo et verso" [I wept and sang; I cannot change my style, but day and night I vent through my tongue and my eyes the sorrow accumulated in my soul]. In the *Trionfi* he reflects that in Eternity he will be known as "chi pianse sempre," he who ever wept; at its close Laura is "quella ch'ancor piangendo canto" [she of whom, still weeping, still I sing] (*Tr. Eter.* 95, 97).

67. *Petrarch's Africa,* trans. Thomas G. Bergin and Alice S. Wilson (New Haven, 1977), book 1, 20–24. On the significance of this passage, see Also Bernardo, *Petrarch, Scipio and the "Africa"* (Baltimore, 1962), 200; Thomas M. Greene, "Petrarch *Viator:* The Displacements of Humanism," *Yearbook of English Studies* 12 (1982): 50.

68. For this poem as the vindication of the position of the Petrarchan persona Franciscus at the close of the *Secretum,* see Renato Caputo, *"Cogitans fingo": Petrarca tra "Secretum" e "Canzoniere"* (Rome, 1987), esp. 109–16, 160–65.

preghiere oneste / l'adoro et 'nchino come cosa santa" [and with chaste prayers I adore it and bow to it as to a holy thing] (228)—yields in the final canzone to the homage and submission offered to the Virgin: "Con le ginocchia de la mente inchine / prego che sia mia scorta" [with the knees of my mind bent, I beg you to be my guide].[69]

But "Vergine bella" offers more than this: the revision of the poet's story revises too the familiar topos of the *donna / sole*. The poem opens with an address to the Virgin who is clothed with the sun and crowned with stars, "di sol vestita, coronata di stelle." This image, directly recalling a passage of the Apocalypse commented throughout the Middle Ages and recurrent in Marian poetry and art, inaugurates in the final canzone a program in which the familiar polarities of light and darkness are reinterpreted to bring together the divine light and the lady. The argument in this canzone is frequently cast in images of light: the Virgin is first among the wise virgins of the Biblical parable "and with the brightest lamp"; it is she who illumines this life as well as adorns Heaven. Most significantly, the Virgin in whom the "sommo Sole" was incarnate is the intermediary between earthly and heavenly light; the divine light that "hid itself" in the Virgin is incarnate in Christ, the Sun of justice.[70] The divine light shines within and through the Virgin, the "shining noble window of Heaven"; thus the Virgin, replacing Laura as object of the poet's devotion and his praise, opens rather than closes the vistas of his love. The Virgin of the final canzone is not only beautiful, not only pure, not only compassionate: her invocation as *advocata nostra* establishes a new relation through which the poet may yet hope for his salvation.

It is in its repeated references to Christ that the final poem of the *Rime* proposes finally a realignment of the essential structure of the poet's story, of the triangle of sun, beloved lady, and poet established in the opening poems of the collection. As the mythological model relates Apollo and the poet in their love for Daphne/Laura, in this poem the Virgin is identified as the beloved both of the deity and of the mortal, a relation stressed in the praise directed to her in the opening stanza: "al sommo Sole / piacesti sì che 'n te sua luce ascose . . ." [(you) so pleased the highest Sun that in you He hid His light . . .]. Laura, in her mythological identity with Daphne, had been loved by the sun, in the

69. Theodor E. Mommsen suggests that Petrarch probably adopted this unusual phrase from an apocryphal section of the Latin Vulgate; in his Testament, written about the time he transcribed "Vergine bella" into Vat. lat. 3195, he prays to Christ "with the genuflexion of this very soul." See *Petrarch's Testament* (Ithaca, 1957), 16–17.

70. See Williamson, "A Consideration of 'Vergine bella'," 219–22: "The light shining forth from the sun within Mary establishes the logical antecedent of all that follows, i.e., that through her God's grace can be obtained."

guise of Apollo.[71] Now the Virgin, with an emphasis repeated in the
further allusion to the incarnation:

> Vergine sola al mondo, senza esempio,
> che 'l Ciel di tue bellezze innamorasti,
> cui né prima fu simil né seconda:
> santi penseri, atti pietosi et casti
> al vero Dio sacrato et vivo tempio
> fecero in tua verginità feconda.

(53–58)

[Virgin unique in the world, unexampled, who made Heaven in
love with your beauties, whom none every surpassed or even
approached: holy thoughts, merciful and chaste actions made a
consecrated living temple of the true God in your fruitful virgin-
ity.]

This passage, partly topical, is similar in this respect to the prayer that
Saint Bernard addresses to the Virgin in the opening of the last canto of
the *Paradiso:* " 'Nel ventre tuo si raccese l'amore, / per lo cui caldo ne
l'etterna pace / così è germinato questo fiore' " ["In thy womb was
rekindled the Love under whose warmth this flower in the eternal peace
has thus unfolded"] (*Par.* XXXIII, 7–9). Petrarch's declaration that
Heaven was enamored of the Virgin's "bellezze," however, which takes
precedence over the evocation of her piety and her chastity, combines
with the opening address to the "Vergine bella" to establish a paradigm
that may more readily be set against the mythological paradigm relating
Apollo to Daphne and the poet to Laura.[72] In reassigning the roles that
related the poet to Apollo and to the *donna / sole,* "Vergine bella"
establishes a new triangle bound by love. Instead of closure, it affords a
new opening whose importance has yet to be considered, bringing at last
to the fore the figure of Christ.

71. See Cesare Galimberti, "Amate dal sole (R.V.F. XXXIV, CLXXXVIII, CCCLXVI),"
in *Miscellanea di Studi in onore di Vittore Branca,* I (Florence, 1983), 432–43.
72. We recall that "atti pietosi e casti" have been attributed to Laura herself; for a direct
formulation in a poem not far distant in the arrangement of the *Rime* from the canzone
addressed to the Virgin, we find her acts depicted as "piene di casto amore et di pietate"
[full of chaste love and pity] (351).

6

COSMOLOGIES

The canzone to the "Vergine bella," closing the *Rime sparse* with a devout and comprehensive recasting of the alternative between divine love and the love of Laura, has confirmed for many readers the imperative to locate the lyric collection in relation to the great Christian itinerary of sin-repentance-redemption. It was precisely this, Martinelli proposes, that governed Petrarch's reconstruction of his existence according to the phases of a progressive conversion to God, this the project that guided the collection and arrangement of his vernacular fragments into an exemplary story of man's experience from the fall to the redemption within the great overarching design of salvation history.[1] It was not by chance, according to another authoritative summary, that Petrarch began systematically to bring together his vernacular lyrics and to make them public only when he realized following Laura's death that he could organize and thereby justify them within a traditional structure of sin, repentance, and redemption.[2] In such a reading, the critical point in the poet's exemplary itinerary is of course the death of Laura, because it is presupposed that, with her death, "everything changes": her role changes, from unwitting temptress *in vita* to heavenly guide *in morte;* the poet's response changes, from a love dominated by concupiscence to a *caritas* that inspires his thoughts of Heaven.

Yet if we take our cue for the reading of the poet's story, both prospectively and retrospectively, from the principal structural indices of its organization, it is evident that this postulated comprehensive linear

---

1. Bortolo Martinelli, *Petrarca e il Ventoso* (Bergamo, 1977), 225, 223, 226; 251–59; 271–72. For a dissenting view, see Raffaele Amaturo, *Petrarca* (Bari, 1971), 354.
2. Emilio Bigi, Introduction to Francesco Petrarca, *Opere,* ed. E. Bigi and G. Ponte (Milan, 1963), xxv.

development does not adequately account for the framing of the collection with two poems from which Laura's name is absent—poems in which, moreover, the experience of the poet's love for Laura receives, implicitly or explicitly, a negative valorization. Thus Foster, who protests the harshness of the treatment accorded Laura in "Vergine bella," is obliged to devalue the proemial poem as well, concluding that in its failure to account for the dimension of a mature adulthood engaged in a salutary friendship with Laura it is "inadequate as a summary of the book it purports to introduce."[3] And indeed, seen in this light, both *Rime* 1 and the closing canzone appear strangely detached, even estranged, from the collection as a whole; Foster cites as evidence the poet's proclamation in the opening sonnet "that he is *now* very different from the man he was *then*," when he wrote the lyrics to which the reader's attention is invited.

The speaker of *Rime* 1, however, does not assure us that he is *altogether* different; nor is the lack of definitive resolution in this poem, which is both epilogue and prologue to the collection of *rime sparse*, unique in Petrarch's corpus. The debate of the *Secretum* too is inconclusive;[4] the close of the letter recounting his ascent of Mount Ventoux finds him "only in part different."[5] Consider, on the other hand, the introduction to his collection of *epistolae metricae*, in which spiritual transformation is again a theme. Here too Petrarch recalls the wounds inflicted by Amor; here, as in the proemial poem of the *Rime*, he introduces the work to follow as an account of his tears and his suffering; here too he looks back over that earlier experience. Now, he says, he seems to himself another person: "My mind, now at peace, shrinks with horror from past anguish; and rereading what I once wrote, it is another's voice that I seem to hear."[6] The poet of the *Rime sparse*, on the contrary, will not shrink from the experience of his love for Laura, but relive it and cherish it in its recording; when he hears "other voices," they will be admonitory voices urging a change in his course; and at the end of the collection he

---

3. Kenelm Foster, *Petrarch, Poet and Humanist* (Edinburgh, 1984), 46–47.

4. Ugo Dotti observes that the striking *novità* of this ending lies in its lack of a conclusion, its acceptance of profound uncertainty and fluctuation; see "Miti e forme dell''io' nella cultura di Francesco Petrarca," *Revue des Etudes Italiennes* 29 (1983): 74.

5. For the connection between these two texts and *Rime* 1, see Victoria Kahn, "The Figure of the Reader in Petrarch's *Secretum*," *PMLA* 100 (1985): 163: "In all three works the moment of conversion is deferred by the act of writing itself."

6. *Metr.* I, 1, 62–65; cited by Foster, *Petrarch, Poet and Humanist*, 50. The near-contemporary composition of the preface of the *Metrice* and the proemial sonnet of the *Rime* is argued by Francisco Rico, " 'Rime sparse,' 'Rerum vulgarium fragmenta': Para el titulo y el primer soneto del *Canzoniere*," *Medioevo Romanzo* 3 (1976): 108–11.

will not have achieved that confident "peace of mind," that *pace* for which he will implore the Virgin. The phrasing of "quand'era *in parte* altr'uom da quel ch'i'sono" of *Rime* 1 initiates the poetic record, not of a complete, but of a partial transformation and calls attention to its partiality, one whose nature is left for the disquieted reader to discover.

Both the proemial sonnet and the insights of the preceding chapters suggest that the itinerary of the *Rime*, rather than a journey from sin to redemption, is that from the embracing of an illusion to the end of illusion. Moreover, the privileged sets of oppositions and alternatives examined in the preceding chapters suggest that the relation between the two parts of the collection is marked not by difference but by sameness. Canzone 264 at the start of Part II contains no mention of Laura's death;[7] what it does contain, as we have repeatedly noted, is the focused recapitulation of the oppositions that mark the poet's state throughout Part I, and these are not to end with the death of Laura.[8] It is not with her death that the poet's "errore" first framed as the "primo giovenile errore" of *Rime* 1 comes to an end, not the death of Laura that effects the rectification of his course. We have seen that in Part II as in Part I the poet seeks consolation and the vestiges of Laura's presence in her familiar landscape. Both *in vita* and *in morte* it is her beauty that enamors him, the sweetness of her voice to which he is attentive; in both parts, expectation and hope—to see Laura again, to be reunited with Laura— are in constant tension with memory, the past in constant tension with the future.[9] The thematization of time's passage and its explicit confirmation in the temporal markers of the anniversary poems in both Part I and Part II only heighten the sameness that marks the poet's responses to Laura *in vita* and *in morte*. "There is so little reorientation," observes Peter Hainsworth, "that Part 2 seems overall a more concentrated, darker rewriting of Part 1, its transposition into a minor key."[10] The illusions of

7. Like the division into two parts, it may antedate her death by perhaps a year; see the chronological reconstruction of E. H. Wilkins, *The Making of the "Canzoniere" and Other Petrarchan Studies* (Rome, 1951), 150–53. Francisco Rico, however, affirms that both the composition of *Rime* 1 and the bipartition of the collection follow the death of Laura and are probably assignable to 1350; see " 'Rime sparse,' 'Rerum vulgarium fragmenta'," 102–16, and Foster's endorsement in *Petrarch, Poet and Humanist*, 98–100. For the critical debate, see Bortolo Martinelli, *Il "Secretum" conteso* (Naples, 1982); Hans Baron, *Petrarch's "Secretum"* (Cambridge, Mass., 1985).

8. Hence Marguerite Waller: "The death of Laura is fortuitous to this alteration, and . . . does not inaugurate a change of the sort necessary to the process of integrating and transcending the past." See *Petrarch's Poetics and Literary History* (Amherst, Mass., 1980), 83.

9. For this "dialectic of a bipolar opposition," see Gianfranco Contini, *Letteratura italiana delle origini* (Florence, 1970), 613.

10. *Petrarch the Poet* (London, 1988), 163.

Part I are reflected and refracted in the illusions of Part II: his cherished fantasy of Laura's longing for him, his hatred of life and desire for death, his reproaches to her when she fails to ease his pain, his praise of her incomparable beauty (as incomparable in Heaven as on earth) and of her sweet speech that banishes all other concerns—all these *in morte di Laura* are mirror images of his varying responses to the elusive Laura celebrated *in vita*.[11]

These many correspondences strongly suggest that the structural relation between the two parts of the collection is not linear but in a special sense specular.[12] In both parts, groups of texts that may be characterized as intermediate structures between the micro- and the macrostructural levels[13]—the sonnets of "l'aura," the series of poems evoking Laura's presence in Valchiusa, those in which her appearance is recorded either in visions or in dreams—organize the carefully elaborated sets of correspondences.[14] The substantial diachronic evidence of the evolution of the *Rime*, moreover, offers suggestive insights into this organization, disclosing that, as Petrarch continued long after the initial division into two parts to revise components of each, to add new ones and to rearrange their order, he simultaneously elaborated thematically correlated series of poems in Part I and Part II. This procedure, as De Robertis observes, is a *mise en abyme* of the definitive arrangement of the *Rime* as a whole.[15]

---

11. Teodolinda Barolini in an important essay casts this relation in terms of the relative narrativity of the two parts of the collection: "in part I narrative is avoided because the goal is to stop time, resist death; in part 2 narrative is invoked because in order to preserve her as she was he must preserve her in time. . . . When she is alive, he needs to cancel time. When she is dead, he needs to appropriate it." See "The Making of a Lyric Sequence: Time and Narrative in Petrarch's *Rerum vulgarium fragmenta*," *MLN* 104 (1989): 37.

12. For a variety of other applications of the term and a typology of specular discourse in narrative, see Lucien Dällenbach, *Le récit spéculaire: Essai sur la mise en abyme* (Paris, 1977).

13. See Cesare Segre, "I sonetti dell'aura," *Lectura Petrarce, III, 1983* (Padua, 1984), 59.

14. For the latter series in Part I and Part II see Robert M. Durling, *The Figure of the Poet in the Renaissance Epic* (Cambridge, Mass., 1965), 78–83. Segre analyzes the series of "l'aura" (194, 196, 197; 320–21) in "I Sonetti dell'aura," esp. 70–71. On Valchiusa, see Chapter 2 above on 107–18 and 279–82. As Oscar Büdel observes, Laura's visionary appearances still *in vita* anticipate her dream-appearances in Part II; see "*Parusia Redemtricis:* Lauras Traumbesuche in Petrarcas *Canzoniere*," in *Petrarca 1304–1374: Beiträge su Werk und Wirkung*, ed. Fritz Schalk (Frankfurt, 1975), 37, 39.

15. Domenico De Robertis, "Contiguità e selezione nella costruzione del canzoniere petrarchesco," *Studi di Filologia Italiana* 43 (1985): 51. He examines the first two *carte* of Vat. lat. 3196, representing the critical period in the construction of the collection when Petrarch assumed from his scribe Giovanni Malpaghini the task of copying components from this "codice degli abbozzi" into Vat. lat. 3195. Rosanna Bettarini concludes of Petrarch's near-contemporaneous additions to both parts that their elaboration is not only

Drawing the consequences of these conclusions, there is yet another sense in which specularity inheres fundamentally in the *Rime sparse*. We have seen that in both Part I and Part II the poet appropriates from Scripture a language and an imagery that suggest the quasi-religious nature of his response to Laura; we have seen too that the paradise created about the figure of Laura, *in morte* as well as *in vita*, is a rival to the heavenly Paradise, and that her radiance, illuminating his world, dazzles him and renders him oblivious to the divine light. Now we must follow the implications of those observations: the overall structure of the *Rime* too combines multiple elements whose ideational coherence is reliant on a specular construct, and for its origins we return once again to the beginning of the story.

While the proemial sonnet has the traditional function of exordium, *Rime* 2–5 apply the rhetorical *initium narrationis* to the collection as a whole.[16] Together sonnet 2 and 3 afford an account of the *innamoramento* that substantially conforms to the recommendations of a medieval rhetoric that, in addition to the identification of personae, included among the "topoi of the thing" the answers to questions: Why? Where? When? How? The mythological model in these two poems affords an immediate answer to the questions How? and Why? as the armed attack on a disarmed victim is carried out by a conventional Amor seeking vengeance for prior resistance. The questions concerning place and time, however, lead in turn to further distinctions: Where? gives rise to an *argumentum a loco*, When? to an *argumentum a tempore*. In the *Rime* the question of place, not addressed in the introductory poems, will soon be engaged in those that follow, while the answer to the question When? is revealed here with particular emphasis, to mark the time of the *innamoramento* as determinate for all future experience.

We may insist on the coordinates *a tempore* and *a loco* because Petrarch insists on them in telling his poet's story. The nouns *tempo* and *loco* are among the most frequently used in the *Rime sparse,* and most often they occur in combination without further modification to designate the coordinates of the *innamoramento.* In the prologue scene of the *Trionfi,* where Petrarch tells essentially the same story, they again mark its inception. "Da quel tempo . . . Da indi in qua . . . Da indi in qua"— from that time, from that moment 'til now—the protagonist of that poem

---

parallel but specular; see "Perché 'narrando' il duol si disacerba (Motivi esegetici degli autografi petrarcheschi)," in *La critica del testo* (Rome, 1985), 318–19.

16. Rico, " 'Rime sparse', 'Rerum vulgarium fragmenta'," 107. That Petrarch was attentive to such rhetorical precepts is evident, he points out, in the prologue to the *Familiares;* cf. G. Billanovich, *Petrarca letterato, I: Lo scrittoio del Petrarca* (Rome, 1947), esp. 49.

recapitulates his long experience of love (*Tr. Cup.* III, 112–20),[17] and the memory of "that day" leads the protagonist into the "closed place" where the dream vision is to occur:

> Al tempo che rinnova i miei sospiri
> per la dolce memoria di quel giorno
> che fu principio a sì lunghi martiri . . .
>   Amor, gli sdegni, e 'l pianto, e la stagione
> ricondotto m'aveano al chiuso loco
> ov'ogni fascio il cor lasso ripone.
>
> (Tr. Cup. I, 1–3, 7–9)

[The season when my sighing is renewed had come, stirring the memory of that day whereon my love and suffering began . . . Springtime and love and scorn and tearfulness again had brought me to the Vale Enclosed where from my heart my heavy burdens fall.]

In the lyric collection, both place and time are more narrowly indicated in a sonnet constructed of the elements of the *innamoramento:*

> Benedetto sia 'l giorno e 'l mese et l'anno
> e la stagione e 'l tempo et l'ora e 'l punto
> e 'l bel paese e 'l loco ov' io fui giunto
> da' duo begli occhi che legato m'ànno.
>
> (61, 1–4)

[Blessed be the day and the month and the year and the season and the time and the hour and the instant and the beautiful countryside and the place where I was struck by the two lovely eyes that have bound me.]

The temporal dimension, indicated here in an insistent rhythm balanced by first a widening scope—"giorno mese anno"—and then a progressive narrowing, arrives at last not only at "l'ora" but at the precise moment, the "punto," of the *innamoramento*. The spatial element is similarly depicted: while the "bel paese," sometimes annotated simply as Provence, could presumably include Avignon, we have seen that consistently

---

17. The apparent monotony, well motivated because of the primordial significance of "that time," is judged harshly by Umberto Bosco; see *Francesco Petrarca* (Rome, 1973³), 231.

in the *Rime* it designates Valchiusa; thus the progression *a maiore ad minus* of "bel paese" and "loco" would refer us first to Valchiusa, then to the exact site of the fatal encounter. The familiar terms again directly identify the *innamoramento* in a poem that singularly heightens this combination through its adaptation to the sonnet form of the lexical intensification characteristic of the sestina:

> Quando mi vene inanzi il tempo e 'l loco
> ov' i' perdei me stesso, e 'l caro nodo
> ond' Amor di sua man m'avinse . . .
> . . . così di lontan m'alluma e 'ncende
> che la memoria ad ogni or fresca et salda
> pur quel nodo mi mostra e 'l loco e 'l tempo.
>
> (175, 1–3, 12–14)

[When I remember the time and the place where I lost myself, and the dear knot with which Love with his own hand bound me . . . from afar she so ignites and kindles me, that the memory, still fresh and whole, points out to me that knot and the place and the time.]

These are the coordinates of an occurrence, "ov' i' perdei me stesso" [where I lost myself], whose gravity will become apparent only later in the ordering of the poems.

Curtius explains the rhetorical categories of place and time: "the former . . . is concerned with discovering proofs in the character of the place where the matter in question occurred," mountainous or level, frequented or lonely, etc. The issue is similar for the *argumentum a tempore:* when, in what season, at what time of day.[18] We have already explored the suggestiveness of place in the *Rime*, locating the poet's experience in Valchiusa or alternatively, eventually, in the *selva*. What "proofs" are then offered the reader in the temporal designation of the *innamoramento?* That the two renderings of *Rime* 2 and 3 define a single event is signaled by syntactic parallelism: "Era . . . quando" [It was . . . when] sets up identical indications in the two poems of circumstance and temporal location.[19] Yet in one sense, as Petrarch's readers have

18. E. R. Curtius, *European Literature and the Latin Middle Ages*, trans. Willard Trask (New York, 1953), 194; "in medieval theory the technical terms *argumentum a loco, a tempore*, which stem from the forensic topics of proof, are transferred to the rules for nature description."

19. See Marco Santagata, "Connessioni intertestuali nel *Canzoniere* del Petrarca," *Strumenti critici* 9 (1975): 89.

pointed out, the two versions are incompatible. The former represents Amor's attack as a vendetta and describes the poet's futile attempt to activate his higher faculties in his own defense, the latter suggests the implications of that attack for the moral state of the protagonist and fixes its prospective function in the spiritual history central to the *Rime* as a whole. The first presents a "laic" version of the event, the second a spiritual occasion.[20]

In the *De inventione*, a founding text of the rhetoric known to Petrarch, Cicero recommends that the nature of an act or an interior state be suggested with relation both to time, conventionally subdivided as we have seen, and to *occasio*, "occasion," in turn subdivided in three *genera: publicum, commune,* and *singulare.*[21] In the *Rime* that occasion is powerfully suggested in the opening section of poems, as sonnet 3, situating the *innamoramento* on the anniversary of the crucifixion, supplants the initial Ovidian scene of the poet's wounding and locates it within a broadly Christian frame, one in which the *argumento a tempo* assumes a particular burden of "proof."[22] It was because of the liturgical occasion, the poet tells us, that he found himself undefended: "Tempo non mi parea da far riparo / contr' a' colpi d'Amor" [It did not seem to me a time for being on guard against Love's blows], and as a consequence Amor found him "altogether disarmed." Early commentators found in this protestation a largely successful attempt to exculpate the unhappy poet,[23] in keeping with the expectations of a medieval society in which variations on the "Truce of God" had for generations been proclaimed for major periods marked by the liturgical calendar. On a Good Friday, in the *Conte del Graal* of the twelfth-century French poet Chrétien de

20. See Dutschke, "The Anniversary Poems," 88, and the discussion of Fredi Chiappelli in "Le thème de la *defectio solis* dans le *Canzoniere: Variatio intus*," in *Il legame musaico,* ed. Pier Massimo Forni (Rome, 1984), 165–66.

21. See M. Pastore Stocchi, "I sonetti III e LXI," *Lectura Petrarce, I, 1981* (Padua, 1982), 16.

22. On the import of the juxtaposition of poems 2 and 3, see Dennis Dutschke, "The Anniversary Poems in Petrarch's *Canzoniere*," *Italica* 58 (1981): esp. 88. Ricardo J. Quinones notes that throughout Petrarch's writings his attentiveness to dates is part of a "larger impulse to bestow meaning on existence," such that "the 'when' of an event is an important part of its significance"; see *The Renaissance Discovery of Time* (Cambridge, Mass., 1972), 110, 113.

23. The commentators were particularly attentive to the rhetorical functions appropriate to an exordium; see Pastore Stocchi, "I Sonetti III e LXI," 16–17. Gesualdo in particular marvels at the occurrence: "Who would ever have thought that this could happen to such a lofty spirit," he demands, "on that most holy day . . . ?" See *Il Petrarcha colla spositione di Misser Giovanni Andrea Gesualdo*, in A. Soletri, *Le vite di Dante, Petrarca e Boccaccio scritte fino al secolo decimosesto* (Milan, 1904), 425.

Troyes, an armed Perceval elicits the incredulous reaction of a group of penitents:

> "Certes, il n'est raisons ne biens
> D'armes porter, ainz est granz tors,
> Au jor que Jhesucris fu mors . . ."
> "Hui ne deüst hom qui Dieu croie
> Armes porter ne champ ne voie."[24]

[Surely, it is neither right nor good, but rather a great wrong, to bear arms on the day Jesus Christ died . . . Today the man who believes in God must not bear arms in field or road.]

The general opprobrium attached to the bearing of arms on Good Friday lends a particular resonance to Petrarch's depiction of the *innamoramento* as a scene of wounding, and the juxtaposition of the poet's unarmed state on that occasion with the account of Amor's armed attack in the preceding poem appears in this context highly portentous: the metaphorical wound inflicted by Amor, deriving from a radically different register, is sharply contrasted to the wounds of Christ, in memory of which a secular yet quite literal violence is proscribed. *Rime* 3, with its implicit inculpation of Amor, sets off the poet's private suffering against the redemptive love and suffering of Christ.

Consider then two juxtaposed sonnets later in Part I where the wounds of poet and Christ are brought into a similar relation. The benediction of the *innamoramento* in *Rime* 61 cited above, including among its enumerated circumstances not only the time and place but the familiar elements of Amor's attack—"l'arco e le saette ond' i' fui punto, / et le piaghe che 'nfin al cor mi vanno" [the bow and the arrows that pierced me, and the wounds that reach my heart]—adopts the lexicon of religious celebration in a rhetorical strategy current in the vernacular lyric.[25] The religious implications of its insistent repetition in this poem, however, are reinstated and confirmed in the next sonnet, "Padre del ciel," as the poet pleads for divine aid to escape from Love's bondage. The startling contraries represented by these two poems exemplify more than the interference between courtly and religious registers in the collection.[26]

---

24. *Le Roman de Perceval ou Le Conte du Graal*, ed. William Roach (Geneva and Paris, 1959), vv. 6258–60; 6299–6300.

25. For the *incipit* of this poem as a commonplace, drawn by Petrarch from a generalized rhetorical tradition rather than from a single model, see Pastore Stocchi, "I Sonetti III e LXI," 6–7.

26. For that interference, see for example Mariann S. Regan, "Petrarch's Courtly and Christian Vocabularies: Language in *Canzoniere* 61–63," *Romance Notes* 15 (1974): 527–31.

They exemplify too the consequence of the initial occasion: the crucifixion and the *innamoramento,* associated in *Rime* 3, are radically dissociated here, as it were divided between the two juxtaposed poems. In the benedictions of *Rime* 61 there is no mention of the liturgical circumstance; in the penitential sonnet 62, as in a reading of the event from the other side of the mirror, Amor is the poet's "duro avversario," his harsh adversary, and his submission to love a pitiless yoke, "dispietato giogo."

To explore this juxtaposition we may turn to a poem that despite its strategic placement has received little close comment. In fact, from its placement *Rime* 4 assumes a singular importance: following the two contrastive accounts of the *innamoramento* in sonnets 2 and 3, the reader awaits a confirmation of the light in which to cast that occurrence, a possible mediation. The poem speaks first of Christ, then of the lady:

> di sé nascendo a Roma non fe' grazia,
> a Giudea sì, tanto sovr' ogni stato
> umiltate esaltar sempre gli piacque.
> Ed or di picciol borgo un sol n'à dato,
> tal che natura o 'l luogo si ringrazia
> onde sì bella donna al mondo nacque.
>
> (4, 9–14)

[He, when He was born, did not bestow Himself on Rome, but rather on Judea, so beyond all other states it pleased Him always to exalt humility. And now from a small village He has given us a sun, such that Nature is thanked and the place where so beautiful a lady was born to the world.]

The grammatical subject of these statements is God himself, repeatedly identified by periphrasis in the preceding verses as "Que' che"—He who created the earth and the planets, He who came to earth to reveal the truth to mankind; the author of this new gift is that "fattore" of the created world who is God and at the same time the crucified Christ in the preceding poem. Sonnet 4, like sonnet 3, predicates a collective response that is heightened in a relational reading: the common sorrow of the anniversary of the crucifixion is now replaced by an implication of rejoicing in the poet's profession of gratitude for a magnificent gift; and in that gift, following the symbolic linking of Christ's suffering and that of the poet in *Rime* 3, Christ's birth is linked to Laura's through the humble origin chosen for each by God.[27] Here in the opening of the

27. On the boldness of the combined evocation of these two epiphanies, see Pier Massimo Forni, "Laudando s'incomincia: Dinamiche di una funzione petrarchesca," *Italian Quarterly* 23 (1982): 21.

collection, in verses that bear a distant echo of the Scriptural celebration of the Divine Advent—"or di picciol borgo un sol n'à dato"—Petrarch announces not the *lumen Christi* but the birth of Laura, the advent of the lady whose light will illumine his personal world.[28]

The suggestion is disquieting, and particularly so, as Peter Hainsworth notes, in the resolution of such hyperbolic compliment into the bare literal identification of this new gift as "sì bella donna."[29] Its startling effect is perhaps attenuated somewhat if we recall the tradition within which Petrarch develops his representation of Laura. As an example, consider a remarkable sonnet by Lapo Gianni:

> Sì come i Magi a guida de la stella
> girono inver' le parti d'Oriente
> per adorar lo Segnor ch'era nato,
> così mi guidò Amore a veder quella. . . .

[Just as the Magi guided by the star turned toward the East to adore the Lord who was born, so Love guided me to see that one. . . .][30]

Petrarch in turn, in a poem that has occasioned considerable commentary, compares his search for Laura's "true form" to the arduous pilgrimage undertaken by one eager to see Christ's image in the Veronica:

> et viene a Roma, seguendo 'l desio,
> per mirar la sembianza di colui
> ch'ancor lassù nel ciel vedere spera.
> Così, lasso, talor vo cercand'io,
> Donna, quanto è possibile in altrui
> la disiata vostra forma vera.

(16, 9–14)

28. See the discussion of this poem in Thomas P. Roche, Jr., *Petrarch and the English Sonnet Sequences* (New York, 1989), 22–25. Peter Hainsworth comments that this first instance of Petrarch's many castings of Laura as sun-figure "is hidden away in the twelfth line of the poem and its potentially dramatic effect is minimized"; see "Metaphor in Petrarch's *Rerum vulgarium fragmenta*," in *The Languages of Literature in Renaissance Italy*, ed. Peter Hainsworth et. al. (Oxford, 1988), 6. The network of comparisons in both poems 3 and 4, however, renders it not only dramatic but daring, and portentious for the poet's story to be told in the *rime sparse* to follow.

29. Peter Hainsworth, *Petrarch the Poet* (London, 1988), 156–57.

30. Cited in Antonio Lanza, *Studi sulla lirica del Trecento* (Rome, 1978), 76. Lapo's poem may, he suggests, echo a sonnet by Guittone, "Con più m'allungo, più m'è prossimana," in which the simile of the guidance of the Magi also appears.

[and he comes to Rome, following his desire, to gaze on the
likeness of Him whom he hopes to see again up there in Heaven.
Thus, alas, at times I go searching in others, Lady, as much as is
possible, for your longed-for true form.]

Here, as in Lapo's sonnet, the daring of the comparison is conditioned
and as it were shielded by the simile, which allows us to compare, not
the lady and Christ, but the questing journeys of those who seek to
contemplate the "true image" of one or the other.[31] In *Rime* 4, however,
there is no simile: the conjunctive "Ed or" that likens the "picciol borgo"
of the lady's birthplace to the humble setting of Judea establishes an
ambiguous but powerful analogy between Laura and Christ.

The analogy itself, of course, is not unprecedented. In the *Vita Nuova*
Amor explicates a scene in which Beatrice is preceded by another lady
named Giovanna but commonly called Primavera: while the latter name
means that she will precede Beatrice (*prima verrà*) on this occasion,
Giovanna too signifies "she will come first," for it derives from Gio-
vanni, "who preceded the True Light, saying *Ego vox clamantis in
deserto: parate viam Domini*" (*VN* XXIV).[32] The status accorded Laura
in her denomination as "sola un sol, non pur a li occhi mei / ma al
mondo cieco che vertù non cura" [alone . . . a sun, not merely for my
eyes, but for the blind world, which does not care for virtue] (248) is
reaffirmed *in morte*, as Dante had marked the death of his lady with a
lament for the loss suffered by the city of its "beatrice."[33] In the *Rime*
the emphasis on the time and place—even the hour—of Laura's death,
the commemoration of its anniversaries, the insistence on death as the
soul's separation from the body all suggest that she, like Beatrice, has
hagiographic models.[34] In connection with her death the poet again
evokes the eclipse of the sun's light that indicates the universal response
to the crucifixion in sonnet 3: "et in un punto n'è scurato il sole" [in the

31. See Waller, *Petrarch's Poetics and Literary History*, 25. Here Petrarch offers a more
secular version of the comparison between the lover separated from the beloved and the
pilgrim traveling to see the Veronica implicit in *Vita Nuova* XL; see Charles S. Singleton,
An Essay on the "Vita Nuova" (Baltimore and London, 1949), 23.

32. For the nature of the analogy, see Singleton, *An Essay on the "Vita Nuova,"* esp.
22.

33. For this status of Beatrice, see Singleton, *An Essay on the "Vita Nuova,"* and Enrico
Proto, "Beatrice beata," *Giornale Dantesco*, 14 (1906): 60–89.

34. See Michael Lauwers, "La mort et le corps des saints: La scène de la mort dans les
vitae du haut Moyen Age," *Le Moyen Age* 94 (1988): esp. 30, 33–36. Yet more suggestive
for the staging of the scene of Laura's death in the *Trionfi* is the model of the saint's
preparation for death, serene and surrounded by the appropriate community (see 26–27).

same instant the sun is darkened] (268).[35] Again his verse echoes the account in Luke 23, "et obscuratus est sol," and again the loss assumes cosmic proportions: "Lasciato ài, Morte, senza sole il mondo / oscuro et freddo . . ." [Death, you have left the world dark and cold without the sun] (338, 1–2); "Nel tuo partir partì del mondo Amore / et Cortesia, e 'l sol cadde del cielo . . ." [With your departure Love left the world and Courtesy, and the sun fell from the sky] (352, 12–13).

From the correspondence of the time of Laura's death with that of the *innamoramento*, noted in the commemorative inscription in Petrarch's Virgil manuscript presumably intended for his eyes only as well as recorded in sonnets included among the *rime* (211, 336), readers have concluded that Petrarch inscribes her death "under the sign of Christ's resurrection."[36] This "calendar time" is resonant with liturgical time: April 6, the "dì sesto d'aprile," *feria sexta aprilis* was associated in the medieval commentary tradition, not only with the crucifixion, but with the creation of man and with the Fall.[37] In sestina 142, where the alternatives that subtend the poet's story are most clearly defined, we found the two unmodified terms "tempo" and "loco" recurring together: "ora la vita breve e 'l loco e 'l tempo / mostranmi altro sentier di gire al cielo . . ." [now the shortness of life and the place and the season show me another pathway to go to Heaven . . .] (142). Here, however, the set of spatial and temporal circumstances indicate not the inception of his love but an apparent providential design inciting to a change of course. An earlier component identified a place where a demonstration of the means of ascent to Heaven occurred:

> L'aspetto sacro de la terra vostra
> mi fa del mal passato tragger guai
> gridando: "Sta' su, misero, che fai?"
> et la via de salir al ciel mi mostra.
>
> (68, 1–4)

35. In contrast to an early draft of this poem that limits the application of the motif to the poet's state, the final version with its strong Biblical echo emphasizes a universal sorrow; see Chiappelli, "Le thème de la *Defectio solis*," 167, 176–78. It is important to recall that in the *Vita Nuova* the portentious phenomena accompany the death of Beatrice, not in the report of its actual occurrence, but in the poet's fevered dream.

36. See Foster's discussion of the conscious decision to link the two because of the sacred associations of the date (*Petrarch, Poet and Humanist*, 53–54), and Bortolo Martinelli, " 'Feria sexta aprilis': la data sacra nel Canzoniere del Petrarca," *Rivista di storia e letteratura religiosa* 8 (1972): 483–84.

37. See Carlo Calcaterra, *Nella selva del Petrarca* (Bologna, 1942), 209–45; Martinelli, " 'Feria sexta aprilis'," 449–84.

[The holy sight of your city makes me bewail my evil past, crying: "Get up, wretch! what are you doing?" and shows me the way to mount to Heaven.]

Addressed to a Roman friend, these verses suggest by analogy that the privileged place to which Petrarch alludes in sestina 142 is Rome. If we further associate that place with the privileged liturgical time of Holy Week, Gorni suggests, the alternatives posited in *Rime* 142 assume a ritual symmetry: the story begun on a Good Friday would after many years here conclude on that same occasion,[38] and thereafter the poet would follow the example of a Laura whose triumph over the world will be affirmed in one of her last dream appearances near the end of the collection in words that echo those of Christ: "io giovene ancora / vinsi il mondo et me stessa . . ." [I when still young conquered the world and myself] (359).

But of course the story does not conclude here, just as the poet's love for Laura does not conclude here. In the *Secretum* Augustinus cautions that "Nothing so much leads a man to forget or despise God as the love of things temporal, and most of all this passion that we call love," and his explanation offers a remarkable key to the relation between that spiritual analysis and the poetic fiction of the *Rime sparse*. The accuracy of his analysis, Augustinus insists, is borne out by a familiar phenomenon: that to the passion of love, "by the greatest of all desecrations, we even gave the name of God, without doubt only that we may throw a heavenly veil over our human follies and make a pretext of divine inspiration when we want to commit an enormous transgression."[39] This condemnation has its Augustinian authority in the *Confessions*, in particular in a discussion of the dangers of pagan texts that depict the amorous exploits of lascivious gods.[40] Here, however, focusing on the single figure of Amor—"Quem proprio quodam nomine Amorem, et . . . Deum etiam vocant"—Augustinus's indignation erupts to lay bare a whole

---

38. Guglielmo Gorni, "Metamorfosi e redenzione in Petrarca: Il senso della forma Coreggio del Canzoniere," *Lettere Italiane* 30 (1978): 9–10; see also Marco Santagata, "Il giovane Petrarca e la tradizione poetica romanza: Modelli ideologici e letterari," *Rivista di letteratura italiana* 1 (1983): 58–61.

39. *Petrarch's Secret,* 131–32.

40. For Petrarch's relation of his own youthful experience to that of Augustine as informing his allusions to pagan gods in the *Rime*, see Sara Sturm-Maddox, *Petrarch's Metamorphoses: Text and Subtext in the Rime sparse* (Columbia, Mo., 1985), 96–99. Thomas Hyde evokes the same passage of the *Confessions* in relation to the *Trionfi;* see *The Poetic Theology of Love: Cupid in Renaissance Literature* (London and Toronto, 1986), 62–63.

poetic tradition in which the classical Cupid is appropriated as the ruling divinity of an amorous universe.

The appropriation is so common as to appear almost insignificant in the poetry of the later Middle Ages. Yet while many poets merely borrow Ovidian conceits to represent subjective emotion, others gradually elaborate around the figure of the classical Cupid what Thomas Hyde identifies as a poetic theology of love, locating Amor "in a fictive world in which his divinity is constitutive rather than merely a local trope for the force of erotic desire."[41] Dante addresses this practice explicitly in the *Vita Nuova*, thematizing the anxiety that accompanies the personification of Amor in a fiction that claims for itself an ontological status transcending fiction. His own portrayal culminates in the painstaking explication of the personification. The attribution of speech to love "as if it were a human being," he reminds us, is merely a figure like others, not to be used by those who cannot "justify what they say; for it would be a disgrace if someone composing in rhyme introduced a figure of speech or rhetorical ornament, and then on being asked could not divest his words of such covering so as to reveal a true meaning" (*VN* XXV). In the *Commedia* he returns to the practice and to its origins, commenting in the setting of the Heaven of Venus on the ascription of "folle amore" to astral influence and through it to classical deities:

> Solea creder lo mondo in suo periclo
> che la bella Ciprigna il folle amore
> raggiasse, volta nel terzo epiciclo;
> per che non pur a lei faceano onore
> di sacrificio e di votivo grido
> le genti antiche ne l'antico errore;
> ma Dïone adoravano e Cupido,
> questa per madre sua, questo per figlio,
> e dicean ch'el sedette in grembo a Dido . . .
>
> (*Par.* VIII, 1–9)[42]

[The world was wont to believe, to its peril, that the fair Cyprian, wheeling in the third epicycle, rayed down mad love; wherefore the ancient people in their ancient error not only to her did honor

---

41. Hyde, *Poetic Theology*, 29. See chap. 2, "Medieval Developments," where the tensions inherent in this elaboration are examined in the *De Amore* of Andreas Capellanus, the *De planctu naturae* of Alain de Lille, and the *Roman de la Rose*.

42. For this passage as an example of a "Christian critique of paganism by 'demythologizing'," see Kenelm Foster, "Dante's Idea of Love," in Thomas Bergin, ed., *From Time to Eternity: Essays on Dante's "Divine Comedy"* (New Haven, 1967), 90–92.

with sacrifice and votive cry, but they honored Dione and Cupid,
the one as her mother, the other as her son, and they told that he
had sat in Dido's lap . . .]

The Augustinus of Petrarch's *Secretum* would endorse this analysis: in
his indictment cited above, all the protestations of the poet in the *Rime*
concerning wounding, helplessness, and compulsion, all his prayers to
Amor and his addresses to him as Signore—all are unmasked at one
blow. In the *Trionfi*, where the Amor who first appears on a triumphal
chariot is much like his counterpart in the *Rime*, Petrarch himself
dramatizes such an unmasking. Here, as if citing Augustinus, the narra-
tor's guide identifies this figure as a creation of human passions in terms
that Augustinus would again surely approve:

> "Ei nacque d'ozio e di lascivia umana,
> nudrito di penser dolci soavi,
> fatto signor e dio da gente vana."
>
> (*Tr. Cup.* I, 82–84)

[Idleness gave him birth, and wantonness, and he was nursed by
sweet and gentle thoughts, and a vain folk made him their lord
and god.]

He is nurtured by these amorous thoughts much as the poet's heart was
nurtured by his sighs in the proemial sonnet of the *Rime* in that time of
his "primo giovenile errore," and it is a pertinent commentary on these
verses that in the *Trionfi* "errori," along with "sogni" and "immagini
smorte," decorate the triumphal arch of the god Amor (*Tr. Cup.* IV, 139–
40). The contrast between Petrarch's redefinition and Dante's, however,
is striking: Dante defines it historically in terms of pagan belief su-
perceded by Christian revelation,[43] while Petrarch internalizes it, as does
Augustinus, as an inclination of the human psyche. More harshly in the
same vein, this Amor, worshiped by the "vulgo," is defined as the
creation of feeble intellects, of "tardi ingegni rintuzzati e sciocchi" (IV,
89–90).

In the combination of proemial poems that afford the *initium narra-
tionis* of the poet's story, the rhetorical locus *a persona* in fact yields not
two personae, but four: not only the poet and Amor, explicit in *Rime* 2;
not only the lady, implicit in that sonnet and explicit, "Donna," in *Rime*

---

43. On Dante's rejection of this "errore," see G. Vallese, "L'evasione cortese," in his
Studi di letteratura umanistica da Dante ad Erasmo (Naples, 1964²), 11–36.

3, but Christ as well. In these poems that sketch the myth of origins of the poet's love for Laura, the interference of registers immediately suggests an interference of religious ideologies. As the event of the *innamoramento* is set against the anniversary of the crucifixion, a new god comes to dominate the poet's spiritual universe. Not only will he continue to recur to the conventional attributes and strategies of Amor to account for the *innamoramento* and its enduring consequences: it is Amor in whom he will place his hope and to whom he will address his lament and his prayer. It is Amor who will guide, Amor who will constrain, Amor who will punish or promise reward.

Any poetic theology, Hyde observes, "implicitly claims for itself the status of Scripture. That claim makes poetic theology equivocal and unstable. Reading it becomes a moral problem, a temptation."[44] In the *Rime* that problem is sharpened, as we have seen, by the appropriation of the language of religious devotion to render the poet's experience of love and his praise of Laura. Looking more closely at the deity who rules the poet's spiritual universe, moreover, we find that his depiction not only implicitly claims the status of Scripture but recalls Scriptural models.[45] Petrarch's Amor is an omnipresent deity, one to whom all thoughts are known:

> Amor, che vedi ogni pensero aperto
> e i duri passi onde tu sol mi scorgi,
> nel fondo del mio cor gli occhi tuoi porgi
> a te palese, a tutt'altri coverto.
> Sai quel che per seguirte ò già sofferto. . . .
>
> (163, 1–5)

[Love, you who see openly my every thought and the harsh steps where you alone guide me, reach your eyes to the depths of my heart, which appears to you but is hidden from all others. You know what I have suffered in following you. . . .]

The Biblical background is similarly perceptible in numerous other poems among the *Rime;* under both the positive and the negative aspects

44. *Poetic Theology,* 37. For the ambiguities inherent in the conflation of pagan and Christian love imagery by poets, as well as in the readings *in bono* and *in malo* of the Christian mythographers, see esp. 29–31.

45. Dante's portrayal of Amor in the *Vita Nuova* twice awakens Biblical echoes: in chap. III the narrator records a dream vision in which a lord "of powerful aspect" appears within a fiery cloud, in an episode filled with allusions to the Book of Ezekiel; in chap. XII the "young man clothed in whitest garments" that he seems to see sitting at his side as he sleeps recalls heavenly angels of the New Testament. See Hyde, *Poetic Theology,* 48–49.

of a god both benevolent and hostile, Forster points out, the attributes of the Old Testament God of Israel are transferred by Petrarch to the god of love.[46] Not infrequently these echoes are blended with the conventional language of courtly poetry, as in the casting of Amor as an aggressive archer, "Amor mi à posto come segno a strale" [Love has set me up like a target for arrows] (133), that evokes Lamentations 3:12, "posuit me quasi signum ad sagittam."[47] In another poem not far distant in the ordering of the collection, that same god multiplies the afflictions visited upon his faithful follower, prompting the latter's appeal to all enamored souls to see how sorely he is tested: "deh, ristate a veder quale è 'l mio male!" [ah, stay to see what my suffering is!] (161). This is a god, as the poet both exults and laments repeatedly, from whom there is no escape, "l'alto signor dinanzi a cui non vale / nasconder né fuggir né difesa" [that high lord before whom one cannot hide or flee or make any defense] (241).

In the *Triumph of Cupid* this deity rules over a "folta schiera" or thick flock of his followers (I, 35) as a hard master "che tutto 'l mondo sforza" [who dominates the world] (III, 125). The image is fully congruent with that of the imperious Amor in the *Rime,* against whom the poet levels this accusation late in the collection:

> in quanto amaro à la mia via avezza
> con sua falsa dolcezza,
> la qual m'atrasse a l'amorosa schiera!
>
> (360, 25–27)

[to how much bitterness has he trained my life with his false sweetness, which drew me to the amorous flock!]

In the *Rime,* however, there is another divinity, one who rules over the world not through the exercise of force and a weapon of wounding but with a "pietosa verga." While the poet of the *Triumph of Cupid* becomes part of the "amorosa greggia" or flock of Amor (IV, 9), Christ too has a flock, and it is here that the poet of the *Rime* hopes to find refuge:

> I' mi fido in colui che 'l mondo regge
> et ch'e' seguaci suoi nel bosco alberga

46. Leonard Forster, "Petrarch's *Solo e pensoso* and the Omnipresence of the Deity," in Klaus Hempfer and Gerhard Regn, eds., *Interpretation: Das Paradigma del Europäischen Renaissance-Literatur* (Festschrift für Alfred Noyer-Weidner) (Wiesbaden, 1983), 236–38. He cites in particular *Rime* 35; 129; 145; 163; 306; and both *Psalms* and *Amos.*

47. On the *compenetrazione* of Biblical original and Petrarchan text, see Marco Santagata, "Prestilnovisti in Petrarca," *Studi Petrarcheschi,* n.s., 2 (1985): 96–97.

che con pietosa verga
mi meni a passo omai tra le sue gregge.

(105, 42–45)

[I rely on Him who rules the world and shelters His followers even in the wood to lead me now with merciful staff among His flocks.]

These verses, as Fenzi points out, are the exact reversal and sublimation of the situation of the poet among those conquered by Love, the "vinti d'Amore," in the *Trionfi*.[48] The welcome accorded by the Good Shepherd has been foreshadowed in a poem in which, as we have seen, the metaphors of choice are prominent:

ché più gloria è nel regno degli eletti
d'un spirito converso, et più s'estima,
che di novantanove altri perfetti.

(26, 12–14)

[for there is more glory in the realm of the elect for one converted spirit, and he is more esteemed, than for ninety and nine others who are just.]

Here the poet's appeal to all those "who praise Love in rhyme" anticipates the amorous chorus of vernacular love poets to whom our poet himself will serve, he confides in a later sonnet, as a well-known example. Particularly noteworthy, then, is the opening of that poem:

Più volte Amor m'avea già detto: "Scrivi,
scrivi quel che vedesti in lettre d'oro,
sì come i miei seguaci discoloro
e 'n un momento gli fo morti et vivi."

(93, 1–4)

[Many times had Love already said to me: "Write, write in letters of gold what you have seen, how I change the color of my followers and in one moment make them dead, or alive."]

---

48. E. Fenzi, "Per un sonetto del Petrarca: R.V.F. XCIII," *Giornale Storico della Letteratura Italiana* 151 (1974): 504–5.

This exordium evokes the privileged condition of one to whom a god, or God, has entrusted the transmission of a marvelous vision of hidden truths;[49] it is the privileged condition of the lover who will in a later poem see in Laura's eyes "quel che mai non vide / occhio mortal, ch'io creda, altro che 'l mio" [what no mortal eye ever saw, I believe, except my own] (127). It is this same Amor, called upon late in Part II to elevate the poet's mind along with his style as he attempts to praise adequately a Laura now become immortal, who dictates to him a revelation concerning Laura's physical beauty that encompasses all of human history:

> "forma par non fu mai dal dì ch'Adamo
> aperse li occhi in prima; et basti or questo,
> piangendo il dico, et tu piangendo scrivi."
>
> (354, 12–14)

> ["there has never been a form equal to hers, not since the day when Adam first opened his eyes; and let this now suffice: weeping I say it, and do you weeping write."]

In other poems Amor presides over a secular religion which in its very terms evokes its sacred counterpart. The poet who exclaims that Laura "was surely born in Paradise" sighs, " 'How did I come here and when?' thinking I was in Heaven, not there where I was" (126), and in a later poem he will remember with what wings he had come to be there: the agent is identified now as "Amor, ch'a' suoi le piante e i cori impenna / per fargli al terzo ciel volando ir vivi" [Love (who) gives wings to the feet and hearts of his followers to make them fly up to the third heaven] (177). The oppositional value in this attribution is evident in the opening poem of Part II, for there it is God who may provide the wings, not for the lover's thoughts of Laura, but for his intellect: "mille fiate ò chieste a Dio quell'ale / co le quai del mortale / carcer nostr' intelletto al Ciel si leva" [a thousand times I have asked God for those wings with which our intellect raises itself from this mortal prison to Heaven] (264).[50]

While it is Amor who assumes the status of divinity in this universe, and while it is Amor who "gives" the poet Laura—" 'a costui di mille / donne elette eccellenti n'elessi una' " ["for this fellow out of a thousand

---

49. See Fenzi, "Per un sonetto," 496–97, who cites recalls of *Purgatorio* XXXII, 104–5, and *Paradiso* XVII, 128.

50. This prayer of course recalls the echo of Psalms in the penitential sonnet 81: "Qual grazia, qual amore, o qual destino / mi darà penne in guisa di colomba, / ch'i' mi riposi et levimi da terra?" [What grace, what love, or what destiny will give me wings like a dove, that I may rest and lift myself up from earth?].

excellent, choice ladies I chose one"], he declares in the great debate of canzone 360—we recall that his power over the poet is achieved only through the agency of Laura, and that agency is affirmed in the first poem to associate the *innamoramento* with the anniversary of the crucifixion. Let us return once more to that explanation:

> Era il giorno ch'al sol si scoloraro
> per la pietà del suo fattore i rai
> quando i' fui preso, et non me ne guardai,
> ché i be' vostr' occhi, Donna, mi legaro.
>
> (3, 1–4)

[It was the day when the sun's rays turned pale with grief for his Maker when I was taken, and I did not defend myself against it, for your lovely eyes, Lady, bound me.]

The solar light, absent in obedience to the cosmic sorrow, is a reminder on the liturgical occasion of the "true" light, that of Christ.[51] But that light, profoundly evocative *because of* its absence, is not the only light in this poem: present instead are the eyes that are to be proclaimed the exclusive source of light for the poet in a very large number of poems among the *rime sparse*. The juxtaposition both initiates and contextualizes the poet's story: here, in the darkness of a day saddened by the death of Christ, shine the eyes of the lady.[52] Not only does the occurrence occult for the enamored poet the significance of the sacred event. It is in relation to liturgical time that the *innamoramento* is first inscribed "in time" in *Rime* 3—"tempo non mi parea di far riparo / contr' ai colpi d'Amor"— and it is this occasion that initiates the ritual chronology of the collection, as the splendor of Laura's eyes shining in the darkness initiates a new "sacred time."[53] The poet will go on to create his own sacred calendar,

51. For Patristic citations and discussion, see Martinelli, " 'Feria sexta aprilis'," 459–63.

52. In a further opposition, the sun's rays are "pietosi," while Laura, whose eyes now bind the poet, will be depicted "senza pietà"; in sonnet 44 she is addressed as "voi che mai pietà non discolora" [you, whom pity never makes pale]. See Pastori Stocchi, "I sonetti III e LXI," 18.

53. Pastore Stocchi proposes that Petrarch's insistence elsewhere in the *Rime* on the astral coordinates of the inception of his love make of sonnet 3 the marker of a dual sacred time, in which the sacred liturgical time is opposed to an astrological one; thus we would find already present in this sonnet the enigmatic kernel of his story, the error of having desired a sacred time entirely his own ("I sonetti III e LXI," 21–22).

marking its stages and commemorating its anniversaries in the ritualistic structures of a private cult.[54]

The setting of that cult, of course, is Valchiusa, that "solo al mondo paese almo felice" [sole in the world, rich, happy country] (226), his private "sacred place": "tu paradiso, i' senza cor un sasso, / o sacro, aventuroso et dolce loco!" [I am a stone without a heart, but you are a paradise, O holy, lucky, sweet place!] (243). In "Chiare, fresche, et dolci acque" (126), his desire to be buried in this landscape, adopting the conventional terms of *disprezzo* for the secular world to evoke the consolation of a final "riposato porto," makes of it a private hallowed ground. In Part II of the *Rime,* this landscape now bereft of Laura's informing presence becomes not only the setting but an integral part of his cult of Laura: "tal che pien di duol sempre al loco torno / che per te consecrato onoro et colo" [so that full of grief I return always to the place that I honor and adore as consecrated to you] (321). Just as Laura's poet creates his earthly (and his Heavenly) paradise in a free invention around the splendor of her beauty, so is that beauty accepted as the evidence afforded mortals of Heaven, as in his praise of her portrait by Simone Martini:

> Ma certo il mio Simon fu in Paradiso
> onde questa gentil donna si parte;
> ivi la vide, et la ritrasse in carte
> per far fede qua giù del suo bel viso
>
> (77, 5–8)

[But certainly my Simon was in Paradise, whence comes this noble lady; there he saw her and portrayed her on paper, to attest down here to her lovely face]—

a gesture that, for all its stilnovistic tonality, nonetheless recalls the witness of Saint Paul that he had indeed "seen" Paradise.[55]

In this rival paradise, nothing else is seen, nothing else heard, nothing else desired: nothing else is necessary. From Laura's eyes Amor rains down "un piacer sì caldo . . . ch' i' non curo altro ben né bramo altr'esca"

---

54. For Petrarch's myth of Laura as private religion, see Glauco Cambon, "L'eterno femminino petrarchesco: Magia e impotenza della metafora," *Italian Quarterly* 23 (1982): 14; on the "calendrical liturgy," see Gianfranco Folena, "L'orologio del Petrarca," *Libri e Documenti* 5 (1979): 6.

55. It was "per recarne conforto a quella fede / ch'è principio a la via di salvazione" [that he might bring thence confirmation of that faith which is the beginning of the way of salvation] that Saint Paul, according to Dante's pilgrim, visited Heaven (*Inf.* II, 29–30).

[a delight so warm that I care for no other good nor desire other bait],
the poet tells us (165), and a closely following sonnet finds him nourished
in a visionary Heaven:

> Pasco la mente d'un sì nobil cibo
> ch'ambrosia et nettar non invidio a Giove,
> ché sol mirando, oblio ne l'alma piove
> d'ogni altro dolce, et Lete al fondo bibo.
> Talor ch' odo dir cose e 'n cor describo
> per che da sospirar sempre ritrove,
> ratto per man d'Amor (né so ben dove)
> doppia dolcezza in un volto delibo.
>
> (193, 1–8)

[I nourish my mind with a food so noble that I do not envy Jove
his ambrosia and nectar; for when I merely gaze, oblivion rains
into my heart of all other sweetness, and I drink Lethe to the
bottom. When I hear things said and write them down in my
heart, so that I will always find them to sigh about, rapt by Love's
hand I know not where, from one countenance I drink in a double
sweetness.]

"Ratto per man d'Amor"—ravished by Love, rapt into Paradise; the
language of the mystics is heard in these verses.[56] The allusion to the
sustenance afforded by this "cibo" echoes once again the experience of
Dante's pilgrim in the Earthly Paradise:

> Mentre che piena di stupore e lieta
> l'anima mia gustava di quel cibo
> che, saziando di sè, di sè asseta . . .
>
> (*Purg.* XXXI, 127–29)[57]

[While my soul, full of amazement and gladness, was tasting of
that food which, sating of itself, causes hunger for itself . . .]

56. They recall too the *raptus Pauli* (2 Cor. 12: 2–3); see Domenico De Robertis,
"Contiguità e selezione," 53, who adds that the "ambrosia et nettar" associated with Jove
in this same poem are the conventional literary equivalent of "eterna vita" and "Dio" in
sonnet 191.

57. The connection is noted by Paolo Trovato, *Dante in Petrarca: Per un inventario dei
dantismi nei "Rerum vulgarium fragmenta"* (Florence, 1979), 72.

That echo, however, when fully contextualized, discloses not similarity but difference: the pilgrim too is gazing into the eyes of his lady; but her gaze is turned, not to him, but to the griffin at the center of the allegorical procession, and his rapture is occasioned not by her eyes but by what he sees reflected there, the marvel of the "doppia fiera" that figures the two natures of Christ, human and divine. Petrarch substitutes the image of Laura for that of Christ in terms of this metaphorical "cibo," much as he had declared, in a poem in which the divine vision is directly invoked, that he would wish to be nourished by the life-giving sight of Laura:

> Et se non fusse il suo fuggir sì ratto,
> più non demanderei; ché s'alcun vive
> sol d'odore et tal fama fede acquista,
> alcun d'acqua o di foco, e 'l gusto e 'l tatto
> acquetan cose d'ogni dolzor prive,
> i' perché non de la vostra alma vista?
>
> (191, 9–14)

[And if its fleeing were not so swift I would ask no more, for if some live only on odors, and the fame of it is believed, and some on water or on fire, satisfying their taste and touch with things that lack all sweetness, why should I not live on the life-giving sight of you?]

In the *De vera religione*, Augustine warns that the splendor of worldly objects promises us a false paradise: deceived by a light that is merely mortal, ephemeral, we seek to extend it infinitely.[58] The expansion of the light emanating from Laura is much like the expansion of her image to fill all visible space, and the proliferation of the laurel's image to fill all landscape. For Petrarch's poet this light assumes almost hallucinatory proportions:

> stando in se stessa à la sua luce sparta,
> a ciò che mai da lei non mi diparta;
> né farò io, et se pur talor fuggo,
> in cielo e 'n terra m''à racchiuso i passi,
> perch' a gli occhi miei lassi
> sempre è presente, ond'io tutto mi struggo.
>
> (127, 90–95)

---

58. *De vera religione* 20; see Dotti, "Miti e forme dell' 'io'," 80.

[remaining in herself, (she) has scattered her light in order that I may never depart from her; nor shall I, and if at times I flee, in Heaven and earth she has circumscribed my steps, for she is always present to my weary eyes, so that I am all consumed.]

This light of Laura that fills the cosmos discloses once again that her identification as *donna / sole* is more than compliment.[59] To her eyes is attributed the power to alter or even to reverse the order of nature:

> et non so che nelli occhi che 'n un punto
> po far chiara la notte, oscuro il giorno,
> e 'l mel amaro, et addolcir l'assenzio. . . .
>
> (215, 12–14)

[and I know not what in her eyes, which in an instant can make bright the night, darken the day, embitter honey, and sweeten wormwood.]

Late in the collection, Fortune will describe the precocious portents of this presence in recalling an infant Laura:

> "Et or carpone, or con tremante passo,
> legno, acqua, terra o sasso
> verde facea, chiara, soave, et l'erba
> con le palme o coi pie' fresca et superba
> et fiorir coi belli occhi le campagne,
> et acquetar i venti et le tempeste
> con voci, ancor non preste,
> di lingua che dal latte si scompagne."
>
> (325, 81–88)

[And now crawling, now with trembling steps, she made trees, water, earth or stone green, clear, or soft, and with her hands or feet the grass fresh and proud, and with her eyes she made the fields blossom, and with the words not yet ready of a tongue that was barely weaned, she quieted winds and tempests.]

59. See Gerard Genot, "Pétrarque et la scène du regard," *Journal of Medieval and Renaissance Studies* 2 (1982): 10–11, who points out that the frequent comparison of her eyes to the sun might appear mechanical except for the fact that this image is based on a psychology, a physiology, a cosmology, and a theology, from each of which it explicitly draws certain elements.

In this way her depiction as miracle finds its place too in Petrarch's myth of origins as the incarnation of springtime, beneath whose feet flowers bloom.[60] In this *bimba taumaturga* who regenerates nature, as Cambon observes, we find the personal myth of a Petrarch who saw in Laura the genesis of his world.[61]

Like one who sees God in all of Creation, the poet sees Laura in all of creation, in its beauty a reflection of Laura's beauty; and in this, Noferi points out, God's place is occupied by Laura.[62] God and Laura as objects of his desire both motivate a striving whose failure to reach its object he wearily acknowledges in strikingly similar images of aborted flight.[63] The categories of this experience evoke those of Christian experience precisely through the closeness with which they afford parallels. Let us compare Augustine's celebration of the eternal light: "When first I knew you, you raised me up so that I could see that there was something to be seen, but also that I was not yet able to see it. I gazed on you with eyes too weak to resist the dazzle of your splendour. Your light shone upon me in its brilliance, and I thrilled with love and dread alike."[64] So does Petrarch's poet look upon Laura, in love and dread alike, protesting that his mortal eye is blinded by her splendor: "né mortal vista mai luce divina / vinse, come la mia quel raggio altero" [nor did any divine light ever vanquish mortal sight, as does mine that high ray . . .] (151); early in the collection her eyes are celebrated as ". . . que' duo lumi / che quasi un bel sereno a mezzo 'l die / fer le tenebre mie" [those two lights, which made my darkness into a clear sky at noon] (37), rendering a passage of the *Confessions* in which it is the Beatific Vision that will turn dusk to noonday.[65] Another often-cited example assimilates the contemplation of Laura to the categories of the Beatific Vision, calling to mind the Pauline "peace of God":

60. Eugenio Battisti notes the resemblance of this Laura to Botticelli's Primavera, a figure who originates in a revival, due to Poliziano and Lorenzo de' Medici, of Petrarch's "simbologia floreale"; see "Non chiare acque," in *Francis Petrarch, Six Centuries Later: A Symposium*, ed. Aldo Scaglione (Chapel Hill and Chicago, 1975), 328.

61. Cambon, "L'eterno femminino," 13, 14.

62. Adelia Noferi, "La canzone CXXVII," *Lectura Petrarce, II, 1982* (Padua, 1983), 17.

63. Adelia Noferi cites three poems widely separated in the collection as the measure of "this type of interchangeability of Laura and God as (unattainable) objects of desire": sonnets 81 ("Io son sì stanco sotto 'l fascio antico"), 163 ("Amor, che vedi ogni pensero aperto"), and 335 ("Vidi fra mille donne una già tale"); see "*Voluptas canendi, voluptas scribendi:* divagazioni sulla vocalità in Petrarca," *Paradigma* 7 (1986): 19–20.

64. *Confessions* VIII, 10.

65. *Confessions* X, 5. See Nicolae Iliescu, *Il Canzoniere Petrarchesco e Sant'Agostino* (Rome, 1962), 120.

Pace tranquilla senza alcuno affanno,
simile a quella ch'è nel ciel eterna,
move da lor inamorato riso.

(73, 67–69)

[Tranquil peace without any trouble, like that which is eternal in Heaven, moves from their lovely smile.]

The three "canzoni sorelle" in praise of her eyes, as Foster observes, all exemplify a theology of Grace in which the source of a secular grace is the lady's gaze: "Fugge al vostro apparire angoscia et noia, / et nel vostro partir tornano insieme . . ." [At your appearance anguish and pain flee, and at your departure they return together . . .] (71).[66] In the achievement of this direct vision, the poet records, "Conobbi allor sì come in paradiso / vede l'un l'altro. . . ." [I learned then how they see each other in Paradise] (123).

"For now we see in a mirror dimly, but then face to face. Now I know in part; then I shall understand fully, even as I have been fully understood" (1 Corinthians 13:12): the Pauline affirmation, echoed also by Augustine in the passage of the *Confessions* cited above, constrains the reading of Petrarch's verses. Let Richard of St. Victor explain the character of contemplation, which is to "adhere with wonder to the object which brings it joy": "The matter of our contemplation always depends upon and is developed by some one thing, while the soul of [the] contemplative gladly dwells on the beholding of his happiness, while he endeavors always to return to it or to hold himself motionless in it for a long time."[67] It is that endeavor that is recorded in "Chiare, fresche, et dolci acque" (*Rime* 126), where the nullification of time again suggests the Beatific Vision.[68] Consider then another ecstatic record of the vision of Laura:

Sì come eterna vita è veder Dio
nè più si brama né brama più lice,
così me, Donna, il voi veder felice
fa in questo breve et fraile viver mio.

---

66. Foster, *Petrarch, Poet and Humanist*, 69–70. Earlier readers, it should be noted, praised this and similar formulations for a Platonic inspiration: see the summary of critical reactions in Ettore Bonora, "Le 'Canzoni degli occhi' (LXXI-LXXII-LXXIII)," *Lectura Petrarce, IV, 1984* (Padua, 1985), 319–26.

67. Richard of St. Victor, *Selected Writings on Contemplation*, trans. and ed. Claire Kirchberger (London, 1957), 139–41.

68. See Durling, *Petrarch's Lyric Poems*, Introduction, 23.

Né voi stessa com' or bella vid' io
giamai, se vero al cor l'occhio ridice,
dolce nel mio penser ora beatrice
che vince ogni altra speme, ogni desio!

(191, 1–8)

[As it is eternal life to see God, nor can one desire more, nor is it right to desire more, so, Lady, seeing you makes me happy in this short and frail life of mine. Nor have I ever seen you as beautiful as you are at this hour, if my eye tells my heart the truth, oh sweet hour that makes blessed my thoughts, that surpasses every high hope, every desire!]

It does not *lead to* the Beatific Vision: as the poem makes explicit, the experience is sufficient unto itself, excluding all other concerns.[69]

To this Laura, moreover, are attributed functions proper to God. The lady of the metamorphosis canzone, who punishes the poet's expression of his plaint, is likened in her response to his humble plea for mercy to God judging souls:

Et se contra suo stile ella sostene
d'esser molto pregata, in lui si specchia,
et fal perché 'l peccar più si pavente;
ché non ben si ripente
de l'un mal chi de l'altro s'apparecchia.

(23, 127–31)[70]

[And if, contrary to her custom, she allows herself to be begged long, she mirrors Him, and does it that sinning may be more feared, for he does not repent well of one sin who prepares himself for another.]

69. Etienne Gilson underlines the fundamental differences between the exaltation of the lover's experience in courtly poetry and that of the mystics; see *La théologie mystique de Saint Bernard* (Paris, 1934), appendix 4: "Saint Bernard et l'amour courtois" (193–215). On the implications of the theme of ecstatic vision in the *Rime*, see Kenelm Foster, "Beatrice or Medusa," *Italian Studies presented to E. R. Vincent*, ed. C. P. Brand, K. Foster, and U. Limentani (Cambridge, 1962), 41–45; Mary Barnard, *The Myth of Apollo and Daphne from Ovid to Quevedo: Love, Agon, and the Grotesque* (Durham, 1987), 95–101.

70. On the highly unusual nature of this passage and its echoes of Dante "comico," see Santagata, "Il giovane Petrarca," esp. 25.

In other poems Laura is described in terms that in devotional texts figure the relation between God and the individual soul. To her the poet attributes the fructification of his soul: "io per me son quasi un terreno asciutto / colto da voi, e 'l pregio è vostro in tutto" [in myself I am as it were a dry soil tilled by you, and the praise is yours entirely] (71). She sees within that soul, reading its innermost, unspoken desire:

> Ma voi, occhi beati, ond'io soffersi
> quel colpo ove non valse elmo né scudo,
> di for et dentro mi vedete ignudo
> ben che 'n lamenti il duol non si riversi.
> Poi che vostro veder in me risplende
> come raggio di sol traluce in vetro,
> basti dunque il desio senza ch'io dica.
> Lasso, non a Maria, non nocque a Pietro
> la fede ch'a me sol tanto è nemica!
> et so ch'altri che voi, nessun m'intende.
>
> (95, 5–14)

[But you, blessed eyes, from whom I received that blow against which no helm or shield availed, you see me entirely, without and within, even though my sorrow does not pour forth in laments. Since your seeing shines in me as a sunbeam penetrates glass, let my desire suffice, without my speaking. Alas, Mary and Peter were not harmed by faithfulness, which to me alone is hostile! and I know that besides you no one understands me.]

The "fede" of the final tercet here suggests more than a conventional protestation of the lover's faithfulness. Its power derives from the explicit renewal of its origins in the vocabulary of religious devotion, as well as from the exemplary faith to which it is compared: that of Mary Magdalen and Peter, those who loved Christ, those rewarded by him. An equally startling casting of Laura occurs in Part II of the collection, in the words that he imagines her glance to have spoken on the occasion of their last encounter: " 'Rimanetevi in pace, o cari amici; / qui mai più, no, ma rivedremne altrove' " ["Peace be with you, dear friends; never again here, no, but we shall see each other again elsewhere"] (328). While the plural "amici" refers here to the poet's eyes, to which Laura's eyes are speaking, this rather strained usage preserves the full evocative power of the absent text: that of the Gospel in which Christ, on the occasion of the Last Supper, speaks to his apostles concerning the imminent Passion.

When the poet declares that he turns always to Laura's eyes "come a fontana d'ogni mia salute" [as to the fount of all my health] (73), the ambiguity of the Italian term "salute" as both "health" and "salvation" warns us that here too Laura is "in the place of God," and the threat of idolatry incurred by such projections hovers closely over other poems of the collection depicting the self-conscious constitution of Laura as an object. This process, as Durling has demonstrated in a seminal study, is that performed upon the phantasm of the lady in "Giovene donna sotto un verde lauro" (*Rime* 30) by the lover's obsessive meditation. The designation of the resulting image as "my idol sculpted in living laurel" is thus to be taken seriously: metaphorically sculpted of precious materials by the lover, "it is an idol because he worships it instead of God, and meditates on it instead of on God."[71]

In "Giovene donna" we find too an unexpected new definition of the long-pursued object of desire, one now immobilized as the "duro lauro / ch'à i rami di diamante et d'or le chiome" [the harsh laurel that has branches of diamond and golden locks]. Consider then an earlier enigmatic reference to the laurel as destination:

> sol per venir al lauro onde si coglie
> acerbo frutto, che le piaghe altrui
> gustando affligge più che non conforta.
>
> (6, 12–14)

[only to come to the laurel, whence one gathers bitter fruit that, being tasted, afflicts one's wounds more than it comforts them.]

The loss and frustration of this culmination of the protagonist's pursuit is of course guaranteed by the mythological subtext in which Apollo is his precursor. Yet, as in "Giovene donna," an abrupt change of focus confronts the reader: the impersonal "si coglie" and the indeterminate "altrui" of this final tercet, following verses that dramatically render the poet's pursuit, suggest that this immobile object is a sacred plant with the communal connotations of a cult.[72] The mention of wounds, while recalling the conventional depiction of the *innamoramento* in *Rime* 2, recalls also the initiation of a cult in celebration of Laura; it places the poet's personal and idiosyncratic pursuit in an altered perspective, in

---

71. "Petrarch's 'Giovene donna'," 11, 15.

72. See Giuseppe Velli, "La metafora del Petrarca," in his *Petrarca e Boccaccio: Tradizione, Memoria, Scrittura* (Padua, 1979), 44–45.

which the consequence of reaching the laurel assumes the importance of a provisional judgment.[73]

What the pursuer and celebrant finds upon reaching the laurel is bitter fruit, "acerbo frutto." The botanical detail is foreign both to the Ovidian account and to its medieval allegorizations, particularly those in which the plant stands for viginity, which emphasize on the contrary its nonbearing nature.[74] Another medieval reading of the myth of Apollo, Mann reminds us, might have prompted an association of the laurel's bitter fruit with the theme of vainglory;[75] others have noted instead a moral or spiritual resonance.[76] In Petrarch's poem, however, where a literal reading produces absurdity,[77] another association is particularly suggestive: bitterness is a term which recurs frequently in medieval characterizations of the Fall. In a transposition of the taste of the forbidden fruit to its universal consequences, Dante presents Adam as ". . . 'l padre per lo cui ardito gusto / l'umana specie tanto amaro gusta" [that Father because of whose audacious tasting the human race tastes such bitterness] (*Par.* XXXII, 122–23).[78] Precisely because the laurel is not generally associated with fruit to be eaten, the taste of its fruit may evoke the gustatory metaphor of mystical language adopted and developed from Scriptural topoi.[79] It is an opposition known to Petrarch from

73. In canzone 23 the poet attempts to reconstitute his experience in rhymes because "cantando il duol si disacerba." On this "disembittering," see Waller, *Petrarch's Poetics and Literary History*, who contrasts it to Dante's use of "acerbo" and "maturo" to describe the preconversion self and the redeemed self in the *Commedia* (85).

74. See for example the *Ovide moralisé*, ed. C. De Boer (Amsterdam, 1915), I, 3197–3200, where it is the plant that remains green in all seasons just as virginity must "verdoier / Et vivre sans fructifier" [flourish and live without bearing fruit]; the single exception, in this sense "contre nature," is the Virgin herself.

75. In this explanation Apollo figures allegorically "the man who, seeking fame and vainglory, is left only with bitter berries"; see Nicholas Mann, *Petrarch* (Oxford and New York, 1984), 59.

76. See Adelia Noferi, "Note ad un sonetto del Petrarca," *Forum Italicum* 2 (1968): 203; Dorothy Gabe Coleman, *Maurice Scève, Poet of Love* (Cambridge, 1975), who finds that these lines are "an allegorical way of saying that he is dragged down by the effect of his passion; he is forced to eat the harsh bitter leaves of the bay tree" (123).

77. Velli points out the vast "apertura metaforica" of these concluding verses ("La metafora del Petrarca," 44).

78. For discussion of this tradition and other examples, see Manuela Colombo, "Note sul linguaggio amoroso dei mistici medievali e Dante," *Letture classensi*, XIII (Ravenna, 1984), 89–109. Dante also employs the metaphor to suggest the opposite of this postlapsarian state as heavenly bliss; see *Inf.* XVI, 61–62; *Purg.* XXVII, 115–16; *Par.* III, 37–39.

79. Augustine, Noferi notes, had frequently cited and developed these same biblical metaphors; see "Note ad un sonetto del Petrarca," 204. See also Richard of St. Victor: the soul "thirsts for God when she desires to experience what that inward sweetness is that inebriates the mind of man, when he begins to taste and see how sweet the Lord is" (*Selected Writings on Contemplation*, 223).

Augustine, in terms whose relevance to his poet's story is immediately apparent: "The good things which you love are all from God, but they are good and sweet only as long as they are used to do his will. They will rightly turn bitter if God is spurned and the things that come from him are wrongly loved."[80] In the *Rime* the laurel's bitterness, like the lack of comfort afforded, suggests again its inadequacy in relation to what the early poems first imply and then identify as "altro amor."[81]

The lover's worship of his idol is explicit in a later sonnet, in which the laurel is not sculpted but rather implanted in his heart:

> Fama, onor, et vertute et leggiadria,
> casta bellezza in abito celeste
> son le radici de la nobil pianta.
> Tal la mi trovo al petto ove ch' i' sia,
> felice incarco! et con preghiere oneste
> l'adoro e 'nchino come cosa santa.
>
> (228, 9–14)

> [Fame, honor, and virtue and charm, chaste beauty in celestial habit, are the roots of the noble plant. Such do I find it in my breast, wherever I may be, a happy burden, and with chaste prayers I adore it and bow to it as to a holy thing.]

The final verses leave no doubt as to the nature of this gesture; the lofty nature of the "roots" of the plant cannot guarantee against its appropriation as an idol by the lover.[82] Are we not to hear in this listing of its qualities the echo of another listing, in a poem not far distant in the *Rime*, where the *innamoramento* has been defined as an entry into the labyrinth?

80. *Confessions* IV, 12. Augustine continues: "Why do you still choose to travel by this hard and arduous path? There is no rest to be found where you seek it."

81. The second meaning of *acerbo* as "unripe," attested elsewhere in the *Rime* as in the *Commedia* to indicate youthfulness as opposed to the "etate matura," would not alter the connotation of a fruit not to be eaten, not to be enjoyed. This is the reading inherent in the contrast advanced by Maurice Scève between his own *innamoramento* "en Automne" and that of Petrarch's young protagonist; see Joann Dellaneva, *Song and Counter-Song: Scève's "Delie" and Petrarch's "Rime"* (Lexington, Ky., 1983), 25–29.

82. Robert Durling adds to the expressions of idolatry the poet's professed willingness to adore Laura in a dark cell in *Rime* 206; see *The Figure of the Poet in the Renaissance Epic* (Cambridge, Mass., 1965), hr n. 12. P.R.J. Hainsworth points out that the praise of the laurel "and the assigning to it of virtues such as nobility, honour, truth, and purity prove as questionable as the celebration of love and the human Laura"; see "The Myth of Daphne in the *Rerum vulgarium fragmenta*," *Italian Studies* 34 (1979): 41.

Vertute, onor, bellezza, atto gentile,
dolci parole ai be' rami n'àn giunto
ove soavemente il cor s'invesca.

(211, 9–11)

[Virtue, honor, beauty, gentle bearing, sweet words brought us to
the lovely branches, that my heart may be sweetly enlimed.]

Thus the laurel, Laura's tree, figures along with the lady herself in the
oppositional structure of the poet's story. While there are other shelter-
ing trees in the *Rime*—it is in the shadow of a beech tree, a "bel faggio,"
that the poet, hearing an admonitory voice, reflects on his wayward state
(54)[83]—it is the laurel that is praised for its protective shade. That shade,
as we have seen in Chapter 3, also constitutes a zone in which extraordi-
nary events occur, and in this it is not unlike the fig tree beneath which
Augustine's conversion occurs. Petrarch himself was aware of the possi-
bility, perhaps the inevitability, of the comparison: in the *Secretum*, as
Freccero points out, it is Franciscus who responds to Augustinus's recall
of his conversion with mention of "that life-giving fig tree, under whose
shadow this miracle happened to you," and it is Augustinus who replies:
"I should hope not, for neither myrtle nor ivy, nor even that laurel dear
(so they say) to Phoebus, should be so welcome to you."[84] To evoke the
tree as protection, however, is to awaken echoes of a widespread topos
of Biblical origin.[85] The exegetical tradition, upon which Petrarch draws
in his own Penitential Psalms, explains that man enjoyed a favored
position "beneath the tree" in Eden, but that after the Fall Adam and
Eve hid themselves beneath another tree, attempting to hide from the
justice of God; later, exposed to the full sun of divine justice, man was
to find shelter again beneath the tree of the Cross.[86] "To rest comfortably

83. On this "faggio," see E. Proto, "Per un madrigale del Petrarca," *Rassegna critica
della letteratura italiana* 16 (1911): 107; P. Courcelle, "Sonnets de Pétrarque et *Confessions*
augustiniennes," *Latomus* 23 (1964): 347; Vincenzo Dolla, "Il 'ciclo' dei madrigali e la
struttura del *Canzoniere* petrarchesco," *Esperienze letterarie* 4 (1979): 68.

84. John Freccero, "The Fig Tree and the Laurel: Petrarch's Poetics," *Diacritics* 5
(1975): 37.

85. On its patristic background, see Etienne Gilson, "Sub umbris arborum," *Medieval
Studies* 14 (1962): 149–51; "Sur deux textes de Pétrarque," *Studi Petrarcheschi* 7 (1961):
35–50.

86. See Genesis 3:8. The apple tree as a type of Christ, affording respite from God's
wrath, was a stereotype in sermons on the Song of Songs; see Stanley Stewart, *The Enclosed
Garden* (Madison, Wis., 1966), 72–73, 86–87, and on Christ's tree as the only tree offering
true repose in its shadow, see Quinones, *The Renaissance Discovery of Time*, 124. For the
legend that the Cross was made from the wood of the Tree of the Knowledge of Good and
Evil, see Emile Mâle, *The Gothic Image*, trans. Dora Nussey (New York, 1958), 186–88,
and the summary of the legendary history of the Cross in Stewart, 75–86.

in the shade of the wrong tree," Robertson summarizes these medieval interpretations, "amounts to the same thing as to make a home in Babylon."[87]

Augustinus' reminder is well taken. The fig tree was a scriptural emblem of conversion, while the laurel as a symbol of poetic superiority is claimed for Petrarch alone.[88] In "Giovene donna," the first of the anniversary poems commemorating the *innamoramento* that took place on Good Friday, the alternative between a secular and a religious cult is more directly suggested as the iconography of Laura and her tree is implicitly juxtaposed with the iconography of the crucifixion, the outstretched arms of Christ on the Cross with the outstretched diamond branches of the laurel; "in theological terms," Durling suggests, "the lover's idolatry is measurable in his being turned toward the wrong tree . . . , a tree with a woman under it."[89] The opposition of the laurel tree to the Cross is suggested again, along with other oppositional elements of the poet's story, in the alternatives posited in sestina 142. Invoked along with "altro amor" are "altri rami," in opposition to those branches that have throughout the poem been those of the beloved laurel, its "leggiadri," "bei," "primi," invescati," and finally "amati rami." Here Petrarch does not follow the tradition of moralizing allegorical readings that offered a reconciliation of the secular laurel with the spiritual aspirations of his protagonist.[90] Particularly suggestive, on the other hand, is the well-known Good Friday hymn "Pange, lingua," which evokes the laurel in connection with the triumph of the Cross.[91]

In both secular and devotional texts, where it figures prominently as a reminder of man's sinful state, the Cross was regularly evoked to inspire a crisis of awareness, a turning toward God. It is precisely thus, in the *Conte del Graal* cited earlier, that years of aimless wandering devoted to

87. D. W. Robertson, Jr., "The Doctrine of Charity in Medieval Literary Gardens: A Topical Approach Through Symbolism and Allegory," *Speculum* 26 (1951): 32.

88. See Freccero, "The Fig Tree and Laurel," 34–35, 37–38.

89. Robert Durling, "Petrarch's 'Giovene donna sotto un verde lauro'," *MLN* 86 (1971): 18–19. On the relation between *Rime* 30 and 62, see also Dutschke, "The Anniversary Poems," 89.

90. In Pierre Bersuire's interpretation, for example, the laurel embraced by Apollo signifies the cross "embraced in the body" by Christ the sun of justice. For the medieval moralizing readings of Daphne's transformation, see Yves Giraud, *La Fable de Daphné: Essai sur un type de métamorphose végétale dans la littérature et dans les arts jusqu'à la fin du 17e siècle* (Geneva, 1968), 94–126.

91. Gorni, who cites this tradition, suggests that other elements of the oppositional series of the sestina also allude to the crucifixion: "other leaves" to the crown of thorns (replacing the laurel crown desired by the poet), "other hills" to Golgotha ("Metamorfosi e redenzione," 10–11).

feats of unmotivated chivalric prowess come to an end for the young Perceval. Encountering penitents and asking them what day it is, he receives a reply which is not without interest for the case of Petrarch's poet lost in his own oblivion:

—"Quels jors, sire? Si nel savez?
C'est li vendredis aorez,
Li jors que l'en doit aorer
La crois et ses pechiez plorer,
Car hui fu cil en crois pendus. . . ."[92]

["What day, Sire? Then do you not know? It is holy Friday, the day when one is to adore the cross and weep for one's sins, for today He was hung upon the cross. . . ."]

In a similar fashion Petrarch's poet prays to God on Good Friday as he marks the anniversary of his *innamoramento:* "reduci i pensier vaghi a miglior luogo, / rammenta lor come oggi fusti in croce" [lead my wandering thoughts back to a better place, remind them that today you were on the Cross] (62). The "pitiless yoke" that characterizes the experience of love in this poem is the same as that "yoke of bondage" with which Richard of St. Victor characterizes the lover's state, and in *Rime* 62 the poet follows the course urged by Richard as the sole possibility of resolution. "I can find no other remedy in this state of misery," Richard writes, "but to look to the divine clemency and implore His mercy. . . . If there is no way of escape left that you can actively pursue, call upon Him who is able to do all things."[93] Petrarch's "Padre del Ciel" closes with the appeal for a salutary meditation on the crucifix- ion as that remedy most likely to correct the erring and errant thoughts of the poet, and these thoughts will remain of Laura *in morte* as they had been *in vita,* defining his *passio* as "Amor, che m'à legato et tienmi in croce . . ." [Love, who has bound me and keeps me in torment] (284). "Remind them that today you were on the cross": the prayer that closes "Padre del Ciel" retains its urgency throughout the collection, positing an antidote to the obsessive love of Laura.[94]

For the protagonist of the *Commedia,* whose plight the situation of

---

92. *Le Roman de Perceval ou Le Conte du Graal,* vv. 6266–70.

93. Richard of St. Victor, *Selected Writings on Contemplation,* 216, 218.

94. The meditation on the cross to which devotional texts urge the Christian on Good Friday is particularly suggestive in regard to the poet's dilemma: it is invoked in the struggle against the concupiscence of the flesh. See Martinelli, " 'Feria sexta aprilis'," 466, and for Petrarch's attention to the ritual of the cross, see his *Petrarca e il Ventoso,* 297.

Petrarch's poet in many ways recalls, divine aid is forthcoming: Dante's limping pilgrim, the beneficiary of the intervention of three heavenly ladies and of Virgil's tutelage as well, sets about the long and laborious business that will finally enable him to ascend, not only to the shining mountaintop, but to Paradise. The poet of the *Rime*, however, is both a wood-wanderer and a labyrinth-wanderer, and no clear divine signs mark a possible exit. The "primo giovenile errore," already suggestive in the proemial sonnet of moral responsibility, will be redefined as an "errare":[95]

> Allor errai quando l'antica strada
> di libertà mi fu precisa et tolta,
> ché mal si segue ciò ch'agli occhi agrada;
> allor corse al suo mal libera et sciolta,
> ora a posta d'altrui conven che vada
> l'anima che peccò sol una volta.
>
> (96, 9–14)

> [I went wrong when first my former path of freedom was cut off and blocked to me, for it is ill to follow what pleases the eyes; then my soul ran free and unbound to her harm, now she must go at another's behest, though she sinned only once.]

The exploitation of literal and metaphorical "erring" continues until the final segment of the collection, where the poet will summarize the fate to which Amor has subjected him: " 'Cercar m'à fatto deserti paesi . . . et ogni error che' pellegrini intrica' " [He has made me search among wildernesses . . . and every wandering that entangles travelers] (360). That wandering is dramatically refocused in the retrospective definition of the poet's love as "un lungo errar in cieco labirinto" [a long wandering in a blind labyrinth] (224).[96] As Petrarch well knew, his classical poets had also associated "errores" with the figure of the labyrinth; it was

---

95. On the relation of the two terms, see Martinelli, *Petrarca e il Ventoso*, 277–79. For comment on "errore" in *Rime* 1, see A. Jacomuzzi, "Il primo sonetto del *Canzoniere*," in *Letteratura e Critica: Studi in Onore di Natalino Sapegno* (Rome, 1977), 48; A. Noyer-Weidner, "Il sonetto I," *Lectura Petrarce, IV, 1984* (Padua, 1985), 350–51.

96. Gaetano Cipolla notes that this labyrinth has the value of an emblem in its representation of the passion of love; see "Labyrinthine Imagery in Petrarch," *Italica* 54 (1977): 267. Cf. Adelia Noferi, "Il Canzoniere del Petrarca: Scrittura del desiderio e desiderio della scrittura," *Paragone letteratura* 296 (1974), who observes that the perimeter of the *Canzoniere* is in reality the perimeter of a labyrinth (6).

characterized by Virgil as the "inextricabilis" and "irremeabilis error."[97] The doubling of physical and spiritual erring is central to Augustine's reading of Virgil: describing his response to the *Aeneid*, he refers to that work not by its title but as *Aeneae errores*, confirming the perceived analogy with his own youthful delusions represented in turn as exemplary of the wanderings of errant mankind.[98] In the *Confessions*, deviation from the proper path is a fundamental metaphor for straying from God.[99] In the *Rime* the entry into the labyrinth closes the poem (211) that contains the fullest disclosure of the date and time of the *innamoramento*.[100]

In the *Secretum*, confronted with the penetrating analyses of Augustinus, Franciscus cites Cicero in defense of his love for Laura: "If I err I err here willingly, and I shall never consent to part with this error as long as I live."[101] The poet of the *Rime*, of course, repeatedly acknowledges his error and desires to abandon it. The death of Laura, however, does not alter his course, although early in Part II he urges a new direction upon his disconsolate soul:

> cerchiamo 'l Ciel se qui nulla ne piace,
> ché mal per noi quella beltà si vide
> se viva et morta ne devea tor pace.
>
> (273, 12–14)

[Let us seek Heaven, if nothing pleases us here; for we ill saw that beauty if living and dead it was to rob us of peace.]

Engaged in its backward longing and its backward turning, the soul does not listen: his wandering thoughts and his heart once again "arm them-

---

97. For a similar designation in two of Petrarch's *epistolae metricae*, see Cipolla, "Labyrinthine Imagery," 274–75. "Labyrinthia claustra, / erroresque novos . . . carcer habet," Ovid describes it; cited in E. H. Wilkins, *Studies in the Life and Works of Petrarch* (Cambridge, Mass., 1955), 117.

98. *Confessions* I, 13. See John O'Meara, "Augustine the Artist and the *Aeneid*," *Mélanges offerts à Mademoiselle Christine Mohrmann* (Utrecht and Antwerp, 1963), 256–61.

99. In *The City of God*, Augustine explains that the disobedience of Adam and Eve instituted in the history of mankind the "period of erring" (XIV, 11). See the suggestive comments of Timothy Bahti relating these passages to the accusations leveled by Augustinus in the *Secretum;* "Petrarch and the Scene of Writing: A Reading of *Rime* CXXIX," *Yale Italian Studies* 1 (1980): 56–57.

100. The final tercet of this poem was revised to include the date, throwing this closing statement into greater relief. On this correction made five years before Petrarch's death, see Cipolla, "Labyrinthine Imagery," 267–68.

101. *Petrarch's Secret*, 112. As Victoria Kahn observes, this citation leads to a discussion of the moral status of examples; see "The Figure of the Reader," 160–61.

selves with error" (274), and it is in the refound Laura that he continues to place his hope and to seek consolation. In the second commemoration of her death he exults in her renewed dominion (278), and the dominion of Amor too resumes: it is Amor, as we have seen, who once again guides his steps as he returns to Valchiusa early in Part II, reinstating the relation defined in Part I in "Di pensier in pensier, di monte in monte / mi guida Amor" (129).[102] Many poems and many journeys later, in *Rime* 354, Amor is still addressed as "Signor," and the poet entreats his aid to speak of the Laura now in Heaven; even as he acknowledges that he should fix his eyes in a safer place, he continues to confess himself in Amor's service (355). The long story of his ills past and present that he at last dares to address to a sympathetic Laura recounts how "di dì in dì, d'ora in ora, Amor m'à roso" [day by day, hour by hour, Love has gnawed at me] (356), and Laura's admonishment in her final dream appearance, urging him to seek God's help if "another" is overpowering him (359), implicitly acknowledges Amor's continuing domination. In the following poem, the great debate in which the poet submits his case to the adjudication of Reason, Amor appears once again in full personification as "quel antiquo mio dolce empio signore" [my old sweet cruel lord] to defend himself— and ably—against his longtime victim, who proclaims his continuing bondage emphatically in verbs of the present tense:

> ché vo cangiando 'l pelo,
> né cangiar posso l'ostinata voglia.
> Così in tutto mi spoglia
> di libertà questo crudel ch'i' accuso.
>
> (360, 41–44)

[For my hair is turning, but I cannot turn from my obstinate will: this cruel one whom I accuse despoils me of all liberty.]

Amor appears twice in the three penitential poems that precede "Vergine bella." In the first of these, following Laura's pious advice, the poet avows himself "fuor di man di colui che punge et molce, / che già fece di me sì lungo strazio" [out of the hands of him who pierces and heals, who once made of me such a long torture] (363) and turns instead to God:

102. Note again the contrast with the *Vita Nuova*, where Amor is first deliberately established as an abstract entity, then identified as Beatrice herself (*VN* XX, XXIV). At this point he disappears from the narrative, even before Dante's explanation of his status as a mere figure of speech. For discussion, see Robert Pogue Harrison, *The Body of Beatrice* (Baltimore, 1988), 49–52.

et al Signor ch'io adoro et ch'i' ringrazio,
che pur col ciglio il ciel governa et folce,
torno stanco di viver, non che sazio.

(363, 12–14)

[and to the Lord whom I adore and whom I thank, who governs
and sustains the heavens with His brow, I return, weary of life,
not merely satiated.]

In the next poem, his summary of his years of burning and weeping
dominated by Amor is a final explicit confirmation that Laura's death
did not mark a radical change in his course:

Tennemi Amor anni ventuno ardendo
lieto nel foco et nel duol pien di speme;
poi che Madonna e 'l mio cor seco inseme
saliro al Ciel, dieci altri anni piangendo.

(364, 1–4)

[Love held me twenty-one years gladly burning in the fire and full
of hope amid sorrow; since my lady, and my heart with her, rose
to Heaven, ten more years of weeping.]

This Amor, it should be noted, is identical to the powerful deity of Part
I of the collection. One cannot, the sonnet seems to tell us, serve two
masters:[103]

Omai son stanco, et mia vita reprendo
di tanto error che di vertute il seme
à quasi spento; et le mie parti estreme,
alto Dio, a te devotamento rendo
pentito et tristo de' miei sì spesi anni,
che spender si deveano in miglior uso,
in cercar pace et in fuggir affanni.

(364, 5–11)

[Now I am weary and I reproach my life for so much error, which
has almost extinguished the seed of virtue; and I devoutly render
my last parts, high God, to You, repentant and sorrowing for my

---

103. For "Signor" as key term in these poems, where it is redirected from Amor to
God, see König, "Das letzte Sonett des *Canzoniere*," 247–48.

years spent thus, which ought to have been better used, in seeking peace and fleeing troubles.]

Here in the final anniversary poem of the collection, the twenty-one years passed burning *in vita di Laura* and the ten subsequent years passed weeping are all years centered in Laura, and all are implicated in the penitential declaration.[104]

The regret and sadness for these wasted years recalls his lament in "Padre del Ciel" when already, marking the eleventh anniversary of the *innamoramento*, his prayer was uttered "dopo i perduti giorni, / dopo le notti vaneggiando spese" [after the lost days, after the nights spent raving] (62). Yet more insistently, it recalls the proemial sonnet of the collection.[105] Among the persuasive correspondence with *Rime* 1 are "le vane speranze e 'l van dolore," the vain hopes and vain sorrow that recall the years when Amor kept him "full of hope amid sorrow," and the next and final sonnet affirms that the hope long placed in Amor will at last be vested instead in God: "'n altrui non ò speranza" [I have no hope in anyone else] (365). In *Rime* 1 the retrospective "ben veggio or" assesses the poet's "primo giovenile errore"; in *Rime* 364 he confides that "mia vita reprendo / di tanto error" [I reproach my life for so much error].[106] Once again shame, once again repentance: then "'l pentirsi," now "pentito e tristo." Measuring the correspondence across the span of the intervening *rime sparse*, both poems close with "conoscere": "'l conoscer chiaramente / che quanto piace al mondo è breve sogno" [the clear knowledge that whatever pleases in the world is a brief dream]; "ch'i' conosco 'l mio fallo et non lo scuso" [for I recognize my fault and I do not excuse it]. These recalls heighten the essential difference between the two components: *Rime* 1, addressed to "voi ch'ascoltate," invokes an audience expert in matters of love, from whom the poet hopes to find "pietà, non che perdono"; *Rime* 364 is addressed to God, in a prayer for

104. On the element of weariness that achieves particular prominence in these final sonnets, see Jill Tilden, "Spiritual Conflict in Petrarch's Canzoniere," in *Petrarca 1304–1374; Beiträge zu Werk und Wirkung,* ed. F. Schalk (Frankfurt, 1975), 312–13. The contrast of *pace* and *affanni*, notes Dutschke, "recapitulates the central theme of the anniversary poems, conflict between human and divine love" ("The Anniversary Poems," 96–97).

105. Iliescu proposes that *Rime* 2–4 as "prologue" sonnets stand in special relation to the final three sonnets, *Rime* 363–65; see *Il Canzoniere Petrarchesco e Sant'Agostino,* 100–104 (citation, 101–2).

106. The passage, Francisco Rico notes, is an adaptation of Cicero's *Tusculanes,* a clear statement of Stoic doctrine that opposes the purturbation of conflicting passions to the certainty and tranquility attainable only by the philosopher; see " 'Rime sparse', 'Rerum vulgarium fragmenta'," 125, and for the importance of this doctrine in other works by Petrarch, see 126–31.

salvation. In this sense the proemial sonnet is the secular version of *Rime* 364, which opens the way to a fully penitential sonnet from which Laura is absent, and to the great canzone addressed to the "Vergine bella."[107]

The poet's continued devotion to Laura *in morte* belies his affirmation in the first of the anniversary poems following her death: "L'ardente nodo ov'io fui, d'ora in ora / contando, anni ventuno interi preso / Morte disciolse . . ." [That burning knot in which I was hour by hour caught for twenty-one whole years, Death has untied . . .] (271). This sequence is confirmed instead in the *Trionfi*, where the *innamoramento* is again correlated with Laura's death: "L'ora prima era, il dì sesto d'aprile, / che già mi strinse, et or, lasso, mi sciolse: / come Fortuna va cangiando stile!" [April the sixth, it was, and the first hour, when I was bound— and now, alas, set free! Surely the ways of fate are strange indeed!] (*Tr. Mor.* I, 133–35). But here we find in germ the most significant difference between the casting of the story in the *Trionfi* and that in the *Rime sparse:* in the former, the "dì sesto d'aprile" does not evoke the crucifixion. In the *Trionfi* the principal personae are not four but three: Amor, Laura, and the poet. Laura *in vita* conquers Amor, binding him ignominiously in chains, and thereafter inspires the poet's meditation on Eternity. Banished is the opposition of registers that constrains the reading of the poet's story in the lyric collection and that, as we have seen, constitutes one of its principal anxieties. Despite the ready availability and ecclesiastical sanction of triumphal imagery associated with the Cross,[108] in the *Trionfi* the event of the crucifixion, which in the *Rime* sets Christ's redemptive suffering against the poet's amorous passion, is strikingly absent.[109]

In the *Rime sparse*, the poet's story opened upon the *innamoramento* as a scene of wounding that intruded upon a sacred anniversary. In its

107. Petrarch indicated the reordering of the last thirty components in marginal numbers added to Vat. Lat. 3195. See Wilkins, *The Making of the "Canzoniere,"* 122ff., and A. E. Quaglio, *Al di là di Francesca e di Laura* (Padua, 1973), 33–56. For the last sonnets as a sequence closing Part II of the *Rime*, see Bernhard König, "Das letzte Sonett des *Canzoniere*," in *Interpretation: Das Paradigma der Europäischen Renaissance-Literatur*, ed. Klaus Hempfer and Gerhard Regn (Wiesbaden, 1983), 239–57.

108. See Robert Baldwin, "Triumph and the Rhetoric of Power in Christian Art, 450–1520," in *"All the World's a Stage": Pageantry and Spectacle in the Renaissance*, ed. Barbara Wollesen-Wisch and Susan Munshower (University Park, Pa., 1989).

109. See Sturm-Maddox, *"Arbor vittoriosa triunfale:* Allegory and Spectacle in the *Rime* and the *Trionfi*," in *Petrarch's Triumphs: Allegory and Spectacle*, ed. Konrad Eisenbichler and Amilcare A. Iannucci (Ottawa, 1990). Waller suggests that the Christocentric model itself is absent from the poem, noting that "the only trace of the Christ event" is "the mention of his empty tomb which the contemporary Christian world has abandoned to the Saracens"; see *Petrarch's Poetics and Literary History*, 130.

secular cosmology Laura is the desired source of mercy, the source of reward, the "fonte di pietà," the fountain of pity (203). Redefining his dilemma in the poem that opens Part II, the victim of Amor finds the outstretched arms of Christ still open: "Quelle pietose braccia / in ch'io mi fido veggio aperte ancora" [those merciful arms in which I trust I see still open] (264). But that affirmation is immediately followed, like most of the affirmations of alternatives or admonitory interventions in the collection, by "ma . . ."—"but"—reinstating the dilemma. Already in "Padre del Ciel," however, the rememoration of the crucifixion had intimated the sacred source, not only of pity and consolation, but of healing: the sacrificial wounds of Christ, commonly represented as wells or fountains of pity and of mercy, related by the medieval tradition that identified both the Fall and the crucifixion as occurring on the *feria sexta aprilis* to the wound common to the descendants of Adam.[110]

It is in this perspective that the final canzone closes the circle to complete the framing of the poet's story. Here Christ, not Laura, is defined as "il Fonte di pietate" (366), and here the final mentions of wounding occur. The first is a moving but largely conventional allusion to the Virgin's sorrow at the scene of the crucifixion, at the sight of the "spietata stampa / ne' dolci membri del tuo caro figlio" [the pitiless wounds in your dear Son's sweet limbs]. This, of course, is the scene of the universal "pietà" in *Rime* 3, and it returns us to the scene and the occasion of the beginning of the poet's story, when the sun's rays were paled "per la pietà del suo fattore." But wounding too is evoked again, now more directly, in his final prayer to Mary:

> Vergine gloriosa,
> donna del Re che' nostri lacci à sciolti
> et fatto 'l mondo libero et felice,
> ne le cui sante piaghe
> prego ch'appaghe   il cor, vera beatrice.
>
> (47–52)

[O glorious Virgin, Lady of that King who has loosed our bonds and made the world free and happy, in whose holy wounds I pray you to quiet my heart, O true bringer of happiness.]

110. For this topos in medieval literature, see Douglas Gray, "The Five Wounds of Our Lord," *Notes and Queries* 208 (1963): 50–51, 82–89, 127–34, 163–68. Citing the protagonists of both *Sir Gawain and the Green Knight* and *Pearl*, Paul Reichardt notes "the paradox that the only remedy for their moral vulnerability is the sign of Christ's vicarious suffering, his wounded body"; see "Gawain and the Image of the Wound," *PMLA* 99 (1984): 159.

The liberation of mankind, and personal liberation as well: to the *antiche piaghe* are opposed the *sante piaghe*. Here the poet's story, initiated on a Good Friday, at last finds its closure: while the resolution of his spiritual anguish has not yet been granted, these verses that invoke first the promise of man's liberation from the consequences of original sin acknowledge also the direct relevance of Christ's wounds to the wounded poet's dilemma.

In his *De quatuor gradibus* Richard of St. Victor offers an explanation of the phenomenon of love that begins, like the *Rime*, with the depiction of the *innamoramento* as a wounding: "the first stage of love is the wounding, when the lover first notices the object; the second is the binding, when the lover is bound to the object; in the third the object becomes unique, the only one capable of satisfying the lover's desire; in the fourth, the love becomes infinite and therefore, unless the object is God, insatiable."[111] Insatiable: so had Augustine in the opening words of his *Confessions* stated the premise for the entire retrospective narrative to follow, "our heart has no peace til it rest in Thee." So too will the poet of the *Rime sparse* offer a final recapitulation of his experience:

> Da poi ch' i' nacqui in su la riva d'Arno,
> cercando or questa et or quell'altra parte,
> non è stata mia vita altro ch'affanno.
>
> (366, 82–84)[112]

[Since I was born on the bank of Arno, searching in this and now this other direction, my life has been nothing but troubles.]

Richard's text reads almost like a program for the unfolding of Petrarch's lyric collection: that unique object of desire, not only elusive and unattainable but finally in opposition to the single object that might afford satisfaction, is pursued throughout the *Rime* with a fervor—and adored with a devotion—of an order due to God alone.

In the opening poem of Part II the poet draws the consequences of his love for Laura:

---

111. The summary of the *De quatuor gradibus violentae caritatis* is that of Bruce Comens in "Stages of Love, Steps to Hell: Dante's *Rime petrose*," *MLN* 99 (1986): 160.

112. The *Rime*, like the *Confessions*, closes with an appeal for "pace." See the observations of Iliescu, *Il Canzoniere petrarchesco e Sant'Agostino*, 96–97; Georg Rabuse, "Petrarcas Marienkanzone im Lichte der 'Santa Orazione' Dantes," in *Petrarca 1304–1374: Beiträge zu Werk und Wirkung*, ed. F. Schalk (Frankfurt, 1975), 249–50.

> Ché mortal cosa amar con tanta fede
> quanto a Dio sol per debito convensi
> più si disdice a chi più pregio brama.
>
> (264, 99–101)

[For the more one desires honor, the more one is forbidden to love a mortal thing with the faith that belongs to God alone.]

But God is not the only deity whose authority is acknowledged in this poem. Here too is Amor: "mi sforza Amore / che la strada d'onore / mai nol lassa seguir chi troppo il crede" [Love forces me, who never lets anyone who too much believes him follow the path of honor]. The "fede" with which he loves Laura and the "crede" that is his response to Amor identify a system of belief. And in the final analysis his condition is not radically altered with the death of Laura because the fundamental issue throughout the *Rime*, in Part II *in morte* as in Part I *in vita*, is not the opposition of concupiscence to *caritas* explicitly thematized in the penitential poems: it is a system of belief. In Amor and in the lady who eludes not only his possession but his description and his comprehension the poet places his faith and his hope for reward, first on earth and then in Heaven. His belief in this mortal creature, this "mortal cosa" raised to the status of divinity, is one meaning of his "errore," whose failure he confesses after Laura's death as his harsh fate, his "dura sorte":

> ch'altri che me non ò di chi mi lagne,
> che 'n dee non credev'io regnasse Morte.
> O che lieve è inganar chi s'assecura!
>
> (311, 7–9)[113]

[for I have no one to complain of save myself, who did not believe that Death reigns over goddesses.]

From the beginning of illusion to the end of illusion: the conclusion of this meditation—"or cognosco . . . come nulla qui giù diletta et dura" [now I know . . . how nothing down here both pleases and endures]—recalls in direct terms the end of the opening sonnet of the collection,

---

113. See Dotti, "Miti e forme dell''io'," 84. It is noteworthy that the anxiety of this disconsolate confession of the *Rime* is absent from the *Trionfi;* on the contrary, the chaste companions who attend the death of Laura exclaim, "Vattene in pace, o vera mortal Dea" (*Tr. Mor.* I, 124).

"conoscer chiaramente / che quanto piace al mondo è breve sogno," the clear knowledge that all that pleases in the world is a brief dream.[114]

But the principle of intelligibility is at issue in another way as well.[115] In the Christian semiotics exemplified by Augustine, as Freccero points out, it is the theology of the Word that affords such a principle: it "binds together language and desire by ordering both to God, in Whom they are grounded," always "reaching out for a silent terminal point that lies outside the system."[116] Petrarch's poet instead installs Amor and the lady as the ordering principles of his reading of the world and of his own experience. The Laura represented in *Rime* 4 as a "divine gift" and, in her virtuality, as "a sun," a source of illumination, is thus likened to Christ, whose identity as the "true light" has been suggested in the liturgical allusion of sonnet 3.

Implicit in this analogy is that just as Christ, God's gift of Himself come to earth "a 'lluminar le carte / ch'avean molt'anni già celato il vero" [to illuminate the pages that for many years had hidden the truth] (4), incarnated a new dispensation for mankind, so Laura's birth is a divine advent, one promising a new illumination. As the inception of his love occults the significance of the liturgical occasion, so the light of Laura, redefined in *Rime* 141 as his fated sun, expands to fill his universe, occulting the divine light. Her advent into his life marks his entrance into the labyrinth of desire, and she becomes the instrument of his confinement, his world contracting as her light expands: "in cielo e 'n terra," he confesses, "m'à racchiuso i passi" [in Heaven and earth she has circumscribed my steps] (127). Her own virtue is not questioned, but her effect on the poet is indisputable, for with her death he remains in darkness: that sun, "tornando al sommo Sole, in pochi sassi / chiuse 'l mio lume" [returning to the highest Sun, (she) has closed up in a few stones my light].

We have seen, however, that the poet's love for Laura throughout the collection is marked by an ambivalence in the association of the *innamoramento* with Good Friday.[117] Not only has Laura, as Augustinus insists,

114. See Arnaud Tripet, " 'Voi ch'ascoltate' . . . Poesia e coscienza nel Petrarca lirico," in *Civiltà del Piemonte: Studi in onore di Renzo Gandolfo* (Turin, 1975), 841.

115. For a different but closely related perspective on the issue of Laura's inadequacy as the desired center of the lover's existence, see Waller, *Petrarch's Poetics and Literary History*, 19–22.

116. Freccero, "The Fig Tree and the Laurel," 35. In the *Rime*, Freccero suggests, Petrarch offers us instead a self-contained system, one that "uses Augustinian principles in order to create a totally autonomous portrait of the artist, devoid of any ontological claim" (34).

117. For this juxtaposition as an emblematic oxymoron very close to sacrilege, see Cambon, 16.

detached his mind from the love of heavenly things and inclined it to love the creature more than the Creator, inverting the order.[118] The cult of Amor and of Laura, against which the other voices in the collection warn him, opposes to the Christocentric cosmos one centered in Laura and intelligible only in terms of Laura. The quiet, weary profession "Al Signor . . . torno" of *Rime* 363, closing the first of the series of penitential sonnets that immediately precede his final appeal to the "Vergine bella," is not a conversion, but it is a both a turning, and a return. It returns to that devotion that was the poet's before the inception of his love for Laura, to reinstate an order of intelligibility that alone may illuminate his life, to "illuminar le carte" of his story.

118. To Franciscus's protestation that he had been led to the love of God through love of Laura, Augustinus replies sharply that while "every creature should be dear to us because of our love for the Creator," he has loved God as the creator of Laura (*Petrarch's Secret*, 124–25).

EPILOGUE: WRITING IN THE SHADE OF THE LAUREL

Così cresca il bel lauro in fresca riva,
et chi 'l piantò pensier leggiadri et alti
ne la dolce ombra al suon de l'acque scriva!
                    (148, 12–14)

[Then let this lovely laurel grow on the fresh bank; and he who planted it, let him—in its sweet shade, to the sound of the waters—write high and happy thoughts!]

These verses present us with a curious circumlocution: "he who planted the laurel," of course, is Francesco Petrarca, and in this third-person representation of the self he is penning not only a poem celebrating a plant but a self-portrait. While gestures of this sort are far from uncommon in Petrarch's corpus, whose abundant self-disclosure has afforded a mine for critical inquiry, this one is particularly suggestive because Petrarch did in fact plant laurels. He tells us so, speaking not only through his multiple poetic personae but in his own voice, in his letters and in his manuscript of Palladius's *De agricultura*.[1] His self-representation in sonnet 148 as writing in the shade of the laurel he had himself planted in the familiar landscape of Valchiusa prompts in his reader a heightened sense of encounter, not with a poetic persona, but with the "real" Petrarch who penned the *Rime sparse*.

This apparent intersection between life and literature nonetheless bears

---

1. See Ernest H. Wilkins, *Life of Petrarch* (Chicago, 1961). He tried unsuccessfully to establish laurels in his garden in Milan, and recorded his hope that Boccaccio's presence would bring luck on the occasion of a renewed attempt; see Pierre de Nolhac, "Pétrarque et son jardin, d'après ses notes inédites," *Giornale storico della letteratura italiana* 9 (1987): 409. Two laurels were later planted with ceremony, "solennissime," at Arquà.

further examination. In the Coronation Oration, for example, Petrarch takes a Virgilian text as an introduction to represent himself as poet beneath the laurel, "sub lauro mea." The literary nature of the image is evident too in the miniature that he commissioned for his cherished Virgil manuscript, executed by the Simone Martini who also prepared the portrait of Laura that prompted two admiring sonnets included among the *Rime sparse*. Here a soldier, a farmer, and a shepherd, evoking the myriad talents of Virgil as author of the *Aeneid*, the *Georgics*, and the *Eclogues*, watch as the commentator Servius (identified in Petrarch's explanatory notation) draws back a curtain.[2] The painted gesture reveals the figure of Virgil himself: wearing a wreath of laurel and gazing into the distance, he reclines beneath a tree, pen in hand. The wreath of laurel that adorns the recumbent poet, symbol of the fame that crowns inspired poetic labor, gives visual form to a preoccupation with that symbol in Petrarch's works both Latin and vernacular;[3] "indeed," as Mann comments, "we might even take the reclining poet in the miniature for Petrarch rather than for Virgil."[4] For confirmation we need only turn to the verbal portrait of himself as young poet that Petrarch paints in the *Africa*, the work upon which he rested his major claim to poetic distinction at the time of his coronation. Here, as the Greek poet Homer solemnly foretells to the Latin poet Ennius the greatness of a Petrarch yet to be born, this promising youth is glimpsed reclining, pen in hand, beneath a laurel tree, with whose fronds "he seems about to bind his locks."[5]

In these images Petrarch identified himself mimetically with a bucolic tradition in which poet and thinker seek to distance themselves from city life. The motif of the philosophically and poetically productive retreat into nature was already well established when Virgil used it in his eclogues, which Petrarch sought to imitate in his *Bucolicum carmen*;[6] Horace's verse "Silva placet Musis, urbs est inimica poetis" is cited

2. See *Francisci Petrarcae Vergilianus Codex*, ed. G. Galbiati (Milan, 1930). The commentary of Servius, in smaller characters, encloses the Virgilian text; Petrarch's inscription is in Latin verse on three scrolls included in the miniature. For a suggestive discussion of the relation between the Oration and the miniature, see Joel Brink, "Simone Martini, Francesco Petrarca and the Humanistic Program of the Virgil Frontispiece," *Mediaevalia* 3 (1977): 83–117.

3. See the chapter "Sub lauro mea" in Carlo Calcaterra, *Nella selva del Petrarca* (Bologna, 1942), 89–107.

4. Nicholas Mann, *Petrarch* (Oxford, 1984), 1–2.

5. *Africa*, book 9, 295–300; trans. Thomas G. Bergin and Alice S. Wilson (New Haven, 1977).

6. On the motif of writing poetry under trees, on the grass, or by a spring, see E. R. Curtius, *European Literature and the Latin Middle Ages*, trans. Willard Trask (New York, 1953), 187. See also Renato Poggioli, *The Oaten Flute: Essays on Pastoral Poetry and the Pastoral Ideal* (Cambridge, Mass., 1975), who comments that "the pastoral ideal is rooted not only in a vision of life but also in a view of art and literature" (34).

approvingly by Augustinus in the *Secretum*.[7] The sentiment, however, is not only literary, not generic: Petrarch's citation of Horace follows an exchange in which his persona Franciscus expounds on his hatred of city life in Avignon. The passage in the *Africa*, moreover, adds a significant detail to the classical locus: it is in Valchiusa—"nam longe clausa sub valle"—that the dreaming Ennius is shown the youthful Petrarch.

Petrarch indeed records, in the *Letter to Posterity* that forms his carefully composed autobiographical statement, that it was in Valchiusa that he had been inspired to begin the composition of the *Africa*. In this text, one written late in life and included as the last book of the letters that he collected under the rubric of *Seniles*, he identifies Valchiusa in more comprehensive terms as the locus of his most intense literary activity: "all my little works," he tells us, "were either completed or begun or conceived" there.[8] Both the bucolic vision of his eclogues and the meditative vision of the *De vita solitaria* are explicitly associated with the welcome solitude of his "enclosed valley."[9] Encouraging a friend to visit him there, he describes its natural elements and then suggests that the place has become widely known on account of his own presence, as well as through his verse: he has labored to make it famous, he acknowledges, "not only in my choice of the place itself, but in my rustic dwelling and, I hope, in the stronger mortar of my words and songs."[10]

Thus Valchiusa helps to create the portrait of Petrarch, and Petrarch creates in turn a portrait of Valchiusa.[11] In fact, while his interest in the

7. See Horace's epistle II, 3, and the comments of Oscar Büdel, "Illusion Disabused: A Novel Mode in Petrarch's Canzoniere," in *Francis Petrarch, Six Centuries Later: A Symposium*, ed. Aldo Scaglione (Chapel Hill and Chicago, 1975), 139. Jennifer Petrie suggests that Horace's frugal life of solitude at Tiber may afford a particular precedent for this self-representation; see *The Augustan Poets, the Italian Tradition, and the Canzoniere* (Dublin, 1983), 90–91. B. König, in "Petrarcas Landschaften," *Romanische Forschungen* 92 (1980), notes Petrarch's attention to Horace as lyric poet (252–53; for other probable classical sources of his depictions of landscape, see 273–76).

8. *Letters from Petrarch*, trans. Morris Bishop (Bloomington, Ind., 1966); citation, 9. The text of the *Posteritati* is in Francesco Petrarca, *Prose*, ed. G. Martellotti, P. G. Ricci, E. Carrara, and E. Bianchi (Milan-Naples, 1955), 2–19; for discussion, see Aldo Bernardo, "Petrarch's Autobiography: Circularity Revisited," *Annali d'Italianistica* 4 (1986): 45–72.

9. In a fragment of Latin verse probably addressed to Bishop Filippo di Cabassoles, he describes his "happiest years" spent there as a boy, as a youth, and as a man, and expresses his desire to finish his days there. See Enrico Carrara, "Gli 'Improvvisi' del Petrarca," *Studi Petrarcheschi* 1 (1948): esp. 147. Adelia Noferi calls attention to "the myth, or rather the fable of this peaceful residence"; see *L'esperienza poetica del Petrarca* (Florence, 1962), 91.

10. *Fam.* VIII, 3. See Claudia Berra, "L'arte della similitudine nella canzone CXXXV dei 'Rerum vulgarium fragmenta'," *Giornale Storico della Letteratura Italiana* 163 (1986): 195–96.

11. In one sense, Enrico Carrara notes, Valchiusa is the aesthetic masterpiece of Petrarch's life; see "L'epistola 'Posteritati' e la leggenda petrarchesca" in his *Studi petrarcheschi ed altri scritti* (Turin, 1959), 61.

natural site is well documented—he marveled at its extraordinary beauty, reported his close observation of its various elements, and sketched its landscape—[12] it is in the *Rime* that he paints its most memorable portrait. We have examined its portrayal as "Laura's place," as the locus of the *innamoramento* of his lyric protagonist. But it is also a place for writing, and while later generations were to read the *Rime* for the story of Petrarch's love for Laura, the poet who records that love is less elusive than the lady celebrated in his verse. "Petrarch was too deeply immersed in literature not to end up as a literary character," observes Francisco Rico,[13] and while Augustinus in the *Secretum* lays bare the role-playing of the poet who writes of his beloved laurel as if he were "a denizen of Peneus' stream, or some priest of Cirrha's mount,"[14] in the *Rime* it is as poet in landscape that Petrarch frequently identifies himself to the reader: "Qui mi sto solo, et come Amor m'invita / or rime et versi, or colgo erbette et fiori" [Here I am alone, and, as Love leads me on, I gather now rhymes and verses, now herbs and flowers] (114). *In vita di Laura* and *in morte di Laura*: a later sonnet cited above identifies this fresh, flowering bank as "là 'v'io seggia d'Amor pensoso et scriva" [where I am sitting in thoughts of love and writing] (279).

Like the victim of Amor who pursues an elusive Laura, the poet who writes of Laura in this *locus amoenus* has classical prototypes. The poet of Virgil's first eclogue, reclining beneath a birch in pastoral repose, makes the woods resound with the name of his beloved Amaryllis, and so does the poet of the *Rime* make the valley and the forest of Valchiusa resound with Laura's name: ". . . solo del suo nome / vo empiendo l'aere che sì dolce sona" [with her name only I fill the air which so sweetly sounds] (97). The classical *locus amoenus*, we may recall, was indebted for its designation to Virgil's constant term for "beautiful" nature; it was both "pleasant" and a place "for pleasure." The Virgilian commentator Servius—he who, in the miniature commissioned by Petrarch, pulls back the curtain to disclose the recumbent poet—explains that such places are "loca solius voluptatis plena," and further identifies that pleasure with

12. Petrarch's representations of Valchiusa were noted by Pierre de Nolhac, *Pétrarque et l'humanisme* (Paris, 1907), II, 69–83; for a more recent study and the designs themselves, see Eugenio Battisti, "Non chiare acque," in *Francis Petrarch, Six Centuries Later: A Symposium*, ed. Aldo Scaglione (Chapel Hill and Chicago, 1975), 305–39.

13. Francisco Rico, "Philology and Philosophy in Petrarch," in *Intellectuals and Writers in Fourteenth-Century Europe*, ed. Piero Boitani and Anna Torti (Cambridge, 1986), 65. Mann devotes a chapter to "the life as work of art" in his *Petrarch*.

14. *Petrarch's Secret*, 134–35.

love, "amoenus" with "amor"; in the widely read *Roman de la Rose* it is in such a pleasing place, "le lieu plaisant," that Guillaume de Lorris sets the love initiation of his own young protagonist.[15] Consider then this Petrarchan version, which merits citation at length for the diverse codes that enter into its composition:[16]

> Giace oltra ove l'Egeo sospira e piagne
> un'isoletta delicata e molle
> più d'altra che 'l sol scalde o che 'l mar bagne;
>   nel mezzo è un ombroso e chiuso colle
> con sì soavi odor, con sì dolci acque,
> ch'ogni maschio pensier de l'alma tolle. . . .
>   Et rimbombava tutta quella valle
> d'acque e d'augelli, et eran le sue rive
> bianche, verdi, vermiglie, perse e gialle;
>   rivi correnti di fontane vive
> al caldo tempo su per l'erba fresca,
> e l'ombra spessa, e l'aure dolci estive. . . .
>
> (*Tr. Cup.* IV, 100–105, 121–26)

[Beyond the Aegean's sighs and tears there lies the softest and the gentlest of all isles warmed by the sun or watered by the sea; and hidden in the midst a shadowy hill with fragrances so sweet and streams so clear that from the heart they banish manly thoughts. . . . And the whole valley echoed with the songs of waters and of birds, and all its swards were white and green and red and yellow and perse.]

For the reader of the *Rime* this is unmistakably the familiar landscape of Valchiusa, that of sonnet 148 and so many other poems already reviewed. This depiction, however, is found not in the lyric collection but in the *Trionfi;* it renders, not Valchiusa, but the island of Venus, and that identification is highly suggestive for the nature of the setting in the *Rime* as well. Compare the setting of an early poem *in morte di Laura* where these elements are again conjoined, the summer breeze accompanying the sound of water and birds:

15. This discussion is indebted to Curtius, *European Literature and the Latin Middle Ages*, 192ff.

16. For a discussion of these codes—Provençal, classical, moralizing—see Battisti, "Non chiare acque," 327–33.

> Se lamentar augelli, o verdi fronde
> mover soavemente a l'aura estiva,
> o roco mormorar di lucide onde
> s'ode d'una fiorita et fresca riva . . . ;

(279, 1–4)

[If I hear birds lamenting, or green leaves moving softly in the summer breeze, or the faint murmuring of shining waves from a fresh and flowering bank . . .]

The immediately following sonnet makes explicit the likeness to the haunt sacred to Venus, to affirm that this too is a setting for love:

> né credo già ch'Amore in Cipro avessi
> o in altra riva sì soavi nidi.
> L'acque parlan d'amore, et l'òra e i rami,
> et gli augelletti e i pesci e i fiori et l'erba,
> tutti inseme pregando ch' i' sempre ami.

(280, 7–11)

[nor do I believe that Love ever had, in Cyprus or on any other shore, such sweet nests. The waters speak of love and the breeze and the branches and the little birds and the fish and the flowers and the grass, all together begging me always to love.]

This is indeed Amor's realm recreated in Valchiusa, that enchanted place where a blossom falling upon Laura "girando parea dir: 'Qui regna Amore' " [turning about seemed to say: "Here reigns Love"] (126).

In the *Trionfi* Petrarch passes a harsh judgment on such seductive places. The Isle of Venus is explicitly condemned as a place that retains so much of its fascination—"tanto retien del suo primo esser vile" [holds still so much of its first pagandom], as the protagonist forthrightly puts it (IV, 110)—that it still deceives mankind. The lordship of Amor, we have seen, is a fiction, one born of idleness and wantonness and nourished by human thoughts and desires. Petrarch would have found this realm exemplified in the *Roman de la Rose,* where Amor captures his victims in the garden of Deduit whose gatekeeper is Oiseuse. It is exemplified too by the adventures of a group to whom the narrator of the *Trionfi* pays particular attention among Amor's captives:

> Ecco quei che le carte empion di sogni,
> Lancilotto, Tristano e gli altri erranti,
> ove conven che 'l vulgo errante agogni.

(*Tr. Cup.* III, 79–81)

[Here too are those who fill our books with dreams: Lancelot, Tristram, and the other knights whose wanderings lead the common folk astray.]

Heightened by repetition here are two senses of *errare:* "erranti" were not only the chivalric heroes, but also the *volgo* whose fantasy was engaged by these fictions.[17] Whereas Augustine had associated spiritual and physical erring, in the vernacular tradition *errare* was suggestive both of the experience of love and of its poetry, as in the "amorosa erranza" of one of Dante's sonnets in the *Vita Nuova.*[18]

In this passage of the *Trionfi* Petrarch judges not only a poetic theology but its fictions, and his judgment is not without implications for his own amorous verses associated with the setting of Valchiusa. It is in Valchiusa, as his tears mingle with the waters of the river and the great fountain, that his sighs take the form of *rime*, as he later recalls to a correspondent: "Thus, the flames in my heart spread through my bones and filled those valleys and skies with a mournful, but, as some called it, pleasant tune. From all this emerged those vernacular songs of my youthful labors which today I am ashamed of and repent, but are, as we have seen, most acceptable to those who are afflicted by the same disease."[19] The declaration of shame and repentance recalls that in the opening poem of the *Rime sparse*—"e del mio vaneggiar vergogna è 'l frutto, / e 'l pentersi . . ." [and of my raving, shame is the fruit, and repentance]—and reminds us that the poem in the *Rime* that directly posits the alternatives of "altr'-amor, altre frondi, et altro lume" posits also another literary project, one in which the poet who had devoted his verses to the celebration of the laurel might "far frutto, non pur fior et frondi" [bear fruit, not merely flowers and leaves] (142).[20] Late in life Petrarch pens another rather disparaging characterization of himself as the writer beneath the laurel,

17. See G. Vallese, "L'evasione cortese," in his *Studi di letteratura umanistica da Dante ad Erasmo* (Naples, 1964²), 33. Lancelot and Tristan, of course, were known through these fictions not only as exemplary knights but as exemplary lovers; in this sense Dante's ill-fated Francesca and Paolo of *Inferno* V are exemplary readers.

18. "Tutti li miei pensier"; see A. Jacomuzzi, "Il primo sonetto del *Canzoniere*," *Letteratura e critica: Studi in onore di Natalino Sapegno* (Rome, 1977), 47. There were associations with "errore" as well; see N. Scarano, "Fonti provenzali e italiane della lirica petrarchesca," *Studi di filologia romanza* 8 (1900): 269.

19. *Fam.* VIII, 3, on his *clausa vallis*.

20. In the *Secretum* Augustinus uses these terms to register his concern for the goodness and virtue early displayed by his disciple; see *Petrarch's Secret*, 127. The metaphor is a commonplace in whose background are Biblical loci such as the analogy in the Sermon on the Mount between the good and corrupt works of men and good and corrupt fruit trees, and the cursing of a barren fig tree by Christ (Matthew 21:19).

"not so much a scholar as a lover of woodlands, a solitary, given to murmuring foolishly amid high beeches and, with the utmost presumption, to toying with my little pen beneath a bitter laurel-tree."[21] In the *Rime*, however, the *altro lavoro* that is repeatedly evoked represents the work not produced, *l'opera assente*, while the poet continues to write of the laurel and of Laura.[22] If Petrarch elsewhere records misgivings about his amorous rhymes, in the *Rime* the lordship of Amor continues undiminished until the closing poems of the collection; and the poet-protagonist effects only a temporary escape from his exemplary commission as love's scribe, as Amor will remind him in triumphantly reimposing his dictation: " '. . . di man mi ti tolse altro lavoro, / ma già ti raggiuns'io mentre fuggivi' " [another work took you out of my hand, but I caught up with you as you were fleeing] (93). Thus, in a subsequent poem, the poet will confess that "né le man [sanno] come / lodar si possa in carte altra persona" [nor do my hands know how on paper any other person can be praised] (97).

If we look once again, and closely, at the depiction of the Isle of Venus in the *Trionfi*, we find that while as a *locus amoenus* it shares most of the features of the landscape of Valchiusa in the *Rime*, it lacks the defining feature of that landscape. In *Rime* 148, where our consideration of Petrarch's mythmaking began, the apparent realism of the two lexical sets with which the poem opens—its catalog of rivers filling the entire first quatrain, its five different varieties of trees of which one is found only in this poem and three others are of rare occurrence in the collection—only heightens the uniqueness of a singular river and a singular tree. None of these other trees and rivers, the poet tells us,

> poria 'l foco allentar che 'l cor tristo ange
> quant' un bel rio ch'ad ogni or meco piange
> co l'arboscel che 'n rime orno et celebro.
>
> (148, 6–8)[23]

[could lessen the fire that wearies my sad heart as much as a lovely stream that from time to time weeps along with me, and the slender tree that in my rhymes I beautify and celebrate.]

21. *Seniles* I, 6; trans. in Mann, *Petrarch*, 97.

22. See Enrico Fenzi, "Per un sonetto del Petrarca: R.V.F. XCIII," *Giornale storico della letteratura italiana* 151 (1974): 518.

23. For Petrarch's rejection of the great rivers associated with history and empire in favor of "an equally specific landscape whose mythic meaning is private, and whose river, though nameless, is purer, more potent, and nurtures his beloved laurel tree," see W. H. Herendeen, "Castara's Smiles . . . Sabrina's Tears: Nature and Setting in Renaissance River Poems," *Comparative Literature* 39 (1987): 269–97.

In the classical pastoral setting are typically found a variety of trees, and the choice of one or another assumes a certain thematic importance, as when bucolic protagonists discuss in verse their preference for a tree in whose shade to seek repose. According to the system known to medieval rhetoric as the "rota Virgilii," reflecting the distinction of styles illustrated by the Virgilian texts evoked in Simone Martini's miniature, the beech tree is associated with the *stilus humilis* treating of shepherds, fruit trees with the *stilus mediocris* treating of farmers, and the laurel and cedar with the *stilus gravis* treating of warriors.[24] In the horticultural interventions through which he brought his own property into closer conformity with the conventional pastoral setting, Petrarch himself planted a variety of trees;[25] but he planted laurels in particular, and their favored status is evident in a letter that portrays him as poet in landscape during his final period of residence in Valchiusa:

> Read if you will, my friend, these verses I send to you now
> Written in haste on my Helicon, where I sit on a verdant meadow
> Under a lonely rock that hard by a murmuring brooklet
> Sheltering stands between the laurels I planted for your sake.
> How many times have I bid them to grow, in the hope that one day
> You too would sit beside me in the shade of their sacred branches.[26]

Not only Petrarch, but his poetic personae: the rustic protagonist of the tenth of his eclogues, named Silvanus because he shuns the life of cities for woodland seclusion, becomes in that forest environment a cultivator, not of trees generally, but of laurels—and in particular of a special laurel, to which he professes his indebtedness:

> The laurel gave me my name; my renown was due to the laurel;
> The laurel gave me my wealth for I found myself rich in the forest,
> Having been poor in the fields, and no man was happier than I was.[27]

24. See Curtius, *European Literature and the Latin Middle Ages*, 201, and on the "rota Virgilii," 232. The laurel appears in this connection in the Middle Ages in the *Song of Roland* and the *Alexandreis* of Gautier de Châtillon.

25. In the frequent accounts that he offers of his life in Valchiusa, Mann points out, "his 'translapine Helicon,' as he calls it, is part real garden, but part poetic exercise, for he was careful to plant it with good literary trees such as laurels and beeches which might encourage Apollo and his Muses to wander there " (*Petrarch*, 44). See also Terry Comito, *The Idea of the Garden in the Renaissance* (New Brunswick, N.J., 1978), who observes that "as much as his literary endeavors . . . Petrarch's gardening is a matter of *imitatio*" (59).

26. *Metrica* III, 33, to Francisco Nelli; trans. in Thomas Bergin, *Petrarch* (New York, 1970), 140.

27. *Petrarch's Bucolicum Carmen*, trans. and annotated by Thomas G. Bergin (New Haven and London, 1974).

This singular laurel, of course, does not owe its privileged status merely to its symbolic recall of the ancient's crown of poetry. Nor is it due only to its connection, through the primary mythological subtext, with the transformed nymph in whose memory Apollo had declared it "his" tree. Despite the protests anticipated by Augustinus in the *Secretum* that Petrarch's love for learning had priority over his love for Laura, the poet of the *Rime* celebrates the laurel because it is "Laura's tree"; but Petrarch is at pains to locate Laura's tree in Valchiusa, and in so doing he integrates it into his personal mythology. Unlike the personal myths that psycho-criticism proposes to divulge from the recurrence of obsessive metaphors, Petrarch's are of a highly self-conscious nature.[28] Add a laurel to the classical *locus amoenus*, and it becomes a highly personal place; generate a forest from the laurel, and that forest assumes a particular symbolic suggestiveness. The pastoral poem whose Petrarchan protagonist is Silvanus opens with his exile from the Tuscan Arno to a sylvan place where the currents of the Sorga and the Durenza rivers mingle in the Rhône, where a beautiful laurel had grown on the bank of the river. The allegory that follows, Herendeen observes, gives us "Petrarch's literary and amorous autobiography, in which he recounts his apprenticeship, his rise to fame, and Laura's sudden death."[29]

Consider then the sonnet "Almo sol, quella fronde ch'io sola amo" [Life-giving sun, you first loved that branch which is all I love] (188), one of the most overt invocations of the Ovidian paradigm in the collection. While the poet's love for the laurel identifies him here with Apollo, whom he invites to join him in gazing at the plant, the poem also offers a new and unexpected characterization of its dwelling, its "bel soggiorno," as "quell'umil colle . . . ove 'l gran lauro fu picciola verga" [that low hill . . . where the great laurel was a little sapling]. This interpolation, which passes almost unnoticed in the development of the light-and-shadow imagery that controls the sonnet, is a radical sign of the superimposition of Petrarch's myth of Laura on the myth of Daphne: the laurel now appears not only as the definitive product of a transfor-

---

28. While concerned, unlike the present study, with manifestations of unconscious impulses, Charles Mauron's discussion of associative networks of "obsessive metaphors" disclosed by the study of multiple texts is suggestive for the reading of Petrarch's corpus; see *Des métaphores obsédantes au mythe personnel: Introduction à la psychocritique* (Paris, 1962). For a recent study focusing on Petrarch's Latin works that attempts to advance toward a "psychopoetics" of his writing, see Pierre Blanc, "*Petrarca* ou la poétique de l'ego," *Revue des Etudes Italiennes* 29 (1983): 122–69.

29. Herendeen notes that in Petrarch's own allegorical reading of his first eclogue sent to his brother (*Fam.* X, 4) "we can begin to perceive his desire to create public and private landscapes for his persona" ("Castara's Smiles . . . Sabrina's Tears," 298 and n. 18).

mation, but as a plant that recalls a childhood and a gradual maturation. The Laura/laurel is a fixed point opposed to the flux of the poet's existence, as he confides in a sonnet addressed to the river Po for which an actual voyage is the evident pretext: his spirit, overcoming the movement of the swift current that bears him away from Laura, flies on the wings of its desire back toward the "aurea fronde," the golden leaves of the laurel, the "dolce soggiorno" where it will find repose (180). It has been suggested that Petrarch found a key to his own restless wandering in the myth of the soul's true country;[30] certainly he returns to Valchiusa with the homing instinct of a bird because it is the place both of Laura, and of the laurel.

These images introduce a new affective content that marks the myth as Petrarch's own. This laurel was reserved for him alone:

> Non vide il mondo sì leggiadri rami
> né mosse il vento mai sì verdi frondi
> come a me si mostrar quel primo tempo. . . .
>
> (142, 7–9)

[The world never saw such graceful branches nor did the wind ever move such green leaves as showed themselves to me in that first season. . . .]

These verses remind us that in the myth that Petrarch creates about Valchiusa in the *Rime* something very special happens in "quel primo tempo" in that special place, something that will not only ensure Amor's prolonged dominion but also charge the poet's *rime sparse* with a special meaning. In the recall of the *innamoramento* it takes myriad forms: the poet's soul enters "di primavera in un bel bosco," a beautiful wood in springtime, and finds there a singular presence: "un tenero fior nato in quel bosco / il giorno avanti" [a tender flower had been born in that wood the day before] (214). Or a figure appears of such splendor that he mistakes it for a divinity:

> Daphne, when first I beheld you alone upon the deserted
> Shore of the stream, I knew not if you were woman or goddess,
> Fragrance hovered around your mantle of purple and gold . . .

30. See Comito, *The Idea of the Garden in the Renaissance*, 59. This myth may be evoked in *Rime* 126 in the poet's expressed desire to be buried in Valchiusa, "e torni l'alma al proprio albergo ignudo" [let my soul return naked to this its own dwelling]; see Giuseppe Mazzotta, "Petrarch's Song 126," in *Textual Analysis: Some Readers Reading*, ed. Mary Ann Caws (New York, 1986), 127.

Thus in Petrarch's third eclogue;[31] in the *Rime* the lyric protagonist will recall this phantasm rising from these waters to sit upon the shore:

> Or in forma di ninfa o d'altra diva
> che del più chiaro fondo di Sorga esca
> et pongasi a sedere in su la riva. . . .
>
> (281, 9–11)[32]

[Now in the form of a nymph or other goddess who comes forth from the deepest bed of Sorgue and sits on the bank. . . .]

This image of Laura as a supernatural creature will color even her depiction *in morte*, blurring the contours of the "angelic" Laura in Paradise: he himself is "non pur mortal, ma morto," not merely mortal, but dead, he tells us, and she is a goddess: "et ella è diva" (294). Throughout his life this figure will be for Petrarch both nymph and goddess, not only Daphne but Aurora and Diana. She will be the Sofonisba of his *Africa;* in the *Rime*, as we have seen, she is both Medusa and Eurydice, both siren and *beatrice*. Late in life, in a letter in which he offers an interpretation of the appearance of Venus to Aeneas in Virgil's poem, Petrarch will return to this familiar iconography to identify the goddess, her hair scattered to the wind, as *voluptas*.[33]

In the *Rime* this apparition in most of its myriad guises is sudden, dramatic.[34] Sudden is the appearance of a white doe at sunrise, causing him to abandon everything to follow: "era sua vista sì dolce superba, / ch'i' lasciai per seguirla ogni lavoro" [her look was so sweet and proud

31. *Bucolicum carmen* III, cited in Bergin, *Petrarch*, 141–42.

32. Mary Barnard suggests that the likeness of Petrarch's Valchiusa to the Vale of Tempe, where the encounter of Ovid's Apollo and Daphne takes place, makes of it too a setting for mythical encounters, "a place devoid of historicity and the witness of borrowed mythical fantasies"; see *The Myth of Apollo and Daphne from Ovid to Quevedo: Love, Agon, and the Grotesque* (Durham, 1987), 182–83 hr n. 26.

33. *Seniles* IV, 5, to Federigo Aretino. See the discussion of Adelia Noferi, "La canzone CXXVII," *Lectura Petrarce, II, 1982* (Padua, 1983), 19–20; Battisti, "Non chiare acque," 332–33.

34. Suddenness also characterizes Laura's greeting as recalled by the poet; see Rainer Warning, "Imitatio und Intertextualität: Zur Geschichte Lyrischer Dekonstruktion der Amortheologie: Dante, Petrarca, Baudelaire," in *Imitation: Das Paradigma der Europäischen Renaissance-Literatur* (Festschrift für Alfred Noyer-Weidner) (Wiesbaden, 1983), esp. 311.

that to follow her I left every task] (190).[35] And in this extraordinary occurrence Petrarch took the measure of a singular destiny.[36]

> O mia Stella, o Fortuna, o Fato, o Morte,
> o per me sempre dolce Giorno et crudo . . .
>
> (298, 12–13)

[O my Star, O Fortune, O Fate, O Death, O Day to me always sweet and cruel, how you have put me in low estate!]

If, as has been suggested, the opening poem of the *Rime sparse* establishes the protagonist as fixed in a destiny,[37] it is in variations on this singular experience that he identifies its nature. Other poems assign to him the role of ritual victim: he anticipates a fall "giù ne l'amorosa selva" [down into the amorous wood] (22), that wood in which Virgil situates the souls of those who die for love.[38] The new beauties, "vaghezze nove," of Laura and her surrogate images make of him a dweller in the shady wood, "abitador d'ombroso bosco" (214), erupting into his life and interrupting its course.

This event assumes proportions not only magical but sacral. In yet another rendering of the *innamoramento* the nets of Amor are spread beneath the laurel: "e 'l chiaro lume che sparir fa 'l sole / folgorava dintorno . . ." [and the bright light that makes the sun disappear was lightening all around] (181). This epiphanic experience suggestively recalls Dante's *Paradiso*, where the final vision is described, straining against the professed inadequacy of language: "la mia mente fu percossa / da un folgore in che sua voglia venne" [my mind was smitten by a flash wherein its wish came to it] (*Par.* XXXIII, 140–41). It is like Dante's vision, moreover, in that it is unique, unreplicable. Like the revelation of the laurel in "quel primo tempo," the poet has seen in Laura's eyes that never seen by any other mortal (127). The experience is

---

35. The appearance and disappearance of this creature, "apparve . . . sparve," stage, as B. T. Sozzi points out, the central "event" of the collection as a whole; see "Per il sonetto: *Una candida cerva*," *Studi Petrarcheschi* 8 (1976): 215.

36. Raffaele Amaturo, noting this event as decisive in Petrarch's spiritual and poetic "vicenda biografica," cites *Fam.* XIII, 4: "Cui singulare aliquid nature donum est, in perpetuis laboribus etatem aget;" see *Petrarca* (Bari, 1971), 355.

37. On these "signature poems" in the tradition of the formal *excusatio* of classical love lyric, see Germaine Warkentin, " 'Love's sweetest part, variety': Petrarch and the Curious Frame of the Renaissance Sonnet Sequence," *Renaissance and Reformation* 11 (1975): 18.

38. *Aeneid* VI, 442–44; for the "selva amorosa" as literary metaphor, see Marianne Shapiro, *Hieroglyph of Time: The Petrarchan Sestina* (Minneapolis, 1980), 105.

not one vouchsafed to the *vulgo,* as the reader is reminded late in the *Rime* in tones that address posterity: "Non la conobbe il mondo mentre l'ebbe; / conobbil'io ch'a pianger qui rimasi" [The world did not know her while it had her; I knew her, who remain here to weep] (338). The first of these verses, echoing John's words concerning Christ, exemplifies once again the ambiguity of register of the celebration of Laura *in morte;* the second, setting the poet apart from all the world, reinstates him as unique and privileged witness.[39]

The consequence of this compulsion for Petrarch's poetic ambitions is explored early in the *Rime sparse.* While the Coronation Oration in which he identifies himself as a poet "sub ombra" makes no mention either of his vernacular verses or of Laura, the dynamics of the opening section of the *Rime* create an opposition between the lyric protagonist's anguished love and the *corona poetica* to which he aspires; it is the laurel, "l'onorata fronde che prescrive / l'ira del ciel" [the honored branch that protects one from the anger of heaven] that has denied him the crown "che suole ornar chi poetando scrive" [that decorates those who write poetry] (24).[40] In the extraordinary nature both of the *innamoramento* and of Laura herself, however, he finds the promise of winning that laurel crown. The experience that makes him a privileged witness also makes him a privileged poet, paradoxically affording him the means to inscribe his poetic enterprise within the sanctioned literary tradition. He assures himself and the reader that his lady, singular in her beauty and her virtue, surpasses the heroines of antiquity, that she would have attracted the efforts of its greatest poets.[41] It is by careful design that whereas in the *Africa,* celebrating the hero Scipio Africanus, Petrarch establishes himself in the line of Homer and Ennius, in the *Rime* he likens Laura to Scipio and himself to Ennius because he solemnly undertakes the celebration of this new marvel of unequaled merit:

> Ennio di quel cantò ruvido carme,
> di quest'altro io, et o, pur non molesto
> gli sia il mio ingegno e 'l mio lodar non sprezze!
>
> (186, 12–14)

---

39. On the exceptional destiny claimed by the poet, see Arnaud Tripet, *Pétrarque ou la connaissance de soi* (Geneva, 1967), 187.

40. See Marco Santagata, "La canzone XXIII," *Lectura Petrarce, I, 1981* (Padua, 1982), 66–68.

41. Homer and Virgil would have devoted themselves to Laura's praise; she is worthy that they and Orpheus too sing of her only (*Rime* 186, 187). Amaturo remarks that the choice of the love theme reflects an essential moment not of Petrarch's psychology but of his poetics; see *Petrarca* (Bari, 1971), 355.

[Ennius sang of him an inelegant song, I of her; and ah! may my wit not displease her, may she not despise my praises!]

The conjunction, moreover, was destined, like the love that prompts his verse. If he fears that Laura was entrusted to his celebration by a "stella difforme et fato sol qui reo" [a deformed star and her fate, cruel only in this] (187), her advent into his life was his poetic destiny:

> . . . "Quello ove questi aspira
> è cosa da stancare Atene, Arpino,
> Mantova et Smirna, et l'una et l'altra lira.
> Lingua mortale al suo stato divino
> giunger non pote; Amor la spinge et tira
> non per elezion ma per destino."
>
> (247, 9–14)[42]

[. . . What this man aspires to would exhaust Athens, Arpinum, Mantua, and Smyrna, and the one and the other lyre. Mortal tongue cannot reach her divine state; Love drives and draws his tongue, not by choice but by destiny.]

As we have seen, the project of his "speaking" of Laura in the *Rime* is initially shadowed by the possibility of interdiction, defined not in terms of the lady but of the laurel: "che forse Apollo si disdegna / ch'a parlar de' suoi sempre verdi rami / lingua mortal presuntuosa vegna" [perhaps Apollo is incensed that any mortal tongue should come presumptuous to speak of his eternally green boughs] (5). It was nonetheless to be this poet's destiny to write not only of Laura but of the laurel. Thus he will record its sudden appearance that at once commanded his allegiance:

> Del mar tirreno a la sinistra riva
> dove rotte dal vento piangon l'onde,
> subito vidi quella altera fronde
> di cui conven che 'n tante carte scriva.
>
> (67, 1–4)

[On the left bank of the Tyrrhenian sea, where the waves weep broken by the wind, suddenly I saw that noble branch of which I must write on so many pages.]

---

42. For *Rime* 186 and 187 in relation to the *Africa* see Guido Martellotti, "Stella difforme," in *Tra Latino e volgare: Per Carlo Dionisotti* (Padua, 1974), 569–84. Vincenzo Fera further explores Petrarch's cult of Scipio and of Laura in "I sonetti CLXXXVI e CLXXXVII," *Lectura Petrarce, VII, 1987* (Padua, 1988), 219–43.

It was also his destiny to write in the laurel's shade, and there, he tells us in retrospect, his youthful talent was nourished to fruition:

> L'arbor gentil che forte amai molt'anni
> (mentre i bei rami non m'ebber a sdegno)
> fiorir faceva il mio debile ingegno
> a la sua ombra et crescer negli affanni.
>
> (60, 1–4)

[The noble tree that I have strongly loved for many years, while its lovely branches did not disdain me, made my weak wit flower in its shade and grow in my troubles.]

His literary activity will in turn be identified as the cultivation of the laurel, and from this "ben colto," well-tended laurel he hopes for poetic immortality (30). In a later poem he offers this rather remarkable account of his attention to another laurel planted, not by himself on the bank of the Sorga, but within his heart by Amor:

> Vomer di penna con sospir del fianco
> e 'l piover giù dalli occhi un dolce umore
> l'adornar sì ch'al ciel n'andò l'odore,
> qual non so già se d'altre frondi unquanco.
>
> (228, 5–8)

[My pen, a plow, with my laboring sighs, and the raining down from my eyes of a sweet liquid have so beautified it, that its fragrance has reached Heaven, so that I do not know if any leaves have ever equaled it.]

Just as the origins of this experience of Laura and the laurel are associated with Ovidian myth, with the "sempre verdi rami" sacred to Apollo, so is its ending marked by the myth's negation. The evergreen property of the laurel, unique privilege of the plant most favored in Heaven, is repeatedly affirmed in the collection. It is also in terms of this property, one that protects the tree from time and change while underwriting its status as poetic symbol, that the poet imagines a vengeance for Laura's indifference:

> "Né poeta ne colga mai, né Giove
> la privilegi, et al sol venga in ira
> tal che si secchi ogni sua foglia verde!"
>
> (60, 12–14)

["Let no poet ever gather from it, nor let Jove favor it, and let it receive the sun's anger so that all its green leaves dry up!"]

This display of vengeful frustration is unique in the collection; in the poet's world the loss of the laurel's leaves would be a loss unthinkable and irretrievable, a portent of its destruction. And in the *Rime* that destruction renders Laura's death:

> Al cader d'una pianta che si svelse
> come quella che ferro o vento sterpe,
> spargendo a terra le sue spoglie eccelse,
> mostrando al sol la sua squalida sterpe . . .
>
> (318, 1–4)[43]

[At the fall of a tree that was uprooted as if by steel or wind, scattering on the ground its rich leaves, showing its pale root to the sun . . .]

Like the vision of origins, so now the vision of endings: like the initial apparition, destruction takes various forms. Several of these are brought together in a succession of visionary images in the allegorical canzone 323.[44] Here the ruin of two initial figures, a wild creature and a ship, is followed by four movements. The first depicts the laurel, its terms recalling not only the extraordinary nature of the plant but its spellbinding effect on the privileged observer:

> In un boschetto novo i rami santi
> fiorian d'un lauro giovenetto et schietto
> ch'un delli arbor parea di paradiso;
> et di sua ombra uscian sì dolci canti
> di vari augelli et tant' altro diletto
> che dal mondo m'avean tutto diviso.
>
> (323, 25–30)[45]

43. For the relation of this poem to other versions of destruction, see Antonio Daniele, "Lettura del sonetto petrarchesco 'Al cader d'una pianta che si svelse' (CCCXVIII)," *Revue des Etudes Italiennes* 29 (1983): 43. *Rime* 318 and the laurel stanza of *Rime* 323 are connected through both rhyme scheme and imagery with *Inferno* XIII, the canto of Pier della Vigna; see Rosanna Bettarini, "Perché 'narrando' il duol si disacerba," in *La critica del testo*, Atti del Convegno di Lecce (Rome, 1985), 319. Echoes of Dante's depiction of the suicide wood occur also in *Rime* 288.

44. For a description of this poem in Vat. lat. 3196 and the revisions of this stanza, see Fredi Chiappelli, *Studi sul linguaggio del Petrarca: La canzone delle Visioni* (Florence, 1971).

45. The early commentators Gesualdo and Bembo explained that the "boschetto novo" of the laurel stanza was Laura's birthplace; cited in Charles Roger Davis, "Petrarch's Rime 323 and Its Tradition through Spenser," Ph.D. diss., Princeton University, 1973, 26–27.

[In a young grove were flowering the holy boughs of a laurel, youthful and straight, that seemed one of the trees of Eden, and from its shade came forth such sweet songs of diverse birds and so much other delight that it had rapt me from the world.]

Then a lightning bolt strikes from an ominously darkening sky, brutal in its suddenness—"da radice / quella pianta felice / subito svelse" [it suddenly tore up by the roots that happy plant]—[46]and the two following movements take up in turn other figures familiar to the reader, only to record their annihilation:

> Chiara fontana in quel medesmo bosco
> sorgea d'un sasso et acque fresche et dolci
> spargea soavemente mormorando . . .
> Una strania fenice, ambedue l'ale
> di porpora vestita e 'l capo d'oro,
> vedendo per la selva altera et sola . . .
>
> (37–39, 49–51)

[A clear fountain in that same wood welled from a stone, and fresh and sweet waters it scattered forth, gently murmuring . . . A wondrous phoenix, both its wings clothed with purple and its head with gold, I saw in the forest, proud and alone . . .]

Once again the coherence of the multiple figural representations is established by their familiar common setting. In two closely preceding poems the poet had lamented Laura's absence from her habitual surroundings in Valchiusa—"Vedove l'erbe et torbide son l'acque / et voto et freddo 'l nido in ch'ella giacque" [the grass is bereaved and the waters troubled, and empty and cold is the nest where she lay] (320)—and returned to the metaphor of the nest that had harbored the young Laura to portray his phoenix:

> E' questo 'l nido in che la mia fenice
> mise l'aurate et le purpuree penne,

---

46. The destruction of the laurel is attributed to a violent storm in the tenth eclogue, "Laurea occidens," which locates it in the familiar setting "on the bank of the river," and in *Fam.* VIII, 3. See Michele Feo, "Il sogno di Cerere e la morte del lauro petrarchesco," in *Il Petrarca ad Arquà: Atti del Convegno di Studi nel VI Centenario (1370–1374)*, ed. G. Billanovich and G. Frasso (Padua, 1974), 117–48; Chiappelli, *Studi sul linguaggio del Petrarca*, 68; Sara Sturm-Maddox, *Petrarch's Metamorphoses: Text and Subtext in the* Rime sparse (Columbia, Mo., 1985), 36–38.

che sotto le sue ali il mio cor tenne
et parole et sospiri anco n'elice?

(321, 1–4)

[Is this the nest where my phoenix put on her gold and purple feathers, where she kept my heart beneath her wings and still wrings from it words and sighs?]

In canzone 323 the destruction of the laurel, the fountain, and the phoenix all take place in the forest, the initial "boschetto novo" reappearing first as an idyllic landscape, then as the "selva" suggestive of the alternative setting of the *innamoramento*.[47] Now the clear fountain disappears into a chasm, and the phoenix, finding the waters dried up and the laurel destroyed, destroys itself:

ché mirando le frondi a terra sparse
e 'l troncon rotto et quel vivo umor secco,
volse in se stessa il becco,
quasi sdegnando, e 'n un punto disparse. . . .

(56–59)

[for, seeing the leaves scattered on the earth and the trunk broken and that living water dry, it turned its beak on itself as if in scorn, and in an instant disappeared. . . .]

The self-immolation enacted in this ravaged landscape dramatically renders the interdependence of the various figures. The disappearance of the phoenix is as sudden, as unforeseen as the apparition of Laura that marked the inception of the poet's story. "Ogni cosa al fin vola," everything flies to its end: finally the image resolves into the figure of the lady herself, moving through her accustomed setting: "Alfin vid' io per entro i fiori et l'erba / pensosa ir sì leggiadra et bella Donna . . ." [Finally I saw walking thoughtful amid the flowers and the grass a Lady so joyous and beautiful . . .].[48] This figure is to be destroyed there in turn: pierced

47. Francesco Maggini, "La canzone delle visioni," *Studi Petrarcheshi* 1 (1948), cites possible sources in Ovid for the "sacred beauty" of the place; see 44–46. See also Feo, "Il sogno di Cerere," 136–37. That these four stanzas are linked by the forest to form a single frame for successive events is yet more evident in the version of this verse in Vat. lat. 3196: "In un boschetto novo, a l'un de canti / vidi . . ." [In a young grove, to one side I saw . . .].

48. See Vincenzo Dolla, "Il 'ciclo' dei madrigali e la struttura del Canzoniere petrarchesco," *Esperienze letterarie* 4 (1979): 75, and on this "ultima meraviglia," see Francesco Zambon, "Sulla fenice del Petrarca," in *Miscellanea di Studi in onore di Vittore Branca* (Florence, 1983), 415.

in the heel by a snake, she languishes like a plucked flower and departs, leaving the poet to exclaim that nothing in the world except weeping endures.

How to shore up these fragments against this ruin? A disconsolate poet puts the question in the first canzone following the notification of Laura's death, which opens with the cry "Che debb'io far? che mi consigli, Amore? . . . Madonna è morta" [What shall I do? What do you counsel me, Love? . . . My lady is dead] (268). The question is also raised, in strikingly similar terms, by the loss of the laurel: a closely related poem *in morte*, opening with a recall of the early casting of Laura as Aurora, now acknowledges sadly the inappropriateness of that model once so fondly entertained, for while the aged husband of the goddess may anticipate her return as the diurnal cycle repeats itself, the poet can only exclaim of his own bereft state "ma io che debbo far del dolce alloro?" [but what must I do about the sweet laurel?] (291).[49] An answer to the question is soon to be proposed, and it is not vested exclusively in Amore's urging in canzone 268 that the poet overcome his grief in order to continue his celebration of Laura's name. In *Rime* 318 cited above, the loss of the laurel is compensated by the identification of another laurel, the one within the poet's heart "al ciel traslato," translated to Heaven and no longer subject to physical ruin. It is a consolation much like that offered the protagonist of Petrarch's tenth eclogue, who receives the assurance that his beloved plant has been transplanted elsewhere by the gods. As the evergreen laurel had been a surrogate image of Laura whom he had believed immune from the limits of mortality—unable to believe "that Death reigns over goddesses"—this "living laurel," like the phoenix perennially regenerated from its ashes, is a surrogate for that Laura who "dying on earth has been reborn in Heaven" (331).[50]

This solution "in Heaven" nonetheless remains far removed from the poet who is left on earth to mourn his loss, bereft now not only of Laura but of the laurel and its shade, "che simile ombra mai non si racquista" [for such shade is never regained] (323).[51] He is bereft of hope

49. Rosanna Bettarini explores the relation of the two poems in "Che debb'io far? (*RVF* CCLXVIII)," *Lectura Petrarce, VII, 1987* (Padua, 1988), 187–99. For the "reverberations for the whole collection" of sonnet 291, see Peter Hainsworth, *Petrarch the Poet* (London, 1988), 152–53.

50. Gianfranco Contini, "Saggio d'un commento alle correzioni del Petrarca volgare," in *Varianti e altra linguistica* (Turin, 1972²), 118. This transcendence, notes Zambon, is not exclusively moral or religious: it is the *memoria eterna*, earthly immortality that informs his writing ("Sulla fenice del Petrarca," 425).

51. Cf. his lament for the sheltering "ombra" afforded by both the laurel and his "colonna," his friend and patron Giovanni Colonna, whose death followed that of Laura by some three months: "perduto ò quel che ritrovar non spero . . ." (269).

as well: ". . . or mie speranze sparte / à Morte" [now Death has scattered my hopes] (331). Images of dispersal intensify in the final section of the *Rime* in a crescendo of occurrences of "sparse": the poet's thoughts have been scattered, "sparsi," by time's rapid passage (298); he recalls his years spent roaming the hills of Valchiusa seeking "di vaga fera le vestigia sparse" [the scattered footprints of a wandering wild creature] (304); after burning with love in the presence of the fire, he goes now "pian-gendo il suo cenere sparso" [bewailing the scattering of its ashes] (320). The central image of destruction returns in these sad and weary verses, which, while far from the most poetically successful of Petrarch's meta-phorical representations, nonetheless render his poet's condition as he finds himself abandoned in a world without Laura:

> Ditele ch'i' son già di viver lasso,
> del navigar per queste orribili onde;
> ma ricogliendo le sue sparte fronde
> dietro le vo pur così passo passo.
>
> (333, 5–8)

[Tell her that I am already tired of living, of sailing through these horrible waves, but that, gathering up her scattered leaves, I still follow after her step by step.]

The magical world in which he had followed and celebrated Laura and the laurel is once again the banal world of reality; the forest generated entirely from a single laurel, "sol d'un lauro," resumes its natural state with the disappearance of Laura, the evergreen laurel tree replaced by deciduous variety: "spenti son i miei lauri, or querce et olmi" [my laurels are faded, are oaks and elms] (363).[52]

"Non mi ha lasciato altro che 'l nome," protests the poet, she has left him nothing but her name; but so much is in a name. Dante knew it: in the *Vita Nuova*, whose first chapter reveals the name of Beatrice only to affirm that its significance was not apparent to those who pronounced it, the young protagonist's return to Beatrice following the distraction of the "Donna pietosa" is marked explicitly by the return of her name in his thoughts and in his sighs, where he finds "quel dolce nome di

---

52. See Paola Mastrocola, "Gli 'errori' del Petrarca," in *L'Arte dell'Interpretare: Studi critici offerti a Giovanni Getto* (Cuneo, 1984), 101–2. Mary Barnard suggests that the transformation "carries echoes of mythical beginnings" suggestive of a return to the time "before the laurel" in Ovid's account, when the oak and other trees fulfilled the roles later assigned to the privileged tree as a consequence of Apollo's love for Daphne (*The Myth of Apollo and Daphne*, 108).

madonna scritto, / e de la morte sua molte parole" [the sweet name of my lady . . . penned and many words to tell her death again] (*VN* XXXIX, "Lasso! per forza di molti sospiri"). The two remaining poems of the *libello* both recapture that name, first in the revelation to pilgrims that the sorrowing city through which they pass has lost its "beatrice," then in the vesting in her name of the evidence of his vision of her in Heaven: the final poem concludes of the sublime thought that he is unable fully to render that "So io che parla di quella gentile, / però che spesso ricorda Beatrice" [that noble one is named, I apprehend, for frequently it mentions Beatrice]. It is this vision that inspires the hope with which the volume closes, to say of this lady that which had never before been said of any lady; and if that hope is only to be realized in the *Commedia* to follow, her name recurs in the final sentence of the *Vita Nuova* as he identifies once again "la sua donna" as "quella benedetta Beatrice," the blessed Beatrice who looks upon the face of God.

So too does Petrarch record his hope, while Laura is yet alive, to immortalize her name through his verse: "forse averrà che 'l bel nome gentile / consacrerò con questa stanca penna . . ." [perhaps it will happen that I shall consecrate her lovely noble name with this weary pen] (297). And like the *Vita Nuova*, the collection of his *rime sparse* closes with the promise of speaking of a lady. That lady, however, is not Laura:

> Se dal mio stato assai misero et vile
> per le tue man resurgo,
> Vergine, i' sacro e purgo
> al tuo nome et pensieri e 'ngegno et stile,
> la lingua e 'l cor, le lagrime e i sospiri.
>
> (366, 124–28)

[If from my wretched and vile state I rise again at your hands, Virgin, I consecrate and cleanse in your name my thought and wit and style, my tongue and heart, my tears and my sighs.]

It is difficult not to see in this conclusion, this consecration that addresses first Laura and then the Virgin, not only a palinodic gesture but a final confirmation of Petrarch's rivalry with Dante, echoes of whose own prayer to the Virgin in the *Paradiso* are to be heard in this poem.[53]

Yet while this solution in which the name of the beloved lady is

---

53. For *Rime* 366 as a "canzone di dedica," see Guglielmo Gorni, "Petrarca Virgini (Lettura della canzone CCCLXVI 'Vergine bella')," *Lectura Petrarce, VII, 1987* (Padua, 1988), 212.

suppressed in favor of that of the Virgin offers an ideologically sanctioned alternative to Dante's celebration of his earthly lady, Petrarch does not renounce his own claim to poetic preeminence in the latter domain, and once again his poetic project is illumined by its contradistinction to that of Dante. "Nulla al mondo è che non possano i versi" [There is nothing in the world that cannot be done by verses] (239): this affirmation *in vita di Laura*, in a poem devoted entirely to the lady's resistance and the poet's hope to overcome it through his amorous rhymes, is immediately followed by the acknowledgment of the futility of his effort, of the certainty of failure. His verses are *sparse* like the vestiges of Laura, like his voice and his sighs calling out to Laura.[54] Yet despite the harsh judgment that he repeatedly passes on these verses, despite his laments for their fragmentarity and their failure to capture Laura, the sounds that he scatters calling out her name *in vita* will continue to form her name *in morte*. No, his verses had not persuaded Laura, but the fervent belief in the power of poetry remains. *In vita* he confers his benediction upon his effort to celebrate Laura:

> Benedette le voci tante ch'io
> chiamando il nome de mia donna ò sparte . . .
> et benedette sian tutte le carte
> ov'io fama l'acquisto. . . .
>
> (61, 9–10, 12–13)

[Blessed be the many words I have scattered calling the name of my lady . . . and blessed be all the pages where I gain fame for her. . . .]

And it is precisely this enterprise that Laura urges upon him through the intermediary of Amor in the first canzone following the revelation of her death, as the response to his anguished cry "Che debb'io far?"

> "è viva colei ch'altrui par morta
> et di sue belle spoglie
> seco sorride et sol di te sospira,
> et sua fama, che spira
> in molte parti ancor per la tua lingua,
> prega che non estingua,

---

54. On Petrarch's writing as "distracted," his style "errante," his rhymes "disviate," see Mastrocola, "Gli errori del Petrarca," esp. 104–8.

anzi la voce al suo nome rischiari,
se gli occhi suoi ti fur dolci né cari."

(268, 70–77)[55]

["she is alive who seems dead, and she smiles to herself at her
beautiful remains and sighs only for you; and she begs you not to
extinguish her fame, which sounds in many places still by your
tongue, but rather to make bright your voice with her name, if
her eyes were ever sweet or dear to you."]

The formulation of this plea, whose closing words recall the poet's own
earlier appeal to Apollo to protect the laurel—"Apollo, s'ancor vive il
bel desio . . . et se non ài l'amate chiome bionde . . . già poste in oblio"
[Apollo, if the sweet desire is still alive . . . and if you have not forgotten
. . . those beloved blond locks] (34)—immediately distances the project
from that undertaken by Dante in the *Vita Nuova:* it is attributed to a
Laura who desires that her poet not abandon that celebration of her name
which had already rendered it famous.[56]

Apollo had not forgotten Daphne: the anticipated result of his contin-
ued attention is "una meraviglia," one realized in *Rime* 34 in that
marvelous fusion of Laura and laurel as the lady sits upon the grass
within the shadow of her arms. And so will Petrarch too work his magic
with loss and with time. "Né di sé m'à lasciato altro che 'l nome," she
has left nothing of herself but her name: but even as he confronts the
chasm that separates Heaven and earth, that "altro che" opens a possibil-
ity, a promise. We have seen that in the final canzone of the *Rime,* where
Laura's name is absent, the poet rededicates his love and his verse to the
"Vergine bella"; but the very last poem that Petrarch added to the second
part of the collection opens with a semantically dense recall of Laura/
lauro—"L'aura et l'odore e 'l refrigerio et l'ombra / del dolce lauro et sua
vista fiorita" [the breath and the fragrance and the coolness and the shade

---

55. For this admonition in relation to the poet's undertaking to praise Laura *in vita*, see
Pier Massimo Forni, "Laudando s'incomincia: Dinamiche di una funzione petrarchesca,"
Italian Quarterly 23 (1982): esp. 25–26.

56. Nancy Vickers observes that this Laura is "splendidly narcissistic even in death"; see
"Widowed Words: Dante, Petrarch, and the Metaphors of Mourning," in *Discourses of
Authority in Medieval and Renaissance Literature,* ed. Kevin Brownlee and Walter Stephens
(Hanover, N.H., 1989), 108. The successive versions of the *tornada* of Petrarch's poem,
she points out, recalling that of the first canzone of the *VN* following upon the telling of
the death of Beatrice, bring into sharp focus his rivalry with Dante.

of that sweet laurel and its flourishing sight]—to reaffirm his hope for his verses:[57]

> et se mie rime alcuna cosa ponno,
> consecrata fra i nobili intelletti
> fia del tuo nome qui memoria eterna.
>
> (327, 12–14)

[and if my rhymes have any power, among noble intellects your name will be consecrated to eternal memory.]

His hope, no longer vested in a response from Laura, is vested in the future readers of his *rime sparse*. It is a hope whose locus is not in Heaven but "qui," among us, a hope dramatically refigured in the myth of the poet who writes beneath the laurel in Valchiusa and leaves behind in *rime* the traces, not only of Laura, but of his own passage.

---

57. For discussion of the image of Laura that emerges from the poems added to the *Rime* during Petrarch's last years, see Aldo Bernardo, "La Laura umanistica del Petrarca," in *Il Petrarca ad Arquà: Atti del Convegno di Studi nel VI Centenario (1370–1374)*, ed. G. Billanovich and G. Frasso (Padua, 1975), 7–12.

INDEX